WORK IN PROGRESS

To Anthony Cook
with thanks and hope

David R. Brower
10/94

WORK IN PROGRESS
DAVID R. BROWER

PEREGRINE SMITH BOOKS

SALT LAKE CITY

First edition

95 94 93 92 91 5 4 3 2 1

Copyright © 1991 by David R. Brower

This is a Peregrine Smith Book, published
by Gibbs Smith, Publisher, P.O. Box 667,
Layton, Utah 84041

Design by J. Scott Knudsen, Park City, Utah

Manufactured in the United States of
America

**Library of Congress Cataloging-in-
Publication Data**

Brower, David Ross, 1912 –
  Work in progress / David R. Brower.
    p. cm.
Includes bibliographical references and
index.
  ISBN 0-87905-374-7
  1. Brower, David Ross, 1912 – .
2. Conservationists — United States —
Biography. 3. Environmentalists — United
States — Biography. I. Title.
QH31.B859A3 1991
333.7'2'092—dc20
[B]

The paper used in this publication meets the
minimum requirements of American
National Standard for Information Sciences-
Permanence of Paper for Printed Library
Materials, ANSI Z39.48-1984 ∞

*To David Cornelius Brower
and Anne Kathryn Olsen,
hoping* their *grandchildren
will know a safer Earth.*

CONTENTS

ix

IN A CONGRESSIONAL FIELD HEARING ON WILDERNESS held in Oregon in the late fifties I inserted what I thought could be a Sierra Club credo, improved it a little in the foreword to *This Is the American Earth,* added to it for Friends of the Earth in the seventies, and have been adjusting it ever since. The latest version goes like this:

There is but one ocean though its coves have many names;
a single sea of atmosphere, with no coves at all;
the miracle of soil, alive and giving life, lying thin
on the only earth, for which there is no spare.

We seek a renewed stirring of love for the earth.
We plead that what we are capable of doing to it
is often what we ought not to do.
We urge that all people now determine that
an untrammeled wildness shall remain here
to testify that this generation had love for the next.

We would celebrate a new renaissance.
The old one found a way to exploit.
The new one has discovered the earth's limits.
Knowing them,
we may learn anew what compassion and beauty are,
and pause to listen to the earth's music.

We may see that progress is not the accelerating speed
with which we multiply and subdue the earth
nor the growing number of things we possess and cling to.
It is a way along which to search for the truth,
to find serenity and love and reverence for life,
to be part of an enduring harmony.

PREFACE

A GOOD PART OF MY LIFE, perhaps too much, has been spent looking foreword—writing forewords for the books I had a hand in editing or publishing, quite often books I had urged others to write, on behalf of special places or ideas. The forewords allowed me space (usually I just took it) to explain why the Sierra Club or Friends of the Earth was publishing the book—to show and tell, for example, what was so great about the Colorado River in the Grand Canyon, and why the readers should come to its rescue. Which they did.

Little did I realize, until some reviewers of the first part of my life and times, *For Earth's Sake,* pointed it out, that it would be the readers who needed to be rescued. The autobiography's structure, I thought, would be obvious to all. It wasn't. The second part won't be, either, so I had better explain the so-called structure both parts have in common.

Each is divided into subjects, and each subject has its own internal chronology, or some reasonable facsimile, with a backflash or two mixed in whenever I could get away with it. Now and then I lapse into the hysterical present to see if it helps any. In each book half is new and half isn't. The half that isn't is selected from the piles and piles of material one almost inevitably accumulates in five or six decades of being involved in the word and conservation business—not necessarily in the conservation of words.

In the selection, I thought it would serve some purpose to show what my thinking was while I was growing up, particularly if I thought it was about an idea I believed was my own. Let me quickly add that I am still growing up, and am in no hurry to succeed. I also looked for material that could demonstrate that the environmental movement did not begin with Earth Day 1970, as so many younger people (so delightfully much younger) often allege. Altogether, there would be therein some evidence of how the thinking of my contemporaries, all elders now if they're still around, and my thinking evolved and what good, if any, the thinking did.

It also seemed important to let people know that, in spite of appearances, I did not found the Sierra Club. John Muir got that out of the way in 1892, twenty years before I was born. Nor was Yellowstone the first national park. Yosemite beat it by eight years. Nor was I fired from the Sierra Club staff for fiscal irresponsibility or, as one quite irresponsible person told an Ohio reporter, because I had my hand in the club till. The club, in a way, and Friends of the Earth more so, had a hand in mine, and I preferred it that way.

One thing neither book contains, in large part because it would have destroyed my marriage, is a list of the factual errors about my past, most of them about my role on the Sierra Club staff, contained in several books (take a deep breath):

> *Pioneer Conservationists of Western America* by Peter Wild
> *John Muir and His Legacy: The American Conservation*
>   *Movement* by Stephen Fox
> *Cadillac Desert* by Marc Reisner
> *Playing God in Yellowstone* by Alston Chase
> *The History of the Sierra Club* by Michael Cohen
> *Ansel Adams: An Autobiography*
> *A Story That Stands Like a Dam: Glen Canyon and*
>   *the Struggle for the Soul of the West* by Russell Martin

There are also assorted interviews that make me wonder how often, if ever, reporters get things right. Occasionally, however, they would send me a draft to check for factual errors — and would listen. Douglas Strong did in *Dreamers and Defenders: American Conservationists*. Or they would heed the recommendations of their Facts Editor, when they had one.

But that is more than enough self-justification, which, however indirect, is more boring than useful. I should protest the more common fault: the people who looked at and wrote about my past were almost invariably too generous.

Not nearly so generous, however, as Anne, who has had to live forty-eight years with what is now my past and who graces my present and delights my future. I tried to make it clear, when listing all the things I still want to do and reporting my request three years ago for a twenty-year extension, that I don't want it unless she gets one too.

ACKNOWLEDGMENTS

M Y DEBT TO OTHERS for *Work in Progress* is essentially the same as it was for the first half of this total effort, *For Earth's Sake*. With one major exception, my debt to John McPhee. In going through my bound volumes of *Not Man Apart,* the Friends of the Earth journal, I came upon the 1971 review of *Encounters with the Archdruid* by Stewart L. Udall, our best Secretary of the Interior by far.

Encounters had appeared in three parts in *The New Yorker,* and John McPhee's "Narratives about a Conservationist and Three of His Natural Enemies" had just been published by Farrar, Straus, & Giroux in hard cover at $6.95. The nineteenth printing of the paperback appeared early in 1991 for $8.95 — a measure not only of inflation, but also of how long John McPhee has been explaining me, some would say, better than I do. Stewart Udall's review explains my debt, I must say, the way I should have long ago:

THIS IS A BOOK about Dave Brower, but it is also a book by and about John McPhee — and I know Dave will applaud a commentary that discusses McPhee as much as it does Brower.

John McPhee's credentials as an interpreter of the conservation scene were well established before this book appeared. His earlier book about *The Pine Barrens* of New Jersey was a minor masterpiece, and now with this volume he has stamped himself as one of the most perceptive, penetrating reporters of the environmental crisis.

For those who want to understand the issues of this crisis, *Encounters With The Archdruid* is a superb book. McPhee reveals more nuances of the value revolution that dominates the new age of ecology than most writers could pack into a volume twice as long. I marvel at his capacity to listen intently and extract the essence of a man and his philosophy in the fewest possible words. For example, McPhee's description of Dave Brower's split with the Sierra Club board told me more in ten pages than I had learned from long conversations with several participants. There was a problem of discipline and management, and the personality conflicts were deep and divisive, but Brower also out-grew the Sierra Club: his vision was too broad, his stance too militant for the old guard.

All those who warm their hands before this book are indebted to the editor and publisher of *The New Yorker* magazine. One reason we have a few words like this one is that *The New Yorker* gives its roving writers leeway to pursue people and write books like "Encounters With The Archdruid." I am told McPhee worked intermittently on this *New Yorker* "profile" for nearly two years. It is obvious that it took extraordinary efforts for him to bring the people together and complete the arrangements that made the three "encounter trips" possible. McPhee had the time to write a superior book only because his employers gave him the gift of freedom from assignments and deadlines.

So, three cheers for John McPhee and *The New Yorker*. Let us hope this fine book gets the wide audience it deserves.

Dave's antagonists for the encounters were well-chosen, and McPhee's editorial skill enables the participants to reveal the marrow of a man, or an issue. Park (the geologist) and Dominy (the dam builder) are articulate, formidable men who state their case with power and force. I doubt that either of them is aggrieved by John McPhee's reporting of their ideas and convictions. They are able, single-minded exponents of the conventional wisdom of American progress—and they hold their own so well with the holistic Brower that some readers may think Park and Dominy "won" their bouts with Brower. Charles Fraser is the exception. He not only lost his seashore "development" before this book appeared in print, but he was no match for Brower. He comes across as the bright, cocky rich boy he is in real life. He's a "good developer, but he's a bulldozer type behind the fancy rhetoric."

The climax of the book is the boat ride down the Grand Canyon with Floyd Dominy. Listen to the punches they land as they discuss the proposed Bridge Canyon Dam after a day in the lower reaches of Havasu canyon:

Dominy: It would be beautiful, and like Lake Powell (formed by his Glen Canyon Dam,) it would be better for all elements of society.

Brower: Lake Powell is a drag strip for power boats. It's for people who don't do things except the easy way. The magic of Glen Canyon is dead. It has been vulgarized. . .

Dominy: Don't give me that crap that you are the only man that understands these things. I'm a greater conservationist than you are, by far. I do things. I make things available to man. Unregulated, the Colorado River wouldn't be worth a good God damn to anybody. . . your weapon is emotion. . . For Christ's sake, Dave, be objective. Dave, be reasonable.

Brower: Some of my colleagues make the error of trying to be reasonable. Objectivity is the greatest threat to the United States today.

This, I submit, is great dialogue, an exchange of champions. It is the kind of journalism that makes conservation come alive for any reader. Thanks to this book Dave Brower is a prophet honored in his own time. John Muir died a disappointed man, but few would argue today that he was not the ultimate winner of the argument over Hetch-Hetchy. Brower and his allies have already won some of their own Hetch-Hetchy battles—and in the long run my guess is that Dominy will fare no better with history than the opponents of Muir.

Robert Frost, the old poet who loved paradoxes, used to say, "There is more love outside of marriage than in, more education outside of classrooms than in, more religion outside of churches than in." Dave Brower is not a churchgoer, but on the evidence of this book, he is surely one of the most truly religious men of our time. Now it is our good luck to have a book that tells the story of this remarkable American and his cause.

Not Man Apart, 1971

So now I must acknowledge my substantial debt to Stewart Udall. I was happy to support Morris Udall's candidacy for president, but he was given the opportunity to write the book, Too Funny to Be President. I would be delighted to support Stewart's candidacy anytime he asks. The world badly needs an environmental president in these parts.

The cover of the latest "Archdruid" sports a beautiful Bierstadt of Hetch Hetchy Valley, which reminds me of yet another debt to acknowledge—mine to John Muir, for whom I should do everything I possibly can to see Hetch Hetchy Valley returned, restored as well as possible, to Yosemite National Park, which he desperately wished it to grace in perpetuity. May I suggest that we could use your help?

—D.R.B.

David Brower at his desk in Berkeley. (Photo by Kurt Markus.)

CHAPTER 1

THE SIERRA CLUB BULLETIN

——

T HAT MODEL OF ALL MOUNTAINEERING JOURNALS," were the words the British mountaineer and writer Ronald Clark chose to describe the *Sierra Club Bulletin*. Francis Farquhar had made it so, and I think he hoped when I became editor in 1946 that I would keep it that way. It was a lot for a Harvard man (1912) to expect of a University of California sophomore dropout (x1933 — the 'x' meaning that I would have graduated in 1933 had I stuck around). It was a bold hope on his part, but not exactly a shot in the dark.

The year I was supposed to have graduated was the year of my seven-week backpack trip with George Rockwood, an event of the summer of 1933 that George described, fifty-four years later, as one of the big events of his life. It initiated a series of events, including my joining the Sierra Club and Marjory Bridge (later Farquhar)'s putting me on my first Sierra Club committee, that led to Francis's putting me on the *Bulletin's* editorial board.

What I had already learned about mountaineering, and would learn from the *Bulletin* about publishing, were two of the most important influences in my life. Both engendered a kind of boldness that I would not otherwise have known — boldness that got me into a bit of trouble now and then, but also enabled me to accomplish a few things I would otherwise have deemed impossible. The mountain and the journal taught me that you can get there from here. "There" would include Anne, a family, a home, and a chance still to ride through the Grand Canyon on a well-splashed, oar-driven dory.

It didn't take me long, however, to disappoint Francis. He asked me to review two books for the *Bulletin,* and I totally missed the deadline, a talent I would perfect as years went by. One of the books was *Men Against the Clouds* by Richard L. Burdsall and Arthur B. Emmons. I labored too long flyspecking the technique used in the ascent of Minya Konka, one of the lesser giants in the Himalaya. I was a bit full of all the new experience I had acquired on Mount Waddington's glaciers, in British Columbia, and Francis, when he finally had the opportunity,

1

gently admonished me for worrying so much about technique when I should have concentrated on the achievement. Technique-versus-achievement exercises were not what the *Bulletin* needed.

Nevertheless, Francis delayed publication long enough to include the two reviews and to run my photograph of Mount Waddington as the frontispiece of the 1936 *Annual Bulletin.* I had strained his patience, however, and was retired from the editorial board for a year.

Francis let me earn my way back in 1938, and there was ample time for it, inasmuch as the Yosemite Park & Curry Company had decided to do without me between the fall of 1937 and the summer of 1938 — except for a few photographic assignments. One of these was to make publicity prints for the company, and Marjory Farquhar generously let me use her darkroom in Francis's and her home on Garber Street, in Berkeley. Her darkroom was close to Francis's library, which was where the *Bulletin* articles and photographs were assembled.

Nature took its course. I was looking at photographs and articles, making suggestions, running errands to the printer, reading proof, and learning the elements of publishing from a man who had deep interest in the graphic arts and in mountaineering history, especially the history of the Sierra Nevada. He was justly proud of his and Ansel Hall's first ascent of the Middle Palisade, and vicariously proud of the mountaineering achievements of others. Whenever a mountaineering dignitary approached the San Francisco region, Francis's home was opened to the visitor and all the mountaineers within easy reach. His professional life as a CPA may have been exciting; what mountains brought to him certainly was. That included Marjory. She also loved the Sierra, the Grand Canyon, and their four children as much as he did, and she loved photography more than he. But she never read the *Sierra Club Bulletin,* or so she said.

I read it all. More than that, I had worked on it so energetically that Francis passed it on to me when he felt it was time to retire. He had hoped to pass the baton earlier, but World War II and my stint in the Mountain Troops got in the way. Nine earlier editors of the *Bulletin,* except for William Frederic Badè's reign of eleven years, had served only a year or two. Francis persevered for twenty-one years.

In 1946 I was promoted to captain, released from active duty in the army, and assigned to active duty, unpaid, on the *Bulletin,* concurrently reoccupying my seat in Room 203 at the University of California Press, where I was paid to edit.

August Frugé, the new director of the press, assigned me a most attractive postwar task — revision of *Manual of Ski Mountaineering,* which I had edited for the press as its contribution to military training. That contribution had helped us in the army's mountain training program, and now that program was to help the revision, on press time and payroll, during the first two and a half months of which I was also being paid by the army for accumulated vacation time.

I also signed up in the Army Reserve and became director of the Infantry School, Oakland Army Base — one night a week and two weeks a summer. The university paid reservists during their summer tours of duty, and so did the army. The army also paid first-class rail fare, while I traveled coach, to summer training. I traveled to Camp Carson three years in a row to learn how to climb rocks in a course based on what I had helped teach the instructors. "Brower's Dude Ranch," someone called this exercise.

By May 1946 I was back on the Sierra Club Board of Directors, and in July was once again leading a Sierra Club High Trip in the Kearsarge Pass region of the High Sierra. Time off for High Trips was part of my original arrangement with the press, and the arrangement continued as long as I stayed at the press.

In the Sierra Club I was the kid in the candy store, reaching for every available shelf. There were many committees to serve on, and I seemed ready, as Dick Leonard once wrote me, to take on anything that was easy, interesting, or glamorous. So in addition to being *Bulletin* editor, I served on the Outings, Conservation, Mountaineering, Winter Sports, Place Names, and Visual-Education committees.

Francis Farquhar had devoted twelve years to the *Bulletin* before his twenty-year stint as editor. There had been twenty-seven years of *Bulletin* before that. The first semiannual issue appeared in January 1893. It was published semiannually until 1914 — Francis's first year on it, when it became an annual magazine. In 1923 this was supplemented with the *Sierra Club Circular,* and five years of that, in the *Bulletin's* six-by-nine-inch-plus format, bulk a mere three-eighths of an inch. More information needed to get to the membership more economically, so bimonthly issues of the *Bulletin* began in 1928. For the next eighteen years there were five bimonthlies per year and one annual, which appeared in the month of convenience. The annual carried articles of lasting interest, and delays were tolerable. The bimonthly carried news and pleas for members to act.

Being gainfully employed at intervals, and ungainfully unemployed at corresponding intervals, I had time to be of assistance to Francis on the annual and the bimonthlies from early 1938 to October 12, 1942, when I joined the U.S. Mountain Troops. Editing of the 1941 annual was largely left to me, and of the 1942 annual even more so. Francis had delegated work on the bimonthlies to other members of the editorial board, and I had more time to spend on the annual than the others. In 1940 I persuaded Francis to let us shift the bimonthly from text stock to coated so that we could make further use of our wealth of halftone

3

illustrations from old annuals — boxes and boxes of them stored at the printer's. (The bimonthly slipped back to the old format while I was off to war, and returned to coated paper and illustrations when I returned from service.) The *Bulletin*, especially the bimonthly, carried much of the brunt of the campaign to establish Kings Canyon National Park, and I began to wish in 1938 that it could be issued more frequently. The year 1946 brought me, as the new editor, the chance to publish monthly. Now we could exploit the halftone bonanza faster, and add new photographs, which were particularly helpful in saving the San Gorgonio Wild Area in California and in preventing the loss of primeval forests in Olympic National Park. Moreover, the members received more than twice as much information as they had been getting, and it was twice as timely.

For the first fifty-seven years, the *Bulletin* was preponderantly devoted to the Sierra Nevada — exploration, first ascents, geological and botanical discoveries, national forests and national parks in California — with an occasional foray into other parks on the Pacific Coast and other parts of the Americas. The *Fifty Seven Year Index: Sierra Club Bulletin* makes this clear. It was published in 1952 after a major struggle by George Shochat and Dorothy Bradley — an effort sadly flawed by its having been printed against the grain of the paper, which means that the pages handle like postcards instead of rolling smoothly the way good books should.

That index shows that World War II severed many old connections, but it widened horizons. Hundreds of members had been in the military services and would not forget the far places and problems they had seen.

One sign of the widening happened in 1950 when Dorothy Hill (later Varian) represented the Sierra Club at an early meeting of the Natural Resources Council of America — a forum of many national conservation organizations. In the same year the campaign began to rescue Dinosaur National Monument from proposed dams. The National Park System needed to be completed as well as protected. The postwar surge in club membership, which had tapered, began once more. The *Bulletin* not only kept up, but also had a hand in leading the charge.

As one device to promote new national parks in Oregon and Washington, the club introduced "Wilderness Cards from the Sierra Club," produced by an inexpensive three-color process in four sizes — normal, postcard, giant, and colossal. They were loaded with message, and though not great as examples of the graphic arts, nor widely distributed, they portrayed places beautiful enough to compensate for the quality of the cards. With a backlog now of color subjects, we could bring those color plates to the *Bulletin*. We needed to exploit their varying sizes

4

and, more important, to publish more words per dollar. So we increased the size of the monthly to eight-and-a-half by eleven inches.

By 1955 we had learned from Ansel Adams and Nancy Newhall, in their superlative exhibit, "This Is the American Earth," the importance of counterpoint in image and text. So January 1959 brought a new look to the monthly *Bulletin*. Handsome Weiss initials proclaimed "SIERRA" in red capitals just over an inch high. Three-eighths-inch capitals were big enough for "CLUB BULLETIN" in black. Under this was a color photograph by David R. Simons of Trapper Lake, above the Stehekin Valley in the North Cascades of Washington. Below this we quoted an economist:

A world from which solitude is extirpated is a very poor ideal. . . .
Nor is there much satisfaction in contemplating the world
with nothing left to the spontaneous activity of nature.
John Stuart Mill, 1806–73

Here we had the first "deep-economist," to be followed in February by a reasonably deep-ecologist, Allen Morgan, in what was to be the war cry of the sixties: "What we save in the next few years is all that will ever be saved." The color cover, also by David Simons, was of the old mining road in Stehekin Valley, with Trapper Mountain in the background. The cover warned of "Crisis in the Northern Cascades," and the issue contained six pages of articles, photographs, and a full-page map illustrating that crisis. The map, also by David Simons, showed the North Cascades National Park he and the club wanted, of which we have so far achieved only part.

As an example of innovative conservation ideas launched in the *Bulletin*, the lead article in that February issue was entitled "Toward a Historic Step Forward in Conservation," with a supplementary heading, "Vast land exchange proposed by the Sierra Club 'a masterpiece of constructive thinking.'" A federal commission had proposed transferring forty-six million acres of Interior Department (BLM) land to the Forest Service and the Sierra Club, at my suggestion, counterproposed transferring six million Forest Service acres to Interior for national parks. Six pages were devoted to our counterproposal, beginning with a letter from club president Harold C. Bradley to President Dwight Eisenhower. The letter began:

"Dear Mr. President:
"The Hoover Report and Nelson Rockefeller's commission on forestry consolidation have urged a transfer of lands from Interior to Agriculture. We understand that the Bureau of the Budget is actively considering the proposal to transfer 46.6 million acres from the Bureau of Land Management to the Forest Service.

5

"We believe it may be desirable and feasible to compensate for this transfer, in whole or in part, by exchange from Agriculture to Interior of certain lands in which recreational, scenic, scientific, educational, and historic, values are now, or soon will become, paramount.

"As an example of an area eligible for such exchange, we suggest the Lake Chelan-Glacier Peak unit of the Northern Cascades of Washington, long recognized as one of the nation's greatest scenic and recreational resources, and the equal of any existing national park. . . . We hope you will agree that this may be a historic opportunity for a great step forward in conservation — a still wiser use of federal lands."

The Sierra Club enclosure listed some potential exchanges — sixty million acres from Interior to Agriculture, six million from Agriculture to Interior, and described five possible ways to make the exchanges. One of these was presidential proclamation of National Monument status. We listed the major scenic monuments established by presidential proclamation between 1906 and 1956: thirteen by President Theodore Roosevelt, five by Howard Taft, seven by Woodrow Wilson, six by Warren G. Harding, five by Calvin Coolidge, four by Herbert Hoover, and thirteen by Franklin Roosevelt, who was not to be outdone by an earlier Roosevelt.

There followed a page and a third of advantages and disadvantages of the proposed exchanges, and a page and two-thirds of comment from leading conservationists. All in all, the presentation was a substantial one, well deserving, I thought, of the encomium, "a masterpiece of constructive thinking."

The response showed that Gerald D. Morgan, deputy assistant to the president, was not quite ready for the idea. Copies had been sent, however, to the secretaries of Agriculture and Interior, the budget director, and the chairman of the Outdoor Recreation Resources Review Commission. "As you know," Mr. Morgan explained, "this Commission is charged with inventorying and evaluating the outdoor recreation resources of the Nation."

The Sierra Club did indeed know. The commission was the direct result of the Sierra Club's having proposed a national scenic resources review three years earlier.

The Department of Agriculture dispatched its assistant secretary to the West to protest the club's idea as an evil land grab, and the Forest Service took steps to try to gag the club's executive director, who was still deeply involved with the *Bulletin*. The gag effort was partly successful, briefly, so far as it concerned me.

The exchange proposal has not yet got off the ground, and still ought to.

The annual magazine continued in its smaller format, but in steadily broadening content, until 1964. That year's annual stepped up to the monthly's format. The color, this time, was superb — as good as could be produced in the United States or, at the time, anywhere else. It exploited the color work which Karl Deschutter, of Antwerp, and Barnes Press, of New York City, had produced for the Sierra Club's exhibit-format books. Thereby club members were kept currently aware of the club's book-publishing effort. They could see what was coming, and they ordered enough copies in advance of publication to make the books, and the mission they served, financially feasible. There was little other advertising in the *Bulletin*, and income from this advertising was directly related to the club's purpose or was derived from it. Twenty years later the name *Sierra* would be substituted for the old *Sierra Club Bulletin*, the frequency would be reverted to bimonthly issue, and half the content would become income-producing advertising, predominantly of interest to people traveling to far-off places, and about what they wore, rode in, or were photographed with.

There was still another annual magazine in 1965. It repeated and augmented the success of 1964. The two were probably America's most beautiful magazines. The next year ended before an annual could be assembled, and so did 1967. But in 1968 we caught up. If you can find one — the combined *Sierra Club Bulletin/Annual Magazine* for 1966–68 — in a used bookstore somewhere, grab it. In its content and in its graphic art, it is far and away the best. It is not "the model of all mountaineering journals," because the descriptions of climbing mountains had given way to describing ways to save them. But it was the last Sierra Club annual, and I think Sierra Club members are the losers, even though hardly a handful know what they have lost. The Sierra Club could certainly use a yearbook again, perhaps by that name rather than *Annual Magazine.* Tradition need not sound archaic.

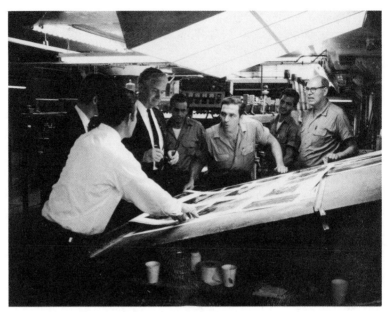

Discussing the press check at Barnes Press.

At the Friends of the Earth exhibit, Frankfurt Book Fair. Edwin Matthews, Dave Brower, Eric Schindler, and others.

CHAPTER 2

ABOUT BOOKS

―――

EARLY INFLUENCES

―――

NOT BEING AS LITERATE AS MY WIFE, then or now, I had to be read to at the age of seven, and the first book I remember having been read to me was *The Adventures of Bobby Coon,* by Thornton W. Burgess, who wrote it for reading at bed-time. In 1919, a year after it was published and a year before my mother lost her sight, she read it to me. I looked over her arm at Harrison Cady illustrations. A little later I saw what Beatrix Potter was doing for Peter Rabbit. Even now, for all the years that have passed, and in spite of the two holes made in our roof by grub-hunting raccoons, and the depletion of our mosquito control by the raccoons that raid our fish pond at night, I am incapable of not liking them — and equally incapable of liking Mr. McGregor.

I didn't even mind cyclones when I learned what one did for Dorothy as Miss LaGrange read to our second-grade class about the wonders of Oz. Reading the other Burgess bedtime stories to myself, I learned to think the way wild animals are presumed to think, and reading Ernest Thompson Seton's *Wild Animals I Have Known,* I learned and cared about the rough time they were having. John Muir's *My First Summer in the Sierras* and Clarence King's *Mountaineering in the Sierra Nevada* fleshed out in print what I had learned about the Sierra from car-camping with my parents and their other three children.

Stewart Edward White's books on his Sierra travels prepared me for getting wet there and liking it. John Adams Comstock's *Butterflies of California* presented one of my favorite subjects beautifully and expen-sively (the public library's expense). Geoffrey Winthrop Young's *Mountaincraft* and Guido Rey's *The Precipice* and *The Matterhorn* told of the skill needed and the drama felt in high mountains.

Mary Austin's *Everyman's Genius* was put in my hands by Edith Rockwood, my friend George's mother, and taught me, as the title explains, that there is a bit of genius in everyone and I had better dig to see if I had any, and use it.

I was imprinted.

Words are a poor substitute, as they say, for pictures, but words were what I had to use to describe for my mother the things she could no longer see. When she could still see the hills, her face told me how much she loved them. Now I told her about her hills as I helped her walk there, and wrote about mine. In a way, I was writing not only for the *Sierra Club Bulletin,* but also for her.

Very briefly in 1933, and at length in 1934, I described my first extensive wilderness trips to the Sierra. The second piece, "Far from the Madding Mules," was good enough, when heavily edited by Francis Farquhar, to appear as a full article in the 1935 annual magazine number of the *Bulletin.* That was what led to my being appointed to the *Bulletin's* editorial board.

That year I met Walter Starr at the Farquhars's San Francisco home, and saw the beginnings of a Sierra Club book, *Starr's Guide to the Muir Trail,* being assembled by Walter from the assiduous notes made by his son Pete before he fell to his death in the Minarets. I had already met Ansel Adams in the Sierra and had seen how excellently his photographs were reproduced, along with the first-rate typography Francis insisted upon, by one of San Francisco's top firms, Taylor & Taylor.

Everything was falling together, but there was still a fall or two to come. By 1941 I had put enough authors and photographers and printers and words and pictures and bulletins together to persuade Francis to recommend to his brother Samuel T. Farquhar, manager of the University of California Press, that I be given a chance to be an editor there. Working with Harold A. Small, editor of the press, I fell in love, platonically, with editing. I also fell in love with Anne, also editing and simultaneously winding up the thirteen years it would take her to graduate from the university I had already dropped out of.

Mix them all together and you have a book addict who likes to play with other people's words and pictures, see them combined, distributed, and absorbed, particularly on subjects related to wildlife and mountains. Within a few years you would also have the father of four children, all of whom like words and pictures and wildlife and mountains, and whose mother told me, two years before Kenneth was born, "I wish I could amuse you more than I do." She did. Shortly after our fortieth anniversary she said, "I think you ought to get married and have a family." I had.

What led to that was all the time and some of the energy I spent away from home gathering some of the thoughts loosely assembled here, more of that time and energy being spent on books than on anything else. My too inevitable series of questions became: Do you have a problem? Do you want my help? Can you write a book about it, or find someone who can? How soon?

That led to many books. And those books led others to question me: Would you like to write a book about my problem? Will you read a manuscript about my problem? Or, here are five hundred color slides that I think should be made a book of, and do you know anyone who would like to write it?

Now the question is: Here are bound galleys of a book we are about to publish; would you like to say something nice about it for the jacket?

But that is ahead of the story. How about a particular book, an important one? How did it begin? How did it proceed? What good did it do? Let *This Is the American Earth* answer the questions.

THIS IS THE AMERICAN EARTH

ANSEL ADAMS, in his and the century's late teens, assisted Francis Holman as custodian of LeConte Lodge, built by the Sierra Club in Yosemite Valley in memory of Joseph LeConte, a club pioneer. For that reason, and many others, Ansel became attached to the lodge. When the National Park Service complained to the club about the lackluster quality of the program the club was conducting in the lodge, Ansel accepted the challenge. He sought the advice of Walter Starr, a former president of the Sierra Club who was at the time serving as president of the Yosemite Park & Curry Company. They, assisted by Nancy Newhall and her experience with the Museum of Modern Art in New York City, came up with the idea of placing a major conservation exhibit in the lodge. This coincided with my having become executive director of the Sierra Club just two years before, in 1952, and my also having gotten to know Ansel quite well when I was serving as publicity manager for YP&C Co. in 1935 and 1937. In a minor way I got into the act. Ansel and Nancy were certainly well informed in conservation matters, but I had by now become a professional in the business and could add some of the things I had learned to what they already knew about the blending of word and image.

By 1955 a spectacular exhibit was ready for the lodge. It consisted of twelve four-by-eight-foot panels on which the history of American conservation was displayed gloriously. There were forty photographs by Ansel and an equal number from a host of other photographers whom Ansel and Nancy knew from their work together. Image sizes ranged dramatically — from what Nancy called little jewels to prints made dynamic by being several feet wide. These were interspersed with Nancy's flowing text. Here and there were a few natural objects — a

11

butterfly, a shell, or the exquisite sculpture of ancient weathered wood from the High Sierra.

It took genius to fit all the panels in the little lodge, but the genius that had put the exhibit together would not fail now, and the exhibit was fit. But not just in LeConte Lodge. By now a great many of Ansel's and Nancy's friends knew about the project, and copies of the exhibit were ready to appear simultaneously in the California Academy of Sciences in San Francisco and were also to be traveled about the world, in various languages, under the auspices of the Smithsonian Institution. "This Is the American Earth," a most spectacular exhibit, was on its way.

Exhibits are an important way to publish. Huge audiences may come. They also go, and the impression they leave behind is in individual minds and not easy to recapture. They are a little bit like the television program — pre-video recorders — that headed off for interstellar space, never to be known about again unless there should be someone on the far side of that space. What could make them retrievable? A book, of course. A book has a few virtues of its own. It is usually thought out carefully in advance. It is designed, printed on paper that should last quite a while, distributed widely, one hopes, standing on its own, spine and all, on a bookshelf, read and available to be reread, the images of its pages often so well fixed in one's mind that one will remember with some precision where a given passage was in the book — early or late — and whether it was on a right- or left-hand page, topside or other. If you are in my house, where there are more books than several lifetimes would give one time to read, there is a fair impression of what room and what shelf and what color spine hides the reference you are looking for. There what you want to know is. If you have any luck at all, there it will be for year upon year, until you forgetfully lend the book to a forgetful person or until your house burns down.

"This Is the American Earth" needed to be rescued from its exhibit mode where people might wander in at the beginning of it, or the middle, or the end, and not comprehend its context. It needed to become a book. And not just because it was an exhibit, but because it was an exhibit without precedent. There had been many conservation exhibits, albeit none of this magnitude, but none had put conservation, later to be renamed environmentalism, in its context. The full sweep was in it — the earth's beginning, life's first moves, the brief story of our ancestry, what we received and what we left behind us in the past, and what now, with new and possibly unmanageable capabilities, we were about to do. And it was not simply a story in words alone or in images (I still am willing to say 'photographs' alone, but in what the two art forms could do in counterpoint. The words were good enough — indeed, Alfred Knopf considered publishing the words alone — but when the words were read in the context of the image, something new sprang off the page, synthesized in the reader's mind in the reader's own way, and there was an unexpected power in the collaboration. Let's hear it for the book!

How big should this book be? There were examples in some of Ansel's earlier books, one done for a western bank, others done on Ansel's camera in the national parks and in Yosemite, formats that he and Nancy Newhall had worked out. We settled on a trim size of ten and a quarter inches by thirteen and a half. What we were looking for, if an exhibit was to be simulated in a book, was a page size big enough to carry a given image's dynamic. The eye must be required to move about within the boundaries of the image, not encompass it all in one glance. Ideally, we should have published the book in four-by-eight-foot panels. But there were a few problems in trying to be that bold. So we settled for a portable size that would later feel at home on a coffee table. I thought it would be useful to call that size *Exhibit Format.*

The exhibit was born in Ansel's studio and darkroom on Twenty-fourth Avenue in San Francisco, and it was to the studio we went to transform the exhibit into a book. We lost track of the numbers of times Nancy came west from Rochester, New York, or Ansel came down from Yosemite, or I took the shorter trip from the downtown office of the Sierra Club out to the studio. Visitors streamed by endlessly.

Virginia Adams was the hostesses's hostess. I have never met a hostess who exceeded her ability to make people feel that they were the people Virginia had wished so long and so hard to see. Each contributed to the creative effort, if only by appreciating what was happening.

One problem persisted. How was the book to begin? In the exhibit, the show began wherever the visitor happened in on it, whether it was panel one or panel twelve. By the time all the panels had been seen, the message got through. But a book would be expected to be organized in a traditional way, with beginning, middle, and end. It was in Seattle, where I had gone to attend a conference, taking the text with me (there was no need, happily, to take the photographs; I carried them all in my mind) to spend any spare time I could on last-minute notes on how to put the book together, that a brilliant idea popped into my head. What the book needed was a prelude — a long statement to precede the foreword. But how could this be done? The United States Register of Copyrights had a definite idea about a book's beginning. There could be a half title, a title page, and, on the verso of the title page, the book's copyright notice must appear. Could there be exceptions? I telephoned the Washington office. There was no official objection to having several pages of material preceding the title page, but the copyright notice must still appear on the verso of the title page.

Thus began the extended prelude idea that was to mark many of the Exhibit Format series — in the Sierra Club and elsewhere. I think the idea was also picked up for films. The audience now has the excitement of trying to determine when the show starts. I had not intended it that way — not for the movies, anyway. But there was purpose for it in the book.

The book takes seven pages to get under way — four photographs and fewer than two hundred words of text. Like the exhibit, the book opens with Ansel's *Sierra Nevada from Lone Pine, California.* Below it are Nancy's words:

> *This, as citizens, we all inherit.*
> *This is ours, to love and live upon,*
> *and use widely down all the generations of the future.*

Powerful words, a powerful image — these set the stage, stated the challenge. Next, facing Ansel's Nevada Fall, Yosemite National Park, and its burst of water comets, is Nancy's text outlining humanity's need and problem, as her poem continues, scanned as she believed it must be:

> *In all the centuries to come*
> *Always we must have water for dry land, rich earth*
> *beneath the plow, pasture for flocks and herds, fish*
> *in the seas and streams, and timber in the hills.*
> *Yet never can Man live by bread alone.*
> *Now, in an age whose hopes are darkened by huge fears —*
> *   an age frantic with speed, noise, complexity*
> *   an age constricted, of crowds, collisions, of*
> *   cities choked by smog and traffic,*
> *   an age of greed, power, terror*
> *   an age when the closed mind, the starved eye, the*
> *   empty heart, the brutal fist, threaten all life*
> *   upon this planet —*
> *What is the price of exaltation?*

That spread ended with a question the waterfall echoed. More questions, vital ones, followed:

> *"What is the value of solitude?*
> *of peace, of light, of silence?"*

For answers, she gives us Ansel's *Fern in Rain, Mount Rainier National Park,* and *Lake MacDonald, Evening, Glacier National Park.* Finally her prelude asks,

> *"What is the cost of freedom?"*

and Eliot Porter's *Bird in Flight,* a tern, flies away from the sky of Ansel's *Clouds and Peaks, Glacier National Park.* The fanfare works.

14

The photographs magnify the words, and the words return the compliment. A new dimension is added, each art building on the other, as the mind adds its own increment of time.

The double-spread title page follows. Two lines of thirty-point Arrighi type, the italic face that blends with Bruce Rogers's elegant Centaur, carry Ansel's and Nancy's names, and floating under it, expanded Centaur capitals, "THIS IS THE AMERICAN EARTH," spread across both pages. Above them is a photograph not in the exhibition, Ansel's *Half Dome, Winter, Yosemite Valley*. This is an image I found in his file and fell in love with.

It is all clean and simple. The book won a Fifty Books of the Year award from the American Institute of Graphic Arts, with special mention of my title spread. The title spread was duly followed, at long last, by the copyright notice, dated 1960.

Next came the foreword, the first of many in which I seem to have gone on in greater and greater length. This one was written August 23, 1959, in Lupine Meadows in the Tetons. Our family was staying in a cabin there, now gone, as guests of Dick and Pat Emerson. Our stay there was flavored with martens that ran through the attic throughout the night, and an event that tumbled us out into the night to see what was happening to the Tetons themselves when a major earthquake shook Yellowstone. Next morning something less dramatic caught my eye:

A MILE OF MOUNTAIN WALL spills out of the Wyoming sky beyond a wide meadow, a meadow edged with wonder this morning when a small boy's excited cry *moose!* woke us and we watched mother and calf leisurely browse their way downstream, ford, and then disappear into a tangle of cottonwood, aspen, fireweed, and lodgepole. They were not exactly a graceful pair, for nature had something else in mind than mere grace of line when the moose was designed. But they graced the place where we saw them and added to it a new dimension of wildness and of space. A moose needs a lot of wild space and here she found it, in a place that is just about as much the way it was when trappers first saw it as a place could be and still be part of a national park a million people see each year.

It was three years ago that the boy saw his first moose here. Now his age had doubled without a moose having recrossed his ken; yet he knew exactly, without hesitating a moment, what the cow and calf were and with no rack of antlers to guide him. The image fixed well, as wild images do, on that perfectly sensitized, but almost totally unexposed film of his mind. The same thing would happen to any other small boy, given the chance, and the composite image of a thousand such

15

experiences would enrich his living in the civilized world so thinly separated from the wildness the boy was designed to live with.

But where will the chance to know wildness be, when this boy is himself a father, when a generation from now he is seeking out a place in which to expose his own six-year-old to wonder? How much of the magic of this, the American earth, will have been dozed and paved into oblivion by the great feats of engineering that seem to come so much more readily to hand than the knack of saving something for what it is?

Man's marks are still few here, but they are being made faster and faster. The cabin hewed with patient care has mellowed, and the road to it has not burgeoned beyond the two tracks that led there when it was new. The stream has claimed the bridge that once crossed it; twenty-year-old pines grow on one of the approaches, and beavers have built and used and abandoned a lodge on the other. The power line is hardly more permanent than the fence that fell and now moulders in the meadow. The highway is so far away that the drone of cars can hardly be heard above the stream music. Silence closes in soon after the sight-seeing planes pass by the front of the great range.

But each year these silences are briefer. The throng that comes, grows larger, needs more, and the forest and meadow make way to accommodate them. Wider highways speed people through faster and crowd out the places where the cow has dropped her calf for all the generations since the ice retreated, and where the trumpeter swan could inform her cygnets of those few things the evolutionary force had not already told them. Here where the blue vault arches over the wildest and least limited open space and beauty, even here man's numbers are taming and limiting with greater and greater speed, heedless of the little losses that add up to deprivation.

Again and again, the challenge to explore has been met, handled, and relished by one generation — and precluded to any other. Although Thomas Jefferson argued that no one generation has a right to encroach upon another generation's freedom, the future's right to know the freedom of wilderness is going fast. And it need not go at all. A tragic loss could be prevented if only there could be a broader understanding of this: that the resources of the earth do not exist just to be spent for the comfort, pleasure, or convenience of the generation or two who first learn how to spend them; that some of the resources exist for saving, and what diminishes them, diminishes all mankind; that one of these is wilderness, wherein the flow of life, in its myriad forms, has gone on since the beginning of life, essentially uninterrupted by man and his technology; that this, wilderness, is worth saving for what it can mean to itself as part of the conservation ethic; that the saving is imperative to civilization and all mankind, whether or not all men yet know it.

Ansel Adams probably knew this in his marrow when he first began to capture the image of wilderness with his camera. Wilderness, let's say, responded unstintingly to this understanding; if a cloud were needed for a given composition, or a highlight or a lowlight, wilderness would provide it, in exactly the right place, to reveal not only breadth and width, but depth and feel too.

The symbiosis went uninterrupted for some twenty-five years and led to this book's conception. The book was assisted when the National Park Service expressed a wish that something functional be done with the little building the Sierra Club had in Yosemite Valley as a memorial to Joseph LeConte, a pioneer conservationist. Ansel Adams suggested an exhibit of photographs and text that would combine to explain what national parks were really all about.

He was offered substantial help by Walter Starr and the California Academy of Sciences and asked Nancy Newhall to lend "just for a week or two," he thought, her skill with exhibits and text so apparent in her work with the Museum of Modern Art and in her books. She felt an immediate need to bolster her understanding of the conservation force and its origin. One good reference led to another, each revealing still more about that force — and about still more references — until the text could give the exhibit such scope that both artists knew that a book must emerge too. But first Nancy Newhall would go back still further in the collection of great photographs and the record of important ideas, then come back through them, selecting, compressing, arranging, and restating, at last achieving a stirring counterpoint of images, on film and in word, that can reveal in the whole what all the parts could only suggest.

The exhibit itself, although it has turned out to be only a prelude, enjoyed a worldwide audience through the offices of the Smithsonian Institution and the United States Information Agency.

This Is the American Earth epitomizes what the Sierra Club, since its founding in 1892 by John Muir, has been seeking on behalf of the nation's scenic resources and needs to pursue harder in the time to come. The book is by far the most important work the club has published, and the debt is enormous to Ansel Adams for his inspiration of the book, his photographs, and his guidance, and to Nancy Newhall for the organization of the book and the power of its text. It is a stirring book.

It needs to be stirring, stirring of love for the earth, of a suspicion that what man is capable of doing to the earth is not always what he ought to do, of a renewed hope for the wide, spacious freedom that can remain in the midst of the American earth, at least spacious enough, in the uncounted years, for a moose to drop her calf and coax it far down along the stream to browse and splash and play and lead a small boy to wonder.

This Is the American Earth, 1960

17

IT IS ONE THING TO GET THE MATERIAL together for a book. It is another to find financial assistance, a printer, a distributor, and a salesman. In 1959 the Sierra Club's publishing experience consisted primarily of publishing a superior journal, the *Sierra Club Bulletin,* and occasional guidebooks. The annual gross income ranged between one and two thousand dollars.

Ansel and Nancy put us in a different arena. For one thing, the photographs required superb reproduction. That would not come cheap. Nor would the typography, which required a matching elegance. We could find no commercial publisher who wanted to accept enough of our ideas, or their cost. We tried three whom we thought might carry out the task we had in mind. None was ready enough.

Fortunately, the advance work by Ansel, Nancy, and me had all been accomplished on other budgets. Thanks to the generosity of Marion Randall Parsons, who had always been interested in Sierra Club publishing, there was a small fund to start with, but the printer would need far more than that. One of Ansel's photographer friends was Dick McGraw, whose father Max, of McGraw-Edison, could easily come up with assistance if he were persuaded it was a good idea. He was persuaded, and we had an outright gift of fifteen thousand dollars and an interest-free loan of another ten thousand.

We needed a co-publisher and Paul Brooks was our first choice. As executive editor of Houghton-Mifflin he had co-published with Virginia Adams two of Ansel's books. On November 29, 1958, I wrote Nancy Newhall from Boston, immediately after my encounter with Paul, paraphrasing him, then setting forth my goal for the book:

What you people seem to be after, then, is an art book. We would have a devil of a time getting rid of our 5,000 copies at $12. Many bookstores don't handle art books and we don't have very good connections with photographic stores, who could also help. Anyhow, your art book could only convert the converted. We would much rather see 50,000 or 100,000 copies sold to spread the conservation message more broadly, where it's needed, to an audience only a very few of whom would detect the difference between the costly and the commercial reproduction and between the lavish and the modest format. (And we could pay no higher, for finished books, than 30 percent of the final selling price and would be leery of any advance subscription-selling campaign on your part of the edition.) So I see no role for H-M in this book as you have planned it.

I told Paul that the subsidy was provided to give us top-quality work and to assist our own revolving fund for conservation publication. I left the door open a crack pending developments in New York in my inquiries of Photogravure and Color, etc. But I now feel free to work out any other program that can meet our original objectives. Let me restate them as I see them now:

1. We want nothing to interrupt the alchemy that will result from the combination of a text packed with power and mood on the one hand and the full impact of superb big photographs on the other.

2. We will strive for a big audience for the few superb books we can make. Our (see, I cut myself in!) book will be out on display in homes, where friends will look at it and talk about what is says. It will be prominent in all waiting rooms we can reach with this message: "Why not let the people who are waiting to see you look at something beautiful, stimulating, and important instead of outdated magazines. If you are a doctor, this book can start the cure!"

3. We can still seek the opportunity of broad distribution through (a) book clubs who want a prestige item (that will beat hell out of the *Columbia Encyclopedia*) and (b) class paperback edition if we think a miniature can do any job at all — later on.

4. We will remember that this dream of wide distribution is still only a dream — and still remember that every damned thing in this world that has great value came from a dream and not from an accounting department, or from bland ideas blandly published. (Is my bias showing?)

5. Art books by no means necessarily reach the converted. They reach the most urbane people of all, to whom Bourbon comes from a bottle, not from a rippling sweep of grain, diluted with the waters that come from wilderness. They need reminding. They lead. Reminded, they'll lead better. They'll remember longest what is stated with greatest impact, and damn it that is what our book is going to have.

6. We shall nevertheless be mindful of some major problems in production and distribution that still lie ahead and which are going to require some creative energy too. Ideas, please. For example, E. R. Squibb and Co. gave the initial distribution, free to doctors, of Robert Osborne's *Leisure*. Then the publishing world beat a trail to Squibb's door asking permission to publish commercially. We could do worse!

Our search for a printer ended in New Jersey, with Peter Convente of Photogravure and Color Company. His gravure samples had the quality we needed. For added brilliance we wanted the photograph image space varnished, and he provided this in not quite the way we wanted. He used the printing plate for applying the varnish, which meant that the most varnish went on the blacks, where we needed it least, and the least on the whites. For all that, we ended up with a surprise: there was an unexpected three-dimensional effect in the photographs. Alfred Knopf was quite impressed with it, and this was just as well, for it was his company that undertook to distribute the book in all but the eleven western states.

Taking a deep breath we ordered ten thousand copies and set the price at fifteen dollars. I knew from an earlier experience with Knopf that it would be useful for us to help sell the book, to Sierra Club members as well as to bookstores in the West. We had reported to club members on the progress of the book, but we had fewer than fifteen thousand members at the time. When Alfred Knopf published *This Is*

Dinosaur for us, I had tried a hand at a promotional brochure and was ready to try again for *This Is the American Earth*. The brochure was the size of an actual double spread of the book, featuring Ansel's *Burnt Stump and New Grass* opposite Nancy's prose, together with a few Polaroid snaps of the team at work preparing the book and some rich promotional prose: "The most important announcement the Sierra Club has ever made."

I believed it and so, happily, did many of the members, who were already well aware of the magic in anything Ansel undertook. The next problem was recording the money that came in. The *New York Times* reviewed the book three times. A Kansas City paper devoted its entire editorial page to the book. Justice William O. Douglas was kind enough to add his name to a claim that I also believed: "One of the greatest statements in the history of conservation." The final chapter appeared as a segment on "The Today Show." The images filled the television screen, accompanied by the text, read by Dave Garroway, and with appropriate musical background. Stewart Udall, then Secretary of the Interior, was ready to look for funds to enable Aaron Copland to write a symphony based on the book.

The public responded. The ten thousand copies were about gone, the interest-free loan was paid back, and a second printing was under way. So was a conservation publishing program that, by the time the Sierra Club thought I would be more useful on some other organization's staff, had added nineteen more exhibit format books to the club's series and had begun four others, two of which the club was to publish and two which others would publish. This was followed by ten in the same format published by Friends of the Earth — all being titles I had a hand in. Not now, but sometime, I should like to explain the trials and tribulations suffered by many hands in all this. There are two others stories to be told instead, and they relate to what *This Is the American Earth* started.

"IN WILDNESS IS THE PRESERVATION OF THE WORLD"

T HE BIG PACKAGE IN THE MAIL was from Eliot Porter. Two albums, slightly larger than exhibit format in size, containing eighty of his color photographs, dye-transfer prints selected from his twenty-year search for subjects to illustrate selections he had made from Thoreau's *Journals* and *Walden*. They were from his exhibition at the Smithsonian entitled "The Seasons." He had taken them to six publishers, all of whom thought the idea of making a book of the show a beautiful one, but much too expensive to undertake. He had sent them to me at Nancy Newhall's suggestion.

By the time I had perused the albums — and I could not think of doing anything else until I had finished the perusal — I was ready to rob a bank if that should be necessary to publish the work. The generosity of Kenneth Bechtel and his Belvedere Scientific Fund made that procedure unnecessary. His decision would not have happened but for the happy intervention of his wife Nancy, a photographer herself, who thought the book should happen. This time it was a twenty-thousand-dollar grant and a thirty-thousand-dollar interest-free loan. That was enough extra help to get the book under way; but the Sierra Club had not yet — it was 1962 — left its California moorings very far, and Francis Farquhar, although a New Englander himself, did not think the Sierra Club should be wandering so far afield in its publishing. "I'll take care of Francis," Kenneth Bechtel told me. The Sierra Club's first color book was under way.

This time we knew where to set the type. I had concluded, for our first exhibit-format books that any typefaces would do as long as they were Centaur and Arrighi set by Mackenzie and Harris in San Francisco. In my earlier U.C. Press and *Bulletin* days I had learned to like Old Style No. 7, Caslon, Bodoni, Baskerville, Janson, Goudy (I had met him), and Weiss initials — and to hate all sans serif faces because they are dull and deny type design its history. With Centaur and Arrighi, however, it was love at first sight, and it endures.

We were baffled, however, about how to find the right color printer. There was one in Hackensack, New Jersey, whose price was very tempting, but the sample printing he gave us showed some serious register problems. Good color work requires accurate registration. The printer was aware of the shortcoming and promised to eat all the sheets that were not in proper register. This might have required an extraordinary appetite. He could print but four subjects at a time, one color at a time, and it was thanks to Bruce Kilgore, a Sierra Club editor, that Mr. Hackensack was spared. "How could he conceivably eat all the trouble he might get into before we discover it?" Bruce asked as we were walking up Fifth Avenue. I started looking for another printer.

We had already thought of Europe, and we checked out printers in Switzerland and Holland. Just how I now forget, but we were to end up in Greenwich Village, or rather in one of its fringes. Barnes Press, on Spring Street, had what we needed — big offset presses that could print four colors at once on sheets big enough to hold sixteen exhibit-format pages. Moreover, their register was unbelievably precise. Hugh Barnes was the president and his brother Jerry the chief engineer. Jerry's goal was to obtain that maximum precision. He didn't want a printing dot to be anywhere else but exactly where it should be. The Barnes brothers also realized that a given sheet of paper, as it passed from one color to another in the four-color procession, became a little bit larger as a result of the pressure on it as the successive colors were printed. So they arranged to have each successive printing plate correspondingly larger, if ever so little, than the preceding plate in the color sequence.

The first color proof sheets were printed on the proof press with no space between the subjects. They were an amazing mass of spectacular color. When the first of those sheets was seen in San Francisco by Denny Wilcher and Bill Webb, who were now part of the team that represented Sierra Club books, they took sheets to their principal bookstores and wholesalers. They created an excitement I hadn't thought possible. Some stores displayed the sheets and began taking orders.

Meanwhile, back at Barnes Press, the final color plates were ready, sixteen pages up in each of five forms. The book was to be single-sheet collated, which meant that color subjects could be grouped on press in whatever way they would print best together. This was important to the final quality, for if a color subject that required a great deal of ink were to be lined up in the same row of subjects with another, but smaller, subject making similar demands for ink, there would be a slight but nevertheless discernible ghost where the larger subject was denied all the ink it needed.

Single-sheet collation would allow the forms, then, to be imposed in an ideal way; but there would be extra work in the bindery, where the piles of sheets would be cut into individual pages, placed in proper order on the collating table, and picked up by the collating women who walked around the table assembling the book piece by piece. To jump way ahead in my story, I have a copy of a much later book, *Everest: The West Ridge,* which was picked up backwards.

But back to the press. The first form was on press for make-ready, in which the final adjustments of plates and ink flow are made. As the press delivered sheets, Hugh Barnes, Eliot Porter, the press foreman, and I watched. The press got up to speed — six thousand sheets per hour at top speed — and a sheet would be pulled from the press and swung or, rather, floated to the light table, there to be scrutinized by all hands, magnifying glass in hand. Ordinarily the instructions for adjustment would be something like "The yellow is out on the lower right edge of the sheet" or "Reduce the blue" or "Cut the red." Hugh Barnes would go along with the register shifts, but concerning the color he would go the other way: "Add more blue" or "Bring up the yellow."

By the time some five hundred sheets were delivered — and there was a lot of beauty there — Hugh pulled me off to the side and said, "Tell us to throw these sheets away and they'll know they have a fussy job. We'll split the cost of the paper with you." I was astonished, but went along with Hugh's advice.

That decision made, I had little more to do than be a spectator. Eliot and Hugh did the critical scrutinizing. Eliot was superb, not only as a photographer, but also as a man who realized the capabilities and limits of a color press. He appreciated the excellence of color registry that exceeded, at times, what he could achieve in making his own dye-transfer printing back in his darkroom in Tusuque, New Mexico. He knew that a press, printing sixteen subjects at a time, with adjustments to what could be corrected row by row, not subject by subject, could not give each subject the individual attention he could give it in Tusuque. He was thus able to accept the inevitable compromise. I know of other photographers who, unlike Eliot or Ansel, could not make that adjustment as they watched press sheets arrive. They drove printers up the wall. Eliot could keep them on the pressroom floor, loving the beautiful work he had brought them to print, loving him, and loving their own work.

So it happened that in a not too well-known press in a fringe of Greenwich Village a book come into being that was to be voted, at the next Leipzig Book Fair, one of the ten most beautiful books in the world.

Before Leipzig had passed judgment, book buyers had spoken their piece. One particular place, the Publix Bookstore in Cleveland, Ohio, kept ordering the book, twenty-five copies at a crack, with extraordinary frequency. I called them up from San Francisco to see what the reason was. The answer was simple: "People keep buying it."

When you price a book at twenty-five dollars (1963 dollars, or about eighty 1990 dollars) you take a deep breath, cross your fingers, pray, hope, and prepare yourself to be considered insane. I did all those things, not necessarily in that order, and was not prepared to believe that the first printing of thirteen thousand copies would be sold before the book was off press, especially a book jacketed with an abstract image of leaves floating on autumn-colored water and bearing the unlikely title, *"In Wildness Is the Preservation of the World."*

Students in various university towns, we learned, were saving up their beer money and buying the book instead of, say, about fifty beers. They were adding the price of another sixteen beers to buy the two two-by-three-foot posters we also printed at Barnes Press, with the same excellent registry and color rendition, to promote the book, thus promoting the book even further by having the posters on the walls of dormitory rooms.

But that is a little ahead of the story. Something else quite amazing to me had happened first. We go now to the Players Club, beyond the fringe of upper Greenwich Village.

Ian Ballantine had invited me there, the Ian who again and again has proved himself one of the publishing geniuses of our time. He is the only publisher I know who does his own market surveying first-hand, so skillfully that he seems to know what readers are going to want before they do. As a result, he has been able to hop from peak to

23

peak in the publishing world, without having to spend a lot of time in the valleys.

Ian was now in his Environmental Mode. He had seen what had happened to *This Is the American Earth* and was happening to *"In Wildness . . ."* and was beginning to happen to several exhibit-format books that were now issuing from the Sierra Club at the rate of two or three per year. He was master of the mass-market paperback. We were in the Players Club because he thought it worthwhile to mass-market quality paperbacks. Mass-market prices were then uniformly less than a dollar. He wanted to increase the size, step up the quality of production, and try out a price of $3.95. He wanted to start a series of miniature exhibit-format Sierra Club books, and he wanted to start that series — which would eventually number seventeen titles — with the two that were already a huge success in their full format.

I agreed, and took back to the Sierra Club a check for twenty thousand dollars as an advance on royalties, thereupon to be scolded for what I had done by the Sierra Club's publications committee. The books were still selling well in hardback, at fifteen dollars for *This Is the American Earth* and twenty-five dollars for *"In Wildness Is the Preservation of the World."* What would this new arrangement of mine do but kill the sales of the hardbacks with this new $3.95 bargain?

They had a point, and I could only hope — and guess — that they would be proved wrong. My own conclusion had been that there were two distinct markets. The full-size exhibit-format books would appeal to the people who could afford expensive art books, and they would still prefer that size and content to reflect their taste. The bargain-size would find a completely different audience — those who cared for books but did not wish to give up that many beers.

As it turned out, I was lucky. The little book not only did not compete with the big book, but it also turned out to be a brochure for the big book, a brochure for which the reader paid. That, at least, was a conclusion that could be drawn from the results. *"In Wildness . . ."* provided the best example. The hardback went into several successive printings, having reached a total sale by 1985 of about seventy-five thousand copies. The rate of sale continued high when the paperback appeared, even though the book was theoretically getting older. And it is my recollection that the sales of the paperback edition, including a second version in larger format, has now approached one million copies. A second edition of the full-sized book was issued and sold out in 1988. A full-sized paperback ("superback," I named it) followed in 1989.

ON THE LOOSE

E LIOT PORTER, THOREAU, NEWHALL, ADAMS, and a host of others were now reaching an audience that had not been reached before. Ian Ballantine thanked me for making him rich. Barnes Press had gained a new group of admiring customers; they used Sierra Club books, in both formats, as their own advertising department. The Sierra Club goals were becoming widely known (my own inexpert survey showed that 40 percent of the new members were coming in because of the books). The club's gross income from books rose from two thousand dollars or so per year to a 1968 total of one and a third million dollars (exceeding four million 1990 dollars).

And Barnes Press was still able to be bold. The second color paperback, *The Place No One Knew: Glen Canyon on the Colorado* (I seemed to like long titles) survived a crisis. It was printed sixty-four pages up, and the first ninety thousand sheets, when I had a chance to look at them, were muddy in color. Hugh Barnes threw them out, but not until we had agreed to split the cost of the paper three ways, Ballantine, Barnes, and the Sierra Club each taking a third. Once again people knew, even on the mass-market quality paperbacks, that Sierra Club books were a fussy job.

There was an exception. One of the series was submitted as a manuscript illustrated by the best color prints money could buy in a drugstore. The manuscript consisted of a Morocco-bound volume containing those prints, which illustrated a text by Terry and Renny Russell intermingled with excerpts from the Russell brothers's favorite authors. One exceptional thing about the text was that it was all in Terry Russell's calligraphy, superbly done. The other exceptional thing was the strength of what the book had to say and the power of the juxtaposition of text and illustration. "Play for more than you can afford to lose and you will learn the game," one of the excerpts said. Another said, "I'd rather wake up in the middle of nowhere than anyplace else in the world." Terry could reach for Winston Churchill and Steve McQueen.

History was repeating itself. Even though the prints were indeed of drugstore quality, their concept was nothing of the sort. Terry, who did most of the writing, was a present-day Thoreau, and given a chance might please Eliot Porter with his photographic skill. The book had to be published.

"This is not the kind of book the Sierra Club should be publishing," the club's publications committee decided. I had protested that I thought it damned well was, and would reach an audience none of our other books had yet sought. No sale. The committee was adamant.

But the committee relented when I brought back the twenty-thousand-dollar check from Ian Ballantine for paperback rights to *This Is the American Earth* and *"In Wildness . . ."* They gave me a go-ahead. Ian liked *On the Loose* very much. So we ordered sheets enough from Barnes Press to make fifty thousand copies of the book — fifteen thousand copies to be hardbound and slipcased for the Sierra Club to sell at $6.95, the other thirty-five thousand copies to come out a year later as a $3.95 paperback.

Ian never got a chance to sell any of those first fifty thousand sheets. The book was so successful they all had to be hardbound. So far the book has approximately equaled *"In Wildness . . ."* in total sales — about seventy thousand hardback, and nearly a million in paperback.

The man who most deserved to enjoy this success never knew of it. When their raft flipped in Desolation Canyon, it was Renny who grabbed something that was floating. Terry didn't and was lost. He had played for more than he could afford to lose. We, not he, learned the game — we who have been lucky enough to experience *On The Loose.* If you haven't, please look it up. Imagine for yourself what this young man might have achieved had he lived.

It is only fair to give Ian Ballantine the credit for knowing what the book would do in the marketplace and also for knowing what might make the publications committee go along.

On a later occasion, when he had persuaded Paul Ehrlich to write *The Population Bomb* (after I had failed to persuade him), Ian said, "Tell your publications committee they have twenty-four hours to approve this as a Sierra Club book or I'll do it by myself."

It took thirty-six, and the book has now sold more than two million copies. The book sold another two hundred fifty thousand copies every time Paul Ehrlich appeared on "The Tonight Show" and talked about it. And he was a favorite guest of Johnny Carson's.

NEW YORK DAYS

"SURVIVAL IN THE SEVENTIES Depends upon You Being Informed," an Ian Ballantine display poster proclaimed. At my suggestion, subsequent versions of it infused the participle and replaced the 'You' with 'Your.' The poster was heralding the importance of a new series of Ballantine paperbacks, the first of which had been so successful that Ian co-published another ten with Friends of the Earth.

Friends of the Earth (FOE) received its initial funding through publishing. The Sierra Club had decided on May 3, 1969, that it no longer needed me on its staff. FOE was founded in New York City sixty-six days later and needed members, but first it needed the dollars with which to look for the members.

26

One of FOE's new directors was Perry Knowlton, literary agent and president of Curtis-Brown. John Schanhaar had been the Sierra Club's sales and promotion manager, and he soon joined me in exile. He was in touch with the publishing world closely enough to know that the McCall Publishing Company was about to go into book publishing. Perry went to talk to them. By October we were at lunch in La Fonda del Sol, where I could always be found at lunch if I was in New York City. To my great regret, that restaurant closed several years ago. It should have been protected as a national historic landmark. Whatever you may have thought of the food (I liked it very much, but how would I know; I was very fond of chilis rellenos and rarely ordered anything else), the design was delightful — the most delightful, so far as I was concerned, of all that Alexander Girard had ever designed. Ask to look at my complete selection of La Fonda del Sol matches and sugars, and join me in my regret at never having stolen some of the glasses in which my Tanqueray martinis, straight up with nothing in them, came.

"Has Mr. Brower made a reservation?" people would sometimes say. And the answer became, "Mr. Brower never makes a reservation." Loyalty has its rewards, and mine at La Fonda is that I had only to wave at the maître d' as I came in from the Time-Life Building plaza and the party I was with would be ushered to the first table that became vacant — more often than not to my favorite table, one that would seat from five to seven people, under a pleasant Girard-designed awning. I hope someone has photographs of the La Fonda permanent exhibit of south-of-the-border art and good recordings of the happenings of the Sunday fiesta there. O Joy Divine of La Fonda!

One recollection I ought not talk about but invariably do was the time the waiter brought the phone to our table and said: "The world knows where you eat lunch. London is calling."

There under the awning were Perry, Bob Stein of McCall, Jack Schanhaar, and I and the almost final draft of a book contract. Perry asked for an added favor or two for FOE, and Bob Stein replied that he didn't want to get hung up on details, and he went along. The contract called for twelve books that McCall would co-publish with FOE in exhibit format. They had noted well the impact the Sierra Club series had enjoyed, and they wanted to be part of more of the same. The contract called for a total payment of advances on royalties of two hundred thousand dollars, equally divided among the twelve books, half to be paid at the time of signing for each manuscript, the other half upon completion and acceptance. A further thirty thousand dollars was an outright grant to FOE to help it grow and thus become an important audience for the books, as the Sierra Club's members (there were then nearly eighty thousand of them) had proved to be. McCall was prepared to co-publish four books a year. Half the royalties would go to author and photographer, the other half was to be shared by FOE, of which I was then president, and the John Muir Institute for Environmental Studies, of which I was then executive director. One of the provisions of the contract was a serendipity of sorts for two Browers — our son Ken and me. Ken had been a key contributor to several of the Sierra Club exhibit-format books, and editor of eight of the twenty. The contract with McCall, we were not displeased to learn, would be valid only if he or I were involved.

While the agreement lasted, we were. Then McCall was sold to Saturday Review Press, which before too long went down the tube. One of the assets they wanted to count as they went down was *Our Fragile Craft,* a book they wanted me to write. I shared with FOE the advance royalty they paid me. What I submitted did not please them, and it simmered slowly on the back burner.

The October harvest of revenue was followed by a project less remunerative but farther reaching. In late November Anne and I were attending an environment conference that had a global agenda. Next to us was Garrett De Bell, an ecologist who, we discovered as we talked, had a great deal to say. Perhaps he remembers just how we got there, but before the meeting was over I had suggested and he had agreed to put together an environmental handbook.

Senator Gaylord Nelson had suggested that April 22, 1970, be proclaimed Earth Day. Ian Ballantine was ready to put the elements together. He dispatched his editor, George Young, to Berkeley to work day and night, a few blocks north of the Berkeley campus, with Garrett De Bell. Now and then I would drop by to see how they were doing and to suggest an inclusion or two. For my foreword — forewords are all I seem able to write — Ian chose part of something I had already written. There was no time to lose and no time was lost. Remember, it was late November when the idea popped up. In late January *The Environmental Handbook* was in the stores. It was not long before a million copies had sold. Royalties were split by the McCall formula — half to the editor, half split between the John Muir Institute and FOE.

Survival in the seventies did depend on your and our being informed, and FOE's survival began. Publishing bore the initial burden. The word was out. So was the name, Friends of the Earth. And not just in the United States. Before the dust had settled, Friends of the Earth was founded in the United Kingdom. One of its first directors was William H. Murray, Scottish mountaineer and author. He was asked to write a text for an exhibit-format book on the Scottish Highlands. Amory Lovins and Philip Evans were to cooperate on *Eryri, the Mountains of Longing.* Ian Ballantine was ready, with a British enterprise of his, to publish an *Environmental Handbook,* British-style, to co-publish a British edition of *The Population Bomb* with FOE, and to assist with a further spreading of the word, abroad this time, in France and Sweden. Things were moving. Books were the transport.

OVERSEAS

"THE ENVIRONMENTAL MOVEMENT is getting banalized," Ian Ballantine observed, as he watched the list of environmental titles grow and the audience of environmental books diminish, together with his own interest in adding to the list. "Then why not publish Banaltime Books," I quipped, with hope. Ian smiled, but didn't want to try to repeat a success. He had already helped the Sierra Club with calendars, posters, mass-market paperbacks, high-quality paperbacks, and, overriding all this, a unique-in-publishing Ballantine savvy. He would try once more.

Werner Linz, of Herder and Herder, thought there would be a market for books that looked like exhibit format, but were smaller — down from ten and a quarter by thirteen and a half inches to the size that most presses could of necessity handle with maximum economy, eight and one half by eleven, letter-size in the United States. *The Earth's Wild Places* was the series title used for McCall's FOE books. The new series would be titled *Celebrating the Earth*. Werner, Ian, and I would team up. We would follow the *On the Loose* formula. Fifty thousand sheets, fifteen thousand in hardback originally, the remaining thirty-five thousand in paperback a year later, the hardback royalties to Herder and Herder and FOE, the paperback to FOE-Ballantine. Fifteen dollars for the former, six ninety-five for the latter, four titles a year.

We were off and running with the first three — *Only a little planet, Song of the Earth Spirit,* and *Of all things most yielding.* Partway through, Werner moved to McGraw-Hill, taking the remaining titles with him. The hardbacks did fairly well, the paperbacks very well, going into further printings. Further reprintings of several of the FOE exhibit-format books were arranged by Werner Linz. He had also figured out how to bring into print two of the exhibit-format books left stranded when Saturday Review Press failed — *Guale: The Golden Coast of Georgia,* and *Micronesia: Island Wilderness.* Two more titles were to appear: *New England's White Mountains: At Home in the Wild* and *Wake of the Whale,* the first in cooperation with the Appalachian Mountain Club and the New York Graphic Society, the second with E. P. Dutton and Hutchings in the U.K. They added another eighty thousand to the number out on the shelves or about to be there.

It is easy to toss off numbers, like eighty thousand books on the shelves, and to forget where the books come from, once the conclusion has been reached that a book should be written, edited, perhaps illustrated, and designed. The book, after all, must be printed, bound, and sold.

The writing is a difficult subject for me to discuss, since I never learned enough about it to write with the inevitability, say, of Wallace Stegner. In my one attempt to edit him I found I could neither add a word nor subtract one without doing damage.

That I do not write with any trace of inevitability will be attested to by Anne Brower, Bill Travers, and, in particular, Heather Bennett. Her patient pleas and initially intransigent responses would be most helpful to other editors, if not writers, and should be published separately (and privately). I can say this about editors, thanks to my half-century of desultory editing, some of it almost ruthless, of almost everyone but myself.

Concerning illustrations, I was spoiled early by the wealth of superb material created by Ansel Adams, Edward Weston, Cedric Wright, Philip Hyde, Eliot Porter, and, as the years sped on, by Morley Bear, Dave Bohn, Patricia Caulfield, Steve Crouch, William Curtsinger, Norman Dyrenfurth, Phillip Evans, William Garnett, Joseph Holmes, Nancy and Retta Johnston, Richard Kauffman, Gerhard Klammet, Martin Litton, Amory Lovins, John Chang McCurdy, James Rose, Galen Rowell, Renny and Terry Russell, Martin Schweitzer, Lowell Sumner, James Valentine, Robert Wenkam, Brett and Cole Weston. My book-publishing efforts would have gone nowhere without them.

Francis and Samuel Farquhar and August Frugé made me aware of book design and designers — Robert Washbish, the Grabhorn brothers, Frederick Goudy, Amadeo Tommasini, Nancy Newhall, Ward Ritchie, and Adrian Wilson — aware enough to win a few awards for what I had learned from them.

When it comes to printing, I am thankful to have survived all the printer's ink I breathed between 1938 and 1978 — black ink in the first fifteen years and the rest in colors, probably more toxic, for the next twenty-five. I have not overcome the addiction and would recommend against my being autopsied.

If I were paper, I would love letterpress and the sensuous impressive kiss of real type — and having that impression caressed by a loving hand. I would not object to gravure. I would feel quite cool about offset, in which the ink-to-paper affair is over so soon that a one-night stand would, by comparison, have an element of perpetuity in it.

If, however, I were not paper, but an exacting customer, I would feel very good about the four-color offset presses of Barnes Press in New York, Carlisle in San Mateo (if Richard Kauffman was watching over it), his own home press, Garrod and Lofthouse in Crawley (and it isn't far from London), Imprimerie Réunis in Lausanne, and, above all, but with no slight intended to the foregoing, of Mondadori Editores in

Verona, my favorite city (and not just because our battalion in the Tenth Mountain Division liberated Verona in April 1945).

As I looked back on my life and times with books and ask, "Would you do it again?" I conclude that there would really be no point in watching a book be printed unless the press were in Verona, close enough to the old city that you could stay at the Due Torre Hotel, an international treasure in Italy whether or not the Italians know it yet. True, I had a momentary infatuation with Assisi a few years ago — understandable in anyone who is as fond of wildlife as Saint Francis was — but I got over it, and will remain loyal to Verona, Mondadori, and the Due Torre forever.

I first encountered Mondadori at the Frankfurt Book Fair in 1968. They wanted a chance to print Sierra Club exhibit-format books and offered to produce a few sample color separations from *Everest: The West Ridge* to show how good they were, and how low their prices were. A re-encounter was delayed by three events: first, by my parting company with the Sierra Club staff; second, the McCall Publishing Company corporate relationship with Imprimerie Réunis in Lausanne; and third, by a new source of color separations Hugh Barnes found for us — Karl De Schutter, in Antwerp.

Visiting Antwerp to check color proofs for the Galapagos, the Brooks Range, Maui, and Wales brought me in touch not only with great separations but also with some of the finest meals in my life. Karl knew exactly where to find them, aboard ship in the harbor. He also knew where best to accommodate Anne (when she could come) and me — his and Paula's beautiful home, situated in what we called De Schutter National Park, their splendid and extensive garden. We never learned how to imitate Paula's skill in decorating her home, in midwinter, with fresh blossoms. Somehow she could break the winter rest of freshly pruned branches and make the buds think "It's Belgium, it must be Tuesday in May."

I visited Lausanne often while our books on the Alps and Brooks Range were being printed. It was a pleasant train trip from Geneva, the InterContinental Hotel was right across from the station and only the martinis were too expensive, the Metro to the shore of Lac Léman was next door, and it was but a short walk to the best fondues I ever toyed with. Eric Schindler, FOE's Swiss representative and an excellent photographer in his own right, joined me in Lausanne to learn how to apply his skills to the overseeing of book printing. I was never able to persuade Imprimerie Réunis to varnish the photographs. Through the years I had learned about the importance of varnishing from Taylor & Taylor in San Francisco and the Gillick Press in Berkeley. They were in turn inspired by what Ansel Adams had taught R. R. Donnelly, in Chicago, about platemaking and varnishing, which was to make history in Ansel's book, *The Sierra Nevada: The John Muir Trail*. Lausanne insisted on laminating instead of varnishing — beautiful, but far more expensive and unnecessarily so.

One of the most important events in Lausanne was a visit from Edwin Spencer Matthews, Jr., an attorney I had gotten to know when he helped the Sierra Club keep Huntington Hartford's proposed bar and restaurant out of Central Park, across from the Plaza Hotel. Edwin moved to Coudert Frères in Paris. Having learned about the founding of FOE in New York and of my happening to be in Lausanne, he took the next train to see what we could do to help the founding of Friends of the Earth sister organizations in other countries and to help book publishing become an important function in the new organizations. He was critical to the founding of Les Amis de la Terre in Paris, Jordens Vanner in Stockholm, and FOE-U.K. in London. In London, at the organizing meeting he had arranged at the Traveler's Club, it was decided that Edwin, Barclay Inglis of Scotland, and I would be the guarantors of FOE-U.K. That was incidental. What was important was that we met Amory Lovins and Phillip Evans there. Amory was the author and one of the photographers for a proposed book, *Eryri, the Mountains of Longing,* and Phil was the other photographer. The book would save Snowdonia National Park from an open-pit mine and would help Amory decide to disclose the ecological and financial threats of nuclear power and to revise world energy strategy instead of finishing his doctorate at Oxford, where he was a don at Merton College. Edwin would go on to be the most important international FOE advocate and promoter of European editions of FOE books (my file of the tissues of his FOE letters is three inches thick!) and to become the second president of FOE-U.S.

Phil Evans could get to Verona from Wales more easily and more often than I could from Berkeley, and he did too in the course of Modadori's printing of seven Joseph Holmes calendars, a William Curtsinger whale calendar (of poster size), three books in FOE's new series, Celebrating the Earth, and ten books, counting reprints, in the series The Earth's Wild Places.

Phil, Amory, and Edwin were all mountaineers, and in differing ways I think we found that publishing is as challenging as mountaineering. Any lowering of physical hazards is more than offset with financial risks, and risk is essential to achievement. You can fall in both, and I did, but the appeal has not been diminished one whit.

In Verona, between stints of watching press runs at whatever time of day or night a run was ready to watch, I attended the comings and goings of swifts — birds mountaineers never tire of — bird-watching either from my various Due Torre windows or after a walk through charming streets, some of them Fiat-free, from the restaurants along the human-foot-polished marble walks adjoining the Arena. I got pretty good at predicting when the last swift would desert the evening sky, but I never learned when the first swift would dash into the morning.

I should have done better about mornings, because it was Ami Guichard, our printer in Lausanne, who awakened me to the importance, in the affairs of living creatures with eyes, of late evening and early morning light. Dusk gentles you into a dark that has stars to look at, a night with good sleep in it, readying you for the rich colors that mark the advance of the new day and light up your senses at a speed they were long ago attuned to. Ami didn't say so, but I'll add it. Electric lights and television screens are what the devil dreamed up to drive nature's light away from people.

The presses in San Francisco, San Mateo, Kingsport, Crawley, Antwerp, Lausanne, Verona, Berkeley, and Greenwich Village did their best to bring that light back, and I am grateful to all the people who helped me watch it happen. It is a long, long list.

Now, as for selling books, my favorite line came from Joe Biggins when he was sales manager at the University of California Press — "Anyone can write a book, but it takes a genius to sell one."

Of the Sierra Club series of twenty books, four hundred thousand copies were sold. Round the FOE total to seven hundred thousand, most of them priced at twenty-five dollars or more in original printings, with some of the reprintings at about fifteen dollars, or a rough average of twenty dollars. So book buyers had paid some fourteen million dollars to burden their coffee tables. Nearly four million Ballantine color paperbacks at an average of five dollars, half a million posters at four dollars, four million Ballantine mass-market paperbacks at a dollar each, the beginnings of the spectacular success enjoyed by Sierra Club calendars and the faint echo of this in FOE calendars, another million, and finally what the Mead Corporation did with excerpts from the books and of some of my paragraphs in their school and office supplies, for another ten million. Add it all up, I said to myself from time to time, and what do you have to show for your effort in conservation publishing?

The numbers? About twenty million people spending some fifty million dollars in the marketplace to read the Sierra Club and Friends of the Earth message at the buyers's expense. Roughly 40 percent of that went to the bookstores, of course. And perhaps 30 percent of the remaining 60 went to the printer. The promoters got their share too, but what they did spread the message far beyond the final purchasing audience, if only in bits and pieces.

In the aggregate, I argued to doubters (and there were many), this was a fairly good shortcut to fund-raising. What do you do with the funds you raise? I asked, and stayed to provide my own answer. You hire writers, speakers, printers, distributors, and public relations experts to spread your message at your expense. Publishing spreads it at the readers's expense.

I was persuaded. Who else?

That is a hard question to ask, unless you raise funds for a survey and believe what it tells you. I know what I would like to think. The books were there, treasured somehow by those who bought them, perused or perhaps even borrowed and read, and perhaps returned, by their friends, recycled by being reread, reviewed, the books's messages being spread by what the reviewers said, used as reference for other writers and speakers, filmmakers, talk-show hosts, conferences, hearings, and barroom brawls.

One of my pleasures is going to better bookstores and looking at the high prices those exhibit format books now bring — sometimes five or six times the original price. If the booksellers have forgotten to mark them up, I buy them back. *The Wall Street Journal* once described them as a good investment. On this I welcome their advice.

IN PRAISE OF THE BOOK!

LET US RE-EMPOWER THE BOOK! Free the world from the treadmill of television and radio, which requires the captive audience to race along at the producer's pace, their own sense of position lost. No chance to reread a sentence because of its power (or because it wasn't clear enough the first time), no chance to look up from a page and contemplate, returning to the page when you want to without losing the continuity, no chance to read a paragraph aloud to spouses, whether or not he or she wants to hear it, no chance, if you are a proper book vandal, to make some sort of mark on the page, or file your protest there, or to note the page number on the back fly so that you can find the passage again, no chance, if it is an exhibit-format book, to build a special bookcase, as my friend Dick Emerson did, on which you can display one of the beautiful spreads, or several, as part of your living-room decor, no chance to put the book longingly on the shelf, telling it "I shall return."

The book is something well worth getting addicted to. Television (and radio) can make no such claim. Yes, you can videotape a program, but you know what happens. If you are addicted to television, you will never find time to look at your videotapes. But don't misunderstand me. I have nothing against video recorders. There is one at the office and there are five at home. What is secretly in my mind, I suspect, is that I have them so that I can record television, and, having recorded it, never have to look at it. Or so that I can use my video cameras for taking notes to be edited someday. . . .

Yes, a book. But what book? What publishing giant? What scheme for sending the book on its errand and having it accepted when it arrives?

Let's start with the giant, and with two of my model giants — Alfred and Blanche Knopf. I am sorry that I never met her and met Alfred, with delight, only in his dual role as publisher and as a member of the National Parks Advisory Board; but I knew what they accomplished, in general, and would welcome the chance to learn more from those who knew the Knopfs well. What they mean to me, as models, is that they sought out and were willing to take a chance and publish things they knew needed to be published, not because it was about Garfield or those other cats, or because there had been a market survey in which buyers at Dalton or Walden believed the book would sell in great numbers.

They had a boldness that is an endangered species. William Shawn had it at the *New Yorker*. Who else would have done what he did with John Hersey's *Hiroshima,* or Rachel Carson's *Silent Spring,* or other pieces that required the space other journal editors cannot find.

And what happened to Alfred Knopf, Inc.? It became part of Random House, which is part of what now, and what or whom next? What happened to William Shawn's *New Yorker?* It has been sold; and although his ideas may be immortal, he isn't, and they may suffer in his absence. Ian Ballantine? He lost his control of Ballantine Books because he was too successful. I think I remember the numbers — an annual gross sales rising from three million to five to eight to eleven to fourteen to seventeen, and a sudden dearth of the capital necessary to fund the growth. At that point his hope of co-publishing the exhibit-format books, in the smaller format that would continue the Sierra Club success, vanished, and with it, I think, McCall's hope to continue book publishing. Vanishing at the same time was Ian Ballantine's hope of producing four titles a year, in paperback, of the Celebrating the Earth series. A few million dollars in sales of those titles would have done the environmental movement no harm. Ian would not have had to scramble for other sustenance, nor would McCall, or Saturday Review, or Herder and Herder, or Friends of the Earth. For the want of a nail the war was lost. The need for profitability had prevailed. Nor is it likely soon not to.

Can the Real World be friendly to books? A good question, and having no particular basis for knowing the answer, I'll leap to one. Yes, it can be friendly to books, and it will be because it must. Some tithing will be required. When RCA or Gulf Oil or ARCO or T. Boone Pickens, to pick names at random, elect in a friendly or unfriendly way to take over a publishing firm, let them set aside a tithe, or even more, in their budgeting for the publishing of books that may, or more likely may not, fit in the Dalton/Walden Procrustean bed. Let them get medals for it, possibly a Nobel Prize, for being part of a new organization, Leveraged Takeover Artists for Social Responsibility.

Concerning the books I like best — those related to the development of human cultures consonant with survival of their life-support system — I have some suggestions about what this tithe might be invested in beyond the creative and technical increments of getting a book out. The further investment would be in outlets. And I would like to see a few friends get together and develop the outlet idea that needs to be franchised and to fly.

Earth Island Centers (see pp 223) would celebrate books in ways imaginative people could dream up. Have refreshments nearby, not so near as to spill on the books. Add exhibits, meeting space, music, craftsmanship such as exhibited in the things Virginia Adams brought to the Ansel Adams Gallery in Yosemite, or Tom Wrubel and Elise White brought to the Nature Company in the San Francisco Bay area, or David Gaines brought to the visitor center on Mono Lake's shore in Lee Vining, east of Yosemite, or you might dream up that I would like to hear about, if we could just talk.

What we want to see happen in these centers is what used to happen in The Firehouse when Howard Gossage infused it with his own kind of magic. The Firehouse was an architectural achievement in rehabilitation on the respectable side of Broadway in North Beach. Howard, of Freeman, Mander, and Gossage, had his office in a high-ceilinged room on the second floor, a room big enough for a dozen people to meet in, or more if the occasion called for more. You knew, because their names were on the broad high wall opposite the window, which dignitaries, past or imminent, had met there. People who were sober enough could use the ladder and write their names, or remarks, on high.

The place was a hotbed of ideas, none of them tired. On very special occasions the whole firehouse was part of the party, and there would be a Mariachi band adding to the ambience. If you wonder why I have a special feeling for the place, this is the reason: When Friends of the Earth was launched, in the fall of 1969, with no money in sight, Howard said to me, "This is your office. Pay rent when you can."

So there should be Earth Island Centers all over, meeting places, an ambience that creativity cannot escape, mailing lists of people who need to know what meeting or exhibit or book or author is on deck to celebrate, to help the celebration change things that need to be changed — even the minds of people in politics. At least one Earth Island Center per town. Eventually, one per home.

When that happens, books will be back.

I know of no barroom brawls over the books I had anything to do with the publishing of, nor brawls anywhere else. There have been, however, extended boardroom or committee-room arguments and some long-lasting estrangements. Most of them, it seems to me, have resulted from a lack of understanding of how to overcome the frequent criticism voiced in conservation meetings: We are always just talking to ourselves.

I have two objections to that oft-heard remark. First, we don't talk enough to each other to half understand one another.

The other objection, at least in my encounters, is that when you plan to talk to a much larger audience, as, for example, by publishing a book about an important item on your agenda, the board or committee is too likely to say, "Isn't there a better way to spend the money?" I have lost a lot of votes by answering, "No."

I lost so many votes in Friends of the Earth meetings that the publishing program died there a year after I left the presidency. The FOE inventory of both series, The Earth's Wild Places and Celebrating the Earth, was sold at remainder prices in order to handle a cash crunch, leaving nothing to support what we called our smaller "cause books," and FOE's ability to reach out and touch someone else was badly handicapped.

At the Sierra Club the publishing program slowed only briefly upon my departure. When Jon Beckmann became the club's publisher, he persuaded the club's board of directors that he needed a three-year commitment and got it. This enabled him to find authors, give them time to write, provide time also for the editors, designers, printers, and sales force to play their roles well, and a program emerged with strength and diversity that continues to serve the club well, and the environmental cause too.

Perhaps it is futile. Perhaps print must give way to electronic publishing. Perhaps there is not going to be time, anymore, to read anything more demanding than the headlines in the morning's news and advertisements. Perhaps there isn't even time for that, and people's overburdened senses must settle for what comes easy on the television screen or quickly in the news broadcasts they have time for thanks to gridlock. Perhaps there isn't time even for that, but only for commercials where time is so precious that the advertiser is forced to edit out the space between words, and radio commercials sound as if they were read by an auctioneer. Human ears and nerves do not need that many words delivered with so little meaning in so little time.

Must all these changes come about? Not if we say no.

We must say no, recognizing that the book is the antidote to the global cerebral paralysis television is creating. All too often television is no more than an incessant flow of information that comes and goes without the recipient's having to do anything with or about it.

I had a chance to address the alternative — Nature Writing and Value Formation — at a conference held by the Meadow Creek Project, in Fox, Arkansas. The story goes that even the people who live in Fox don't know where it is, so there is no point in my giving the coordinates here. Besides, I don't know where it is either.

The project itself, the brainchild of David Orr, is housed in an amazing center overlooking, as the name suggests, Meadow Creek, a beautiful spot in the Ozarks where ideas are tested for sustainability. I was fortunate in being asked to find my way there or, rather, to let Sam Passmore pick me up at the Little Rock airport and drive me there, on two occasions.

NATURE WRITING AND VALUE FORMATION

I DECIDED THAT THE BEST THING for me to talk about on my second visit to the Meadow Creek Project was what books had done for me and for places I cared deeply about.

IT IS EASY TO DEFINE NATURE WRITING — at least I think it is — but abstractions hang me up. So I have about as much trouble with 'value' as I do with 'parameter,' 'paradigm,' and 'holistic' (Les Pengelly defines holistic as a noun, an adjective, and a substitute for thought).

Sam Passmore suggests I talk about political value. Fair enough. Let me talk about ethical value too. There must be some others. Perhaps you can find some in what follows. My trouble is that Duke University Press gave me a manuscript to review; I was thrown off by the author's using 'values' fifty-six times in a single chapter. In my mind the word 'values' became water dripping off a roof into the same old holes, to quote Senator Biden.

The earliest nature writer affecting me was Thornton W. Burgess and his bedtime stories. His writing bent this twig early. My bent twig never got straightened out. Nature still gets a high place in my system of values. Once a forester friend of mine, the venerable Emanuel Fritz, told a group of people to whom he was explaining redwoods, "Nature never does anything right." I have had a hard time listening to anything else he has had to say ever since.

I was feeling good about animals, thanks to Burgess, when Ernest Thompson Seton, in *Wild Animals I Have Known,* made me feel sad about the series of tragic endings to the lives of the animals his book tells about. I am sure they had a role in my becoming a conservationist.

38

Next came Clarence King (after I had gotten over reading about nature in the Tarzan and Mars books) to tell me about *Mountaineering in the Sierra Nevada*. I liked the nature he wrote about well enough to do something about it, like trying to trace his steps in the Sierra at Reflections Lake and on Mount Tyndall.

There were many other nature writers whose work I read and collected diligently — they wrote about another kind of nature — mountains, and how they were to be climbed. They motivated me into extensive fieldwork, into climbing thither and yon from 1930 to 1956, and trekking or strolling in wild places ever since.

Then came John Muir, the mountaineer whose legacy is the American conservation movement. I have just finished writing a foreword for a Sierra Club edition of Muir's *The Yosemite*. And indeed, through the machinations of a heavenly hacker, I found a message from John Muir on my lap-top computer and telephoned it to the Sierra Club directors meeting in San Francisco. I will read it to you.

"My Dear David Brower,

"You have made no attempt to get in touch with me, which I can understand. I hear, however, that in a recent book you have been called 'the John Muir reincarnate,' and I thought I had better get in touch with you. There is a young man here who has told me how to do it. I think he was called a hacker on earth.

"I will make the message brief.

"As you know, the loss of the Hetch Hetchy Valley to the money-changers of San Francisco was one of the greatest disappointments of my life, and I saw little point in remaining on earth after the valley was lost. It was dammed in no small part thanks to a Secretary of the Interior I had thought was a good man.

"Now a Secretary of the Interior who you think is a bad one — and I can understand why — has suggested that the dam be taken down and the great valley be restored. It will be a glorious day when the recovery begins, and each succeeding day will be more glorious as each of the outcast denizens of the valley, the flowers and trees and birds and other wildlife, come back home.

"Would you kindly convey to the Sierra Club that the hesitancy of some of its leaders in accepting the idea of restoring the Hetch Hetchy has caused me renewed grief. Would they rather curse a man for his demonic sins than reward him, and all people who revere nature, for his demonstrated virtue?

"I hope the leaders of the Sierra Club will overcome their hesitancy and renew their commitment to the ideals for which I founded the club. It would hurt me greatly to be required to resign as founder of the club.

"Please convey my respects to Lee Stetson. His interpretation of me has cleared up a great deal of my uncertainty about who I was. I hope any hesitant club leaders will listen to him and clear up their own confusion.

"Yours very sincerely,

"John Muir"

Long before that unbelievable message, Muir's books awakened me to the detail of the Sierra. He aroused my interest in reading the footprints of glaciers and other denizens, faunal and floral, of my favorite range of mountains, Muir's "Range of Light," the Sierra Nevada. He had a great deal to do with my becoming a full-time environmentalist, and was thoughtful enough to found the Sierra Club so I could get paid for my work.

The main point to remember is that the life and letters and books of John Muir made an enormous difference in attitudes toward nature in America, and even more enormous global differences are needed.

An important part of nature writing is what it contributed to one of the most important American institutions, the national park idea. Essence of the idea is that we set aside special places on the earth where we can admire what we find there instead of what we can do to it. Muir espoused the idea well, and has been considered the father of the national parks. The idea, however, had already been written about well enough to provide political support for establishing national parks when their time came.

The extent of this writing first came to my attention in "Yosemite, the Story of an Idea," written for the 1948 *Sierra Club Bulletin* by Hans Huth. This article turned out to be the précis of his book, *Nature and the American,* published by the University of California Press. I had nothing more to do with nature writing until World War II ended in northern Italy.

Let me now indulge, if you will, in show-and-tell time. Let's face it. What I know about nature writing has come, for the most part, from my being publisher and general editor of books for the Sierra Club and Friends of the Earth. My show-and-tell exhibit consists of some examples of the forty books of the same genre I had a hand in between 1955 and 1979, shortly after which FOE shut its publishing program down.

I have a minor role in the Sierra Club's publishing now, serving on its Publications Committee and trying to get the club to continue my bad publishing habits.

The principle purpose of these books, for the club and for FOE, was summarized neatly by Ian Ballantine, who provided great help to our effort, as we were to his. He told me I had made him rich; he enriched the Sierra Club and Friends of the Earth. Ian said I had put together books that made people fall in love with places, that told them of the threats to those places, and explained what they could do about those threats.

Meadow Creek Talk, 1987

I read some of my favorite excerpts from the books — about Thoreau's wanting an entire heaven and an entire earth; Nancy Newhall's explanation of wilderness; my poetry from Point Reyes; Eiseley's on the "Judgment of the Birds" and on the need for a gentler, more tolerant people, and about our being compounded of dust and the light of a star; Jeffers's wanting organic wholeness and not man apart from that; Terry Russell's thoughts about how beauty and adventure could be found; and William H. Murray's on commitment. Before reading the excerpts, almost all of them man-centered, I composed a foreword in four lines:

I wonder where the women were.
The world was just for him, not her.
Perhaps the best solution is
To think of Earth as hers, not his.

One of the books had changed the country's and my own way of thinking about environment, several had resulted in additions to the national park and wilderness systems, and three had helped get national parks created or protected elsewhere on Earth.

Concluding, I said we needed more of this kind of publishing and, pointing to *Restoring the Earth* and *Our Common Future,* urged all to work on the subject of restoration, the best way toward any future at all.

Robert and Kenneth Brower walking through the destruction at the realigned Tioga Road in Yosemite c. 1952.

CHAPTER 3

FROM CINEMA TO VIDEO

H
OW DOES ONE REACH OUT TO OTHERS, to teach, or to learn simply from the very effort of reaching out? Forget ESP for the moment, or other forms of magic.

It's back to the old adage, "One picture is worth a thousand words," and take it from there. Since films pass by the projector's shutter at twenty-four frames per second, an hour's movie is worth eighty-six thousand four hundred words. I thought you'd like to know.

That statistic had nothing to do with my interest in film. Like many others, I started out with a box Brownie, with fixed focus and three different exposure opportunities. It was not going to make me famous. Neither would the vest-pocket Kodak I bought from Harry Best, Virginia Adams's father, nor several interim cameras, including a Graflex, a Rolleiflex, a Voightlander, a Zeiss Super Ikonta B, a Polaroid, a Hasselblad, a Yashica, a Nikon or two, an Eastman 16-mm, a Bell & Howell, and a Bolex. There are thousands of black-and-white negatives and color slides, including some of Dufay Color if anyone remembers, and miles and miles of 16-mm Kodachrome that nothing is likely to come of. But it was fun running all that film behind all the assorted lenses, thus avoiding the necessity of having to remember what I was seeing.

At least, my own diversion of playing at photography for my own amusement, which is what I play the piano for, gave me the opportunity to meet and talk reasonably intelligently with people who worked with photography as an art or as a form of journalism.

Home movies did not come into my life until I started rock-climbing with the Sierra Club and a film was made of the first ascent of the Higher Cathedral Spire by Jules Eichorn, Dick Leonard, and Bestor Robinson. It was black and white, silent, and reasonably exciting, but what I remember best was one of the titles: "A choice of routes are offered." If I could do nothing else, I could at least help edit.

In an early film I was in front of, not behind, the camera. Bestor Robinson recorded our 1935 attempt on Mount Waddington in Kodachrome. That was probably Kodachrome's first year, and not its best. All the color has by now vanished except for the magenta.

In 1936, soon after I had moved from Mount Waddington to being publicity manager for the Yosemite Park & Curry Company, I began to learn about 16-mm cinematography from Clifford Nelson, who was making a film, *Riders Over Volgelsang,* to promote travel to Yosemite's High Sierra camps. Music and narration were added to the silent footage, and I had a hand in that. From Cliff I learned some early rules about cinematography. Do not pan unless it is absolutely necessary, and then don't do it. The camera is supposed to photograph action, not be the actor. If, however, you insist on panning, do so to follow the action. If there is no action, pan only from left to right, the way you read, and start with a good composition, pause on a good composition, and end on one. If I played the camera like a fire hose, he added, he'd have me shot.

I remembered this in the summer of 1937, when I made my own first film of a trip in the Yosemite High Sierra. The excuse for it was that my boss, Stanley Plumb, was an ardent fisherman and assumed that there were others like him who could be persuaded to fish in the High Sierra. The title of the film was *Fishing High,* and was his suggestion, as I remember it. The film was shown a few times for evening entertainment at Camp Curry, and I narrated it. To drop yet another name, I encountered Walt Disney, an ardent lover of Yosemite, with the company's 16-mm camera in hand, and learned from him a trick every cinematographer knows, but I didn't. If you want to reverse the action, simply hold the camera upside down when photographing the action, and splice the film in right-side up.

Whenever I could borrow a movie camera and afford film, I photographed climbing, summer and winter, from 1937 to 1942. Berkeley's now-famous rocks — Cragmont, Indian, and Pinnacle — had not yet had their key handholds covered with chalk or their key footholds polished by human footgear. We were not environmentally sensitive, however, to what pitons were doing to the rock; we were more interested in our own safety. Our favorite recreation was not climbing, but falling — and seeing how smoothly we could belay a fall to a halt. Dick Leonard insisted that we become the world's safest climbers. The biggest intentional falls were at Indian Rock, where a climber (or should he be called a victim?) would leap into space and fall free some twenty feet before the belayer could begin to check the fall. I enjoyed jumping and photographing equally. When Morgan Harris and I made the first ascent of The Arrowhead, on Yosemite's north wall, he and I photographed each other on the climb and Dick Leonard supplemented our footage by telephoto. Unfortunately for the film, nothing spectacular happened. If it had, I would probably have missed the shot — just as I did when I was being paid to photograph an ascent of the Higher Cathedral Spire and stood with my mouth open, not my lens, when Oliver Kehrlein fell.

SKY-LAND TRAILS OF THE KINGS

I MANAGED SOMEHOW not to use the film trick Walt Disney taught me in the mountaineering films. Cliché though it is, the trick never failed to bring laughs when I used it in *Sky-Land Trails of the Kings*. In a simple-minded sequence, some young Sierra Club High Trippers paused to go swimming, and Bruce Meyer dove into shallow water and pretended that his head was stuck in the mud. With camera upside down, I photographed two of his friends tossing him into the water, and later spliced the scene in right-side up, thus having them catch him as he emerged. Audiences are so hungry for humor in environmental films that they will probably laugh at anything.

Sky-Land Trails had a more serious purpose — helping the campaign to create Kings Canyon National Park. Dick Leonard and I photographed it in the course of the Sierra Club High Trips of 1939 and 1940 as they traveled through the high country of the Kings River Sierra. Dick Stitt, with whom I had worked briefly on a film on Yosemite's four seasons, lent me a superb Bell & Howell with a full turret of lenses. I was then in good enough shape to carry that heavy outfit on a traverse of the North Palisade, and am happy that I shall not have to do it again.

In 1939, as chairman of the Sierra Club's San Francisco Bay Chapter, I was able to persuade the chapter to buy a Bell & Howell sound projector. In its active life, it helped save Kings Canyon. *Sky-Land Trails,* in its 1939 and 1940 versions, was shown again and again all over California, and once in the Longworth House Office Building in Washington. Charlotte Mauk, the club's conservation secretary and long a board member, found the right record music, the most fitting being *The Moldau,* which, had Smetana only known, could accompany the Kings River fully as well as the Moldau. "Afternoon of a Faun," "The Swan of Tounella," and "Enchanted Lake," tone poems, were unspecific enough to fit the various moods of the film. I would introduce the film on stage, then retreat to the projector, to which I had plugged in a turntable and microphone, and sell Kings Canyon National Park for the next hour. I certainly sold myself on the idea.

It was not always possible for me to accompany the film. We made a copy and I wrote out a narration for others to use if they wished, listing music that Charlotte Mauk had recommended and that I invariably used. Although I never throw anything away, I can rarely retrieve what I have collected. What I prepared for *Sky-Land Trails* is an exception, but I'll spare you.

We got the park, in spite of the opposition of the California Chamber of Commerce, the state legislature, the U.S. Forest Service,

The Wilderness Society, and the National Parks Association. In my opinion, the Forest Service orchestrated the opposition within the state and almost persuaded the Sierra Club to oppose the national park proposal. The Forest Service has always been loathe to donate national forest land to the National Park Service.

The Wilderness Society and the National Parks Association, calling their shots from Washington and lacking on-the-ground appreciation of the Kings River High Sierra, insisted that there be no park at all if the park could not include the Tehipite and South Fork canyons of the Kings River — each of them a yosemite in its own right. Thanks to the good work of Arthur Blake, Irving Brant, Harold Ickes, and Franklin Roosevelt, the High Sierra portion of the Kings River watershed, including General Grant Grove of giant sequoias, was set aside in 1940 and the two Kings River yosemites were added many years later. It is not my nature to like delays, but this one delay in saving the canyons worked. Had the high country not been saved first, it might not have been saved at all. The plans for dams in the finest sky-land sanctuaries could all too easily have been put into effect under Forest Service administration. In Kings Canyon National Park, they are as safe as people can make them.

Skis to the Sky-Land

SKI MOUNTAINEERING DESERVED a film of its own, and the Sierra Club film *Skis to the Sky-Land,* which I photographed in the winters of 1940 – 41 and 1941 – 42, climaxed in a winter ascent of Bear Creek Spire. Its subclimax was a shot of a ski in unmarked fresh snow — of no particular interest until the ski started moving by itself. Shortly thereafter Milton Hildebrand, who had built himself a covered snowtrench to sleep in before the night's snowfall, emerged into the morning sunlight after a comfortable and quiet night's sleep.

I traveled all over California showing the film, playing records and narrating as I had for the Kings Canyon film, the biggest audience again being at Wheeler Hall, on the Berkeley campus. The film has been transferred to videotape, and I am still looking for new copies of the 78 rpm records I used — and something to play them on — in this age of 45s, 33s, CDs, and no 78s. I particularly want to find the European 78, "Echojodel."

ROCKS, OWLS, AND SNAKES AT SENICA

IN THE SPRING OF 1944 I finally had a camera of my own, simply by refusing to give it back to my brother Ralph when he came to visit the Seneca Assault Climbing School in West Virginia. I assured him that I needed it more than he did, paid him for it, and began photographing our Seneca activities. I combined new footage with the old — from Berkeley, Yosemite, and Shiprock — to entertain and educate the troops on the Seneca days when rain, snow, or sleet kept us indoors. We lightened up the showings with my other movie scenes of ice skating on our stretch of the Potomac, or the antics of the barn owl, garter snake, and billy goat (dressed in GI fatigues) that shared our Seneca digs briefly. The owl had been blown out of its nest and fared very well in camp on the mice and other tidbits the troops found for him. He even had a sense of humor, ruffling his feathers into full combat array and striking fiercely at any finger proffered him, but never really biting. He finally took off into the wild, but returned from time to time for another mouse.

The snake amazed the camera and all of us by her skill (we didn't know how to sex either the owl or the snake, so I am assuming either sex) by traveling along a taut metal clothesline. She became a spinning spiral but pressed forward regardless. We climaxed the film with an outrageous banquet, huge steaks grilled over chestnut coals, and unconscionably relished in a day when, owing to rationing, ordinary citizens could not find such morsels at any price. Raffi Bedayan, our volunteer supply officer, knew how to get items that were beyond the reach of Maneuver Area headquarters. I still do not know how he got the steaks. Probably in exchange for a few flashlight batteries.

Forty-four years later, with my cameras gathering dust, I was at Tennessee Pass again, above where Camp Hale was, looking at names with my camcorder. It paused at the names of five of our Seneca instructors who did not come home from Italy. They and a thousand unlucky colleagues are remembered on the Tenth Mountain's own Vietnam wall at the pass. War's senselessness hits hardest when it wastes one's own friends.

WILDERNESS RIVER TRAIL

IF HAROLD BRADLEY'S FILM of his 1952 family trip down the Yampa and Green rivers in Dinosaur National Monument could trigger my determination to keep dams out of the monument, what could the Sierra Club produce to motivate people not so easily excited? Perhaps a professional film instead of a family effort, or a little of both. Charles

Eggert, a professional, had made a film on Dinosaur for the National Parks Association — a film concentrating on the dinosaurs but not on the rivers. The dinosaur quarry was not in danger and the rivers were. Was he interested in endangered rivers?

He was, and gladly accompanied the first of three river trips, each with sixty passengers, the club had persuaded Bus Hatch to run through Dinosaur in the summer of 1953. To demonstrate that these were not dangerous trips that could be enjoyed only by suicidal river buffs, I took Ken and Bob along, who were then eight and six. They and the rivers performed beautifully.

I had a brilliant idea for an opening sequence as I dropped by Charlie's studio in Red Cliff, New York, to watch the editing. We would have people discussing the Dinosaur issue, go to a map, the camera would zoom in on Echo Park and Steamboat Rock, the voices as people talked about the map would be drowned out by the noise of an airplane's engine, and the scene on the map would dissolve quickly into an actual overflight of Echo Park.

Brilliant, but Charlie wouldn't buy it. He didn't need to. What he finally produced was brilliant enough. A joyful trip for people of all ages, two little lads exploring enticing places from riverside camps, spectacular colorful cliffs passing by, some exciting rapids, quiet camping, then a switch to the threat, with Clair Leonard's music, composed and performed on the Bard College pipe organ, augmenting each sequence. Mr. Leonard's music lets you know who the villain is when the dams, power lines, and tacky development come on screen. The Bureau of Reclamation knows, too, and has said that *Wilderness River Trail* (of which there were fourteen well-circulated copies) was the most effective weapon we had in saving Dinosaur National Monument from those who coveted the wildness in its rivers.

TWO YOSEMITES

O N MAY 15, 1955, with five hundred feet of color film to expose, I visited Hetch Hetchy with Philip Hyde and ended up with an eleven-minute special, *Two Yosemites,* which could bring people to tears. The film and a brochure revealed the truth about the scenic benefits the Bureau of Reclamation was promising that its proposed Echo Park and Split Mountain dams would bring to Dinosaur National Monument. The film shows what nonbenefits the O'Shaughnessy Dam, flooding Hetch Hetchy Valley, have brought to Yosemite National Park. My movie footage and Philip Hyde's devastating photographs later appeared in the Sierra Club book, *John Muir and the Sierra Club: The Battle for Yosemite,* by Holway Jones (1965), which also included an adaptation of the narration from the film:

THIS IS THE STORY OF TWO YOSEMITES. One was the Hetch Hetchy Valley hardly anyone knew. It was one of the most beautiful valleys in the world. Handsome cliffs and waterfalls in a charming setting. Trees to frame the vistas, meadows to look at and to look from, natural beauty under foot and to walk by — a setting with open space, living space, that a million people might see and enjoy every year. It was very much like the Yosemite Valley the world knows today, just a few miles to the south.

The other yosemite is Hetch Hetchy Valley today, but the setting has gone.

Hetch Hetchy was a remarkable storage vessel, with a fine dam-site where the walls crowded together. It was dammed to enable Mocassin Creek powerhouse, in the Sierra foothills, to generate some kilowatts for San Francisco — at the cost of the nation's scenery. They said the dam would be "easily covered by grasses and vines."

John Muir, the Sierra Club, and other conservation groups fought hard against this destructive park invasion. San Francisco argued that without this water it would wither; it must have this cheap power; there were no good alternatives; and the dam would enhance the beauty of the place and make it more accessible. "The greatest good for the greatest number." Teeming San Francisco against the few people who had yet visited Yosemite.

Fifty years ago, San Francisco won. This once-beautiful valley, part of a national park, was flooded.

Philip Hyde took these pictures May 13, 1955. The reservoir was down one hundred eighty feet, but sixty feet higher than it had been May 1. In June it would probably fill, then start right back down again, for it is a fluctuating reservoir, as most power and storage reservoirs must be. Its zone of ups and downs, between high water and low is a region of desolation. Nothing permanent can grow in it.

This zone is ugly enough at the dam. At the head of the reservoir it is worse. There this much drawdown means two miles of desolation. We walked a mile up into it. Although it was still very early in the season, sixteen hundred people came into Yosemite Valley that same day. Two came to Hetch Hetchy, and we didn't come for pleasure. Who would?

What you see here is what you see at most fluctuating reservoirs and what no one should see in a park. Stumps where the basin was cleared. Stumps and more stumps, exposed and re-exposed until silt finally buries them. The stream — it was one of the most beautiful in the Sierra — is silted in. Tuolumne Falls is covered. The banks are silted. The flat living space is silted, and as soon as it is dry enough, it is on the move — a dust bowl, from the silt that sloughed off the canyonsides when the reservoir was full. The river brings still more each year, and wind-blown scum collects in the eddies of what was sparkling river.

They had circulated touched-up pictures of an artist's conception of a pretty lake, always brimful. San Francisco's mayor wrote, "The scene will be enhanced by the effect of the lake, reflecting all above it and about it, in itself a great and attractive natural object." Secretary of the Interior James Garfield testified: "In weighing the two sides of the question, I thought that it should be resolved in favor of San Francisco, because this use of the valley would not destroy it as one of the most beautiful spots in the West. It would simply change the floor of the valley from a meadow to a beautiful lake."

Congressman Englebright added: "As it is a lake, it will be one of great beauty; there will be fine fishing in it, and boating, and so on, which would make the lake an improvement to the park." . . .

There were alternative sites. The day of atomic power *could* have arrived [!] with Hetch Hetchy still beautiful. But the Secretary of the Interior accepted the city's claim. He had made a "careful, competent study" and no other way would do.

The alternatives, which would have harmed no precious scenery, remain unused. And for the million people who come to Yosemite each year to enjoy it, perhaps a thousand approach Hetch Hetchy — to turn away from its tragic drabness. Why should they stay? To pack in and camp here? To let the children play in the meadows? To fish in this stream? To breathe the clean mountain air? Could this ever have been beautiful?

Above the waterline is a clue to what beauty could have remained. Colorful lichens, miniature gardens of mosses and ferns — these bring life to the rocks and rills. Near a promontory where a summer house was built for city officials, well above the fluctuation zone that dominates every broad vista, is a pitifully small flat area — too small for camping and almost as unattractive as the dead zone. On a nearby slope along a dead-end trail, we can find remnants of the former beauty of the place. A temporary stream runs a few feet through this isolated garden and drops into a desolate zone of rock, sand, and stumps. A patch or two of grass remains above the high water line, but there will never be grass enough or vines enough to conceal the dam. We found that even this little bit of grass was spoiled by the high-water debris and the monotonous view.

Across the valley the main falls are still there, shining in the springtime. But where is the setting? Where is the pulsing heartland of this place? It is gone. It is gone beyond the recall of our civilization — thanks to the dam, where plaques praise the men who took so much from so many for all our time.

We know from those who saw Hetch Hetchy before it was destroyed that Yosemite Valley is its nearest counterpart. Hetch Hetchy's cliffs were like Yosemite's, free of bleach and water stains, unspoiled, set in forests, forests where you could walk by the shaded streams.

Yosemite tells what a setting means everywhere you look. Here you can see what the trees which are now stumps ought to still be doing for Hetch Hetchy — providing a place to stroll, to relax, to listen, to see clear water glide over clean rocks, to catch the sun sparkle, to breathe fragrant air, to rest where the river pauses, to feel renewed, to know the beauty of natural things.

Yosemite cannot meet today's recreation needs, let alone tomorrow's. The future will find abundant power outside the parks — parks for which there are no alternatives. So many of the parks are now overcrowded — certainly Yosemite is. And Hetch Hetchy could be giving to millions, for ages, much of what Yosemite gives. Its waters could have remained an inspiration in their beautiful natural setting and then be put to practical use downstream — just as Yosemite's river is.

The cliffs, the groves, the streamside, the whole setting — what do they mean to man? Something that you can neither measure in dollars, nor replace with dollars. Hetch Hetchy's setting is irretrievably lost to all of us and to all generations. It need not have been.

In 1916 Congress put up a sign to prevent any more tragedies like this one. It was the National Park Act, which says to park exploiters, "Do not enter." We'll do well to remember Hetch Hetchy, where once was too often.

Two Yosemites, 1955

Eighty years later there is a movement to restore Hetch Hetchy Valley. I hope this film can help that movement, and that Yosemite visitors will help by carrying away as souvenirs small pieces of O'Shaughnessy Dam as soon as they are made available.

WILDERNESS ALPS OF STEHEKIN

B UOYED BY THE SUCCESS of *Two Yosemites* and how it helped the campaign to save Dinosaur, and buoyed further by my enthusiastic support, fanned by David Simons and Grant McConnell, for a North Cascades National Park, I was delighted when Grant's close friend and summer neighbor in Stehekin, Abigail Avery, contributed five thousand dollars for a film to help the cause. Two summers' effort produced the footage, and Charles Eggert helped me unscramble it to produce *Wilderness Alps of Stehekin.* It won an honorable-mention award in international competition, and the Sierra Club sold one hundred twenty-five copies of it. Howard Zahniser liked it well enough to run my narration in *The Living Wilderness,* and I liked the narration well enough to include it

51

in *The Wild Cascades,* a Sierra Club exhibit-format book by Harvey Manning. I still like it well enough to include it here:

THE NORTHERN CASCADES country was once, all of it, wild as the sea — the wild, shining sea, shaping the earth through the ages, never the same, yet not to be changed by man, who long ago learned to accept it for what it is even as we are now learning not to change some of the wild land, but to keep it natural, to seek from it answers to questions we may yet learn how to ask.

Can we set apart unmanaged, unspoiled, enough of these places? Can we spare the stillness of a rain forest, where trees can live out their full span and return to the earth they came from? All that lives here repays in full for value received, nourishes as it has been nourished. Scores of centuries built this, a cool, green world, hushed as a prayer. Man could wipe it out in a decade. Or consecrate it as a park, not to be impaired, a place where all generations could come to know the dignity of nature.

In the Northern Cascades, there is an alpine wilderness that belongs to our national gallery. Such places are the last of our primeval landscapes, the few surviving samples of a natural world, to walk and rest in, to see, to listen to, to feel the mood of, to comprehend, to care about. There isn't much of it left. What there is is all all people will ever have, and all their children. It is only as safe as people, knowing about it, want it to be.

But do enough people know about it? We didn't, and went in to look it over. We had heard about the region and about a conflict between those who wanted to use raw materials and those who wanted to preserve natural beauty. We weren't prepared for what began to unfold — an amazing wilderness of rugged alps built in grand scale, unique, unsurpassed anywhere in the United States.

Our first trip in was a flight — too hurried, too cut off, too unreal for us to feel the country or remember the shape of the waves of the storm-tossed sea of peaks. We knew it was great country, big country. We also saw that its size alone could not protect it. On the west side men were already clear-cutting the last virgin forests, getting timber and pulp from forested avenues of approach needed very much as primeval setting and living space to look at and look from. Crossing Cascade Pass, in the heart of the wilderness, we were but a few miles from other wild forests, also wanted for their timber, but needed as setting too.

There are many entryways. In Stehekin the road starts at a handsome lakeshore and dead-ends in paradise. It connects with no highways and doesn't compete with any. The few cars on it know each other by their first names. It is seldom far from the river, and if you stop for a close look, no horn blows behind you. Great trees tower over the road.

Flowers and grass grow alongside it and between the wheeltracks. It's bumpy enough to slow you down to *see* the roadside. It doesn't cut in and shoulder its way through. It treads softly, in no hurry to someplace else; it's there already.

One day we met friends who knew the country we had flown over, to see from a soft cushion, through a window, and far away. They had felt it underfoot. They had spent the time you need to spend, in our speed-shrunk world, when you want to feel the size of space, when you want perspective. You can earn the best of what this country gives, they said, only if you do it yourself. So they walked the trails, and climbed where no trails were, carefully where the tundra was steep; they reaped the special rewards of those who walk where no one has walked before.

And so it was that one day our trail climbed grassy canyonsides to a small shelter in its own private alp below the pass. We only had time that day to explore a lower side trail for a mile or two, to see what a wilderness forest is like when man leaves it to its own wondrous devices. We walked waist-deep in ferns, quietly, looking backward on the eternity that has made this forest what it is. We found the camp a wonderful base for strolls high above the pass, a chance to enjoy the world of tundra and tarns. We had never seen better country to walk in. Everybody explored the alps, poked along the parklike high trails, wandered through the miles of grasslands, let the mountain wind blow away flatland cares.

Almost everybody got out on a glacier, too — the Whitechuck Glacier's flat ice field is made to order for beginners. And we kept looking for a hole in the mist through which to glimpse the monarch of this country, Glacier Peak — the same Glacier Peak we had flown around and soon would walk around to see from Image Lake, the really classic view in the unspoiled Northern Cascades. Then we watched the cloud cap, the strange lenticular cloud that the wind blows through, leaving the cloud there.

Everywhere there were wild gardens. And here, deep in the heart of the little-known alps, seemingly remote, we met at noon a friend who had left New York City late the night before, a whole continent away. Our friend had come up one of the west-side avenues into the mountains.

We remembered our own avenue, up through virgin forest with huge trees, almost a rain forest, still as a cathedral, in it a clear stream from an unscarred watershed, clear in spite of the northern weather. The northern traveler, as we knew, is seldom bored by blue skies. But then, monotonous fair weather can't build mountains like these, and their glaciers and forests and flowers. We liked the way the mountains looked and discovered how to like what made them that way. Don't scurry for cover and miss the show. Stay out and be part of it! Not on a high peak, of course. But take a walk down in the sheltered valley. So we walked out into it, heads up, and felt the freshness the rains bring, saw new patterns, smelled the wet leaves, now washed and cool, and we looked up to see the old contest between the crags and the mists. Oh, we got wet and our feet squished a little in our boots. But what never gets wet can never get dry. We got both. We never came back from one of our walks feeling only half alive. I guess the children knew it all the time, and I rediscovered it — epidermis is waterproof and the rain is only water. And that strange tingling — that was just my circulation, circulating. I had almost forgotten the feeling.

But now we were close to the pass, making camp, our own mountain world spread out around us, each clump of trees a timberline penthouse, each room perfectly air-conditioned. You can't beat a camp on these timberline gardens, with sunset on the high peaks. Never mind what the cook has mixed up. If it doesn't look too fancy, wait till it gets dark and you won't have to see what you're eating while you trade stories around the campfire far into the night.

Dawn brought a flush to Glacier Peak. The sun will light all this mountain land soon, and we hope it will always reveal wilderness there — in the avenues of unspoiled forest, in the flashing waters of the sidestreams and the river, in the friendly lower gardens and the grassy alplands, up at timberline and in tundra, on the glaciers and peaks.

Other people will want to be walking our trails, up where the tree reaches high for the cloud, up where the flower takes the summer wind with beauty, and the summer rain too. They will want to discover for themselves the wildness that the ages have made perfect.

They have a right to discover wild places, I told the children, just as we did — and your children and theirs too. They *can* discover them, but only if we keep some wildness in between the shining seas, only if man remembers, in his rising tide, not to engulf his last islands, of wilderness.

Wilderness Alps of Stehekin,1958

We won, almost. When the Glacier Peak Wilderness becomes part of the national park, where it certainly belongs, we can delete the 'almost.'

THE PLACE NO ONE KNEW

THE 1960 WINTER OLYMPICS made a heavy environmental impact on Squaw Valley, but there was a compensating advantage — I was able to buy a complete 16-mm Bolex outfit, carefully used in photographing the Olympics, at a bargain price. It had wide-angle, normal, and short telephoto lenses on its turret, and a still longer telephoto when I needed it. Best of all, the finder looked through the camera's lenses, not a lens of its own, which is exactly what I needed. My ability to calculate parallax, and thus avoid cutting off heads or feet or the critical part of a close-up composition, somehow never matured.

The Bolex was at its busiest in Glen Canyon, where I futilely tried to make amends for my having, in blissful ignorance, advocated a Glen Canyon dam even higher than what the Bureau of Reclamation wanted to think of building, a higher dam that would have devastated even more of what was once the most beautiful place on earth, no exceptions.

Year after year, while we still could, we flew from Page, Arizona, the town built to build Glen Canyon Dam, to a spot on the map called Hite, Utah, where we were ferried across the Colorado to our put-in point and taken downriver by not-yet professor of economics Dick Norgaard. Dick already loved Glen Canyon as devoutly as we soon would. The main canyon was wonderful enough. The side canyons were designed to make heaven an anticlimax for anyone who might go there, and I never tired of trying to capture their magic on film.

Unfortunately, the side-canyon heavens were not very well illuminated. What I needed had not been invented yet — a camcorder that had almost no use for light. Cathedral in the Desert was the most frustrating, if the most magnificent, place in the Glen Canyon complex. There was but a narrow slice of sky — Wallace Stegner's term — above it, and it kept most of the light to itself. I would open my Bolex's fastest lens wide and shoot at a speed of eight frames per second with the fastest film I could get, and still miss the beauty and the magic. The film I chose also had the disadvantage of duplicating poorly. Eastman had built it for people who dared show their master film until it wore out. I wanted never to show the master. I had learned that much from professionals.

All in all, there are some three miles of color film of Glen, and not all of them disappointing. They are in a vault awaiting a technology that can transfer them to videotape in a way that captures the splendor I saw and no one will ever see again. Let me know, if you hear of it, when that technology arrives.

IF YOU ARE A GROWN MAN and don't want to cry, or see other grown men cry, avoid at all costs the slide show on Glen Canyon that Phil Pennington and Chuck Washburn assembled from their record of what Glen Canyon was, and was to lose. In summer and winter they and their kayaks traveled the main stem and probed the side canyons. The map in Eliot Porter's book *The Place No One Knew* lists 105 side canyons. Our family explored a few — most memorable of them Moqui, Lake, Wilson, several along the Escalante, including Cathedral in the Desert, and, back on the main stem, Hidden Passage, Music Temple, Twilight, Oak, Forbidding, Rainbow Bridge, Aztec, Driftwood, Cathedral, and Little Arch, with the architectural miracle and subdued lighting of its ultimate inner sanctuary. Many of the very finest we missed entirely, too many because we were too late.

Phil and Chuck didn't miss. In some of the most spectacular places, canyons where you had to have a flashlight at noon, or swim through mysterious pools in semi-darkness, or squeeze through side-ways in the narrowest places, or find colors you could not believe where the upper walls, themselves out of sight, intercepted the colors you expected and reflected surprising hues your way — in these places Phil and Chuck recorded qualities of light and sculpture you could not find anywhere else and can now find nowhere at all. Wallace Stegner tells of "the sudden poetry of springs." In the side canyons you found the flow-ing poetry of stone. It has been silenced.

The Pennington-Washburn slide show ran for forty-five minutes, music, birdsong, and all. Beauty, history, a touch of adventure, then the smashing blow. Their final trips witnessed the rising of the reservoir behind Glen Canyon dam, the dead body of water named Lake Powell after the man who discovered the canyon the rising flood was destroy-ing. The narration speaks of the junction of the Colorado and the San Juan, or of Cathedral Canyon's entrance, or that of Hidden Passage, the screen revealing the unspoiled beauty, whereupon the narrator recites a series of dates as the screen shows the slack water, rising and obliterat-ing. "This featureless cove of Lake Powell" — it is indeed featureless — "was Dove Canyon." The 'was' is spoken slowly. The screen shows the old sculptured Navajo sandstone walls. An uncanny bluish tinge is rico-cheted by walls high above, lit by the sky, but unseen.

What has happened to Glen Canyon, the narrator says, is what is planned for the Grand Canyon, while the screen bears the bad news of technology's imminent blitz. Finally, the retrospective look, the way it was, poignant music, a final fade, and the lilting song of a canyon wren, its sweet notes gliding down the wren's own musical scale, down into silence.

The slide show required equipment and people that could not eas-ily be assembled and shipped around. Could we make it into a 16-mm movie? Larry Dawson thought we could and proved it splendidly. He back-projected the slides and explored them with his camera, panning up and down, zooming slowly in, and in one side canyon skillfully zoom-ing in and dissolving from scene to scene in a way that has you moving up the canyon with him. He drew upon some of my text from *The Place No One Knew* to supplement what Phil Pennington had written. Altogether, Larry squeezed the forty-five minutes down to twenty-six, gaining power with this economy. It is a superb achievement, and we were ready to make copies and send them all over. Larry also produced a 35-mm version that could be shown in theaters. He observed that theater audiences did not applaud when the film ended, and not just because there was no "The End" title. They were in grief. I have seen the film scores of times. If there has been a long lag between viewings, I find my own grief once again hard to handle. And I'm not alone.

Since it is so much easier to carry a VHS cassette than a heavy can of film and a projector and speaker, I have had my copy of *Glen Canyon* transferred to video, and it works quite well wherever I find a friend with a VCR, which means almost everywhere. There's one problem. The studio making the transfer thought the film was over when the screen went dark, and somehow lost the last notes of the canyon wren. I've got to find them.

GRAND CANYON

*T*WO *YOSEMITES* AND THE SLIDE FILM on Glen Canyon told clearly what ought not happen to the Grand Canyon. They said nothing about what was happening in the Grand Canyon. The Sierra Club book, *Time and the River Flowing,* said a great deal about both. But we needed a film for those who preferred the screen to the printed page.

Martin Litton had more film of the Grand Canyon than he knew what to do with. How could we squeeze enough of it into half an hour? Jeff Ingram, then the club's Southwest representative, took on the task. He had already been enormously helpful in the campaign to defeat the Grand Canyon dams proposed for Marble Gorge and Bridge Canyon. His mathematical skills learned at M.I.T. revealed major errors in the calculations of the Bureau of Reclamation. Would these skills come to his aid as he produced a film?

Now and then I looked over his shoulder, even as I had when, with Martin Litton, I first began to learn what the Grand Canyon itself, at river level, was like. If you have walked down the Bright Angel Trail from the South Rim to the river, the best escape is not to struggle back up, but to thumb a ride down to Lake Mead. That is what I did. Jeff had been in Martin's boat all the way down from Lee's Ferry, and I squeezed in.

Jeff and I collaborated on the narration for the film, but the writing, with a few gems borrowed from Martin, was almost all Jeff's, and reveals his love of the place:

WHEN YOU THINK OF THE GRAND CANYON, what comes to your mind? Do you think of being in it, or gliding by the great rock walls that mark off an immensity of space for your spirit to soar through? Do you think of the widening of the space as seeps dissolve the old limestone and tributaries wear away the still older sandstone? Do you think of the living river, basic to all, as it deepens the Canyon, gouging and scoring its way through rock transfigured by two billion years of heat and weight?

Do you think of the water bringing the elements of life to each canyon garden? Of the plants, growing in the sand, pointing up the subtle color of the rocks, contrasting delicately with the seeming harshness of the Canyon?

Do you think of exploring to find out what the Canyon has tucked away? Do you think of riding its river, urged and tugged by the power of its current, challenging, magic, alive?

The river is the most complete host for a visit to the Grand Canyon. It will carry our boats for us, keep our supplies cool and moist, amuse us and sometimes excite us as it glides us into a walled-in world where layer after layer of old rock rises up until the great Redwall limestone dominates Marble Gorge. The river feeds the gardens that nourish the myriad insects, all providing for the birds and animals, freely moving, yet dependent upon the river shore to live.

The streams, here lucid, there turbid, support tiny collections of living things, each carrying out its errand, in a small world where water, rock, plant, and animal continually work out ways of getting along as part of the universe of the Grand Canyon.

The change of natural things still succeeds, here subtly, there dramatically. We can succeed here too, as visitors, delighting in the aromas we can coax from a stove and fire of our own making. We can let the living river succeed with us, feel its grip, and hear river music with no whining motor to drown it out. We can go ashore, feel its texture underfoot — and sometimes take our footprints with us. We can be awed by the enormity of what looked small only because the Canyon can dwarf everything within it.

Redwall Cavern, the largest cave open to view in the Canyon wall and reached from the river, could seat fifty thousand people. But let Redwall Cavern be found in quiet; let it be lonely.

These reckless, heaven-ambitious peaks,
These gorges, turbulent-clear streams,
this naked freshness,
These formless wild arrays,
for reasons of their own,
I know thee, savage spirit —
we have communed together.
Walt Whitman

Rapids happen because of big rocks and little, young, old, and incredibly ancient, down from Hermit, and Hance, Badger, from

Tapeats and Kanab and Stone Creek, and Shinumo and Coconino. They assemble in order, gather together so the Colorado can sand them down and take them away, in the natural, relentless leveling of the land.

Rapids have a spirit of their own, good to commune with if there is a boatman along who knows that the river can be fun, but isn't to be trifled with. Your knuckles may get white, but after the first rapid or two they relax. Then a good thing can happen. The spirit of the rapid and your spirit become one. You exult and your boat dashes on it, turning, climbing, plowing, powered by the river and guided by a nimble oar, rampaging on to the end, where in whirlpool and surges the river finds its pieces and pulls them together again.

What use are rapids? What use are we if we remain indifferent to challenge? What are we worth if we won't feel exhilaration?

Side streams that bring the rock down reveal the story of the canyon as only a side stream can, attenuating the strata that the river cuts so sharply.

Row hard at the last minute and you can beach your boat where the muddy Colorado receives the crystal waters of Tapeats Creek. Climb a little, and Tapeats will guide you to its best-known, best-hidden tributary, Thunder River. We can watch Thunder foam out into the light, giving no hint of its dark beginning under the high Kaibab Plateau, where snow fell and melted, and rain trickled into limestone. In black narrow vaults the waters convene and tumble out in cascades to water one of the finest gardens in Grand Canyon. Like Cedric Wright, "We are aware, lying under trees, of the roots and directions of our whole being. Perceptions drift in from earth and sky. A vast healing begins."

Elves' Chasm is easy to reach from the river. It hides its falls and pools. There are more and more for those who look. [Here Jeff remembers our first ascent of the upper reaches of the chasm.] The truth Loren Eiseley wrote becomes clear: "If there is magic on this planet, it is contained in water."

Like Thunder Creek, Deer Creek is not in the national park. It ought to be. Havasu is protected in the national park — as long as the park is protected. The way we come in is tight and narrow where the creek has worn down through. Or take the trail from the rim and be drawn down by the beauty the stream promises and constantly creates, good to look upon and equally good to feel.

And there are more and more side canyons, too many for a lifetime, but not too many for the lifetimes of those who will find their way here, to discover what Thoreau believed would always be awaiting us, "a world visibly recreated in the night."

To explore, to be within and part of the wildness of this place, to begin to learn what it can tell, confirms the idea that some land should be left unimpaired, that all people might come and enjoy it for what it is — the national park idea.

You never tire of trying to understand how the river did it, chiseling, smoothing, bringing new forms out of the old stone, when its only tools are living water and the finest sand. The round earth turns and follows its course among the stars. The river unearths the ancient rock laid down many cataclysms ago. The water dissolves limestone, paving the ancient rock with it where thin streams and seeps of limewater lay down travertine. Grand Canyon National Monument protects some remnants of a time when lava poured over the rim country, filling side canyons, boiling into the river and plugging it. Volcanic tapestries and columns of basalt along miles of the canyon below the Monument are vestiges of the tumult John Wesley Powell imagined: "a river of molten stone running down into a river of melted snow. . . .What a seething of the waters, what clouds of steam!" The heat that melted rocks is now just enough to keep some springs warm. Earth's fire, though banked, is not dead in the Grand Canyon. Nothing is. The Canyon lives.

The talus and the sandbars let the flowers, grass, and cactus live, and the animals that let us see them, and those that do not. The river itself, urgent and coherent, is alive, and there is magic in it.

Deep down in the earth that the river has already delved a mile into you see the life in stone Loren Eiseley wrote about: "The huge stones were beasts, I used to think, of a kind man ordinarily lives too fast to understand. They seemed inanimate because the tempo of the life in them was slow. They lived ages in one place and moved only when man was not looking. Sometimes at night I would hear a low rumble as one drew itself into a new position and subsided again."

The cycle of life goes on. The Colorado and the Grand Canyon live; and in our intimate connection with them, we live.

The dam builders will always be hypnotized by their desire to exploit the Colorado River and its gorge, to drain from the river its energy we have felt. Yet there are other ways of generating electric power. There is no other Grand Canyon.

Can we afford to keep some land free of the contrivances of the world we made? Can we afford places where all we need to do is to walk easily through the world we were made in? Can we afford to set aside national parks? Can we afford not to? Dams or people? You can help decide.

And if you think some land should be left, exalting its own life; if you feel that clouds should not have to contend for space with smog; if you think that somewhere a garden should be able to grow uncultivated; that a pond should be left to itself, to support its own community; if you are pleased to see a stream running pure, glorifying a natural pavement; if you are content to enjoy a river shore, leaving its design undisturbed; if you think a wilderness river should be left dancing, alive and bringing life; if you have come, even a little, under the spell of this place, then this canyon we have seen only a little of, this Grand Canyon, is your Grand Canyon.

Grand Canyon film, 1968

The extraordinarily beautiful film led to a less extraordinary book, *Grand Canyon of the Living Colorado,* edited by Roderick Nash, with unique interpretive photographs by Ernest Braun and, inevitably, a foreword by a congenital foreword writer. It was a Sierra Club/Ballantine book, published in 1970. But it was too late. Grand Canyon had already been saved. It was also too early, but should be remembered, when the new threats emerge.

ISLAND IN TIME

POINT REYES PENINSULA, for all my earlier years, was just where the highest wind velocity in California would turn up if you needed it, and I didn't. This was what one would expect of a mountain man who thought the ocean was a dead place. My lack of appreciation of the ocean did not survive my marriage. It lingered a while in our second son, Bob, whose constant refrain, for a brief period in our family travels, was "I hate the coast." I think he did not truly dislike it, but he did like our dislike of his refrain. Our family movies show him enjoying the coast as well as the rest of us did — especially the Big Sur coast and the Point Reyes Peninsula.

Our family's interest in saving the peninsula was excited by the film Laurel Reynolds and Mindy Willis made for the Sierra Club. I had the opportunity to help edit the final version and was also bold enough to suggest some changes in the narration and to narrate it, having been reasonably successful in *Two Yosemites* and *Wilderness Alps.* I don't know just why, but Mindy Willis vetoed my narrating. Perhaps some lines I tried to change were hers, and she did not want them meddled with. One passage went something like this: "A tufted puffin, its plumes as golden as Alice's hair. We must be in Wonderland!" I wanted to leave Alice out of it. She left me out. Somewhere I still have an audiotape of my narration and will try to substitute it for what was finally used. I would not wish to change anything else. Laurel Reynolds recommended the music and accepted my ideas for applying it in the sound track. A selection of harp music played by Grandjany, from an old seventy-eight, is beautiful accompaniment for a flight of pelicans, ending the film with so much power that I am willing to credit the combination with saving the national seashore. There were, of course, quite a few other forces at work. Looking through the window of opportunity in the Point Reyes campaign was a host of advocates of the National Seashore, including the late Congressman Clem Miller, whose district it is in, the late senator from California, Clair Engle, Secretary of the Interior Stewart Udall, the National Park Service, particularly George Collins of the regional office in San Francisco, the Sierra Club, Conservation Associates, and President John F. Kennedy. The Pacific Gas and Electric Company surely had no objection to having the openness of a national seashore rather than a burgeoning community of condominiums, malls, and estates, just downwind of the nuclear reactor it was proposing for Bodega Head.

But I'll still give major credit to the three brown pelicans that did exactly what they needed to do to climax Laurel Reynolds's final sequence. The light is low, and the three of them are at first barely distinguishable from the dark sea as they play follow the leader in the most graceful choreography pelicans are capable of, and no other bird can match — the quiet glide, skimming just above the surface of the sea, wings fully spread, kept aloft by the lift of wind as the waves push it upward, all this for twice as long as you think possible, then with a few lazy strokes rising just high enough to drop into another long glide. But what Laurel saw them do is rise from the dark sea into a sky with the clouds so beautifully placed that the pelicans remained aloft for the view. They did not know that they were to be lifted and sustained there, again and again, by the music of Grandjany's harp.

I was blown away, before that expression was invented, by this shot the first time I saw it. Laurel had placed it somewhere in the middle of her initial version of the film, but let me put it where it had to be — at the end — and add the music. I want to transfer it to video and have it as a handy antidote if I feel depression coming on. As I play it I will remember what happened, long ago, when I was showing the film to members of the Commonwealth Club, which is firmly in the conservative spectrum, its members not prone to be emotionally swayed by someone's color film. The pelicans blew them away too.

In my note in *Island in Time: The Point Reyes Peninsula*, by Harold Gilliam, I describe something else I like to remember:

"We had just driven over the top from Inverness and down one of the fine ridges dropping to the sea from the forest, a ridge all decked out for spring, with bright blossoms interspersing the salt-pruned shrubs. The children wanted to get down to where the salt came from, to find their own gifts from the sea, to get some Pacific to cool their feet. Their parents wanted to watch what must always have been one of the most exquisite of sights — that of one's own children challenging the wave edges, chasing and being chased, with a new child reflection in a new frame each time another wave makes the wet sand glisten again. Children belong there almost as much as the shorebirds.

"But the man with the hammer at his side shouted over to us, 'You can't park there. That's private property.' How could we get to the beach or up Limantour Spit? 'This is *all* private property, down to the tide line. If you want to get to this beach, go down to Bolinas and walk up offshore.'

"We let the man go back to work on his new house, a long way north of Bolinas. . . ."

When Stewart Udall spirited me into the Oval Office to watch the signing of the legislation creating the Point Reyes National Seashore, I had a chance to tell President Kennedy of that incident, and to point out that the important things are not what we put on that shore but what we find have always belonged there. I was pleased that he seemed to agree, and signed not only the bill, but also my copy of the book. I also left him a copy of the book. If there had been video then, I'd have left the pelicans too.

NATURE NEXT DOOR

THANKS TO THE LATE PROFESSOR ALDEN MILLER, of the Museum of Vertebrate Zoology, University of California, Berkeley, I had an opportunity to work with Robert C. Stebbins on two Sierra Club films, to identify the song of a wren tit, and to learn what mad dogs and Englishmen and a parietalectomized lizard have in common. Are there any questions?

While he was doing graduate work at the museum, Bob Stebbins wrote a paper I was asked to edit. I plunged into the editing with all the enthusiasm I gained from editing climbing articles by Morgan Harris, a most tolerant mountaineering friend of mine and a zoologist friend of Bob's. There are many ways an editor can be helpful, and I used those that worked with Morg on Bob and thought they were appreciated. Until Sam Farquhar, manager of the University of California Press, received a letter from Alden Miller defending his "coerced author," Bob Stebbins, from his coercer, David Brower.

I still don't understand what I had done that Bob himself did not like, but we did have some friendly discussions. I used a softer blue pencil and began to learn things from Bob, about wildlife in the Berkeley Hills we shared, that I had not known. I had been looking at my hills through the eyes of butterflies; Bob used reptiles and amphibians.

Just walking with Bob through Tilden Regional Park, which both of us live on the edge of, is an enlightening experience, and that's where the wren tit came in. I had been hearing wren tits all my life without listening to them, or discerning their dialects, or even knowing who they were. Bob never showed me the pineal seat of the soul, but he did explain the connection between the pineal gland and the parietal eye, which in some lizards is a radiation dosimeter, telling lizards when to get out of the noonday sun that mad dogs and Englishmen wander into.

All this led naturally into our working together on his film and its accompanying booklet, *Nature Next Door* — a new direction for the Sierra Club. Bob photographed it in Tilden, and in the film celebrated the importance of having some nature next door, readily available to school children, letting them find out what every child should know about the care and feeding of ecosystems. I made a few editorial suggestions and completed arrangements for Sierra Club production and distribution. I also supplied no-cost narration, reading the script as if I were Bob. His daughter Mary starred in the film, and thus became my daughter every time the film was shown. We have never met.

Every school ought to have this film — transferred to video, of course — or better yet, should have a wild place nearby where children can produce their own show, and learn what is happening from the very act of producing it.

The flip side is the film Professor Stebbins made when on a sabbatical in Witwatersrand, *No Room for Wilderness*. I left the Sierra Club staff too soon to persuade the club to reach as far afield as South Africa, or to co-produce with the late Tony Beamish a film concerned with the Indian Ocean — *Adabra Alone*. It is time to reach farther still. Wilderness had better never be just a memory, with no room for it around the inn. John Daniel tells why in his poem "Hanaupah Canyon" (in *Common Ground*).

> *That Earth, of all the ways of being*
> *should happen just this way —*
> *what I hold in mind*
> *of the work ongoing here*
> *is a drop of all that I can't know*
> *that fills me and flows through,*
> *as clear and aching*
> *as this water I hold*
> *streaming through my hands.*

CALLING ALL VCRs

IF YOU WANT TO BORROW THEM, my Bell & Howell sound projector and speaker are tucked far back in the kneehole of my desk in San Francisco. My five-foot screen is in the far corner of the hallway leading downstairs to the papers I intend to sort and file — a pile that would measure eight and a half by eleven inches by about twenty stories high if I tried to file them vertically.

I may live long enough to do the sorting and filing, but not to get that projector and speaker out and haul them and the screen and about twenty pounds of film through long corridors and up and down how many stairs in order to make a two-hour showing. I think I'd rather put my two-hour presentation on a ten-ounce VHS cassette and count on finding VCRs wherever I go.

Do not be alarmed. I have no intention of expecting anyone to watch two hours of anything. That's just how much one can cram into a single videotape at normal speed. And VCRs, according to newspaper accounts in mid-1989, are as common as vacuum cleaners, 65 percent of American households having one or more.

Do that many households have bookcases? If so, with room for how few books?

This is not to argue that the book and the film must join the horse in history, but it is to suggest that it is time for people who like the earth to put VCRs to work saving it. They can start by helping me arrange my two hundred fifty or so video cassettes in sensible order and by preparing an index of what is in them.

It's not that I have no idea. Some tapes I just went out and bought. Others were finished, or nearly finished films produced on video by friends; there are Kodak productions with the Sierra Club name on them; several are video transfers of my own early films; one, particularly treasured, is a Japanese documentary based on Kenneth Brower's book *The Starship and the Canoe.* Many are what my own cameras have recorded about our family, with emphasis on two grandchildren. I have recorded several slide shows and hope to do more, but better. Then there are the cassettes of what has gone on at meetings, such as eleven hours each of a two-week session at Lake Baikal, in Siberia, in 1988, and one week at the Fourth Biennial Congress on the Hope and Fate of the Earth, in Managua, in 1989, and another eleven of the Citizen's Summit in Moscow, in January 1990, and another eleven hours' tape of our U.S./U.S.S.R. Save Lake Baikal expedition of August 1990.

It is hard to imagine that other camcorder owners are in as much trouble as I am; but they, too, must be thinking of how to put the exquisite technology they have in hand to practical use in controlling the development epidemic and in preserving the world by preserving its vestige of wildness, as recommended by Henry David Thoreau.

In January 1989 a conference was held at Stanford University with the theme "You Can Make a Difference." Some thirteen hundred people attended to find out how. Anchorman Ted Koppel chaired an afternoon panel that included a top executive of Chevron, Joan Martin-Brown of the United Nations Environment Programme, two whose names have escaped me, and another whose name didn't, me. Ted

Koppel asked each of us to list important changes that need to be made in the United States.

One of Joan's suggestions was that Chevron move its concern for the environment from the public relations department to the operations department, and the audience applauded in approval. They applauded more enthusiastically an hour later when a member of the audience asked what the panel would advise President Bush to do. Joan quickly listed about ten great recommendations, and concluded with "And when he has finished this, have him call me."

When my turn came I asked Ted (I hadn't met him before, but TV is a first-name business), "Do you want a long speech or just a couple of sound bites?"

"Not a long speech," he replied; "maybe a couple of long sound bites."

I gave my worry list: global warming, acid rain, the ozone hole, loss of biological diversity, the addiction to unsustainable growth, and added one more:

"We need to reform television, which is causing cerebral gridlock across America."

There was prolonged applause, so the discussion went on at length. Ted noted how sharply the network television audience was falling off owing to competition with cable and VCRs. I thought this would change if the networks expected more from their audience than rampant consumption. I told him briefly of the added competition I should like to see come from something like Earth Island Video Journal.

My sound bites were not so long as what follows, but this is what I had in mind and alluded to briefly:

When I learned how to teach as an officer in the Mountain Troops, they drilled into us that teaching consists of Explanation, Demonstration, Practical Work, and Test — E, D, PW, and T so we would remember it. Television stops with E and D, except that it doesn't stop. It is just E and D all day. It is unfair to potatoes to compare them with what therefrom sits on the couch. If there is no practical work and no test, the student doesn't learn. Television must teach as well as entertain. The challenge is to be an entertaining teacher.

I outlined what I thought would set an example, what I would like Earth Island Video Journal to be.

There would be a two-hour cassette every two weeks.

It would open with a warning: "If anyone lets the program run for more than thirty minutes without stopping to do something about what has just been seen, the set will automatically self-destruct."

The content would consist of a twenty-nine-minute feature (allowing one minute to turn the set off), followed by short pieces, ranging from two to ten minutes, covering news, adding some beauty and humor, and including a "Tapes to the Editor" section to keep the nation's camcorders busy, on something beyond weddings and baby's first steps.

The quality would be less than professional to encourage public contributions; content would have precedence over lines-per-inch.

The audience would be VCR owners and friends, with emphasis on friends who would like to see and hear what is too often omitted from national and local programming, for reasons everyone knows: advertisers and major donors must not be displeased by boat rockers. The purpose of the whole exercise is to bypass conventional-media barriers to the airing of important information and to prevent what happens to minds when only the ears and eyes are engaged. The audience should be a do-something party.

Initial distribution could start with Earth Island Centers, Sierra Club chapters and groups, Audubon chapters, and Friends of the Earth branches — these to introduce the opportunity to potential activists. Try for similar groups in the peace, social justice, and others in the sustainable-society movement, hoping schools and universities will join.

The game plan, then, is to gather some people around, start the tape, pausing or repeating as desired (TV doesn't do that), get the point, turn off the set in time, discuss what to do about the issue, and do it. Then back to the screen. At the next thirty-minute break refreshments are permitted. Then back to the screen, and it had better be an upbeat bit.

This has all been explanation, with a meager attempt at demonstration. For practical work, put this book down, think what you can do about the video idea in your community, get on the phone, rattle some cages, and break out your camcorder and rough out a "Tape to the Editor."

There will be a graded test tomorrow afternoon at this time.

Financing is just an administrative detail. Motivation is followed by money.

I dropped this idea on Ted Koppel and urged that he propel the idea along. You have the audience, I said. After a half hour, why not pause and ask your audience to do something about what they have just seen and heard.

His reply came with no hesitation:

"They'd probably go to the bathroom."

Should film be abandoned? Not if you want top quality, can afford it, and don't mind waiting too long to find out what you have photographed.

Abandon books?

Never!

Hetch Hetchy Valley before the dam. (Photo by Jay N. LeConte.)

CHAPTER 4

SCENIC RESOURCES
FOR THE FUTURE

VEN THOUGH I REFUSE TO GROW UP, the years keep adding up, accompanied by increasing mellowness offset by increasing impatience. The impatience is obvious in what I say about foresters. I want to see reform happen in time for me to enjoy it. But where is the mellowness? Perhaps in my learning, belatedly, to try to find out where people who disagree with me are coming from and what is driving them. The Forest Service is coming, of course, right out of the mind of Gifford Pinchot, who believed that everything in the national forests should be for sale (but not to the National Park Service). What is driving the Forest Service? Just the love of the sound of falling trees? Perhaps. More likely, the increasing demand for forest products, including the soaring demand for housing for a burgeoning population, augmented by an addiction to second homes. Combine this with an insatiable requirement that there be more and more paper — to feed copying machines, computer printers, and presses that disgorge newspapers, magazines, and books like this.

These pressures have driven the Forest Service periodically to conduct a Timber Resources Review (TRR), projecting future demand for timber and estimating the resources available to fulfill it. The first TRR to come to my attention did not consider the kind of demand I was to read about in an English language newspaper in Tokyo in 1976. All the world's forests, the story said, were insufficient to meet Japan's need for forest products. Japan at the time was planning an 8-percent annual growth in GNP, without specifying where that growth would find resources to use up to sustain the growth, or even where it would find enough paper to print its annual reports on.

In the mid-1950s, when I first encountered the TRR, I myself had yet to realize that an unending growth in GNP was a no-win situation for our descendants, and ourselves. I did, however, believe that there should be equitable treatment of other requirements of a growing society. Not just timber, but such other resources as water, land, food, and energy. Also a bit of amenity here and there, such as scenic resources, including the beauty of wild things and places.

So I proposed a National Scenic Resources Review, which won the approval of the Sierra Club directors. I talked about it wherever an audience would listen, and was able to persuade myself, as the editor of the *Sierra Club Bulletin,* to publish the article I wrote about it.

WHY CAN'T JOHNNY READ? Because he's only three, our youngest. But he walks quite well for his age. He covered nine of our ten miles of the trail into the Glacier Peak country last summer on his first wilderness trip. That was far enough. Very few miles more, and he would have walked out the other side; none of us wanted to get back to civilization that soon.

John is not much different from other children you know who are his age and who, before you know it, will be voting for president for their first time. The very year they do, this nation will celebrate its two hundredth birthday.

Which brings me to the point. How beautiful will America be then?

And when John is about as old as his father is now — which will happen, God willing, much sooner than he thinks — he'll be able to bid one millennium good-bye and watch the year 2000 come in. In an understandable way, that puts me there too. It gets me to wondering what wilderness will be there for him to walk his youngest into; what wild creatures and natural beauty in a world otherwise filled with artifacts; what choice of scenic experience for a whole crowded land, hardly two generations away.

There aren't many places left where we, ourselves, can choose whether to exploit or leave wild. Although the budget of natural things may have looked unlimited to grandfather, we know it is a finite budget. Wildness is a fragile thing. People can break it but not make it. And we are quite capable, in our own time, of breaking it all — quite capable of using up all the choices America will ever have between saving and spending what is left of its unmarred natural heritage.

Only our own self-restraint, in a way, can assure Johnny and his contemporaries more than a world of ersatz scenery. A recent Reuters dispatch suggests how close that world is. The dispatch tells us that a Paris clinic has found a synthetic equivalent for a month's rest in the mountains:

"Ten short visits to a clinic here will give tired Parisians treatment by oxygen equivalent to a month's rest cure in the mountains, the newly opened Paris oxygen center claims.

"The treatment in rooms decorated with colors to 'suit the condition of the patient' costs thirty-seven dollars [or about two hundred 1991 dollars] and lasts twenty-five minutes for each of the ten visits.

"The center has red rooms reserved for patients who seek the tonic of mountain treatments. Green rooms, said a center official, suggest the quiet of a rest in the country. And blue rooms provide the right atmosphere for the highly strung who would like to take it easy at the beach.

"Each room has artificial windows looking onto giant photographs of soothing land and seascapes and the temperature is regulated with the oxygen to give an impression ranging from balmy days in sunny meadows to invigorating mountain climes. Patients take the oxygen in transparent nylon tents."

I know of no one who is willing to exchange wildness for a synthetic, or who would consciously make decisions today that would leave children only a scenic nylon tent in a Paris clinic, or the two-toned, streamlined equivalent we could expect in the domestic marketplaces. Yet it takes no more than two or three moments of quiet contemplation to demonstrate how fast we are moving in this direction.

While I write, at an elevation of one thousand feet in the Berkeley hills, my eyes are smarting. We built here for the view of San Francisco Bay and its amazing setting. But today there is no beautiful view; there is hideous smog, a sea of it around us. "It can't happen here," we were saying just three years ago. Well here it is. And on the land around us, where just two generations ago people could be born "on a farm in the North Berkeley hills," there isn't room to plant another iris corm when I separate those that are now stifled by crowding. For all this, our planners talk breezily, even happily, of an ultimate population of seventeen million people around the Bay. To enjoy the view? To breathe the clean sea air? To stroll in the park on an autumn afternoon? What park?

"The only thing necessary for the triumph of evil," we are told, "is for good men to do nothing." Some good people are doing very well; those of them who are in the business of transforming natural resources into commodities for the commercial world are planning ahead admirably. The forest products industries and the Forest Service are looking hard at the year 2000, and to meet that year's needs are rapidly adding to our vast tree-crop lands by converting the last of our virgin forests. The agencies that develop water and hydropower are building the dams now that will meet the next century's requirements and are creating reservoirs where the bottomlands were, and the living space for wildlife and recreation. Highway engineers, in long-range plans, are trying desperately to pave pasture fast enough for the new hordes of horses our automotive engineers are placing under millions of hoods — sixty-five million hoods this year, or twice as many as were on the road a decade ago.

The conservationist, however — and by *conservationist* I mean the people (or part of them) concerned with what natural resources do for their spirits, not their bank balance — is not doing so well in making certain that civilization will retain the wild islands that are essential in their tamed world. In the race to the future it seems as if we are riding a detached little red caboose, destined never quite to catch up, resigned to arriving at that future only to find that all the land is already staked out for practicable utilitarian progressive realistic commercial purposes. We need to get out of that caboose and ride the engine instead. Or at the very least to get everybody to ride the caboose and arrive at the same time. And there's a way to do it.

Early in 1956 the Sierra Club Board of Directors proposed a Scenic Resources Review — a full-scale conservationist effort to look ahead as far as the commodity producers are looking. To summarize a summary of it, the Review would provide that public and private agencies combine speedily to find what scenic resources are still left, to make an estimate of the future's need for them, and to devise ways of protecting them in time. The term *scenic resources* is only a convenient shortcut; for our purposes it covers local, state, and national parks, appealing wilderness wherever it is, the wildlife that brings vitality to these scenes, and the vitality, resourcefulness, and creative ability that people regain when they get off the pavement and onto the world. A medium-length definition would be the resources of parks, wilderness, and wildlife and the recreation derived from them. And now let's shorten it to the SRR.

The SRR affects you directly, and poignantly affects anyone you know who is Johnny's age. It relates to what we and his contemporaries will see out of our windows and through our windshields. It has major bearing on what we and he will be able to do on those days when we want to see less of the world as man has remade it and more of it as God made it in the first place. The SRR has meaning in the sights, sounds, smells, tastes, and feelings we ought to be able to know when we head for a far, clean horizon to come to our senses, or to let them come to us.

So much for the general import. What are the specific steps of the inquiry? Let's take them one by one.

1. What Do We Have?

The country's most distant horizons are now less than eight hours apart and the time is shrinking. [In March 1990 it shrank to sixty-seven minutes.] What scenic resources lie between? We need an inventory. We don't have it.

We already know, of course, where our present national and local parks are, but we don't know how many people the key areas of a park can withstand without defeating the aesthetic purposes for which the park was set aside. Nor do we know what areas of park caliber exist which may be set aside to meet the presumably growing need.

We already know what wilderness and wild areas have been designated in national forests, but we don't know their carrying capacity in people. We don't know what wild lands have been designated, or could be designated, in parks, wildlife refuges, on Indian lands, on state lands, or on the public domain in general. For that matter, no compilation exists of where our roadless areas are in this country.

One of the most important categories of scenic resources does not even have a name. It is unlike parks, where you can drive but don't hunt, and unlike wilderness, where you may hunt but not drive; for in this category you may drive and hunt. Its scenic and recreational importance is great, but will be all but obliterated if exploitation of commodity resources is permitted. The Forest Service has designated many of these places as recreation areas; people camp and ski there, or visit resorts and lease summer homesites. But there are many such places on national forest which are not so designated and none of them has strong protection against incompatible uses. We don't know how many there are, or how many people they could accommodate, or how many similar areas there are outside the national parks and forests.

This is not the place to spell out scenic-resource land classifications, but merely to point out the need of their being spelled out. All of us know what kind of scenic place we like to go to when there's a chance; in simplest terms, then, the question on a national scale is, what places like this are there, where are they, and how many people can use them without spoiling them?

2. How Much Space Will We Need?

Assuming that the future will want freedom; assuming that freedom is meaningless without freedom of choice [and is immoral if we take ours from someone else]; and assuming further that tranquility should always be an available choice, somewhere, some time, however briefly — assuming all this, what will our needs be for scenic open space by the year 2000? This is an arbitrary choice of year — it's just the well-rounded year that Johnny should see come in — but it is well within our ken. Many of the nation's leaders can remember well what has happened in the last forty-four years and can thus bring that experience to bear in looking ahead that far. Short though the span of that backward look may be, there is something about it that is terribly important in relation to our look ahead — in those four decades the world mined more of its resources, and used them up, than in all its previous history [Too conservative between 1970 and 1990, *four times more* than in all previous history.]

73

A key man in recreation planning asks, "How can you tell what anybody's going to be doing fifty years from now?" He has a point. A point, but not an answer. Conservationists must do their best at estimating future needs simply because all the resource managers — the commodity producers — are doing *their* best. We don't have to wait on our own research to find out about 2000. The resource managers have estimates of what the population will be, assuming that it will continue its amoeba-like doubling. They have estimates of how much more leisure time we shall be likely to have [they overlooked the homeless] and how much faster we shall be traveling to more distant destinations.

So take their figures and apply them to Yosemite, for example. It's overcrowded now. If the population is going to be twice as great, and the trend shows that each person is likely to spend twice as much peak-season time in national parks by the year 2000, and if we further assume that Yosemite should stand no greater-peak-season overload than it already gets, then we had better look around for scenic space for the three million people who won't squeeze into Yosemite in the year that Johnny takes his youngest out to introduce him to the mountains [but were already squeezed there in 1990].

3. Who Else Needs Space?

Growth brings many problems; competition for space is one of them. An adolescent admires growth; a mature person is more likely to deplore it, for it doesn't seem to happen in the right places anymore. In the adolescent, the thymus turns growth off as soon as the contour is right. The mature person has no such automatic phenomenon to turn to; only judgment and (or) conscience will save him.

Our civilization has yet to show much evidence of a built-in thymus for its adolescence, and we can only hope that judgment and conscience will succor its maturity. There is not yet much embarrassment about the daily homage to the great god Growth, so secure in his chrome-plated niche. This very statement, if it were to be widely read, would probably cause widespread resentment. But does it really miss the truth?

In our commercial world, have we yet seriously questioned the difference between the bigger and the better? Can you find any remorse, on the financial page, in the report that this year's volume was greater than last year's? Is the increase ever expressed as the resources spent from the earth's savings? As a new empty space against the sky that another tree will not fill so well for five hundred years? As thousands of tons of iron ore, never to be renewed, now processed and scattered beyond recovery? Or as millions of barrels of oil, an energy

74

reservoir aeons in the making, exhausted into the atmosphere? Or as fertile lands lost under today's new tract or tomorrow's new freeway while the hearts of cities develop an ominous murmur?

No, there are no questions. This is called progress, and of course these things happen. Perhaps it's better not to think too much about how progress is depriving Johnny's youngest of the best of the world we know.

But we can't dismiss that child. Assuming that we will be some years in devising a new model of progress — one that won't move us ahead so fast, but will carry people longer — we can without much trouble make projections of the future's need for resources, and we can then color in, on our master map, the space which we think should be managed primarily for those resources. This four hundred million acres must grow food; that hundred million should bear a tree crop; these ten thousand miles of streams must be inundated by reservoirs or diverted through penstocks; those mountains must be processed for their ore; these plains paved for industry; those hills recontoured for tracts of houses.

4. Where Are the Conflicts for Space?

Whatever else may grow, and whether the growth is admired or deplored, there is still only one world to count upon and our part of it has firm boundaries. Wherever we might go to look for more space, we could fully expect to bump into someone coming this way on the same quest.

Within our borders there are difficult conflicts already. Final touches are being put on the master plan for controlling the Columbia. There is conflict over the same space by those who are concerned on the one hand with flood control, hydroelectric development, and river navigation and those who, on the other hand, would retain anadromous fish runs, trout streams, wildlife range, national parks, wilderness, and forest recreation. The preliminary plan is well under way for developing California's water. The combatants are essentially the same. A vast sum is being released for highway development — enough to decimate our scenic resources if it is not spent carefully, producing a final product of finer and faster highways to poorer and sadder places, and affording a chance to hurry through what could have been beautiful in order to arrive at a carbon copy of what you started from.

In the forests the conflicts are already legion. The forester's theme, more and more, is "Nature never does anything right," a theme rejected by all who have contemplated the works of two of the greatest foresters, Aldo Leopold and Robert Marshall, who so skillfully showed why we need large preserves to which we can turn from time to time to

75

see if nature was not right after all. The exploitation for minerals still goes on, by and large, subject to one test: Is there mineral there? Seldom it is asked: Is there beauty there, and what would a two or three years' gain in minerals cost in two or three generations' loss in beauty? And finally, for the lands not preempted for farms, cities, reservoirs, power development, forest industries, highways, and mining, there are the signs which say "Keep Out — Military Reservation."

If these are today's conflicts, what of tomorrow's? As we plot those which exist and those which are likely, we see that the master map looks pretty busy. It will be a perplexing map to consider, but we dare not try to escape that perplexity, not unless we wish to resurrect the rejected philosophy of *après moi le déluge*. The important thing is to project all future needs on the same screen with the same projection distance and the same focal length of lens for each scene, and also, to the best of our ability, with the same illumination. Let the light be a cool one.

5. Who Needs the Space Most?

It would be helpful, in resolving the conflicts for space which we see taking form, to have on hand a battalion of people with the wisdom of Solomon. They should also be handy at putting bells on cats. It is easier to suggest criteria for the people on the court than to propose guidelines for decision, but we're in this too far to back out now. So let us ask: For which of the conflicting demands are we most likely to find substitutes?

For example, consider the Northern Cascades of Washington, near Glacier Peak. Here there is a low-grade copper deposit, development of which would bisect one of the primary scenic areas of the entire country, an area equal in caliber to our most magnificent national parks. We are going to run out of inexpensive copper one day and will have to get by with substitutes. We had a taste of what this will mean in the course of World War II, when we were confused a little, but not hurt, by having to use substitutes for copper pennies. Mr. Lincoln lent the same dignity to both, and neither bought more than the other. Our economy went on. Glacier Peak copper can delay our dependence on ersatz copper but a few years. We shall have to find a substitute eventually for gross uses of copper, and our scientists will. But people will never be able to reconstitute the primeval in Glacier Peak once we have breached its superlative redoubt, which we have the tools to do. These are the years of decision — the decision of people to stay the flood of people. We shall have to decide whether to hand the future two voids or one — a world without copper and the primeval, or just without copper [or with all recycled copper].

76

A congressman wrote me that he thought this fifth question — who needs the space most — was a loaded one, designed to get someone else to look for substitutes. He is right. Further, the question should remain a loaded one. The decision needs to reserve the possibility for reversal by a higher court, the next generation, which ought to have a few choices left. A copper substitute or a wilderness? Fewer pages in a newspaper, or a virgin forest? Another button for starting a new kind of appliance, or a jubilant stretch of white water? Faster transportation to more distant housing, or a greenbelt for a city? If we make all these choices, if we use up all this freedom, what is there left for a more crowded world?

We can't be Solomon, but we can remember his most famous decision, and who was awarded the child. Let those who want the wilderness to remain whole phrase the question as they will. A decision adverse to that whole can never be reversed.

Finally, having decided in favor of the future, we need to make sure that the decision sticks; wilderness protection is paper thin, and the paper should be the best we can get — that upon which Congress prints its acts. [Eventually, it should be in the Constitution.]

Who Should Conduct the Review?

There is ample room for difference of opinion about how the Scenic Resources Review should argue its questions, but there seems to be a consensus that the questions need to be asked soon, very soon, and that irreversible decisions relating to natural-resource uses should await the answers.

Various ways of undertaking the SRR are being discussed. What should be the roles of private agencies, of local and state government, of the national executive branch, and of the Congress? An attempt to answer this question with a concrete proposal runs into the difficulties confronting any attempt at positive action — difficulties which should never be underestimated. Nevertheless, a *modus operandi* for the SRR needs to be outlined, and we'll try it, then step aside for constructive suggestions.

Should the review be conducted by private agencies, financed by foundations? Probably not. This is too much the responsibility of all the people. Foundations, with their limited resources might, however, assist with pilot projects or conduct some spot checks. This is a job for the people by the people's agency, government.

Local and state government only? Much responsibility lies here, but a state isn't equipped to act for the nation; the nearer the government, the more accessible it is to advocates of the short-term interest. The review needs the best perspective we can get. And appreciation of a scenic resource often languishes in the minds of those who see it every day. We need a national view of our scene to guide the best efforts of local government.

Then where in the national government should so important a review head up?

The National Park Service has some limited authority under existing law to assist in coordinating national recreation planning, and it is staffed with some of the nation's top people in landscape architecture and recreation planning. But it would probably be a mistake to try to use the Park Service for more than the spark plug; a higher echelon is needed at the wheel. Consider the many agencies concerned: in addition to the Department of the Interior and its lands function, we must take into account the departments of Agriculture (farms and forests), Defense (military land withdrawals), Labor (leisure for working people), Commerce (travel), Education, Health, and Welfare (sociological values), and such other agencies as the Federal Power Commission and the Office of Management and Budget.

This all seems to point directly to a presidential committee or commission, set up under authority of Congress in order to establish a continuity of policy, program, and people to carry on a continuing review. Such an organization is a large order, but are there any who doubt that its creation would receive wide support as soon as the public learns of the need?

While We Wait — A Crash Program

We need an interim, stop-gap step, a *modus vivendi*, while we wait for the public to become informed and for necessary data to be gathered. The premature quality of any crash-program decisions will do no permanent harm if they set aside too much scenery for the time being, whereas the premature exploitation of resources in the absence of the broad considerations proposed in the review could be irreversibly damaging. So many major decisions are imminent that there is certainly not time to precede them with complete programs of research to produce the data we shall eventually need.

Right now, today, however, we have in our bureau chiefs a group of very capable people who can give horseback estimates of the answers to the five questions. In the beginning we can tolerate quite a wide margin of error and make adjustments as the data come in. These people can sketch in the inventory of scenic resources; in time the boundaries can be made more precise. Good sets of figures already exist for estimating the rising demand. We already know quite well what space is wanted for commodity production. That, in a way, is the trouble; that is why scenic-need estimates must be sketched in quickly. Once we have the resulting clear view of the major conflicts for space, we have the National Research Council for counsel on the likelihood of substitutes and their imminence.

There is still no shortcut for resolving the big conflicts. We know that the democratic process can carry on from here. We can rest easy about what will happen so long as we insist that all the cards are on the table before we decide who holds the high one, and so long as we act in the context of a Golden Rule extended to Johnny's contemporaries:

For them, a world as beautiful as ours.

REVIEWING OUR NEEDS FOR SCENIC RESOURCES

In the course of 1956 it has been my privilege to represent the Sierra Club at various meetings about the country and to stress the importance of the concept of the Scenic Resources Review. As far as I could tell, the reaction has been reassuringly favorable every time. The concept adapts itself well to just about every kind of conservation contest we have entered. Perhaps a condensation of part of the testimony I gave will serve two purposes: show in some detail what has been said about several subjects which concern the club — water development, forests, parks, wildlife, wilderness, roads — and clarify their relation to the Scenic Resources Review.

[As of 1991, the French have proved right: *Plus ça change, plus le même chose.* And *Le déluge* is national policy.]

On the Columbia Basin

A typical presentation is the statement made at hearings held by the Army Corps of Engineers in Missoula and Spokane concerning ways to revise earlier plans for control of the Columbia River and its tributaries — an international problem, and very complex. I said in part:

In behalf of the Sierra Club, I am appearing to request that the agencies charged with Columbia Basin water development, as well as other interested groups here, give most careful consideration to planning for the preservation of the Columbia Basin's scenic resources in the course of working out a program of water development. We hope that all groups may work together to assure that the needs of progress are met without sacrifice of unique qualities which are of great importance to the region and to the nation — qualities which cannot be put together again once they have been taken apart.

The Sierra Club is sixty years old. It consists of more than 10,500 members from all walks of life and all parts of the country, but most of them from California. The club has members who are prominent and many more who are not. They share one purpose: to explore, enjoy, and protect the natural scenic resources, including the wildlife resource, which make this land America the beautiful. We are conservationists, all interested in wise use, but especially interested in preserving from development those scarce and special places in our vanishing wilderness which dollars can never replace in kind and for which there will always be human need.

We are a small part of what you might call a national force that has been building to protect the special resource of parks, wilderness, and wildlife. That force is represented, in a way, by the Natural Resources Council of America, of which I am the present chairman. This is a forum of thirty-seven national and regional conservation organizations having a total membership of two million. That force is further represented by the voice of the people themselves, who are realizing in increasing numbers that the few samples we have left of original America must not be sacrificed needlessly.

Witness that public force on the national scene as it was measured in this Congress. In the controversy over Dinosaur National Monument and the proposed Echo Park dam, the Colorado River Storage Project bill was doomed to a seventy-to-ninety vote defeat in the House of Representatives so long as Dinosaur was threatened. The threat was removed, whereupon the bill coasted through with a hundred and twenty-vote majority.

The same force brought a three-to-one defeat at the polls last November in New York state to a proposal to invade part of the Adirondacks which New York citizens wanted to keep forever wild — strong wilderness support in spite of eminent opposition.

The same force showed itself recently at the city level in Eugene, Oregon, where the people chose at the polls not to sacrifice for a power project a beautiful stretch of wild stream, the McKenzie River headwaters. Similar forces are developing rapidly to protect the intangible values of the Rogue River.

All I am trying to say is that we are witnessing a change in the American temper — witnessing a mature realization, in the nick of time, that we must vigorously and dynamically support the preservation of our scenic resources and especially our living wilderness. This doesn't mean that we're building a breed of people who don't like human handiwork; it's just that people are discovering that even the most civilized people need places where they can appreciate what God's handiwork is like, unaided by people. People are recognizing that we cannot forever continue to multiply and subdue the earth without losing our standard of life and the natural beauty that must be part of it.

The Sierra Club believes that the flood-control and power-development needs in the Columbia Basin can be met without jeopardy to important scenic and wildlife resources. There should be optimum use of damsites which do not imperil these resources, no matter whether public or private agencies or a combination of both build on the acceptable sites. These sites should be developed fully enough to meet the overall flood-control requirements with a minimum number of structures. There should be proof that there is no alternative course of action before irrevocable damage is inflicted on the important scenic and wildlife resources.

The club — and this is the general feeling in most other conservation organizations I know of — is in favor of sound water development. However, we consider it not in the public interest in the long run, and therefore oppose, any dam or reservoir proposal which would adversely affect a national park or monument or duly designated [or potential] wilderness area.

Conservationists in general are feeling a growing concern about indirect peril to major scenic resources. For example, the Citizens' Committee on Natural Resources, Washington, D.C., have already voiced conservation opposition to what they are convinced is inadequate development in Hells Canyon. They are not concerned with the public vs. private power controversy. But they are concerned with the threat to major scenic and wildlife values arising from partial development in Hells Canyon. Nearly three million acre-feet of storage is seemingly about to be blocked there. This has already led the Corps of Engineers to seek replacement storage on the Clearwater River, where conservationists are opposing the proposed Bruce's Eddy and Penny Cliffs dams. Likewise, apparently, the Bureau of Reclamation is seeking further control of the Upper Snake River in the tremendously important scenic country above the Narrows, in Wyoming, and in Grand Teton National Park and the Teton Wilderness Area — an effort which conservationists must oppose.

Let me summarize conservationist reasoning here, so that you may understand it even if agreement with it may not be unanimous:

1. It is clear, in the Columbia Basin, that there is not enough flood control now.

2. Remedial action can take four forms:

    a) Flood insurance. This still requires more legislative pioneering; it will not save lives.

    b) Evacuation of flood plain by zoning to prevent new construction or replacement of present structures. This is uphill work, literally and figuratively.

c) Upstream watershed management. Practiced with care, this is good conservation, but it is not effective in controlling the big floods.

d) Flood-retarding structures — midbasin dams and lower basin channel improvement. This action has strong engineering and political backing. We are spending billions on it.

3. To protect scenic resources from flood-control action we must concern ourselves with the effects of dams.

4. The Corps and the Bureau agree that to skim the flood crest from the Columbia River, we need a Main Control Plan, and eventual flood-control storage of 20–30 million acre-feet can be presumed.

5. Scenic resource needs should be integrated with this flood-control need.

6. Whenever storage is provided, someone's special interest will be damaged.

7. The first projects authorized should be those causing tangible damage which can be reimbursed with money; for example, at a cost in dollars, railroads and highways can be rerouted, power generation can be substituted for, and farmland can be replaced in kind [wrong!].

8. The very last to be authorized should be those projects causing damage which no amount of money can replace. This would include damage to national parks and wilderness which people cannot duplicate.

As things stand, in the Columbia River Basin, we seem still to need to provide about fifteen million more acre-feet of usable storage in the Main Control Plan. Conservation opposition has delayed about two million at Glacier View and will probably continue to delay it indefinitely. Partial development plans seem to have blocked three million at the John Day and Priest Rapids sites; partial plans are in the process of blocking nearly three million at Hells Canyon and may well be about to block three and a half million at Buffalo Rapids No. Four if a run-of-the-river plant is built instead of a major storage structure at Paradise; moreover, the smaller development will add greatly to the pressure for major upstream storage in Glacier National Park, either at Glacier View or at Smoky Range. [Clouded thinking.] Conservationists will be forced to oppose both of them.

Thus, to many conservationists, the solution would seem to be to assure full development at Paradise, Hells Canyon, Libby, and in the outlet-works improvement at Grand Coulee, saving the upper reaches of the Flathead in Glacier National Park, the Snake in and near Teton National Park, the Salmon and the Clearwater for scenic and wildlife resources, which in all probability will be in very short supply by the year 2000 [too much an attempt to appear reasonable — at an unreasonable cost to the future].

The Columbia Basin is an especially good area in which to initiate a Scenic Resources Review — a comprehensive plan for adequately protecting now, with an eye to the long-range future, an optimum reservation of the basin's scenic resources of parks, wilderness, and wildlife and their tangible and intangible values for public use, enjoyment, and education.

The plan would consist of a cooperative enquiry by many agencies to develop answers to five basic questions. . . . We believe that the best possible answers to these questions should be sought out before irrevocable decisions are made. Adequate answers are not now available. The nation has immediate need for a broad perspective such as detailed answers to these questions could provide. We believe such a long-range interagency study can be conducted within the framework of present law. Or it may need new legislation. We invite your comment and help.

On the California Water Plan

If there is anything unique about water-development problems in the Columbia Basin, it is the abundance of water there. Scarcity of water, however, doesn't necessarily make it any easier to balance water development against scenic-resources preservation. The contest to prove that natural scenery and water development could coexist in the Upper Colorado Basin was a rugged contest, and very much worth it. California's future will probably see many similarly rugged contests as the California Water Plan, designed to move water from areas of abundance to areas of scarcity, begins to take shape. The relationship of this problem to the SRR is touched in an extract from remarks to the University of California's Fourth Annual Conference on City and Regional Planning at Richmond:

People are recognizing that we must give the most careful consideration to planning for wise use and preservation of our scenic resources — our parks, wilderness, wildlife, and the special recreation which they support. It is my hope that groups such as this one will vigorously seek, and it is my belief that they will find, the means to meet the needs of progress without sacrifice of unique qualities which are of great importance to a city, a region, to the state, and to the nation — and I'm referring to the precious samples of wildness that yet remain, whether in small patches or in large reservations.

The daily papers tell of the recurring threats to these values, and also of the uneasy stirrings of people who don't like what's happening.

Some of you probably saw Dr. Robert C. Miller's recent letter to the San Francisco *Chronicle*, "The LosAngelization of San Francisco," and have seen the *Chronicle* follow up editorially to question the blessings of freeways and to speak of the "tyranny of the automobile."

The same news columns suggest what in some respects might be considered the tyranny of water development. We have read of some of the details of the California water plan, a multibillion-dollar development to meet California's ultimate need for water.

That word *ultimate* should be looked at long and hard. So far as the water plan is concerned, I am not satisfied that we have a good definition of *ultimate*. I don't want to delegate to engineers the working out of the definition, although I have the greatest respect for engineers as builders. Society is quite a bit more than engineering works, however; and I'd like to hear what the philosopher has to say about *ultimate* — or the demographer, or the physician or the psychiatrist or the theologian. I would like to help leave my children something besides what Wallace Stegner describes as "a world mass-produced, with interchangeable parts."

To a water planner, the word *ultimate* means a state population of about forty million, and a Bay Area population of from fourteen to seventeen million. If we continue to consider that growth is the chief element of progress, we're growing fast enough to meet that ultimate terribly soon, and we are planning our engineering works, it would seem, to meet it before it gets here.

I leave it to you to picture the ultimate Bay Area, with perhaps five to ten times the traffic, the noise, and the air pollution, and about one square foot of living space for every five or ten you have right now. If the ultimate Bay Area prospect pleases you, then I would ask you to consider the *post*ultimate which must surely follow — the aseptic world with a photomural on the wall of the oxygen tent to which your grandchildren must retreat for their synthetic outdoor experience.

I should like to make a rhetorical motion — to move that we eliminate the word *ultimate* from our planning, all our planning, and that we substitute therefore the word *optimum*. I think this would result in a very desirable change of emphasis. Not the *most*, but the *best*.

I don't see how we can expect to keep open spaces, scenic and recreational resources, or anything that gives our culture a valuable context, unless we resolve so to shift our emphasis.

For the specific example, let's look at a tiny part of the state water plan. I haven't seen a copy yet, but hope soon to wade through it. Already, however, I know that it contemplates two dams within Yosemite National Park — on the Tuolumne and on the South Fork of the Merced. Yosemite, as most of you know, is already badly overcrowded at times, and our population hasn't hit one-third of the "ultimate" yet, nor has our hoped-for amount of leisure time for travel to national parks. The Sierra Club's short film *Two Yosemites* presents further remarks on this subject. But I just wanted to cite a simple example of what kind of problem we may expect to see multiplied in the complete water plan. More water for more people — at the expense of scenic resources. Not too much thought of the fact that we cannot live by bread alone or water alone, or that reservoirs permanently preempt key living space in a land.

In a state growing as rapidly as this one, we all face a special challenge that requires a careful review of our scenic resources. This will guide us, I think, toward a multiple use of our ever-more-crowded lands. But it won't put conflicting uses in the same place. To each its own place, and always a place for beauty.

California's scenic beauty is something very special. Much of it is still unspoiled. It is an important part of what we need in life besides bread, that we will need still more than we do now, that we will choose to keep if we leave ourselves that choice. Posterity has no vote except in us. Its people must live with what we decide upon now.

To quote Weldon Heald, "God Bless America — Let's Save some of it!"

On Regional Parks

Last September [1954] the San Francisco Chronicle *spoke of the tyranny of the automobile once again, when it editorially lamented "the inertia of bad planning" which "will in time deposit on the Embarcadero a permanent blight" — a double-decked freeway "cutting off the Ferry Building and blighting downtown San Francisco." The editorial concluded:*

"The blight in turn will take an intangible toll from the city through the destruction of aesthetic values. The double-decker freeway will be a living monument to the tyranny of the automobile, a tyranny which has made too many captives to the view that whatever helps move automobiles at the least cost, and hang all considerations of beauty, is right.

"There is a massive problem here for American cities. They need, San Francisco needs, leaders who will recognize it and stand fast to save beauty from the beast." [It took the San Francisco earthquake of October 17, 1989, to hamstring (I hope) that beast.]

The nation's exemplar, Washington, needs them too, to save beauty from the tyranny of pavement. This was the issue before the Senate Committee on Interior and Insular Affairs in February 1955, when I made this statement to the Committee in behalf of the Sierra Club and the Federation of Western Outdoor Clubs:

These organizations believe in parks for today and for the future; they know that the only way we shall have the park areas we shall need for our expanding population is to require ourselves to exercise self-restraint in developing this land.

The main conservation concerns of the groups for which I speak are the national system of parks, wilderness, and refuges. We consider

Rock Creek Park to be part of the national park system in fact as well as in name, part of one of the most beautiful cities of all. When something happens to Rock Creek Park, the bell tolls for all of us, for we are all involved — it is happening to our park, the Nation's park; and it is setting the pattern for parks all over the land, whether they are national, state, regional, or city parks.

Thus, I, a westerner, am concerned about what the present proposals to impair Rock Creek Park will do directly along Rock Creek, and I am also concerned about the effects of action in Washington upon Central Park in New York, Golden Gate Park in San Francisco, and Tilden Regional Park across the bay from San Francisco, where I hope my children will be enjoying a sunny Saturday a few hours from now.

We have great faith in engineers when it comes to engineering, and we believe that engineers can bring about any solution to Washington's traffic problems that Congress requires the engineers to bring about. If Congress, mindful of the irreplaceable values that transcend the engineer's columns of figures, requires the engineers to assume that Rock Creek Park does not exist for transportation purposes, then those engineers are certainly capable of coming up with a feasible solution to transportation needs — whether it be alternate routes, bypasses, a peripheral parking plan, or a reversal of the trend away from mass transportation that has perplexed every traffic engineer in the business. If they should not be capable of coming up with a solution, then we should do well to wait for other engineers who can, for we cannot undo the damage to something unique which would otherwise be destroyed.

Holding fast to a park principle has built an enviable system of national parks for this country. It has also kept Central Park from being subdivided and skyscrapered and has kept it an asset for all New York. Holding fast has kept Golden Gate Park from being covered with row upon row of mimeographed houses that could so easily have blotted out John McLaren's dream. Holding fast will keep Rock Creek Park as a sanctuary for people living in a district where life is so hectic they need such a sanctuary; it will also retain for the National Capital an extremely important and renowned part of its beauty in the eyes of the Nation and the world.

We hope you will act favorably on Senate Joint Resolution 36, and suggest that editorial attention be given to the provisions pertaining to relocation and realignment lest some enterprising engineer find a loophole in the wording through which he might try to drive a truck.

Perhaps Washington's traffic problems will never be solved; but let us be sure while we go through the headaches of trying to solve them that there is a quiet natural beautiful place always there for us along Rock Creek.

This was all that I had intended to say, but a few further thoughts occurred to me during yesterday's testimony. Opponents of the resolution seemed to be of two or three minds on the question of highway versus park; the highway was in keeping with park values and concepts in one part of the park, but not in another, and it would be a good idea, perhaps, to have an expressway all the way through the park — these were the opponents' conflicting views. They seem to underline the need for Congress to make it clear that parks are for park use, and not for highways leading heavy traffic somewhere else.

It was disturbing to see a firm of landscape architects in the position of advocating that an expressway was good because it enabled more people to see a park. If we accept that thesis, parks are doomed everywhere — and we must finally conclude that the more the lanes of traffic and the faster the speed, the greater the use of parks. I hope this committee will agree that a park has far more to offer than what can be seen in a frantic minute or two through a windshield — even a panoramic windshield. Rock Creek Park is already accessible to those who can only drive through it — it has winding, charming roads built with the park as an end in view, not for a fleeting glimpse on the hurried way to someplace else.

It is already unfortunate that the upper meanders of the park are so narrow. Let us show that they will not be made still narrower by pavement that destroys the surface and traffic that destroys the mood. In a way a park is a doughnut, and the place we stand when we use it. Take away the setting, invade the mood, and that hole becomes part of nothing instead of the center of the park. It is a little like this room. We use the floor and the first six feet of space above it; but it takes the rest of the space, and the walls and the ceiling and the decor, to make this a room that has meaning. So it is with parks. By and large it is the part that you do not use for everyday purposes that makes it a park. A park does for you what a park is meant to do when it changes your pace and mood — when you spend a good chunk of the day in it and become part of it for a while, not when, because of a traffic light or a traffic jam, you screech to a stop, then roll down the window for a quick sniff of the great outdoors before someone behind blows a horn.

Because our planners of the past used good vision, a place of Rock Creek's beauty has survived well into the automobile age, of which Bernard De Voto recently wrote, "American culture has made travel by automobile the most satisfactory way and is proceeding to make it impossible." East of the Mississippi and north of Kentucky, he says, "the future has arrived, our mechanical and engineering genius has undone us, and all the institutions of the automobile age are approaching paralysis. For make no mistake about it, the throughways and toll roads are putting an end to what the ads call happy motoring. The density of the traffic and the speed at which it moves destroy the comfort and ease of mind that have hitherto commended auto travel." Mr. De Voto has one more reference to the automobile in his recent *Harper's* piece on public relations artists versus the traveler; he speaks of the time — the imminent time — "when the superhighways have made automobile traffic obsolete."

Rock Creek Park has pretty well survived the automobile so far. We hope that neither the State of Maryland, which controls so much of the National Capital's metropolitan area, nor the Congress, will permit the sacrifice of so much in irreplaceable park value in order to gain so little — if anything — in the moving of vehicles. For here, where the Nation's pulse pounds hard, there are no more havens for all the people where Rock Creek Park came from.

On Roads Proposed for Wilderness

The current tendency to think twice about what freeways or throughways may be doing to us, as well as for us, was preceded nearly twenty-five years by a marked change in our thinking about the relation of roads to wild places. I was sent to Fresno to speak on this subject on before the San Joaquin Valley County Supervisors Association, with particular reference to a proposal to construct a new trans-Sierra highway just south of Yosemite National Park. Excerpts follow:

John Muir, our first president, strongly supported the bringing of automobiles to Yosemite Valley. Too few people knew about the mountains and the parks. If they didn't find out, there would be no force to protect them from destructive exploitation. In its early years, the Sierra Club felt that many new trans-Sierra roads were needed.

In the early thirties that trend of thinking slowed down markedly. That was about the time the first Primitive Areas were set aside in the National Forests. By 1936 the thinking reversed. People realized that an ever-increasing number of automobiles was not a total blessing. They became concerned with Yosemite's fatal beauty — the attraction that was beginning to bring so many people to Yosemite as to jeopardize and destroy its charm.

Nor was it just the hiking clubs who were concerned. In 1936 one of California's most illustrious forums, the Commonwealth Club, completed a full year's study of the question of mountain roads. The following resolution was put to a vote of the entire club membership:

We believe that California's undeveloped high mountain areas have been reduced dangerously near to a minimum for

88

the welfare of the state, and that no further intrusions by the building of roads should be allowed without convincing proof of public necessity.

After reading the comprehensive arguments pro and con which the Commonwealth Club published June 2, 1936, the membership voted the resolution by an overwhelming 650 to 70 — better than 9 to 1. Not so-called nature-lovers, these men, but many of California's most eminent and successful businessmen and leaders.

That was twenty years ago. Today we can be thankful, I believe, that these men took that stand. For despite it, and despite the best conservation efforts since then, our wilderness has shrunk still further, and the number of people who need it has increased far beyond expectations.

Nine years ago the Sierra Club took its present stand. In effect, we support the preservation of the unique wilderness of the High Sierra, whether it was protected by law in the National Parks, by regulation on the National Forests, or merely by the fact that it is not developed. From Tioga Pass on the north to Walker Pass on the south, stretching along the backbone of the state, is the finest, longest wilderness in the country. There are no more where it came from. People come in increasing numbers from all over the nation to see it and travel in it as wilderness. If we keep it there, millions will see and enjoy it that way through the ages — that is, millions, a few at a time. And other millions, whether they have a chance to see it or not, will have a special pleasure in knowing that it is there, for someone, sometime.

If future people decide that this is a luxury they can no longer afford, they can choose to change it. In a few months they can, even with engineering skill no more advanced than ours, undo what nature has taken aeons to build and what people can never restore. They could do this, that is, if they chose to. I hope they don't. The Sierra Club's stand would merely make sure that people of the future have the chance to choose. We ask that no trans-Sierra roads be built between Tioga and Walker passes. We resolved this in 1947. We think that planners, and the engineers who build what planners plan, are ingenious enough to spare this place, the finest wilderness in the land.

In other words, we feel that if this stretch of the Sierra were somehow actually impassable, it would not be necessary to abandon the San Joaquin Valley. Life, development, and progress could go on here. Ways would be found to get the food and fiber for progress around this barrier, or to fly them over it. These alternatives might take a little more time, and cost a little more money. But they would spare what neither time nor money can replace.

Therefore we ask you to base your action on this assumption — the great Sierra wilderness is a barrier against which people, by their own choice, refuse to pit their engineering skill. By our own arbitrary rules of zoning, we will keep our bulldozers, dynamite, combustion engines, wheels — all these we will keep out. All we will pit against this primitive barrier is our own primitive skill, in using our own two feet, or in persuading our pack animals to use four feet.

If you make this choice, if all of us do, we can be assured of special benefits for all time to come. Generation after generation can find recreation and inspiration there. The watershed, so important to you, will be maintained in all its natural protection. Untouched natural processes will continue for us to observe scientifically and to compare with the land we have improved (to see from time to time how we're doing). Wildlife can prosper in this place as it always has. And it will constitute an unmolested reserve, should we ever have to exploit the few commercial resources remaining in this small sample of what America once was.

All this has been fairly general, but I think this general approach is important to our planning of what kind of California we want to have in a more crowded future.

I think I have most of the arguments for a new Mammoth Pass highway in mind — the new recreation area that would be opened up, the access to Mammoth Mountain winter sports, the Hawthorne ammunition route, the escape route in case of disaster, and so on. I think we have good answers for these arguments, and will try to point them out if you wish. We think the answers are compelling.

We hope to persuade you of this: if this road goes in, it is there for keeps, and our finest wilderness is gone for keeps. The people in favor of roads can lose arguments again and again. The people trying to save a superlative bit of wilderness can lose only once. We hope that you will help save this wilderness.

Concerning the problems of transportation, we hope this group will urge a comprehensive study of San Joaquin Valley needs and their relation to the state as a whole. The Division of Highways and the Department of Defense should be brought into the study. They and you should consider how to get maximum effectiveness from the routes already developed — Sonora, Tioga, Walker, and Tehachapi passes and their relation to the chief northerly routes over Donner and Echo summits. The study would need to consider present traffic patterns and the trends that indicate what the future will bring.

I would hope, above all, that the national conservation interest could be represented well in this study. The High Sierra wilderness happens to be in your backyard, and I think in mine too. But it is also the only place of its kind in the nation, one of the most livable, enjoyable places for primitive wilderness travel in all the world.

In a state growing as rapidly as this one, we all face a special challenge that requires a careful review of our scenic resources which can

lead to decisions that won't jeopardize very real future needs. . . .
The Sierra Crest country between Tioga and Walker is something
very special. Most of it is still unspoiled. As it is, we say, please let it be.

On Logging and Virgin Forests

*The Scenic Resources Review derives its name, if not its inception,
from the Timber Resource Review — the "TRR" you hear about whenever
the future of timber production is discussed. The TRR is a recurring study,
the latest edition of which was placed before the public in abstract form this
year in a Forest Service booklet entitled "People and Timber." Shortly after
its precursor appeared — the six pounds of charts, diagrams, and text
which constituted the draft edition — the Sierra Club wrote Secretary of
Agriculture Ezra T. Benson as noted below.*

*This apprehension was expressed in the first part of my letter to Dr.
Richard E. McArdle, chief of the U.S. Forest Service, c. 1954:*

One of our primary interests is in comprehensive planning, as
opposed to piecemeal planning, for the use of our natural resources.
This was expressed in our proposal to Secretary Benson that a multiple-
resource review be undertaken to supplement the Timber Resource
Review to help place the latter in good perspective. We have developed
our proposal further as an interagency Scenic Resources Review, and
this is receiving increasingly wider support. We know that you and the
secretary appreciate the importance of this approach, and we in turn
appreciate Dean Samuel T. Dana's insight and skill in seeking, at the
request of the Forest Service, a program of research that will become an
important part of the broad review the country needs.

There have been some recent controversies between your organization and ours — and others like ours — growing out of competing
and often incompatible demands for the same piece of forest. It is pertinent to point out, however, that these differences are the exception, not
the rule; that vexing though they may sometimes be, they are probably
good for us; and that they all too often obscure the general agreement
and unanimity of purpose we share. For example, the production of timber in the postwar period has almost trebled in California; this has
required excellent resource management, and the Forest Service has
come through notably. In all this, as an off-the-cuff estimate, conservationists have had no occasion to take exception to ninety-nine out of
every one hundred board-feet that have been produced. [Again, I was
trying too hard to seem reasonable.]

There remains that small part of the total where we have conflict,
a part that can be relatively very important to meeting the future's need

for scenic resources. Here any precipitate action has a potential of doing irrevocable damage to irreplaceable natural values. And so much for the preamble.

Regarding the proposed Salmon Creek sale, we cannot understand the rapidity of events which threaten to set the course for the Cannell Meadows working circle and the southern Sierra area, of which this is an important part. Here are the considerations as we see them:

1. Some type of wilderness preservation has been proposed for part of the area in question. Expression of national interest has not been sought yet.

2. A detailed administrative plan that will preserve the primary recreation and wildlife values — for developed, as opposed to wilderness, recreation — is needed for another part. To the best of our knowledge, this does not exist.

3. Timber production for commodity purposes may well be essential for still another part. This has not been proved.

4. Watershed protection is needed for all the area.

5. Other conflicts for key areas are in prospect.

6. Local groups have not had adequate time for study.

7. National groups do not have the beginning of the necessary information for developing their opinions of the national interest.

The feeling of apprehension was amplified in commentary addressed to cooperating organizations, which said in part:

Looking to the year 2000 in its booklet, *People and Timber* (June 1956), the Forest Service concludes: "If we put every acre under good forest management we can have the timber we need, for timber *is* renewable." The same booklet points out also that each of us uses twice as much lumber as a Russian, six times as much as a Frenchman, and far more paper than anybody. The booklet's very last statement is: "The real key to our future timber supply lies in the hands of those *one out of every ten American families* who own our small forests. . . ."

There's a good question to ask. How about *after* the year 2000? . . .

It is the year 2001, let's assume. Every acre is now devoted to good management for timber. But the demand keeps right on rising to use six times as much as a Frenchman (or maybe seven times by then); so we are faced with a shortage of timber. We have already subordinated other forest uses — recreation, wildlife, wilderness, watershed protection — to timber production; we have gone right up to the top, cropping the formerly unmerchantable forests near timberline. We are using more than we can grow, renewable though the timber has been. Now we must resort to substitutes — just as they did after they had finally

92

moved the Cedars of Lebanon out to the sea as ships; just as they did when the forests of southern Italy had gone.

Our children, now in their productive years, are lamenting their forbears' failure to plan better. Why, they ask, didn't we figure back in the fifties on giving equal treatment to the other forest uses? Why didn't we plan things so that some of our recreation would be in natural surroundings, some of our wildlife in a natural habitat, with clear streams from naturally protected watersheds. Why didn't we make the word 'wilderness' mean something — and preserve for them a chance to know, somewhere except on the crags and glaciers, what the natural, God-made world was like? . . .

It's a safe bet that future citizens will need to develop some substitutes for wood products, and that they'll be able to, by the year 2000. It's also a safe bet that they'll be just as able to do so in the year 1990. If speeding up, by a single decade, their search for substitutes means that they will still have good recreation, wildlife, wilderness, and watersheds, who will be the poorer? The decisions that will give the future this choice, or obliterate it, are being made now. Sequoia National Forest is the scene of one of those decisions. Others are coming up — on the Three Sisters in Oregon, around Glacier Peak in Washington, in the Flat Tops in Colorado, in the Gila in New Mexico, to begin to call the list of imminent Forest Service actions.

A little known California area which could have an important future as a scenic resource may have a vital role in setting the pattern of decision. It's your forest and "only *you* can prevent" a wrong decision — you and the millions of others who will share your concern if they learn of it in time.

On Mount Rainier and Mission 66

The need for a Scenic Resources Review was underlined in the course of the recent controversy on Mount Rainier, where the National Park Service has been developing one set of plans for protecting the park in its coming period of heavier use and the concessionaire has felt that a different set of plans would be necessary to allow the public to be adequately served. A hearing resulted from the conflict, and was held in Tacoma by the Senate Committee on Interior and Insular Affairs. The summary of the Sierra Club's position stressed these points:

1. Paradise and Sunrise are the key vantage-point areas from which almost all the visitors to Mount Rainier National Park will obtain their maximum enjoyment of the scenic grandeur of the park — not only of the great mountain itself, but also of the immediate setting and its fragile charm of forested and open slopes. These areas belong to all

the people and are priceless. They are some of the most valuable real estate existing anywhere. Their pricelessness should not be sacrificed.

2. These areas deserve the best possible protection consistent with necessary access. There is evidence that they are now being used too heavily to be able to recover naturally the charm they must retain if this generation is to fulfill its obligation to the next, as the National Park Act requires it to do.

3. Impact upon these areas should therefore be curtailed by any reasonable means to accord with their carrying capacity.

4. Structures to accommodate the inevitable *increase* in travel should be placed elsewhere than in the key vantage-point areas, preferably in places where the structures can (*a*) provide good vistas, (*b*) enjoy safe year-round use, and (*c*) be controlled by the National Park Service with respect to their architecture, surroundings, and use.

5. Structures should not be permitted in key vantage-point areas, or allowed to continue in them, which provide one person a disproportionate share of enjoyment of the place at the expense of precluding another person's enjoying it well or at all.

6. We believe that the following are important considerations:

a) A use should not be excluded merely because everyone cannot enjoy it.

b) Considering that space is limited at Paradise and Sunrise, priority should be given to a visitor center, which is available to all, rather than to a lodge, which is available chiefly to its guests, or a campground chiefly for campers.

c) Parking areas should not preempt for cars the scenic level space that should be available to people who want to get on the land.

d) While the uses listed above may seem conflicting, careful land-use planning may be able to provide for them in different places without impairment other than that consistent with balanced access-area development. A hotel need not be on level, campable ground, but should have a view and can be screened. A visitor center does not require a view or level ground. A campground requires a fairly gently slope, but does not need a view. Parking areas can be situated and landscaped so as to avoid harming the particularly valuable foreground scenery. Roads need not preclude the trails — the primary means of bringing people into close contact with the park.

7. We are confident that the increase in tourist travel to the state of Washington is likely to be substantial and continuing, and that hotel accommodations at Paradise can be continued or eliminated without appreciably affecting the increase in the state's tourist revenue, *provided that* the state and the nation carefully protect the scenic gems which

attract visitors to the state. Whether a superb vista is at a hotel's doorstep or a few minutes' drive away is of minor importance to the nation here. The superb vista is of primary importance, as is the mood of the place from which one sees it.

8. The National Park Service has the special skills necessary for administering these requirements and should keep the public informed of its intentions and its reasons.

We have drawn our conclusions from our organization's sixty-four-years' experience with national-park preservation. We think the conclusions are reasonable. We understand that Mission 66 is working toward these ends, toward solving the difficult problem of preserving and enjoying at the same time. We intend to support, to the best of our ability, the Mission 66 plans that seek those ends. We are confident, Mr. Chairman, that you understand this feeling, and that the Committee on Interior and Insular Affairs shares your understanding, as does the Congress. For the Congress has just reaffirmed its belief, after the great controversy over Dinosaur National Monument, that the National Park System is here to stay, just as the Congress sought to make clear when it created the system in 1916. In the eyes of the world our enduring National Park System is one of America's great achievements. We can produce, we can develop, we can expand our commerce, with all its benefits. We can also show restraint, just as all of us have done and now do when we say —

This is and shall be a primeval national park;
Here we will not second-guess the Great Architect.

(In addition to the statements excerpted here, the Scenic Resources Review was stressed in talks and discussions: at the Conference on Northwest Wilderness, Portland; at the Convention of the Federation of Western Outdoor Clubs, Spokane; at the Annual Meeting of the Natural Resources Council of America, Gatlinburg; before the Channel City Club, Santa Barbara; at the Federal Timber Hearings conducted by a joint Senate-House Committee, Redding, California; and in discussions with Secretary of the Interior Fred A. Seaton, the director of the National Park Service, the chief of the Forest Service, with representatives of Resources for the Future, and at the insistence of the White House with the Bureau of the Budget. Many organizations have resolved in favor of the study: The Wilderness Society asked that it be put in a form to be advocated, and the Izaak Walton League of America is taking the initiative in putting the concept in this form.)

"Scenic Resources for the Future," SCB, December 1956

Ideas flow forth at high speed. Follow-up does not, not mine. I was pleased with the Scenic Resource Review idea and delighted in talking about it. But the pleasure and delight were not enough, and the stage was set for a conversation Howard Zahniser, Joe Penfold, and I had in our favorite lounge upstairs in the Cosmos Club, back in the ridiculous days when ladies must enter the club, if at all, by a side door, and only for dinner downstairs. The Izaak Walton League, Joe told us, was languishing and needed a dynamic project. Then why not, I asked, take the Scenic Resources Review, put it in legislative form, and make it a League project to get it enacted and implemented? Joe agreed, and Zahnie and I were pleased. I am the surviving witness of that event.

Joe changed the name to Outdoor Recreation Resources Review, thereby altering its goal in a way not immediately apparent. The legislation was duly enacted, setting up a commission (ORRRC) and the Bureau of Outdoor Recreation. Laurance Rockefeller chaired the commission, and Joe Penfold was named as one of the civilian members. Secretary of the Interior Fred Seaton, on a trip to San Francisco, asked me to have breakfast with him. There he explained that my name had been considered for the commission I had dreamed up, but others had thought I was too biased to serve on it. My disappointment grew when I later found that the man named in my stead was Bernard Lee Orell, vice-president of Weyerhaeuser Sales Company — the lumber giant.

His bias was not needed, and probably influenced the global continuation of forest destruction in which Weyerhaeuser has played a leading role. I would like to think my bias would have proved more useful, and could have led to a national foresight capability far more valuable than that contemplated by the limited and now defunct Bureau of Outdoor Recreation. For all the review failed to achieve, it did build major support for the National Wilderness Preservation System.

The late years of the Reagan administration launched a similarly limited review that received little public attention, and far too many of the conservation gains begun in the Lincoln administration are left twisting in the wind.

Thirty-five years have passed since the Scenic Resources Review was proposed. The arguments presented for it then remain valid and, if anything, more urgent. Environmental deterioration is accelerating, thanks, in large part, to the arms race, the increase in human numbers, and the over-exploration of resources required to support excessive numbers and appetites. Periodic reviews are essential, expanded to include the need and opportunities for social and environmental restoration.

CHAPTER 5

EARTH NATIONAL PARK

J UDGING FROM WHAT WE HEAR about other planets, we can readily
agree with Jeffers ("It's only a little planet, but how beautiful it
is"). As soon as enough people agree with Thoreau ("In Wildness
is the preservation of the world"), we can take seriously the sky-
head of the advertisement covering a page and a half in the January
1969 *New York Times,* which I dutifully signed and Jerry Mander wrote
most of, beautifully.

New Sierra Club Publications advance
this urgent idea: An international program,
before it is too late, to preserve the Earth as a
"conservation district" within the Universe; a sort of . . .

"EARTH NATIONAL PARK"

I. The Moon, Mars, Saturn...Nice Places to Visit, But You Wouldn't Want to Live There

Any moment now, Man will find himself hurtling around in an
Outer Space so enormous that descriptions of its size only boggle the
mind. (One attempt has put it this way: The size of the Earth is to the
size of the known Universe as a germ is to our entire solar system.)

Yet, we already hear excited talk of locating, out there, a planet
that duplicates the natural environment on Earth, i.e., trees, flowers,
water, air, people; you get our meaning.

The fact is that if we do find such a duplicate Earth out there, it
may be some thousands of years from today. Until then, the only place
in the Universe that will feel like home is Earth, unless *your* idea of
home life could include setting up house on space platforms, or on the
Moon or taking your evening walk with oxygen helmet and space suit.

We haven't got used to thinking about it this way yet, but, as
Astronaut Borman pointed out — for us people, Earth is a kind of inhab-
itable oasis in an unimaginably vast desert.

Also, Earth is a strange sort of oasis, in that quite apart from providing us what we need to live — water, air, sustenance, companionship — this oasis actually *grew* us and every other life form. We are all related.

Darwin, during his famous Galapagos journey, found all life on Earth — from plankton to people — to be part of an incredibly complex interwoven and interdependent blanket spread around the globe. There is no loosening one thread in the blanket without changing the stresses on every other thread, or worse, unraveling it.

So then, if it is life on Earth that most of us are stuck with for the next little while, we had better consider the consequences of what has recently been going on here.

II. Toward a More Moon-like Earth

There was not always enough oxygen to support the existence of Man. It wasn't until green plants and certain ocean plankton had evolved that the natural process was begun by which oxygen is maintained in the atmosphere: photosynthesis.

Man, one would think, has a stake in assuring that this process continues. Consider then, these bits of news:

• In the U.S. alone, oxygen-producing greenery is being paved over at a rate of one million acres per year and the rate is increasing. Also, paving is contagious. Other countries are following suit.

• The oceans have become the dumping ground for as many as a half million substances, few of which are tested to see if the plankton we need can survive them.

• New factories, autos, homes, and jet airplanes have incredibly increased the rate at which combustion takes place — i.e., at which oxygen is used and replaced in our atmosphere by carbon dioxide and carbon monoxide.

The result is a kind of Russian roulette with the oxygen supply. Dr. Lamont C. Cole, ecologist, Cornell University, New York, has said this:

"When and if we reach the point where the rate of combustion exceeds the rate of photosynthesis, the oxygen content of the atmosphere will decrease. Indeed there is evidence that it may already have begun to decline around our largest cities."

There is a bright side: If we should continue what we're doing, overpopulation will cease to be a problem.

Sterile

In only twenty-five years, traces of DDT have found their way into the average American to the extent of eleven parts per million. They are

98

also found in animals, birds, fish, and recently, in notable quantity, in the fatty tissues of Antarctic penguins. (If you wonder about the consequences, similar pesticides have already made sterile a species of hawk and owl in England. Here is the way it works: insects eat sprayed plants, small birds eat them, and then big birds eat *them.* By that time, the insecticide has been concentrated many-fold and the big birds are in big trouble. Now, if we humans were in the habit of eating owls and hawks. . . .)

Aside from the toxic effects on Man and other animals, pesticides like DDT and newer more voguish chemicals eliminate whole populations of certain bacteria and pest organisms.

However, and there is the shocker, *no one in the world knows, when we aim at a particular pest, which other organisms may be eliminated by ricochet.* Someone had better find out.

If some pesticide, herbicide, or defoliant should by inadvertence kill too many of the "nitrogen-fixing" organisms — those organisms that enable living things *to make use of* the nitrogen in the atmosphere — *then life on Earth could end.*

It is that dependent and fragile.

Rampant Technology

The Aswan High Dam was dreamed up to prevent the Nile from overflowing its banks as it had yearly throughout history. (It was thought such a great idea that countries vied for the honor of helping build it, the U.S. foremost among them.) The goals were electricity and year-round irrigation, thus greater productivity. No one, including the U.S., thought much about certain *side* effects, which may ultimately prove the most important:

• Since the natural floods have been halted, life-giving nutrients that were formerly delivered to the land and the Mediterranean Sea are now piling up in a reservoir above the dam, unusable.

As a result the Eastern Mediterranean sardine fishery is already doomed.

As for the land, the lack of nutrients, plus the water-logging caused by old irrigation, plus salinization, *may actually decrease productivity.* Newly irrigated lands have the same fate in store.

• A particular snail has begun to thrive in the warm irrigation canals. The snail hosts a worm which causes schistosomiasis, a debilitating, often fatal disease. In one region around the dam, the incidence of this disease used to be 2 percent. It has now risen to 75 percent.

• At Aswan, we may also see repeated the awful developments at Kariba Dam, East Africa. At Kariba, rafts of hyacinths and reeds have spread over much of the reservoir's surface. It has been estimated that if this growth should cover just 10 percent of the reservoir at Aswan, the plants could actually transpire into the desert air enough water to stop *all* flow into the lower Nile.

Looking at the bright side again: In a few centuries, the dam will fill up with silt, and end its useful life. Then, the river will flow right over it, creating a huge, perhaps lovely, waterfall. Tourists will enjoy the view.

More Improvements
Engineers are improving things everywhere:

• In Alaska, a $2 billion dam is proposed — to bring power to nonexistent industry — which would flood a wilderness and nesting region the size of Lake Erie.

• In Brazil, engineers propose an Amazon dam that would flood a green area as big as Italy.

• In Southeast Asia, a series of proposed Mekong River dams may do for Laos, Thailand, and Vietnam what Aswan is doing for Egypt. *Every* country should be spared such improvements.

III. A Wildlife Preserve Where *We* Are the Wildlife

The speed with which our world is being altered is so rapid that there is no cataloguing it; it is everywhere . . . forests are gone, hillsides eroded and bulldozed, waters filled, and air and water polluted. The implicit assumption is that Man is the Master of Nature, and that losing a wild place or species or plant is of no great importance to us, and never mind the esthetics. But as we have shown, tinkering with the natural order of things can be a dangerous business, *for there is a need to think of the organic wholeness of nature, not man apart from that.* Man's vanity notwithstanding, he is irretrievably intertwined with everything on his planet and therefore must proceed with a degree of caution, until, at last, he has the option of actually leaving Earth.

If, before then, we should so alter our environment that we rid it of ingredients we need for life, then *we* will merely pass the way of other life forms that have become extinct for one reason or another. And, as humbling a thought as it may be, Nature might scarcely miss the people. Things might eventually get back into their own pattern, the natural order reviving. Plankton might evolve; oxygen might re-form in the atmosphere; grass might grow through the pavement and among tumbled columns as it has before.

With all this in mind, you may see that we, the seventy-thousand member Sierra Club, the groups we work with, and the critical publishing project you see outlined at right, are not so much proselytizing on behalf of Nature. In due course, Nature will take care of itself.

Our motives are more selfish, in fact. They are on behalf of our very own lives and the lives of our children who, we feel, have not only the right to live but also the right to live in a world that maintains the natural order enough to continue to feel like home.

We find, therefore, that it is not tenable to confine our activities to local crises in the United States. The problems are everywhere and are doubling by the decade.

And so, we have embarked upon an antidotal new international publishing program to export the view that it is now the entire planet that must be viewed as a kind of conservation district within the Universe; a wildlife preserve of a sort, except we are the wildlife, together with all other life and environmental conditions that are necessary constituents of our survival and happiness.

If you wish to participate and support this approach, general means to do so are suggested at the right.

Thank you.

David Brower, *Executive Director, Sierra Club*

How You Can Further the Idea of "EARTH NATIONAL PARK"

[There followed the all-important coupons — a chance to participate — and to provide names and addresses of participants, together with offsetting income.]

1. Write Mr. Nixon.

A new administration is coming to Washington, and with it the greatest opportunity in history for, on the one hand, far-ranging conservation programs, or, on the other hand, incredible, irreversible, and perhaps disastrous destruction of the environment. We urge you therefore to write Mr. Nixon or forward this coupon to him.

I respectfully urge that you publicly commit yourself and your administration to a program of world leadership in conservation thinking, to wit:

a) Considering the state of things, and the imminent dangers, issues relating to world conservation should no longer be relegated to afterthought status, but should rather be publicly cited as among the critical issues of our time, perhaps the most critical.

b) Nations should place high priority on the development of blueprints for the economics of peaceful stability. Exhortations for a "vigorous, growing economy" by international leaders must be placed in the context of an Earth of fixed size. Only so much growth is possible before the natural balance is destroyed and *all* growth with it.

c) Nations should each establish centers for the advanced study of ecosystems — looking into the science of how everything fits together.

101

d) Nations should have a "Plan for the Reinterpretation of Nature" . . . an educational program to help remind people about *natural* law and order.

e) Nations should cooperate in an immediate program for preserving the last of the Earth's irreplaceable wild areas within a sane kind of world heritage trust. They should also cooperate in *reclaiming* as many as possible of the places not *irretrievably* mauled. The science, technology, and genius of all countries will be needed, as will your leadership.

Thank you.

2. Write your congressmen.

The most effective way to present your views is in your own words by personal letter. Or in lieu of that, send your senators and representatives the following message. It is vital that we all be heard from in some fashion:

Dear Sir: I urge you to support the view that if our environment is to be preserved in anything like its natural state, then all development projects — national and international — must be studied for ecological implications, not merely engineering and economic implications. The dangers to the environment and to all life on Earth — from plants to people — are now too great to ignore. (Your name and address.)

3. Support those few organizations that are working toward the international goals stated herein.

There are many organizations working constantly to stop the degradation of the Earth's environment. *All* are important. We urge you to write them and involve yourself in their programs. For a list of these national and international organizations, with details on their aims, mark the appropriate box in the coupon at right.

The Sierra Club itself has both national and international programs. We are a nonprofit, primarily volunteer organization, founded in 1892 by John Muir, and devoted to Thoreau's thesis that "In Wildness is the preservation of the world."

The Club currently has seventy thousand members around the world, and has offices in San Francisco, Albuquerque, Seattle, Washington, D.C., Los Angeles, New York, and now, London. In addition to such efforts as this, promoting conservation causes through advertisements, publications, and films, the club has an extensive program of outdoor activities and wilderness trips.

If you wish to join the club, learn more about activities, purchase books (a major means of conservation support), or make a donation, kindly use the coupon at right.

The Sierra Club Foundation (see coupon below) is a separate organization devoted solely to scientific, literary, and educational work. Contributions to the foundation are tax-deductible.

To: Edgar Wayburn, Treasurer
Sierra Club Foundation
Mills Tower, San Francisco, California 94104

Dear Sir:

I realize that a publishing project of the magnitude of the Earth's Wild Places (see right, above) will require a heavy capital investment if it is to serve its good purpose. I enclose, as a tax-deductible gift for this purpose, the sum of $_____.

SIERRA CLUB BOOKS

Sierra Club Exhibit Format publications have been called "the most beautiful books in the world" by several distinguished reviewers. They have received frequent honors for design and graphics, and also the 1964 Carey-Thomas Award, as "The outstanding achievement in creative publishing in the United States." (All the series is 10 1/4" by 13 1/2", printed on high gloss paper, in gravure or full color lithography.)

International Series

The prologue publication in our anticipated international series on the Earth's Wild Places is called *Galapagos: The Flow of Wildness*. It is about the islands off the coast of Ecuador that revealed to Darwin, for the first time, an understanding of the flow of life.

Some one hundred books are planned in this series, all of them concerning Earth's still untouched places where there remains the possibility of learning about organic diversity, the genetic pool, the Earth's thin, miraculous biosphere — to learn enough about natural systems so that we may ultimately be able to educate even some benighted engineer friends and send them off to do *good* works without fearing that they'll do us all in while they work.

Several organizations are cooperating in this series. The board of editors consists of representatives of four organizations in England, Switzerland, and the United States, including the Sierra Club.

To: William Siri, Treasurer
Sierra Club
Mills Tower, San Francisco, Calif. 94104

☐ I would like to join the Sierra Club. Here is $14 to cover first year's admission and dues.

☐ Please send further information about the club's conservation activities and wilderness programs, as well as including a complete book catalogue.

☐ Please forward a list of other organizations working toward similar goals.

☐ Here is my contribution of $_____ to help the work of the club (As the IRS has ruled that the club's conservation program involves substantial legislative activity, dues and contributions are not deductible — unless the court or Congress clarifies the law, or you make your check out to the Sierra Club Foundation, which does not involve itself in legislative activities.

☐ Please send the books I have checked, for which I remit $_____.

New York Times Ad, 1969

The final coupon was ten inches deep. It offered discounts varying from 15% to 40%, then listed fifteen of the club's twenty exhibit-format titles, as well as Paul Ehrlich's *The Population Bomb* and *On the Loose*. First on the list was *Galapagos: The Flow of Wildness*, credited to Eliot Porter, Loren Eiseley, John Milton, Kenneth Brower, and others: "Two-volume prologue to the international series, revealing the importance to man of the diversity of the earth's wild places. $45."

Jerry Mander, many others, and I had long conversations about the content. Much of it was drawn from information derived from a conference the Conservation Foundation's president, Russell Train, held at Airlie House, just outside Washington, D.C., to reveal what kind of environmental damage was being caused with the best of intentions by various international aid programs.

The coupon to President Nixon called for the major conservation steps I had proposed and that Justice William O. Douglas had presented to the Ford Foundation (which the Ford Foundation should now dig up and pay attention to — or the MacArthur Foundation; I won't be picky). It also urged the president to support the World Heritage concept. Members of Congress were to be called upon to support what in principal the National Environmental Policy Act was later to provide. The coupon to the Sierra Club treasurer sold Sierra Club memberships and books. The coupon to the treasurer of the Sierra Club Foundation — which had been established in 1960 at my urging but refused to support eligible parts of my work — asked for tax-deductible contributions.

I was particularly anxious to call attention to the club's new two-volume exhibit-format set on the Galapagos Islands, in which the club had invested a quarter of a million dollars. The books urged World Heritage status for the Galapagos. It was also important to recover the

104

club's investment in the Galapagos book, and my attempt to advertise the books to the members and by direct mail had been severely curtailed. So I went to the public, which had responded so well to the Grand Canyon ads, and came up with the block-and Brower-busting book ad. The club's book program was making publishing history. The promotion budget for the fiscal year was a board-authorized $170,000, over which the board had delegated full authority to me. Christmas sales were important to the Galapagos project's success and the Publishing department had been stymied in its efforts to produce them. The only fiscally responsible course — and sound conservation course — was to get the books, and the idea behind them, to readers.

We owed this to Sally Walker, whose grant of her inheritance, $77,000, had made feasible a project initiated by the genius and generosity of Eliot Porter, aided by the energy of John Milton, by the brilliance of Russell Train in proposing the World Heritage idea, made physically feasible by the imagination of Hugh Barnes, put together with the artistry and direct Galapagos experience of Kenneth Brower, a project the scope of which was admired by Jack Macrae, who was to publish much of Eliot Porter's remaining works, and fought for by the Sierra Club's book-publishing staff in its surmounting obstacle after obstacle placed in the way of final club approval of the project.

The ad would cost the book-advertising budget ten thousand dollars, a cost that could be expected to be recovered quickly from contributions and sales, and indeed was more than recovered.

Laurance Moss, nuclear engineer, staunch defender of the Kern Plateau against the Forest Service's plans to log it, was soon to become club president. He understood the bind the club finances and I were in.

"Go ahead. Run it!" he said.

I did.

The day before it was to run I telephoned Jack Schanhaar, the club's sales and promotion manager, and asked him to call club president Edgar Wayburn and tell him of the ad's imminence. Jack didn't. It was unfair to ask him to, but had I called, I feared, I would be directed not to use the authority I had to run it. I was well aware of Dr. Wayburn's earlier displeasure, over a period of a year, with the various ads we had proposed for our North Cascades National Park campaign. In desperation, the North Cascades Conservation Council had to run it. The Sierra Club wasn't permitted to.

So I ran the big ad on January 14, 1969, the twenty-third anniversary of my having been promoted to Captain, Infantry Reserve, and relieved of active duty in the Army of the United States.

Dr. Wayburn thereupon relieved me of my authority as executive director of the Sierra Club. When four other candidates and I decided to run for the club board to change its nuclear-power policy, I was put on leave. By May 3, 1969, I had also been pressed, with unacceptably dire threats, to ask that I no longer be executive director.

So on that day I no longer was. I had not exceeded my authority. I had followed the only fiscally responsible course. I had remained faithful to the club's promise to a major grantor. With help from many people, I had made a commitment to working for the Earth's wild places. I had been insistent, stubborn, shorter and shorter on persuasiveness, unable to communicate with the club membership, a loser along with my fellow nuclear-power critics in our attempt to be elected to the board, and I was making my farewell speech to the staff but not to the Sierra Club. After all, I had long ago paid fifty dollars to become a life member, and Anne and I had later been named patron members.

But there would be good news.

Russell Train's World Heritage idea was proposed to the United Nations by President Nixon. The UN adopted the World Heritage Convention in November 1972. Ecuador designated a Galapagos Islands National Park, which became the thirtieth World Heritage site soon thereafter. And at the end of 1972, the Sierra Club named David Brower an Honorary Vice-President.

The Sierra Club *Galapagos* volumes initiated a new series, *The Earth's Wild Places.* Ian Ballantine published them in smaller format in the quality-paperback series he and I had worked out for the club. The large hardback volumes, slipcased, originally sold for fifty-five dollars and now bring about five times that much — when they can be unearthed.

We founded Friends of the Earth on July 11, 1969. One of FOE's first moves was to contract to publish twelve more volumes in *The Earth's Wild Places.* Ten were published before FOE dropped its book program. Six of them were on places that deserve World Heritage status.

WORLD HERITAGE: AN INRODUCTION

THE CONCEPT OF OWNING LAND is ridiculous, except in law. We are not owners. We are, as Nancy Newhall said, brief tenants. Some of us are more tenacious than others, and can fashion longer strings to impose their wishes on successive brief tenants. For the most part, this hasn't made the earth look any better. The Biosphere Reserve idea, more finely tuned, with increased flexibility (rather a contradiction in requirements, but that makes it more interesting) can help. So can the World Heritage idea, which I have mentioned repeatedly. Perhaps it is time for a more formal introduction.

Labrador as a goal for a Sierra Club outing? It sounded outrageous, but its proposer, John Milton, thought it important, and I supported the idea. It didn't work out. John involved me, however, in another idea that has worked out — the idea that there needed to be a World Heritage System expanding on the national park idea. Under Russell Train's guidance, John was working with Raymond Dasmann, Frank Fraser Darling, and Frank Gregg in the Conservation Foundation. I was swept into the excitement Russ Train had initiated with his World Heritage idea.

That interest began for me in the mid-1960s and continued well into the 1970s. Out of it came a list of one hundred natural areas that deserved World Heritage protection as well as books on the Galapagos Islands and Mount Everest that helped two regions attain protection. A few other books also came but have not succeeded yet.

When I retired as president of Friends of the Earth in 1979, Robert Cahn urged that I renew my interest in the World Heritage. Other goals prevailed, and would probably have continued to prevail had I not been subjected to two shocks that I could not ignore.

First, when I was invited to a conference in the Soviet Union that was considering the protection and restoration of Lake Baikal, I was pleasantly shocked to find a number of Soviet scientists working to include Lake Baikal in the World Heritage. Eliot Porter, once the Sierra Club had started publishing his books, included Lake Baikal as one of the books he hoped to do. In the mid-1960s the chances of getting Soviet permission for such a book were laughable. In 1988 the Soviets laughed at my concern.

The second shock, to which I ought to have been immune, came on May 15, 1989, when a single issue of the *New York Times* reported on residential development plans — no, I'll call them schemes — totaling an estimated twenty-one billion dollars for Queens, Atlanta, and Antelope Valley, California. The rate at which developers were converting what they like to call raw land to a plethora of pavement and condominiums had been bad enough. Now it was utterly appalling.

We have met the enemy, I thought, and it is the developers. All us others must rush to our positions and defend them to the last man (woman ought not be put to such risk). Use whatever tools there are to save amenity from the enemy. At long last demand that there be an accounting for the costs of mindless growth, not just of the benefits. Expand the land-trust movement. Broaden the national park idea. Allow private lovers of the land to defend their love. Protect what can be accommodated in reserves, including a National Biosphere (or Bioregional), Reserve System, and fly the World Heritage flag for all to see.

Unprecedented boldness is required if the protection of nature and natural resources is to prevail over their respective exploitation and

107

extirpation. Let humanity understand that protection is reversible and extirpation is not. A primeval forest exists but once. Paper will not protect it alone. The chainsaw will finish it, unaided. Let the renaissance of ethics begin, and with it a reverence for other life than ourselves and our time.

Robinson Jeffers wrapped it up in a few lines: ". . . the greatest beauty is organic wholeness, the wholeness of life and things, the divine beauty of the universe. Love that, not man apart from that. . . ." There isn't time to spare enough wholeness for all life's future if we plod and saunter at the old rate. We need to brush up on the sprints and prepare for a marathon or two. The World Heritage suddenly has become far more important to survival than I had dreamed it would be. Russell Train probably knew this from the beginning.

Now is the time for the World Heritage Library, in large and small books, on the screen, on cassettes to listen to during gridlock, in concerts, and in world-traveling exhibitions. Let developers henceforth make their mark by recycling the places they already have marked. And may the rest of us opt for the greatest beauty.

But what, in more detail, does the World Heritage consist of?

Russell Train, when he was president of the Conservation Foundation, proposed that there be a World Heritage System; President Nixon presented the request to the United Nations; and in November 1972 the member-states of UNESCO adopted a convention concerning the Protection of the World Cultural and Natural Heritage. As of December 1987, 288 sites had been named to the list and 100 nations had ratified the convention. The Soviet Union added its name in October 1988. Key criteria concerning the convention, excerpted from a booklet published by Environment Canada, are in the paragraphs below:

The Convention provides for a World Heritage Committee.

Compilation of a World Heritage List to include cultural and natural properties throughout the world that are considered to be of outstanding value according to criteria drawn up by the committee.

Preparation of a list of World Heritage in Danger.

Establishment of a World Heritage Fund to provide aid to Member States for World Heritage Sites. Each state adhering to the Convention pays one percent of its contribution to the Regular Budget of UNESCO to the Fund.

Provision of technical and emergency assistance, upon request, to Member States.

General promotion throughout the world of the importance of the Heritage Convention.

Criteria for natural properties:

Properties nominated should: (i) be outstanding examples representing the major states of the earth's evolutionary history; or (ii) be outstanding examples representing significant ongoing geological processes, biological evolution, and man's interaction with his natural environment; or (iii) contain superlative natural phenomena, formations or features or areas of exceptional natural beauty; or (iv) contain the foremost natural habitats where threatened species of animals or plants of outstanding universal value still survive. In addition to the above criteria, the sites should fulfill the conditions of integrity.

Criteria for cultural properties:

Each property nominated should: (i) represent a unique artistic achievement, a masterpiece of creative genius; or (ii) have exerted great influence, over a span of time or within a cultural area of the world, on developments in architecture, monumental arts or town-planning and landscaping; or (iii) bear a unique or at least exceptional testimony to a civilization which has disappeared; or (iv) be an outstanding example of a type of structure which illustrates a significant stage in human history; or (v) be an outstanding example of a traditional human settlement which is representative of a culture and which has become vulnerable under the impact of irreversible change; or (vi) be directly and tangibly associated with events or with ideas or beliefs of outstanding universal significance, and meet the test of authenticity for design, materials, workmanship, or setting.

The World Heritage Convention is one of UNESCO's most popular and important initiatives. The cultural and natural heritage of a nation is one of its priceless possessions. This heritage is irreplaceable, and any loss or serious impairment of it is a tragedy, not only for the nation concerned, but for humanity in general. The member-states of the World Heritage Convention are called upon to promote cooperation among all nations and peoples in order to protect heritage sites that are precious universal treasures.

Only member-states that have adhered to the convention can make nominations to the World Heritage List. These nominations must demonstrate that the site is truly of exceptional universal value, that it meets the criteria imposed by the convention, and that it is assured of adequate protection. Throughout a year-long process of evaluation, candidate sites undergo rigorous scrutiny by experts and by the competent international organizations. The International Council of Monuments and Sites and the International Union for Conservation of Nature and Natural Resources [now The World Conservation Union] advise the World Heritage Committee on cultural and natural sites respectively.

The original list of one hundred sites was concerned primarily with natural areas, not cultural. Some of these have now received protection. The length of the remaining list should not stagger anyone. The public's concern already exists. It awaits an opportunity to be enhanced and organized. The organizing could well use the pattern already existing in the World Wildlife Fund. Support of other existing organizations should be encouraged, including the Nature Conservancy and Conservation International, World Resources Institute, Natural Resources Defense Council, Worldwatch Institute, the Sierra Club, Friends of the Earth International, and Earth Island Institute.

It will be important to enlist people who can help organize this effort. Bill Travers, who has helped organize me into completing my autobio, is my nominee for the multiple task of scouting out places, authors, photographers, co-publishers, and shaping the content and presentation and forever looking for an ever-larger audience. He will need help. I'll offer mine. Any volunteers?

For further information see *Our World's Heritage*, National Geographic Society, 1987, and The World Heritage Convention, UNESCO (Dec. 1987) [a profusely annotated map].

It is fair to remember that
this is not a land that belongs to us.
If we destroy it we destroy something in us.
Its trees can teach us tenacity
and patience and serenity and respect.
Life's urge to survive is the force that
shaped them and their world of wildness,
that made them one of the great miracles.
We, if we are too impatient to care,
can end this miracle, this chain of life
linked to an old eternity when life
first strove to leave the mother sea.
Or we, able to create ideas,
can meet our old material needs
with a different urge —
an urge to preserve what we cannot replace.
Wildness made us; we cannot make it.
We can only spare it.

D.R.B. in *The Last Redwoods* (1975)

CHAPTER 6

THE MILESTONE AT STORM KING MOUNTAIN

———

Success in Getting the Right Candidates in office, and thus making lobbying more fun, is just around the corner — perhaps the corner beyond the corner — and we can have confidence that in the almost-near future we will have better laws. Next comes the question, how do you get them enforced? Once people are almost persuaded to be politically and legislatively active, how can they support environmental defense through litigation?

Phillip Berry and I talked about that on the Sierra Club High Trip in Glacier National Park in 1955. Phil was not out of his teens yet, but he had his eye on law school and what it could teach him about environmental litigation. He was also eager to see a lot more equity in society. Like me, he had gone to Berkeley High School, a quarter of a century after I left it. In my years there, 1926–28, there was one African-American, and he was in my advisory. Now his color prevails there, and was halfway to prevalence during Phil's years. Phil did not like what was happening to minorities. Concerning a new litigational role, we just talked, and nothing happened then, but his role would later be important in the Sierra Club.

The Environmental Defense Fund was first on the front lines early, and EDF's Charles Wurster and Victor Yannacone were on the warpath against DDT. On one of my innumerable visits to New York, Vic found me by telephone. It was probably 1964, when I had been working closely with Barnes Press. Vic was feeling lonely in EDF, had a critical phase of the battle coming up, and needed five thousand dollars immediately. It was a weekend. Weekend or not, I don't carry that kind of money, and neither did my bank account. But to Hugh Barnes, president of Barnes Press, five thousand on a weekend was no problem. He got it for me, whereupon Vic no longer needed it. (Hugh got it back.)

Something closer to home — to the Sierra Club, that is — was happening. Consolidated Edison wanted to build a pumped-storage generating project on Storm King Mountain. That is something that

111

could fit dramatically into the context of my Sierra Club experience in litigation.

STORM KING MOUNTAIN GETS STANDING

SIERRA CLUB MOUNTAINEERS never plotted a route from the west bank of the Hudson River to the top of Storm King Mountain, but Sierra Club lawyers did. It was a new kind of climb. Their legal concerns in the past had been directed mainly to protecting the club's name — registering it to prevent infringement. And the principal task seemed to be to keep a bar in Angels Camp, in the Sierra foothills, from calling itself the Sierra Club Bar. The effort met with mixed success, but little harm was done. Few people were likely to confuse the two.

In the attempt to spare Mount San Jacinto from the environmental impact of a tramway that was to ascend from Palm Springs to the ten-thousand-foot summit, the club invested a thousand dollars in a legal analysis of the club's opportunity to block the scheme in court. No luck. The tramway was built, Governor Earl Warren having tired of vetoing the proposal as successive California legislatures put it on his desk. Three vetoes was his limit.

The National Parks Association ["and Conservation" has since been added to its name] believed the Secretary of the Interior should be required to fulfill the charge given him to protect Rainbow Bridge from the waters that would soon rise behind Glen Canyon Dam as the Colorado River began filling Lake Powell. The law authorizing the Colorado River Storage Project, of which Glen Canyon Dam was the most important part, directed that "the Secretary of the Interior shall" protect Rainbow Bridge National Monument. The law also provided that no reservoir of the project should lie within any national park or monument. When various excuses were made by the Bureau of Reclamation and the secretary, and when, with no opportunity for public participation in the decision, the House of Representatives Subcommittee on Interior Appropriations refused to provide funds for the protection, the NPA went to court to require the government to obey the law. Again, no luck. The association could not demonstrate that it had standing to sue. Economic interests could be protected, but not the public interest in the nation's scenic resources.

A group of lawyers in New York did not think so logical and important a public interest ought to continue being held worthless in the eyes of the court and set about to remedy the situation.

The Scenic Hudson Preservation Society was formed and began to explore ways to win standing for Storm King Mountain. Con Ed had a brilliant idea, from an engineer's standpoint. Build a reservoir high on the mountain and pump some of the Hudson River into the reservoir when Con Ed's steam generators were making electricity with no place else to go; then recapture a good part of that energy by sending the water back down to hydroelectric generators to generate power for sale at peak-demand rates. The energy efficiency was poor, but the economic return would be highly desirable. The Scenic Hudson people believed that an unimpaired Storm King Mountain was even more desirable.

The original legal effort was largely *pro bono*. Alfred Forsyth and David Sive were the principal Sierra Club men involved in the effort, and Al Butzel, in the Weiner, Neuberger, and Sive firm, carried much of the whole burden.

The press was involved, and one of the events that helped involve the press was a cruise up the Hudson by a boatload of dignitaries: Sam Aldrich, Brooks Atkinson, Al Butzel, Carl Carmer, Jim Cope, Ben Frazer, Lloyd Garrison, Bobby Kennedy, Nancy Mathews, Dick Ottinger, Harrison Salisbury, David Sive, and Rod Vandivort: I was aboard too.

My own involvement was peripheral. One thing I like especially to remember was the occasion when David Sive reported that there was a limit to what his firm could do on a *pro bono* basis, and some contribution of dollars was going to have to come from somewhere, preferably the Sierra Club, if he were to be able to stay on the case.

As executive director of the Sierra Club I had a discretionary fund that I thought I understood quite well, but the function of which escaped various club directors from time to time. It started out each year at twenty-five thousand dollars, which I was permitted to use at my discretion for Sierra Club purposes that were not accommodated in the budget. Fifteen hundred dollars was what the Sive firm needed to assure the partners that there was something to draw upon besides their own good wishes. And that is the amount that went to the firm from my discretionary fund. David Sive was delighted. He could thus remain on the case, and few, outside Con Ed circles, regretted it. Environmental interests had been given short shrift in the court at Rainbow Bridge and shortly were to be given even shorter shrift downstream, in the Grand Canyon itself. A win on the Hudson River could help compensate for our losses on the upper Colorado.

The authorization of construction of Glen Canyon Dam opened the door to the Bureau of Reclamation to plan a still more ambitious project, the building of dams in Marble Gorge and at Bridge Canyon, both sites lying within the Grand Canyon. Reservoirs at either site would have an extremely short life were Glen Canyon dam not built first. It will take more than eight cubic miles of mud to put Lake Powell out of action, and the Colorado River will require about three centuries to wash that much silt, sediment, and boulders into it. Without Glen Canyon dam on hand to stop the mud, the Marble Canyon reservoir would have been silted in by the end of the century, had it been built when the Bureau wanted to build it. The Bridge Canyon reservoir would have lasted less than three decades. It was vulnerable to sediment not only from the main stem of the Colorado, but also from the Little Colorado River, which carries very little water but very much mud — approximately half as much as the main stem.

The Grand Canyon battle was a big one, described elsewhere and at length. What made it relevant to environmental litigation is that the Sierra Club, taking the lead in the battle, placed a full-page advertisement in the New York Times. The sky-head read: "WOULD YOU FLOOD THE GRAND CANYON FOR PROFIT?" An accompanying photograph, obtained from the Bureau of Reclamation, contained dotted lines showing where within the canyon the maximum Bridge Canyon reservoir level would reach. The general message of the ad was that the whole idea was a bad one. At the top of the page were coupons telling readers what they could do about the issue. Two of the coupons were addressed to members of Congress. The ad is reproduced in *For Earth's Sake*. Some history was about to be made. Within twenty-four hours of the running of the ad the Sierra Club received a message from the Internal Revenue Service that fatally clouded the club's tax-deductible status, and the club began to think about going to court to rescue that status.

Gary Torre was the club's attorney in the effort, and began compiling an inventory of all the club's activities to show how unsubstantial (substantial legislative activity by tax-deductible organizations not being acceptable to the IRS) a part of its activities the club's legislative work was. The publishing effort was given a major role: publishing was educational, not legislative.

As I recall it, there were varying opinions about how intense the effort should be. The IRS action had not hurt the club, and it had helped the defense of the Grand Canyon substantially.

It had not hurt the club because the club was ready for it. Back in 1959, when the club's board passed the resolution stating that the club's lobbying was only incidental to its program, I worried about how this would tie the club's hands. Conservation decisions that the nation must live with are arrived at through the political and legislative processes. If we decided that our effort in the legislative arena was to be no more than incidental, we weren't going to get very far in our work. I looked at the sources of the club's income. The dues were then nine dollars per year. No one was going to worry about whether a nine-dollar contribution was tax deductible. Income from the publishing effort was not tax deductible anyway, nor was income from the wilderness outings. Tax deductibility was essential for major gifts or grants and for bequests. These, however, were but a small part of the club's annual income. If we were to set up a separate foundation for the club to receive tax-deductible contributions, then the rest of the income — some 80 percent of it — would be available for all the legislative activity the club wished to take on.

I presented this idea to the club's board. Board attorneys Richard Leonard and Bestor Robinson didn't think it would work. Phil Berry, then a law student at Stanford University, took the idea to Professor Phil Neal, who headed the law school, and Professor Neal said it would work. Directors Leonard and Robinson thereupon adjusted their thinking, and the board passed a resolution saying it had no objection to Richard Leonard's heading up a Sierra Club Foundation.

That all happened in 1960. So we were ready for the IRS, and for the failure of our appeal of the IRS decision. The failure would not substantially hurt the club.

In fact, it helped. The story of the clouding of the club's tax status was major news across the country — page-one news in some cities — bringing forth many editorials favorable to the club. What was the IRS trying to do to this little do-good organization that was trying to save the Grand Canyon? People who may not have had any particular love for the Grand Canyon did know how they felt about the Internal Revenue Service. There was a sudden surge in applications of membership. We could argue that we lost tax-deductible gifts, calculated at the average annual rate of such gifts in the past, to the extent that donors had not yet heard of the Sierra Club's new foundation. Our heart, however, was not in our argument. We weren't hurting, and Congressman Morris Udall, staunch supporter, at the time, of damming the Grand Canyon, told me in the quiet of his office that challenging the club's tax status was the worst mistake he made in the Grand Canyon battle.

Once again litigation in behalf of the environment had lost. But this time it had won in the losing. The situation was slowly changing, and the Storm King milestone was about to be added to the stage setting as an article in the *Sierra Club Bulletin* pointed out.

Two Davids, One Goliath

S IERRA CLUB TESTIMONY opposing construction of a pumped-storage hydroelectric plant at Storm King Mountain in the Hudson Highlands by the Consolidated Edison Company was prepared by Executive Director David Brower and David Sive, a lawyer and candidate for election to the club's Board of Directors. Excerpts from the testimony were published in the *Sierra Club Bulletin,* February 1967:

ENTERPRISING DEVELOPERS — whether they favor dam building, power generation, lumbering, mining, road building, urbanization — project future needs for each of the products involved and preempt land, air, or streams for those projected needs. Individuals or corporations give maximum attention to their needs and minimum attention to competing needs.

Their projects, without exception, assume that the present growth in population and in demand for goods and services will continue at today's rate. Almost without exception they assume no growing need for amenity, for the intangible values important to the meaning of America.

They project a continuing population growth of the kind witnessed since World War II, without realizing that such growth cannot long continue without major diminution of important human values, without realizing that this growth must be sharply curtailed soon.

The human and financial resources available for predicting what tangible needs will be — and rapidly committing the land so as to assure that those needs will be met — these efforts are enormously louder and more grasping than those working for equally vital intangible needs.

Hardly anyone pays attention to the law of the minimum, by estimating as accurately as possible which resource we will run out of first, thus precluding any further growth. In California, it will be air or intelligence; I don't know which is going faster, but I can guess.

So we happily propose to convert or dispose of an irreplaceable resource, such as natural beauty, in order to produce low-cost, instant convenience — to amass goods or services that can be obtained by several alternative methods. Some of the alternatives may cost more now, but not in the long run; some may even cost less, if we only could get unpolluted information about their real cost.

Rarely if ever does the public, which must in the end pay whatever the cost is, learn in time what the choices actually are.

Finally, since our civilization grew up in a world that thought many resources were limitless, there is an inertial tendency to continue fine old traditions even though we know they are based upon a fallacious assumption of abundance.

This inertia, in this country, keeps civilization's machine and its developers aimed at the vestige of the American landscape that has not yet felt our machines. And now, alas, we urge the so-called developing nations to follow our bad example.

Perhaps only 10 percent of the contiguous United States is essentially still unaffected by technology, and only about a tenth of that 10 percent is yet dedicated with any firmness to preservation of the native values in that vestige, whatever they may be. The exact figures are not important, but the idea is vital to our future; the real, essential goal for our technology should be to go back over the 90 percent already affected by technology and do a better job.

The last 10 percent of unchanged land is not of large enough magnitude to be vital to our type of existence, or even to permit sustaining of our present rate and direction of growth as far as goods and services are concerned. That 10 percent is, however, of inestimable value to a continuing improvement in American standards of life.

It has been well put by Nancy Newhall that "the wilderness holds answers to more questions we have yet learned how to ask." It should be challenge enough to Americans, with respect to what little wilderness remains, to concentrate on learning how to ask those questions in the ages to come. It should be challenge enough to our technology to do better to, by, and for the lands already altered or disrupted. It is also a challenge to our ability to organize better for the achievement that lies ahead in this field.

It remains true in each of the controversies alluded to that if the resources which some people believe should be preserved are instead utilized for commodity purposes, that conversion will sustain the growth opportunity for the particular use, such as power generation, for but a short period. Thereafter alternatives must be found to sustain progress, and doubtless will be.

The need that ought to be made ever clearer is that it is vital to the public welfare to see those alternatives before a given irreplaceable resource, be it an unspoiled Grand Canyon or the last redwood forest that can make a real national park, is used up. California had to pass a self-limitation act before it could get its allocation from the Colorado River. Instead of trying to forget that limitation, it should pass some new ones. Perhaps all of us can agree, one day soon, that all states should set some limits on something besides speed.

We might all try to make our one pass at this planet as harmless a pass as we can. That could be our finest contribution to the unborn.

Sierra Club Bulletin, February 1967

Law and the Environment, a Conservation Foundation book edited by Malcolm Baldwin and James K. ("Jake") Page, Jr., devotes many pages to Storm King. David Sive's chapter is well worth reading in toto; here are a few fragments:

The task fell to the two opposing intervenors — Scenic Hudson Conservation Conference and the Sierra Club — to prove, under the ordinary rules of evidence, the degree of natural beauty of Storm King. . . . The conservation leaders were Charles Callison, David Brower, Richard Pough, and Anthony Wayne Smith, of the National Audubon Society, Sierra Club, Open Space Action Committee, and National Parks Association, respectively. . . .

[One of the other witnesses was Professor of Art History Vincent J. Scully of Yale University.]

The testimony of the seven experts is a mixture of dry analysis and eloquence. I quote below only the most striking of the eloquence, Professor Scully's description of Storm King Mountain in his direct testimony:

"It rises like a brown bear out of the river, a dome of living granite, swelling with animal power. It is not picturesque in the softer sense of the word but awesome, a primitive bodiment of the energies of the earth. It makes the character of wild nature physically visible in monumental form. As such it strongly reminds me of some of the natural formations which mark sacred sites in Greece and signal the presence of the Gods; it recalls Lerna in Argolis, for example, where Herakles fought the Hydra, and various sites of Artemis and Aphrodite where the mother of the beasts rises savagely out of the water. While Breakneck Ridge across the river resembles the winged hill of tilted strata that looms into the Gulf of Corinth near Calydon.

"Hence, Storm King and Breakneck Ridge form an ideal portal for the grand stretch of the Hudson below them. The dome of one is balanced by the horns of the other; but they are both crude shapes, and appropriately so, since the urbanistic point of the Hudson in that area lies in the fact that it preserves and embodies the most savage and untrammeled characteristics of the wild at the very threshold of New York. It can make the city dweller emotionally aware of what he needs most to know: that nature still exists, with its own laws, rhythms, and powers, separate from human desires."

[Consolidated Edison should have given up right there, and spared itself and ourselves the heavy litigational expense of delaying several more years before throwing in the towel.]

"The clearest and most direct opinion was rendered by Mr. Callison:

"The Hudson River from its origin to the sea is a river of great beauty. Where it flows through the Highlands, from the breathtaking gateway at Storm King Mountain to Dunderberg downstream, the scenery of the river, or from either shore, is supreme. In my opinion this is the most beautiful stretch of river scenery in the United States."

It was a mistake to bring a chauvinistic westerner, worse still a Californian, into such a hearing. I had lived under Half Dome and El Capitan, learned to feel at home on wild cliffs of the High Sierra and Alps, had my imagination exceeded by the land forms of the Plateau Province, where the Colorado River experimented with its sculptor's tools before creating Glen Canyon, itself exceeding in delicacy and innovation what would become known as one of the Seven Wonders of the World, The Grand Canyon. It was a good thing there were New Yorkers to talk to New Yorkers, and that they were able to concede that the Hudson had more to offer than Fifth Avenue.

In view of my rapidly growing concern about environmental restoration, I was delighted with a section David Sive included from his own testimony:

It is this character and "integrity of the Mountain" and the surrounding areas that must be borne in mind in determining the extent to which the Project, and all that goes with it, will mar the natural beauty of Storm King and its environs. If its meaning is changed, in the eyes of those who behold it, its supreme value as a preserver and embodiment of the spirit of the New World . . . to a whole nation particularly the vast millions in its greatest metropolitan area, is forever lost. In that event, no combination of orders of this Commission, funds of the applicant, and skill of its eminent landscape architects, can be any more successful in putting the earth, rocks and trees of Storm King back together again, than were all the king's horses and all the king's men in the case of Humpty Dumpty. Painting concrete green cannot deceive its beholders into believing that it is the handkerchief of the Lord, or, if it can, this Commission should not, in the absence of some overwhelming economic necessity, direct such deception.

"OK, OK, you guys have had your chance — the horses want another shot at it."

David Sive's chapter is entitled, "Securing, Examining and Cross-Examining." One excerpt reveals why it would be a mistake to let him cross-examine you:

Cross-examination of the expert witness of the resource-using agency or company can be fruitful. Such experts, particularly those engaged in planning or construction, still, by and large, do not understand the concept that some parts of the world cannot be improved, or that public policy is not necessarily to have more of everything that we can build.

This pursuit of bigness may not be as dramatically expressed as it was in the words of one of the company's planning experts on cross-examination in the Storm King proceedings — "Any large lake is handsomer than a small lake" — in comparing the proposed immense storage reservoir to the small pond now at its proposed site. Nor may the philosophy of improvement of everything by engineering be stated as clearly as in the following question and answer on cross-examination of a planner of the Storm King project:

Q. "Have you ever in your experience found an area which you decided was so beautiful that you didn't think you could improve it?"

A. "Personally I think practically anything can be improved. In my past experience I have not had any area which wasn't improved or something like that."

[The witness should have heard Theodore Roosevelt's remark about the Grand Canyon: "The ages have been at work on it and man can only mar it." David Sive learned from Storm King a line he used from time to time on the Friends of the Earth board, and I have copied it often: "Suppose we simply didn't build it." He never told me, however, what he reveals in this paragraph:]

"Not too troublesome, but worthy of note is the fact that in the Storm King litigation, Charles Callison was asked questions and gave answers which amounted to an admission that he was a professional conservationist. He was also referred to as a public relations man on the basis of his answers to questions concerning his past. David Brower could not be classified at all by the cross-examiners."

I do not know why they should have been able to classify me, inasmuch as I cannot classify myself. Generally speaking, generalists must avoid being classified. I feel insecure in a cubbyhole ("a snug or confined place, as one to hide or play in" — Webster).

I had known Charles Callison from the Dinosaur days, when he and Stewart Brandborg were with the National Wildlife Federation and persuaded the Federation to oppose the Dinosaur dams. The cross-examiners should have asked him if he, as Audubon vice-president, preferred birds or people. His answer: "I prefer people who like birds."

What was the all-important interim result of all this effort? David Sive again:

. . . The special problems stem primarily from the subject matters of the expert testimony, which are often in the realm of aesthetics.

The Storm King litigation is perhaps the best example. The reversal by the Court of Appeals for the second circuit (in 1965) of the grant of license by the Federal Power Commission was coupled with the remand of the proceedings to the Commission in the now classical language of the opinion of Circuit Judge Paul R. Hays:

"The Commission's renewed proceedings must include as a basic concern the preservation of natural beauty and of national historic shrines, keeping in mind that, in our affluent society, the cost of a project is only one of several factors to be considered."

Economy had to move over to make room for Ecology. The day this happened should be an environmental holiday. Compare the Storm King court's comment with what another court said in December 1962 when the National Parks Association, the Sierra Club, the Federation of Western Outdoor Clubs, and Richard C. Bradley filed suit against Secretary of the Interior Stewart Udall in an effort to enjoin him "to keep open the diversion tunnels of Glen Canyon Dam until he had taken adequate protective measures to preclude impairment of Rainbow Bridge National Monument." The Colorado Storage Project Act had specifically required protection. The Secretary's Bureau of Reclamation had lobbied against funds to provide the protection, and at the conclusion of the hearing, the court, alluding to a suit involving Walden Pond, "predicated on the proposition of Massachusetts law that a person has standing as a citizen by mandamus to enforce a public duty of interest to citizens generally," observed that "This is not the Federal rule" and concluded:

Moreover, if there were standing to sue, the activity involved here is in the discretion of the Secretary. It is not a ministerial duty. The manner in which he should preserve the national monument rests largely in his own discretion. For these reasons the motion for a preliminary injunction is denied.

Dave at the proposed Tall Grass Prairie National Park c. 1975. (Photo by Patricia Duncan.)

CHAPTER 7

CONSERVATION VOTING

F OR THE FIRST HALF OF THIS CENTURY, environmental organizations avoided open political activity. Legislative activity fared
almost as poorly following a Supreme Court decision of 1955
about lobbying. In Monterey, in 1957, a special conference of
the Sierra Club leaders from all over heard me advocate that the club
form a League of Conservation Voters. The audience liked the idea, but
I had not put it in a form they could act upon. Any form would have
perplexed the club's board of directors at that time. They were eager
then to protect the club's tax-deductible status; and if there was anything that was perfectly clear in the Internal Revenue code, it was that
action in favor of candidates, whether they were in office or running for
it, was a no-no.

Concerned about the 1955 tax threat to lobbyists, I asked Warren
Olney, then assistant U.S. attorney general, about the threat. Warren
thought about it while we sipped juleps flavored with mint we had just
borrowed from Martha Washington's kitchen garden. He thought that
the club was "at the bottom of the barrel" concerning any IRS threat. On
December 5, 1959, a worried Sierra Club board passed a resolution,
previously alluded to, while (on the advice of a therapist I was then seeing about how to handle my tensions) I sat in a tranquilized stupor.
When I returned to my normal state of aggression, I was livid. The resolution had these two very troublesome parts:

"No statement shall be used that expressly, impliedly, or by reasonable inference criticizes the motives, integrity, or competence of an
official or bureau."

Fortunately, the Sierra Club was able to think and act otherwise
when James Watt became Secretary of the Interior — and thereby doubled its membership. What bothered me more was this:

It is realized that from time to time isolated bills pending before a variety
of legislative bodies may seriously involve or affect the public preservation principles which the Sierra Club is dedicated to support primarily through educational means. In such individual cases, as a minor and insubstantial part of the
over-all long-term public program of the Sierra Club, the staff is authorized to
support those principles as vigorously and effectively as possible within the law.

123

None of the publications of the Sierra Club shall take "action" with respect to legislative matters by urging Sierra Club members or the public to contact members of a legislative body for the purpose of proposing, supporting, or opposing legislation. Members may be reminded, however, of their constitutional right to petition or to write to Congress, as guaranteed by the First Amendment to the Constitution of the United States.

If anyone erred, the club could tell the IRS that a person had violated club policy as well as IRS regulations — the specific wording was identical — and feel relieved. This would not, however, relieve pressures on the environment that political action could ameliorate. If you must choose between saving the environment and saving tax status, the club was saying, stay out of politics and save your tax status. I strongly disagreed and the honeymoon ended. It was bad enough, I realized on sobering up, to have my hands so firmly tied. But to tie the members' hands too!

At this point in time, John Muir, although not really a revolutionary, was beyond reasonable doubt revolving in his grave. The club had been substantially active in legislation from its founding until the Supreme Court decision alluded to above. The resolution was moved and seconded by Richard M. Leonard and Bestor Robinson, and supported by Ansel Adams, Lewis Clark, Clifford Heimbucher, Stewart Kimball, Will Siri, Cliff Youngquist, and opposed, but only because of the limit on publications, by Elmer Aldrich, George Marshall, Charlotte Mauk, and Edgar Wayburn.

Bolstered by Warren Olney's evaluation, as well as by the prospect of the Sierra Club Foundation, should the Sierra Club lose its tax status, I went on reasonably boldly. That boldness included the Grand Canyon ad written by Jerry Mander that led the IRS to cloud the club's deductible status. Under that cloud the status vanished.

The country reacted, hating the IRS, supporting the club that was trying to defend the Grand Canyon for everybody, and people joined the club in droves. Any losses of deductible income could have been covered by the Sierra Club Foundation, already in existence for six years, had Dick Leonard wanted that to happen. Substantial deductible income was probably lost. But nondeductible income increased.

The club went to court to recover its deductibility. Gary Torre was our lawyer, at Phil Berry's suggestion, and Gary built a lot of his case on the educational value of Sierra Club books.

In 1967, at the board meeting at Clair Tappaan Lodge where Ansel first suggested that I be fired as executive director, Gary argued against continuing the effort to recover the club's deductible status. I urged, successfully, that the club continue its effort — not for the club's sake, because we were doing all right, but for the sake of the rest of the environmental movement, which wasn't. If the club lost to the IRS, I argued, the rest of the organizations, far less well-off, would continue their deepening fear to be active in the legislative arena. And since that was where conservation battles were won or lost, that fear needed to be reduced. Therefore the Sierra Club should continue to fight the case.

In summary, the club was ready in response to retreat from its historical role of environmental advocacy. The creation of the Sierra Club Foundation removed the danger from the club's continuing activism.

The club had lost its tax status, but gained membership in doing so. It need not have lost any deductible grants or bequests, because they could have been channeled into the foundation. The club fought the IRS action to benefit the entire movement, but the club lost. The movement passed through an Era of Timidity.

(Eventually, Elvis Stahr would get the Conable Option through Congress. That option made it possible once again for other organizations to lobby, but only on a scale considerably reduced from what had prevailed prior to the 1955 decision of the Supreme Court.)

Mountaineers learn it early. If one route doesn't work, try another. December 5, 1959, drove me to using books, if not speeches and letters, and to contriving a Sierra Club Foundation to handle the minor part of club income that needed to be tax deductible. Was wimpiness what the board really intended? I think not.

Whatever the intent — and I must not allude to motives, etc., of an official or bureau — it didn't work out that way. The Sierra Club Foundation was incorporated the next year, 1960. The book program took off, with a major boost from Ansel Adams. We took delight in understanding the untenable motives, etc., of the Bureau of Reclamation, we lost our tax-deductible status, grew faster, lobbied harder than ever, refused to compromise, and there are no dams in Dinosaur or the Grand Canyon. By far the greater part of Sierra Club funds are available for full-scale lobbying, in legislative bodies and through the grassroots. And the Sierra Club Political Committee would soon be at work.

The Sierra Club board and its executive director's mutual incompatibility climaxed, fueled by a major nuclear disagreement concerning the siting of the Diablo Canyon reactors, on May 3, 1969.

Walking the plank as a member of the club's staff gave me one of the several opportunities I had been missing. In New York City on July 11, 1969, in the office of David Sive, we founded Friends of the Earth, with the League of Conservation Voters as part of it. In San Francisco on September 16, 1969, we held our first press conference in the old, beautifully rehabilitated firehouse at 451 Pacific Avenue, in space Howard Gossage had made available at no cost to FOE, figuring that before long we could pay rent. The best account of the conference appeared in the *New York Times* September 17, 1969. Larry Davies, who wrote it, had been very helpful in my period as executive director of the club, and had gathered notes on my life and times for the *Times*, not, I was soon informed, for a current use, but for my obituary, when the time came. Neither of us will see it when it runs. I was glad to see this story run:

NATURALISTS GET A POLITICAL ARM

Ex-Sierra Club Chief Gives Details on Voters League

By LAWRENCE E. DAVIES

Special to The New York Times

San Francisco, Sept. 16 — Conservationists headed by David Brower, the former executive director of the Sierra Club, announced plans today to enter the political arena with a new organization.

Mr. Brower said at a news conference that two new international bodies had been established and that a subsidiary of one — a group to be called the League of Conservation Voters — would take part in political campaigns in which the environment was an issue.

He declared that the League of Conservation Voters would enter the campaigns "all the way from local fights to the presidency."

The activation of both the John Muir Institute for Environmental Studies, a nonprofit organization devoting itself to research and education, and Friends of the Earth, a nonprofit membership organization, was announced by Mr. Brower.

The League of Conservation Voters is a subsidiary of Friends of the Earth, of which Mr. Brower is president. He is also director of the John Muir Institute, which is headed by Max Linn, the public relations director for the Sandia Laboratories.

The 'Worst Crime'

Observing that the new groups would complement each other, Mr. Brower remarked:

"The earth needs a number of organizations to fight the disease that now threatens the planet: 'Cirrhosis of the environment.' There is only one environment that will sustain us and other living things we share the planet with. Man's diminishing of the earth is a crime, and the worst one of all is grand larceny against the future."

The John Muir Institute was created, he said, with the financial assistance of Robert O. Anderson, board chairman and chief executive officer of the Atlantic Richfield Company. It was understood that Mr. Anderson's personal gift of $80,000 might be followed by others.

Mr. Brower was the central figure in a Sierra Club fight last spring. He and his slate of directors lost to a conservative ticket, and he resigned as executive director of the conservative organization as the board was preparing to vote him out of office.

At the news conference today, Mr. Brower insisted that the two new international organizations would work with, not compete against, the Sierra Club

126

and other conservation groups. He described the Sierra Club, which claims a membership of 80,000, as "one of our strongest allies."

Tax Status Defined

Mr. Brower said that the John Muir Institute would be a tax-deductible organization, but that Friends of the Earth would not be.

He said he and his associates had chosen not to make Friends of the Earth tax deductible "because it will concentrate on legislative and political action and we plan to be extremely aggressive and noncompromising in our activities."

"Donors will know their money is not deductible," he said, "and they will know the money is going toward the sort of militant activity that I stood for during my last 10 years with the Sierra Club."

Mr. Brower said that Friends of the Earth would have "one or more" full-time lobbyists. He said the regular membership fee would be $15. The fee for membership in the John Muir Institute, he said, would be $50.

Mr. Brower said the conservation organizations would have offices in San Francisco; New York; Washington; Albuquerque, N.M.; Anchorage; Chicago; Honolulu; London; and Morges, Switzerland.

New York Times, September 17, 1969

Having an idea, then, is helpful, but not important in itself. The idea needs to be put in supportable form. That takes something like a lawyer. The form won't move of its own volition. It has to be led, by a leader. Then comes the bad news. Leaders are not quite to be trusted. There must be an administrator, and he or she had better be from the Stanford or Harvard business schools. Administrators want black bottom lines, which require tax-deductible funding. This closes the circle. Absolutely no politics, and very little, if any, lobbying.

The League of Conservation Voters (LCV) would have remained an idea, with enough form not to be amorphous, had George Alderson, first working in Washington for the Sierra Club and now for Friends of the Earth, not told me about Marion Edey. LCV was an idea she liked, and she was ready to put thirty-five thousand dollars into it, nondeductibly. We were off and running. She headed the steering committee. Her strategy was to pick contests carefully at first, try to find those in which a little help would go a long way, and thus show how good we were. It worked. Eighty percent success the first year. We must be nonpartisan, and this was difficult. Republicans were not making it easy. We leaned over backwards. We carefully picked the conservation items we would use to score officeholders and candidates. Congressman Dick Ottinger commented: "I wish we knew in advance what issues LCV is going to score us on." Marion wanted candidates to vote our way, but not if it meant political suicide for them. She picked a good crew and worked indefatigably.

It was soon discovered that for legal reasons LCV had to be separate from FOE. For various other reasons this led to difficult times that can best be described in the next volume of my autobiography, *The Way It Really Was,* a volume not likely to be written.

There is no need for that now. LCV was effective. Its ratings were well reported in the national press. LCV was new. It had a solid environmental aura because its steering committee contained individuals whose identity with their tax-deductible organizations was clear; but it was they themselves, not their identities, who were steering.

Friends of the Earth, with LCV as part of it, was intentionally founded as a civic organization, contributions to which are not tax deductible, although it is tax exempt. Friends of the Earth Foundation was set up to receive deductible funds for FOE work that qualified for such support — a substantial part of its work. FOEPAC would later be founded to be politically active, then disappear in the 1989 merger of FOE, FEF, EPI, and the OS.

But the club's and the similar political arms of Environmental Action are restricted in their communications to their respective memberships. LCV is not. I am hoping that by the time you read this, a new political organization will exist, Earth Island Voters, free, like LCV, to appeal to the entire electorate, but with a broader agenda than LCV's, encompassing environment, peace, and global equity.

CHAPTER 8

THE NATIONAL ENVIRONMENTAL POLICY ACT AND BEYOND

I N JANUARY 1970, the National Environmental Policy Act (NEPA) was signed by President Nixon, giving standing a much firmer footing. NEPA does not require good decisions, Mark Horlings points out, but the process of careful consideration in an open forum. "The assumption underlying process legislation," he adds, "is that good results usually flow from good procedures." Mark, a graduate of Harvard Law School, served as administrative director of Friends of the Earth and became vice-president of Earth Island Institute, until escaping to become attorney general of Palau. His comments appeared in the 1981 edition of *Progress,* in his chapter entitled "The Evolution of Law." He warns: "As NEPA matures, it becomes more common to find impact statements that are in technical compliance but are woefully inadequate in true consideration of issues."

The Environmental Defense Fund was already on deck to make the most of the NEPA opportunity, and the Natural Resources Defense Council was ready to follow suit. I was asked to speak at their founding conference in Princeton on March 21, 1970. David Sive and John Oakes, then editorial page editor of the *New York Times,* were among those in the audience:

MY TITLE: "CAN SURVIVAL BE MADE LEGAL?" My qualifications: I am a sophomore dropout from Berkeley. You are at the mercy of an inexpert.

Six weeks ago I was going to Gainesville, Florida, to speak to the university there. Because I had trusted the Hertz person at Jacksonville to mark the map for me, I went a hundred miles too far, turned around, and was late. At the outskirts of Gainesville is the sign, "Slow down and live." Underneath was the name of the sheriff, but I couldn't read it because I was going by too fast. So are we.

I'll break my remarks down into three parts: The Lawyer and Conservation, Perspective, and What We Need to Do as Soon as I Finish.

"The Lawyer and Conservation" begins in the early 1860s, when some lawyers drafted the language for the first act to set aside a park for the nation — Yosemite. Many of the people who have held the most important conservation job in the country — the Secretary of the Interior — were very able lawyers. The Sierra Club was founded in the offices of an attorney, Warren Olney. William E. Colby, the secretary of the club for forty-four years, was a mining lawyer. He helped draft legislation for the recession of Yosemite to the Federal Government, for a greater Sequoia National Park, for Kings Canyon National Park, and for the California State Parks. The law that became most prominent in Sierra Club history was the Internal Revenue Code. Sierra Club lawyers in the early days were chiefly concerned with protecting the name of the club. They could not protect Mount San Jacinto from a tramway.

In 1955 we really became quite aware of what the law meant to conservation in the Supreme Court decision on *Harris et al., vs. the United States* on the federal lobbying act, which was really one of the landmarks in what happened to conservation in this country. We haven't recovered from that act since. I hope we do.

But the outgrowth of that 1955 action of the Supreme Court was the formation immediately of three organizations in each of which I had a minor role: The Council of Conservationists in New York, the Citizens' Committee on Natural Resources in Washington, and Trustees for Conservation in California. All these were set up to forego tax deductibility in order to permit vigorous legislative work. Each was miserably under-financed. The club had problems, trying to influence legislation and pretending that it was not. Legislative activity was required to save Dinosaur National Monument, pass the wilderness bill, establish the Outdoor Recreation Resources Review Commission and, later, the North Cascades National Park. But organizations were under wraps, seeking cringe benefits.

We joined the suit against the Secretary of the Interior, for not fulfilling the requirements of the Colorado River Storage Project Act to preserve Rainbow Bridge National Monument, but did not have standing. If we had had Dave Sive and Steve Duggan to help us prepare the case, we might then have saved Rainbow Bridge.

We tried to strengthen the Forest Practices Act in California — to get the state to put some teeth in the act. That didn't work. Then came the Grand Canyon battle. In the Storm King case I was glad I had a discretionary fund to help keep the Sierra Club's interest alive. I think the Storm King case is one of the major milestones in conservation law.

Then there is the saga of the Grand Canyon, the IRS, and the Sierra Club. We lost our tax status because our Grand Canyon ad in the *New York Times* contained coupons to send to members of Congress. The Commissioner of Internal Revenue thought that that was so blatant that he clouded the tax status of the Sierra Club and probably cost the club about half a million dollars in deductible contributions. I think Grand Canyon was saved in part by the ire of people against the IRS. People learned about the Grand Canyon who had not known that it was threatened. This included people in the Internal Revenue Service itself, with whom I had my first meeting three days after they clouded our status. They did not know that Grand Canyon was threatened. So I said they should consider the ad as educational, not legislative, and asked them please to write to their congressmen.

We had some other work, then we saved The Grand Canyon anyway — me and a lot of other people — for the time being. We branched overseas a bit and David Sive helped us to set up a Sierra Club Limited of London. There were concerns in the Sierra Club that activities overseas would be *ultra vires* according to our articles of incorporation, and the club closed the office, violating an oral agreement I had to make with the Bank of England.

That brings us up to date on what happened when I was last in touch with what was going on in the Sierra Club. I do know that at this point we have seen the end of the battle of the Kings — Storm King and Mineral King. So the Sierra Club has moved from a point where ABA can mean either the American Booksellers' Association or the American Bar Association. The club is carrying on a number of major cases important to the environment.

For perspective, consider that the Industrial Revolution has run its course for hardly more than two centuries of the two or three million years humanity has been here and the three or four billion years life has been here. The alarming thing about it all is that we have a lot of people around us who write for the financial pages of the *Wall Street Journal* and the *New York Times* and almost any financial page you see, certainly even more so the *London Times,* and they assume that what we have got away with in two centuries as opposed to those billions of years is something we can extrapolate from and continue and can accelerate. I think, as Ralph Nader suggests, they need psychiatric attention. But that's simply because we have a different perspective now from what we used to have. We see the terrible importance of doing something else besides accelerate and accelerate, doubling our speed with which we hurtle toward that cliff which now, I think, we clearly see.

I'd like to explain the horrors of doubling. You are all right on the highway if you double your speed every ten seconds so long as you go from one to two to four to eight to sixteen to thirty-two. That's faster than you can run. At sixty-four you are about right for a highway. That's about what we were doing as we came out of World War II. We have doubled it now to 128 on our attack on this biological wealth, and there are a lot of people saying, "We're all right, Jack, we can double it again." I think we can't. When you are going 128 miles an hour you should have your hands firmly on the wheel, be looking tensely at the road, and be hearing sirens.

I hope the media — excepting the *New York Times,* which has a fair claim to having been interested in the environment for a long time — having just discovered the environment, will stop calling the present interest in the environment a fad. It is not a fad unless survival is a fad.

I think that what we need now is the new environmental law groups. I have been advising young lawyers who ask me what to do to get in touch with David Sive or Jim Moorman, and now I'll tell them to get in touch with you people.

We certainly need to learn how to shift the burden of proof more than we have. We need tax clarification. The conservation force in this country cannot work adequately so long as it's under the inhibition it now is — the assumption that we must not be politically active or legislatively active in pursuit of the goals for which we were organized because of the danger of finding deductible funds withdrawn — assuming that most organizations cannot get by unless they are deductible and exempt. The organizations I work for ride two horses. The John Muir Institute is tax deductible. It is concerned with conferences. Our next is in June, its theme, "Is Survival Economically Feasible?" We are also publishing the series the Sierra Club was not able to continue, "The Earth's Wild Places." We do want to celebrate what we think is the most critical resource, the biological wealth of the planet. All this is tax-deductible. The non-deductible, tax-exempt Friends of the Earth has its name on the title page of those books and others, including *The Environmental Handbook,* which is now a best-seller, a book that we put out on the SST, a book on defoliation, one on reactors, and more battle books. So we publish; we hope to get royalties from that, we hope to have membership, and we hope to be very substantially active in a legislative way without any concern about tax status. We want to be politically active and intervene to try to get some of the good guys in office.

But how do we slow down and live? How do we block the Alaska Pipeline? I think that's the worst threat to wilderness man has concocted, now that the court has put timber destruction temporarily out of the way. How do we prevent massive ocean spills? Every week seems to bring another disaster. How do we stop the use of defoliants and pesticides and the other anti-life chemicals? How do we realize that as we fight other forms of life we are attacking our own life? If you have read the Thomas Whiteside pieces in the *New Yorker* you have seen the indications that in 2,4,5-T there is a contaminant, dioxin, that seems, in tests on chicken embryos, to be a million times worse than thalidomide in causing birth defects. We have been spreading that all over Vietnam and all over our own country throughout the food system, and nobody knew it was happening. When Ralph Nader said it was, the government denied it. Now it has been confessed.

How do we get cars out of cities? I would like nothing better in my own hometown of San Francisco than to see at the city limits, "No private cars allowed." It would be a beautiful city once again. It's not too crazy an idea. How do we get rid of the unnecessary, wasteful mobility we have? How do we free organizations from the IRS? How do we get going on the master plan for the United States that will allow us to use the land the way it ought to be used — the way almost any other country that has survived learned how to use it? How do we end this proliferation of nuclear reactors before we know how to handle the high-level waste? How do we rethink what weapons are for? How do we get the population to decline, bearing in mind that the question of the day remains, how dense can people be? My own answer is that they should be at least half as dense as they are right now. To contemplate a world of half its present population, as most of you know, is not going to be too rugged. That was all the people in the world when I graduated from high school, which wasn't that long ago, and the world worked. We had culture, we had cars, we also had air and drinkable water.

All these abuses must be stopped, and they will be stopped one way or the other. The question is will they be stopped in time, and rationally? The Alaska Pipeline will be stopped, if we build it, as soon as there is a big break, which is the prediction from people I have been talking to, and you watch Lord knows how many million barrels of oil drain out of the pipe between breaks down into the Yukon drainage, into Valdez, into the Bering Sea. Then we will stop it, but why not stop it before we have lost all that valuable wilderness, that valuable resource in the sea? There are other things to do in our civilization than continually accelerate our burning of fossil fuels.

In short, I think we have a good mission that will keep everybody busy, including all the attorneys in this group, going back over the parts of the planet man has already handled, sometimes gently, sometimes quite roughly, going back, stopping where we are and going back and doing better. We can grind up the last of our wildness, the last of our wilderness, and then we will have to stop and go back and do better. But we will have to be doing better in a world that has no wildness anymore, and I don't think we are going to make it in such a world.

To sum up, I think our most important resource is the earth's biological wealth. Our connection from now back the billions of years to life's beginning on earth remains intact in wilderness and its unbroken flow. This we need. If we don't know why we need it, that's just one more measure that we haven't become smart enough yet to ask the right questions. I think we can establish criteria for a feasible and stable economy; I think we can discover alternatives to war; I think we can reenact the Bill of Rights. I think these are some good things to do.

I think we still have a few years to organize on the planet a general global strike against progress in order to force needed change. We can die of caution. Some people may rather die than change their habits, but we don't.

The problem starts in Affluent White America and nowhere else. That's the population problem. One child born in Affluent White America will use fifty times the resources of a child born in Colombia: five percent of the world's people using overall about thirty percent of the world's resources — and looking for a bigger cut and worried about balances of payments when we don't get it. So I think as we enter the decade of the seventies [clouded crystal ball: make it the nineties] we ought to renounce our unwise use of the only planet we are ever going to have. I would like to see growth without reason no longer be the game we play. I would like to see us plan for a tenable future in the battle between a dynamic society and a finite planet. I think in that battle we should act in favor of the planet, at long last appreciate the diversity of living things upon which our own lives depend. The quotation that always informs me, and I hope it always informs you, too, and it should be part of the Pledge of Allegiance to the Planet, is in Adlai Stevenson's last speech, about us, passengers in a little spaceship, preserved from annihilation only by the work, the care, and the love we give our fragile craft. There's the key word and you hardly ever get into it in conferences, but I think it's a good word. Love. It's the one resource that is available in unlimited quantities, and it's hardly ever used anymore. Let's try it a little bit more.

Princeton, March 21, 1970

It would be a sad world indeed if NRDC, EDF, and SCLDF had not been on hand to thwart the manifest goals of the Reagan years and now, apparently, the Sununu years. Perhaps they can all benefit from a happy accident.

In 1986, at a Sierra Club board of directors retreat in Seattle, I urged Rick Sutherland, executive director of the Sierra Club Legal Defense Fund, to put together an exhibit-format book on places that SCLDF action had saved, and to contemplate a whole series of subsequent volumes. I thought they would sell on their own, if beautiful enough, and that he could hardly have a better device for fund-raising. He agreed that the first one was a good idea, but he did not commit himself to subsequent volumes. He was probably trying to avoid my tendency to pour my enthusiasm into an idea, then get someone else to do something about it.

SCLDF's first exhibit-format volume, edited by former *Not Man Apart* editor Tom Turner, *Wild by Law: The Sierra Club Legal Defense Fund and the Places It Has Saved* has appeared, and I will bet that there will be more. EDF and NRDC should do the same. Let them all create the impression that the public needs to grasp — that the government and the Fortune 500, and small corporations too, must be required to adhere to natural law and order, to realize that if the contest is between economy and ecology, ecology must have precedence. It was here billions of years before economists turned up, and there will be no economy in a dead ecosystem. Economists, financial-page editors, justices of the Supreme Court and the International Court of Justice, please note.

Environmental law groups are essential, need generous voluntary public funding, should not be denied reimbursement of costs in suits they win for the public, and should have fewer dark clouds on their horizon — such as what the public is realizing now exist in the storm the present U.S. Supreme Court is brewing up. It is a storm that can worsen severely as the decades pass by — unless.

Unless we do something about the weathervane on every courthouse. It is not the function of the court to hold up a finger to detect where the zephyrs of fad are coming from. But a Supreme Court must recognize an imminent hurricane as it approaches. The biggest hurricane in the history of the earth is coming in fast. The signs are clear in the air and water that are no longer clear enough, in the marks of the earth-beaters, in the footprints of living things that exist no more, with ethics becoming a fossil and with hope and The Bill of Rights becoming a memory.

Public-interest lawyers, rise up. There is legislation to write and pass, public offices to be filled, laws to be enforced, even by regulatory agencies. It is fair to say that peace is at hand, if only it can be made legally preferable.

Garrett DeBell at the UN Association meeting in San Francisco in late November, 19 *Anne and Dave are persuading him to edit* The Environmental Handbook.

CHAPTER 9

PLATFORM PROPOSALS

The First Earth Day, April 22, 1970, was hardly over. Buoyed by the million-copy success of Friends of the Earth's *The Environmental Handbook,* edited by Garrett De Bell, he, Ian Ballantine, and I made the next move. Earth Day revealed what people wanted. But how do we persuade legislators, or get others who can be persuaded, to put these needs in legislative form and vote for them?

We started with *The Voter's Guide to Environmental Politics.* Garrett rounded up twelve authors, added some pieces of his own, and Ian published it in August 1970. Garrett introduced the book with characteristic clarity and grasp:

In *The Environmental Handbook,* we tried to provide an overview of the environmental crisis and a sampling of views on how to avert disaster and develop an ecologically sound society.

This book is an expanded look at one approach — federal legislation. Wherever possible, we have proposed specific legislation for specific problems, from wilderness preservation to the recycling of garbage. But proposed legislation and general goals are only part of what must be done. There have been good ideas in the wind for years which have never been planted in successful bills and germinated into social change.

Much of this book therefore is devoted to reforms which are needed in our institutions, particularly in the United States Congress and regulatory agencies.

It is vital to grasp the connection between the quality of our lives and the internal rules of Congress and congressionally established agencies, which often stifle reform.

Several pages later, after an inventory of problems that are as real today as they were twenty-one years ago, he sums things up:

. . . It would appear that politicians aren't really opposed to survival. It's just that it isn't politically feasible this year.

This book is based on the idea that survival is politically feasible — and if it isn't, we'd damned well better make sure that it becomes so. . . .

It will take a sustained effort . . . to replace the do-nothings with environmentally sound legislators. The idea is not new. It is called Democracy, and sometimes it works.

137

The Voter's Guide included my inevitable foreword, and I am sorry to say it doesn't need much updating. Ian and I added a postscript, "What a Survival Library Can Do for You," because we thought books were of special importance. I added a brief note on twenty-two conservation organizations and then ended the book with five conservation coupons, hoping that readers would cut them out and send them to the president, senators, members of Congress, a major corporation of their choosing, the president of the Equitable Insurance Company, and, to his surprise, a management consultant I knew in McKinsey & Company. I still like the idea, but I am not sure it worked. People just don't like to cut up books. I hope they agree with the Foreword:

THREAT TO THE ENVIRONMENT persists and worsens, in spite of attempts of some shallow journalists to portray concern about it as a fad, and of all too many advertising agencies to create a rug to sweep it under.

Meanwhile, back on the polluted, crowded, endangered, beautiful planet, too few antidotes to the threat have been offered us. Young people and old, new groups and traditional organizations, are working to fill the void. Garrett De Bell, one of the young people, and Friends of the Earth, one of the new groups, are here joined with Ballantine Books and the League of Conservation Voters to spell out how American voters can combine to make a difference. The American voter can learn here how to be the Ralph Nader of his block, how to effect the turnaround essential that is to the survival of our kind, our country, and the planet.

Before, During, and After Elections: Room for Progress

Voting in elections, important as it is, is not enough. The concerned citizen must help to determine the array of candidates selected from on election day, persuade other concerned people to get counted before and on election day, and follow through after the votes are in. After election day, either your candidates or their opponents will be in office. They are not likely to be evil, malevolent, stupid officeholders, even if they are opponents. They are capable of realizing that no one will vote, and no one will be elected, and that all life on the planet is threatened if technology is allowed to dictate when it should seek only to serve.

People who have chosen politics as a career and wish to continue in it must seek a certain amount of consensus if they want to stay in business. They must persuade enough of their fellows to vote with them, or nothing will happen. And they are human enough to be able to do only a few things at a time without help. You may find them a willing recipient of good ideas for legislative progress for which support can be built — either through their own leadership, through the hard work of their limited staff, through the work of the good and bad lobbies, in the District of Columbia, or through your help as a citizen volunteer.

You, the citizen, may have been too busy to follow through. You may have felt you could not afford to join the organizations that can work night and day for your interests.

If we paused and looked around, all two hundred million or so of us, we might agree that too few of us have been willing to set aside time and money to ensure a reasonable chance to live out our normal span. The thought hardly occurred to us that threats to environment were threats to us. There would always be room enough and time — later.

Now we know better. We need only step outside and breathe — and remember how much more enjoyable the process used to be — to realize that concern about the threat to the earth is by no means a fad. The threat is real and pervasive, and it is accelerating.

The good news — perhaps the only good news these days — is that this realization is now widespread enough to supply the necessary power for bringing about reforms. The Constitution foresaw the need for change and provided a route to change. It is possible, we in Friends of the Earth are convinced, to use the good parts of the System to beat the bad parts of the System.

Blueprint for Change

Seeking steps toward reform that could be orderly, just, and swift enough, we met with the editor of the best-selling *The Environmental Handbook* in the pleasing environment of New York's La Fonda del Sol, surrounded by reminders of the charm of native arts and crafts. We reviewed what we would like to do and what we *could* do in time for a "before, during, and after" elections program for voter support of the environment. What could the concerned citizen urge concerned leaders in government and industry to undertake to save the environment — without their committing political or corporate suicide?

We thought it would be a good idea to draw upon several of these leaders for assistance, to ask members of Congress and candidates for election to make a commitment, and then to report to the public on their responses.

We assumed that human beings concerned about racial equality and peace the world over understand that degradation of the planet and of its living resources — including people — is a single, all-encompassing crisis. We all breathe the same air; breathing is still strictly a do-it-yourself exercise. And no one will buy or sell, love or hate, or be white, yellow, red, brown, or black on a dead planet.

139

We assumed also that intelligent people with time to listen already knew full well that the crisis exists. So we would concentrate on proposing solutions needed now, feasible now, and fixable later if they needed fixing.

We wanted to accompany each of the national problems of top environmental importance with a proposal for reform. For each we would state the problem, include draft legislation to correct the problem or begin to, describe alternative ways to meet the need and show why we chose ours, and ask help on each chapter from members of Congress, or a candidate, or perhaps a loser in the election.

Having been in the business a while, we would post warnings in each chapter. We would suggest how the citizen could head off at the pass those who might attempt to vitiate the reforms, such as the people who take out four-color ads in national magazines to explain how their unrestrained pesticides can keep Bambi from a premature death at the hands of a nasty tick. Or those who stress how cars, too, must breathe clear air, and say their gasoline is the best thing there is for clean air. Or the people who send a salesman out on a nationwide speaking tour to push the idea that the U.S. will lose face unless it has a supersonic transport. We would be positive about this, and avoid the temptation to be snide.

A critically important section of the book would be a report on commitment, how members of Congress, or candidates for election, responded to a request for their views on the subjects, including a listing of these who declined to answer. This would be a difficult, ambitious, essential part of the book — so much so that we should try to help phrase answers if asked to, and be willing to build support out in the hustings, for the right answers.

Then, taking a lead from the "What You Can Do" section of the FOE/Ballantine book *Defoliation,* by Thomas Whiteside, we would seek to improve upon what we invented there.

What Are the Further Opportunities?

You can serve as judge of how much of the blueprint we have followed if you will also agree to help us with the next step. Our own feeling is that Garrett De Bell's achievement is superb, and that there is a superb opportunity for improvement by participating readers. We have found it difficult to come up with solutions. The stating of the problem, or restating of it, is much easier. Never underestimate the power of negative thinking: it is always easier to trip people than to stand them on their feet and aim them somewhere.

The Great Gap remains: the statement of congressional commitment. We wanted specific promises to "bite the bullet" and "damn the torpedoes" as opposed to glittering, evasive generality. But such commitment is not yet attainable in quantity.

We think we know why. People in politics who become too predictable have given away in advance one of their greatest powers, their ability to trade. Call it logrolling if you are a spectator, but call it the preservation of essential flexibility if you are a participant in the legislative arena and would like to keep on participating. If you are a spectator, it occurs to us, you should not accuse people in office of being too cynical about committing themselves early until you have exhausted your own imagination — and your own pen and voice — in making it possible for them to be bolder and to lean your way oftener.

Obstacles to Commitment

The routes to making greater boldness possible have many strange roadblocks. Some of the worst obstacles of all are in the Internal Revenue Code.

My own experience convinces me that one of the worst threats to the environment is the present interpretation of the tax laws. The threat is epitomized in what the Internal Revenue Service did to the Sierra Club in the club's attempt to save the Grand Canyon from two proposed power dams. Both dams would be highly destructive; neither was necessary. They would have alienated public property and destroyed the heart of one of the Earth's scenic wonders in the process. Yet the organization that led the defense of the public interest and the saving of the Grand Canyon was, in effect, fined half a million dollars for its effort. The intimidation of traditional conservation organizations gravely weakened their power just when the threat to the environment required that power more than ever before.

The conservation movement is still in that bind.

For reasons that used to be good enough, the IRS encourages the creation of profit which it can tax to support the government. We are not arguing here against taxes; they are our annual contribution to the cost of keeping the U.S. going.

But this approach has left conservationists in peril. Established for public purpose, they could not pursue that purpose in legislative effort — and conservation begins in legislation, is nourished by it, and dies in it — if that effort were "substantial." Webster thinks that something is 'substantial' when it has substance. It is obvious that conservation cannot be of force if it has no substance.

Whatever the IRS thinks substance means, it will not say. So conservation organizations have had to risk their own guess of what the IRS means. To save the Grand Canyon, the Sierra Club took that risk, and the IRS took away the club's tax status. Other organizations could not fail to note the loss.

141

The need is for (1) clear wording of the law, (2) clear guidelines in the regulations, and (3) clear interpretation following adjudication, which will allow the organizations to do what they must. Those groups that have been established to speak for an otherwise voiceless environment, and that do indeed so speak in the public interest, must be allowed to pursue their purpose through any of the three branches of government, or all of them. And they must be permitted to do so without peril to the public assistance they indirectly receive through being tax exempt and tax deductible. They must also be able to comment openly about the environmental promises and practices of officeholders and office-seekers.

Until this clarity comes, there will be organizations like Friends of the Earth and Sierra Club that accept the financial handicap of not being able to seek deductible funds, and do as well as they can. Forgive us for thinking it grossly unfair to have to scrape hard for tiny contributions to finance our effort to save the environment on the one hand, while on the other hand institutions and industries threatening the environment can deduct their costs of influencing the public and the legislators from Income before Taxes.

There are many other tax threats to the environment, such as those tax laws that discourage keeping parts of the environment open, wild, and beautiful. But the tax threat against the people who would band together to get the strength to save the land is certainly a major threat. It is second only to the threat inherent in the still-too-common assumption that more and more people can accelerate their demands upon a finite environment in search of an ever-higher standard of living without demeaning or eradicating standards for life.

Your Role in Building Support for Good Legislators

Early tax reform is essential and — with public support — feasible. It will allow conservation organizations to build public support for sound environmental measures. This in turn will encourage people in politics to risk an unmitigated, open commitment to the environment, and to save their trading of votes for less important concerns.

It is important to remember that the present system is devised to give people in political life the maximum opportunity of reelection. This is an opportunity of which they think highly. Those of us who do not want to enter that life and assume the chores of holding office are nevertheless entitled to protest vigorously the inequities of the present system. We can do so most effectively if we have also worked creatively to build public support for the political leaders who support governmental reform on behalf of the environment.

Citizens working on behalf of the environment need the strength that comes from alliance. They need the good conservative conservationist. They need the newcomer to environmental concern, who must be found in all colors and fields. They need responsible corporation executives who, although they have not always worked wisely, have often worked hard, and have the ability to lead on better routes when they discern them. We need to coalesce, not to splinter, in behalf of the environment.

In attempting to initiate a new growth of citizen activity we have inevitably set forth as new ideas concepts that are merely new to us, but old and tried before by those who have toiled long in the vineyard to rescue and defend the beautiful places we have inherited. If some of what is said here sounds too enthusiastic, please remember that it is better to be naive than to be null. Remember too that at the present disastrous rate of population growth there are enough people added to the world every three years to populate a new United States, and none of them has yet heard what you have heard. Let good things be heard more.

Your Role as an Editor

What could a book like this do better? Where has it succeeded best? The margins are wide, and there are intentional blanks and coupons. Forgetting for a moment that *survival* is an overworked word and remembering that it is an underworked practice, let this be your (political) survival workbook. Mark it up. In the margins, correct the ideas you don't like. Underline and quote those you do. Add yourself, your own genius, the power of your life. If you have time, let us know what we can say better next time. We may agree. We will listen.

Several pages show how you may amplify your voice by adding your force to that of others whose ideas are close to yours. Join with others for strength. If you belong only to your own-personal-self club, you limit yourself too much, and may need more company.

Value, if you will, the diversity — the essential diversity — of the organizations that try to stand guard for you when other duties consume your time. Support several of them. A dozen may not be too many; the cost of a beer or of a soda a day would support organizations that would make survival part of your budget.

The Survival Office in Your House

We have some suggestions for your consideration:

Build a survival library and a Write-Your-Congressman-and-Editors room in some nook of your house.

Write in this book and tear appropriate pages out of it. At very little cost we can supply another.

Gather a few friends in your house to help do these things if you'd rather not be alone in the effort. Your house could be the local office of your chosen organization. Ask about it!

Make the next version of this book better if you have time to.

Make the next election a better one for your having followed up on the current one, with whatever ideas this book has given you or which you have given us.

We do not underestimate your power, and hope *you* don't.

The first goal, let us suggest, is to predict a tenable future for this planet, and then to marvel at what a big difference your own concerted effort will make. Remember Rachel Carson — who did her homework, minded her English, and *cared.*

There are many variants of a few irrefutable themes to develop in the course of persuading good people to change course:

1) *People have not yet had time to learn enough.* In the week of Creation (using *Genesis* time), our kind arrived only three minutes before midnight on the sixth day, upon a world that had worked quite well without us all the previous week.

2) *Progress does not consist of ever-increasing speed,* whether it be of air travel, of the using up of coal, oil, and gas, of the pollution of air, or of the broadcasting of poisonous chemicals that the environment has not learned to cope with.

3) *There are limits.* We cannot constantly double anything. We can let technology grind its way through the last bit of natural beauty and wildness and then be forced to turn around and repair our damage. Or we can, as rational beings, turn around sooner while there is still natural beauty and wildness around us serving purposes we may some day be wise enough to understand.

4) *In diversity is strength.* Biological stability, beauty, and wealth derive from complexity. For example, if somehow the Appalachian forests had been simplified to chestnut, the blight would have obliterated the entire forest. But there was diversity, not a monoculture; although the chestnut is gone, we still have the forest. The lesson is almost unheeded. We can learn it now.

5) *We often forget our second great attribute.* Through the ages we have aggressively manifested our territoriality. We have also manifested love, the inexhaustible resource.

Conclusion

Any of the foregoing that sounds didactic was written either out of habit or out of guilt, but that does not purge it of validity. Thoreau said, "What is the use of a house if you haven't got a tolerable planet to put it on!" The push for a tolerable planet is on!

What a Survival Library Can Do for You

Books in a "Survival Series" should provide the best possible information, written for intelligent people, about the principal current threats to the environment that urgently demand remedial action. They should encourage support for the further research that will always be necessary as long as people revere technology and seek to anticipate its consequences. Proper application of science and humanity will sometimes show that we had better not do what mere technology tells us we can do. They should also urge action now, based on what is already known, to prevent using a given technology in advance of assurance that it will not inflict lasting harm.

The "What You Can Do" department of such a series is important, but the book is the thing. Each book needs to fill what has been a gap in publishing. Ordinarily, books take too much lead time to be of current value. They need to be sped up so that vital information — the abstract (the contents page and the promotional material), the detailed exposition (the text itself, with such illustrations as there are available), and the documentation — can become a readily available part of the concerned citizen's working library. Many magazines require more lead time than such books do, and those that are published on a news-magazine schedule rarely have enough space to provide all the material you may need at hand. And in all but the best organized of homes, magazines have a way of being topped by succeeding issues so rapidly that the lode-bearing strata are lost to all time and to the *Reader's Guide to Periodical Literature* — which is not often in many home libraries.

Such a series needs to be reviewed, interpreted, and enlarged upon in the very media whose limitations we have remarked upon, but nevertheless value very highly for their own unique and indispensable role in letting people know enough about what is happening to their environment in time to save it.

Herein is retrievable information for you to put to good use.

Ian Ballantine, President, Ballantine Books
David Brower, President, Friends of the Earth

The Voter's Guide contained coupons that outlined a course of action. People who had the time could state their views far better than coupons do, but coupons can be a first step, and lead to other steps. Coupons are fine, letters are better, and nonalienating letters are best.

In each coupon, we supplied the address (unless it is for the reader's own senator and member of Congress, whose name their own city hall should know) and a paragraph or two to start them out. We left it to them to add the "sincerely yours" and their own name and address; we also left room for them to add their own note, and hoped they would.

145

"The mark of the concerned citizen," we said, "will be the absence of these pages from the back of your book (or your own note, where appropriate, that you wrote your own). It will help us next time to learn how you made out this time."

The President [then Richard Nixon]
The White House
Washington, D.C. 20500
Dear Mr. President:

I have been reading The Voter's Guide to Environmental Politics and hope you have had a chance to read it too. I am impressed with the statement of various environmental problems, and with the solutions put forth in several of the chapters.

The book speaks of the difficulty of getting men in political life to commit themselves in detail in behalf of such proposals as the book makes — or to commit themselves against the proposals.

To respond in detail to the book would require a book in itself, and that might be a good idea. Meanwhile, it seems to me that a clear indication of your thinking on the issues mentioned would be of inestimable value to the world. Could you undertake this?

I share the concern you have expressed in your several statements about the environment; about the population crisis, about a policy for the oceans of the world, and about governmental reorganization that will assure a far more searching review of projects that threaten the environment than was ever before conducted. I am also deeply concerned about some of the steps that have been taken in spite of your statements.

Since whatever happens to this planet happens to all of us, can you suggest steps that I myself could take to help end this crisis?

The Voter's Guide also provided similarly worded coupons to go to the readers' senators and representatives — or to candidates the readers thought should replace them.

Another coupon, aimed at the president of one of the largest corporations in the world (one of the Fortune 500), had a different approach:

Having learned from The Voter's Guide to Environmental Politics that a man who is obliged to steer the affairs of a major corporation, and who stands a good chance of dying early of excess tension or of ulcers by virtue of his responsibilities cannot be all bad, I have a question for you: How do you feel about the solutions proposed in the several chapters of The Voter's Guide?

I suppose there should be a second question. Since we share a finite planet in which all kinds of growth cannot go on forever without something's bursting (whereupon we may all leave the planet together), what kinds of growth do you think we must continue, what kind taper off, and what kind reverse?

These questions are extremely difficult; but so is the problem. From your perspective, and with your influence in channeling money, the lifeblood of the economy, you have the opportunity to make a major contribution to not only the economy, but also to survival.

146

I hope your corporation will consider becoming a corporate member of Friends of the Earth.

I added another coupon addressed to a friend, who as could be expected, was surprised. Mr. Don Clifford of the McKinsey & Company, Park Avenue, New York:

Dear Mr. Clifford:

As you are a partner of what is perhaps the most prestigious management-consultant firms there is, and since you also are a partner who has shown concern about what is happening to the environment, I am sending you a copy of the letter I just sent to the president of one of the largest corporations.

This corporation may not be a client of yours, but you are probably well aware of their work. Could you let me know what people in consultant work can do to further some new thinking about the problems and solutions set forth in The Voter's Guide to Environmental Politics?

Your answer may fill a book. Perhaps Friends of the Earth would be pleased to be joint publisher of it, if that is what happens.

We also included a coupon to the president of a major insurance company:

I have just read The Voter's Guide to Environmental Politics and its presentation of problems and solutions. An idea has occurred to me that ought to interest you. The insurance companies of America, out of sheer self-interest, should be eager to see recovery of the environment take place as rapidly as possible because a sick environment is a bad investment, and people live progressively shorter lives the sicker it gets.

Perhaps you have never looked at it this way, but it seems to me that the conservation organizations of America are in a very real sense doing your work for you and deserve your support — especially those that cannot receive tax-deductible gifts as a charity but which can be recompensed for services given.

Do you see any logic in this suggestion, and could you come to the aid of the environment in such a way?

The Voter's Guide, 1970

The Voter's Guide sold but one-fifth as many copies alas, as *The Environmental Handbook,* and we had not prepared ourselves to draft the legislation we were asking for.

Seven years later we tried another voter's guide, a handbook for a sound environmental platform, we thought, for either major political party, with broadened scope. It was a full-sized book (8½ by 11) instead of a mass-market paperback, a Friends of the Earth book. We refused to believe that environmental publishing had been banalized. In a scenario resembling Garrett Hardin's "Tragedy of the Commons," hosts of publishers loaded bookstores with titles like ours, and there weren't enough book buyers to go around. Everyone suffered from the imitative, which proved a sad substitute for the innovative. Hugh Nash, who had edited the *Sierra Club Bulletin* and was FOE's senior editor for *Not Man Apart*, edited the new volume. We called it *Progress As If Survival Mattered: A Handbook for the Conserver Society,* a subtitle we had borrowed from the Canadians and their own name for environmentalism. We wanted our platform book to appear every four years to do what it could about presidential-election platforms. It was profusely illustrated, with three times as many words as *The Voter's Guide,* but unfortunately had only one-tenth the distribution. Ballantine could finance mass-market distribution. FOE couldn't by itself. Besides, Ballantine's voter's guide cost ninety-five cents. Ours had to be priced at $8.95 to break even.

We were most gratified by the response, especially from *Library Journal:* "As a guidebook for citizen action . . . as an all-around introduction to the ills and successes of our planet, it should find its way into the homes of almost anyone who reads more than the Sunday comics." The book went through four printings; became a staple in environmental education programs; got into the hands of hundreds of members of Congress, senators, newspaper editors, and activists; and, we hope, showed more than a few people that being an environmentalist meant having plans to make life better now and in the future. We hoped other countries would adapt the plans to their own needs.

The new foreword was just as long, but different. I signed it all, but Hugh Nash wrote the first third of it:

WHAT KIND OF COUNTRY DO YOU WANT? What kind of world? What kind of neighborhood on a small planet? If you have asked yourself such questions, we think you will like this book. If you haven't, we think you need it.

The kind of country and world a growing number of people want — and indeed, the kind we all require for sheer survival — will be less populous, more decentralized, less industrial, more agrarian. Our anxiously acquisitive consumer society will give way to a more serenely thrifty conserver society, one which relies most on renewable resources and least on the irreplaceables. Recycling will be taken for granted and planned obsolescence won't. Nuclear proliferation will be viewed in retrospect as a form of temporary insanity. We will stride confidently and lightly along the soft solar energy path so ably scouted out by physicist Amory Lovins. Restless mobility will diminish; people will put down roots and recapture a sense of community. Full employment will be the norm in a sustainable, skill-intensive economy, and indoor pollution where we work, now fifty times higher than outdoors, will no longer be tolerated. Medicine's role in curing disease will shrink as preventive medicine grows and leaves fewer and fewer diseases. Corporations will no longer demand the right to dispense cancer to you. People will turn on TV less and turn on their own senses more, and be better informed of, by, and for the natural world that made them. Parks and wilderness areas will be recognized as legal "persons," as corporations and ships already are, to ensure their permanent and productive survival. Science (and applied science, or technology) will pay more than lip service to elegant solutions, that is, solutions that achieve desired results with the utmost economy of means. Growthmania will yield to the realization that physical growth is wholesome only during immaturity, and that to continue such growth beyond that point leads to malignancy or other grim devices that keep the planet from being suffocated with a surfeit. The earth will not swarm with life, but be graced with it.

Whatever kind of country and world people decide they want, the next question is, How can they get it? Probably by gaining a new understanding of politics. Politics is democracy's way of handling public business. There is no other. We won't get the kind of country in the kind of world we want unless people take part in the public's business. Unless they embrace politics and people in politics.

Embrace politicians? Yes. Why not? Theirs is, in essence, an honorable calling. When we treat it accordingly, we will deserve politicians who honor their having been called. There is public business to be done. We need to help the men and women who have chosen to undertake it.

Thoreau asked the transcendent question about the use of a house that lacked a tolerable planet. A growing number of people see that the planet is less and less tolerable because its beauty — and let "beauty" epitomize all the things that make an environment excellent and the earth a rewarding place to live upon — is being lost more and more rapidly.

Suppose that one of this growing number of politicians is a presidential candidate and wished to make excellence of environmental quality *the* campaign issue. What kind of platform would such a candidate choose to run on? Or suppose a new political party arose, dedicated, as Friends of the Earth is, to natural law and order. Suppose that party dedicated itself to preserving, restoring, and equitably using the earth and its resources, mineral and living. And suppose it knew that if "progress" continued to depend upon wiping out irreplaceable resources, such progress could not last long. Imagine, then, a party dedicating itself to timely rethinking and corrective action. What would the platform be like?

Questions like these occurred to us in 1970 and we tried our hand at a voter's guide for environmental protection. It was pretty good. Early in 1976 we asked ourselves more questions, better ones. We hoped at first to produce an instant book on the environmental issues of the day, a "platform book," and to challenge candidates in that election to state publicly which of our planks they could stand on and which they feared they would fall between. It is still an appealing idea. It might make the

149

earth's health more of an issue. Since the natural laws upon which environmentalism is based can only be perceived, and can never be amended, a book perceiving those laws well should have lasting value. It could also serve as a yardstick against which to measure the environmental literacy and commitment of a candidate, a party, ourselves, and yourself as understanding evolved.

Having determined to proceed, we asked who should write what. We began with what. A few FOE staff members selected handfuls of topics. Which brought us to who. Which who? Outside experts, whose knowledge was already proved but whose likelihood of meeting deadlines wasn't, and whose broad philosophy might prove to be temporarily tangential? Or insiders, who share their philosophy with us, are familiar with our deadlines, and who had proved themselves able to dig hard in the fact mines? It is risky to assume that knowledge is acquired more easily than philosophy. We took the risk, and drew upon the talents of FOE officers, members, staff, and advisory counselors. Some of them are recognized authorities in the fields they write about. All care, and all know how to do their homework.

We recommended a basic chapter outline and suggested that the authors concentrate on what environmentalists believe rather than why. Consequently some parts may read a little the way tablets brought down from a mountain do, but lack divine authentication. We added counterpoint — pertinent material from other sources which, by itself, would make an environmental anthology of lasting value.

The most important challenge to each author was the outlining of feasible, unfrightening, tempting steps toward a sensible goal. It was tough. All environmentalists, it goes without saying, are opposed to evil and in favor of good. If a dam is evil they oppose it. That is a positive action from a river's point of view. But no one should underestimate the difficulty of putting together an appealing series of positive actions. Most of the public must understand why, how, and when before the whole society will let a politician move to spare its environment and save itself.

It is so hard that the people who put such a series of steps together and stick with them are candidates for hero and should be included in the sequel to John F. Kennedy's book *Profiles in Courage*. The greater the number of needed causes you espouse, the greater the chance of displeasing somebody. Cheap shots are easy. You can positively oppose cancer, heart disease, multiple sclerosis, inflation, unemployment, forest fires, and pneumonoultramicroscopicsilicovolcanokoniosis and never lose a vote. But if you oppose exponential economic growth, however lethal it is, you are not liked by the Conventional Wisdom set. If you take a position for or against abortion or gun control, you divide your constituency and may conquer yourself.

Conservation organizations, like candidates, have political needs to face. We are aware of the risk to FOE as we try to delineate sound environmental views of the many aspects of society we discuss here. It is perilous to take that risk but more perilous not to. We will pin our faith on your intelligence as a lay citizen who cares. Though you may not share our view in all aspects, we ask you to remember that consensus can be carried too far. It can produce not only a dull world, but also an endangered one. Opinions need to differ. As long as they do, you will know people are alive, awake, and still in honest search of truth. And you will remain young in the important sense — still able to listen, ready to change your mind, and willing to avoid being the Practical Man Disraeli worried about, who could be counted upon to perpetuate the errors of his ancestors.

Let us propose a grading system. If you agree with, say, 75 percent of what we propose, we'll give you a passing grade, and you can give us one. That's close enough, and qualifies you and us for working together. We probably should.

We freely concede, and think you will, that getting a world to change course will require powerful motivating forces, and we hope to discern them in time. As Dr. Daniel B. Luten (chemist, lecturer on resources, and a FOE director) has said from time to time: Too many people would rather die than change their habits. Almost all of them think the society exists to serve its economy. Too many of them mistake growth for progress. Almost no one understands the extraordinary demands as we now pass from an empty Earth to a full one. We have been slow, as we look at the rising population, to ask how dense people can be. We know the planet is lone and finite and that finite things have limits. But we have preferred denying them to facing them. Or we have looked for an escape to some greener colony in space.

People who sense the humor in Dr. Luten's way of putting the vital questions can be cheered. For surely the dawn of new perceptions is breaking. We see that there are better things to do than polarize ourselves. We do not get anywhere by trading epithets, doomsayer versus doommaker, or charging each other with degrees of elitism. The fatal addictions, whether on one's home lot or one's hemisphere, can be diverted with patience and love, and probably no other way. Before the child in us will give up the lethal toys forged by mindless growth, that child must be offered something else, attractive as well as beneficial.

Our ultimate goal herein is to find an alternative to the most lethal of the Great Powers' toys and to what led the powers to fashion it — to find that alternative in time. Nuclear proliferation is that deadly toy. Nobody wants it. No leading power has lessened the pressure to use it. The Stockholm International Peace Research Institute has predicted that within nine years thirty-five nations will have the capability of making nuclear weapons and nuclear war will be inevitable. But not if humanity says no. [Revision time: after thirteen years, nine nations apparently have the bomb, the superpowers have fifty thousand or so, and a bright student can make one. There are some forty surrogate wars going on right now, each capable of igniting the big one.]

No, for example, to the export of nuclear reactors, which the United States is encouraging to help a dying industry, perpetuate a myth, and improve a negative balance of payments. This is tantamount to the export of nuclear weapons capability, as Indira Gandhi quickly proved. Adding new refinements to the ways nuclear weapons kill (our neutron bomb and the inevitable Soviet answer to it), devising multilateral alliances that tip an uneasy balance and increase the desperation of anxious rivals, eases no fateful tensions. Pursuing with a Strangelove gleam a radioactive technology that demonstrates its uncontrollability in ever more disconcerting ways helps no one relax. A new danger develops. The worsening prospect produces a fibrillation of will, a sense of futility or of brave acceptance. People who might have sought a way to safety turn back instead. Hope yields to despair. As C. P. Snow admonishes, despair is a sin.

The United States, and we think only the United States, can lead the world back from the nuclear brink to which we led it, with the best of intentions, in the first place. The U.S. can do so, however, only if we step back ourselves and thus persuade other peoples we are to be believed. We are not stepping back, but rushing forward again to get the business before someone else does. [Still tragically true in 1991.]

Nobody needs that business, and those who think they do ought to try to learn a different trade. People can bring about great changes once they construe the difficult problem to be a challenging opportunity. As an example of such public achievement, consider the National Environmental Policy Act (NEPA). It moved the United States from an old danger to a new safety. One of Mr. Nixon's good deeds was to sign it and name Russell Train to oversee it as the first director of the Environmental Protection Agency. NEPA became our finest export.

Environmental victories do not, however, stay won by themselves. They require much vigilance and renewed persuasion. The NEPA victory made many enterprising businessmen so uneasy that they set about trying to weaken it without realizing how important it will be to them in the long run if it is kept strong. The first weakening came when Congress, urged on by the oil companies, left NEPA bleeding after the Alaska pipeline controversy, in which Spiro Agnew broke the tie vote in the Senate the wrong way. NEPA requires strengthening if the environment is to remain whole and productive — a requirement as real for corporations as it is for people. It will pay all segments of society well to look searchingly at the social and environmental consequences of a new proposal to alter a piece of the earth. They should also, as NEPA provides, look as hard at the consequences of a fair range of alternatives designed to serve the broad interest instead of the narrow one.

One alternative, rarely considered, can be "Thanks a lot but forget it," coupled with a list of such benefits as would derive from letting things alone — a list that can sometimes be amazingly long. Another alternative is to consider the advantages of exploiting a given resource later on, or more slowly. Alaska's oil, for instance, could be budgeted to last for the next two or three centuries instead of the next two or three decades. A nation that took from the *Mayflower* until now to get where it is should not rule out, by wiping out, the resources that could get it through another three and a half centuries. Our consideration could well extend to a far-distant future and spare our heirs the need to isolate the nuclear radioactivity generated for our convenience. If Iodine 129 had been so isolated three hundred million years ago at the bottom of the Redwall Limestone formation in the Grand Canyon, it would be safe about now to let it touch living things whose genes should be left intact. It would be fair to do for our genes what our genes have done for us. That way we would not tinker with them. We would revere the miracle in them instead.

Such reverence could let us learn from history, especially from recent, telling history in Alaska. There is a poignant moral in that history, as we in FOE, having been involved in it since we began, can testify. Sadly, we predicted present consequences all too well in our books *Earth and the Great Weather: The Brooks Range* (1971) and *Cry Crisis! Rehearsal in Alaska* (1974). It is useful to remember the things lost to Alaskans and to all others because, while too many citizens were preoccupied, Congress relaxed its own judgment and ruled out the court's opportunity to check the administrators. This brought a host of evils upon us. Alaska's last remaining wilderness can belong to all the generations we can conceive of — people who will need wildness in their civilization. It has been split into lesser pieces. Its greatness cannot now be put back together by any number of generations. Its wildness pours out through the wounds, and the skin shrinks back. Your children may not miss what is gone. Like a fully unraveled sweater, what is gone leaves no trace. We cannot measure our own success proudly if it consists of a growing number of things our children will never be allowed to miss.

The unraveling of the Earth's heritage of resources can be stopped, we think, by the attitudes and steps our contributors espouse here. People do not have to go on being profligate with resources that are not to be renewed. We can drop out of the lead in the race to see who can make the Earth less livable fastest. We would then have a chance to persuade the Soviets and Japan, or other contenders, to think the old race is not worth the trouble.

Ours was quite a binge. We were not alone in it. The earth's people can still escape the tensions that continuation of the binge will intensify, tensions that threaten the survival of all we or anyone else care about most. We cannot escape by forging on, resolutely and regardless, driven by the unmitigated inertia of outworn habits, until we have forced ourselves over the brink in the giant step for mankind no one needs. When you have reached the edge of an abyss, Alwyn Rhys said in Wales, the only progressive move you can make is to step backward. Or turn around, and step forward. Progress, if survival matters, can then become a process that lets people find more joy at less cost to their children and to the earth.

We might even aim at something better than mere survival. As Ivan Illich observes, survival can take place in jail. We can instead seek the steps toward, and rewards of, applying conservation conscience to many fields of human activity. There is still an opportunity to treat the earth as if we knew we ought to do this, and we have told ourselves that this book will help discover how. So, take it from here, please. Tell us about the gaps that you would like to see us try to fill in the next edition.

What kind of country do you want? What kind of world? More of the old Preempt-the-Resources Game? Or one fulfilling the hope Adlai Stevenson crystallized in Geneva, July 1965, in his last speech:

We travel together, passengers on a little spaceship,
dependent upon its vulnerable reserves of air and soil;
all committed for our safety to its security and peace;
preserved from annihilation only by the care, the work
and, I will say, the love we give our fragile craft.
We cannot maintain it half fortunate, half miserable,
half confident, half despairing,
half slave to the ancient enemies of man,
half free in a liberation of resources
undreamed of until this day.
No craft, no crew can travel safely
with such vast contradictions.
On their resolution depends the survival of us all.

The resources that can be liberated without being exhausted are human spirit and love. They can bring the resolution. You can effect the decision. You have the gift. You can pass it on.

DAVID R. BROWER, President
Friends of the Earth
September 4, 1977

The first edition of *Progress* was priced at $8.95 and we sold twenty thousand copies. There were 320 pages and nineteen contributors. The next edition, published in 1981, contained 456 pages, had thirty-five contributors, and was no thicker — more information per pound of pulp. The price went up to $14.95 and the distribution dropped to ten thousand. It lost money, was worth it, and deserved better.

There was double jeopardy for those who bought it: it included my old foreword, and added a new one:

———

FRIENDS OF THE EARTH and the League of Conservation Voters, initially part of FOE, were founded in 1969 in order to augment programs in conservation publishing, political action, legislative lobbying, litigation, and international environmental efforts that were initiated in the course of my seventeen years as executive director of the Sierra Club. FOE now has nearly 25,000 members in the United States and 175,000 in its sister organizations in twenty-six other countries. We work as closely as we can with senior and junior organizations in all twenty-seven. We are pleased to have had a major hand in forming the Environmental Liaison Center in Nairobi, which brings some fifteen hundred citizen organizations into an environmental network with the United Nations Environment Programme.

Energy, and the social and environmental effects of the search for energy and of its development and use, is one of the predominant concerns of our multi-national enterprise, as well as of the Friends of the Earth Foundation and the Foundation's International Project for Soft Energy Paths. Soft paths are Amory Lovins's idea, which FOE has been fortunate to be able to contribute to and help promote: soft energy paths would supply all the energy industrialized and developing societies need, using renewable energy primarily, fossil fuels transitionally, and nuclear power not at all. It is one of the solid routes toward world peace. There needs to be much more attention paid to it by environmental organizations — indeed, by all institutions that care about the future.

There isn't enough concern yet. In the debate between John Anderson and Ronald Reagan on September 21, 1980, Mr. Anderson singled out three important problems before the country that until that moment had not been considered in their debate; the danger of atomic war, a policy for using the world's natural resources, and nationalism. Those problems were but feebly considered in the campaign as a whole. Energy is deeply involved in each of the three.

National energy policy has been, for the past decade at least, a policy of strength through exhaustion. Both major parties are in a contest to see which can achieve exhaustion faster.

Our national nuclear-energy policy is leading directly toward nuclear war and is recklessly fostering the illusion that there can be a limited nuclear war that won't hurt anybody very much, or at least won't hurt buildings very much. This is a race to oblivion that nobody needs.

Our national policy for the world's resources is to use them up as fast as they can be found, insisting that our 5 percent of the world's population is entitled to one-third of the world's resources. We threaten those who disagree, and then are a little perplexed that many countries are beginning to think that they cannot afford the U.S. any more.

Our national policy on nationalism, in a shrinking world that can afford less and less of it, is directly out of Robert Ringer, advocate of taking care of Number One and winning through intimidation. Intimidation is no longer what it once was, before terrorism and taking hostages came into vogue.

We have eight suggestions about energy and ecosystems:

1. The national energy goal needs a new look. Expecting renewable energy to provide only one-fifth of our energy budget by the year 2000 is too conservative. The nation is ready, we think, to try harder.

2. If the nuclear investment continues to be so excessively high, we will not persuade less-developed countries that we are serious when we try to persuade them to move to soft energy. The best salesmen are those who use the product themselves. If we don't persuade these countries, the threat of nuclear proliferation will accelerate and get out of hand, and the danger that the world will stumble into nuclear war, even if it doesn't mean to, becomes unacceptably high.

3. If we continue even our present excessive use of irreplaceable fossil fuels — much less increase that use as our present synfuel excitement would have us do — we endanger the air we breathe, the crops we eat, and the shores we love. The danger is not just from global changes in climate, or from acid rain and snow, but also from the toxic metals fossil fuels release which the earth's life-support system cannot handle. Small cars are not a panacea, even if they get one hundred miles per gallon. Ecosystems can be destroyed as surely by being overrun by mice as they can be by being overrun by rats. Cars, small and big, produce particulate emissions, including rubber, asbestos, and metals. And pavement grows where food ought to.

4. We need to moderate our love affair with the car. It will not be easy. (This I know directly; there was only one of the twelve cars I have owned that I did not love, together with the places they took my family and me.) We are still, too many of us, no more logical than the Vancouver car dealer who defended the big cars he sells by saying, "Why not? The Cadillacs and Rabbits are all going to run out of gas together."

5. Considering the liquid-fuel problem, we should require the Army Corps of Engineers and the Department of Energy to put the trains back on the track (put the tracks back first). We dare not wait too

long. The rescue will require energy. The energy budgeted for the disastrous MX missile proposal could get the trains well under way and add to national security instead of diminishing it.

6. Before going too far on gasohol, we need careful research about just how much energy can be siphoned away from the earth's biomass without *(a)* taking food away from people who cannot outbid big-car owners for it, and *(b)* crippling the essential recycling of nutrients. Energy is needed to fuel "the slow, smokeless fires of decay" which keep the soil alive. We should look harder at what is happening to soil, the most important energy converter of all. If you count food and fiber, which most of us still use, more than half the nation's present energy is solar, much of it filtered through plants. We daily dispose of an unconscionable amount of what it takes to support the photosynthesis that lets us live on this planet. Soil is not old-fashioned. It is essential. Yet we blow it away, wash it away, pave it over, compact it, and strew it with hazardous wastes and witches' brews. We can no longer dare to destroy three million acres per year of our best agricultural soil, and who knows how much more of our forest soils.

7. Remember how much too often the free market has given us its message too late. Ask the passenger pigeon. Ask Detroit. Politically popular though it has been to bad-mouth government, it is still true that government of and by the people still speaks best for the people. For all Madison Avenue's skills, corporations don't yet quite do as well for the people, and probably won't until it is as easy for them to look into the distant future as it is for them to look at the next quarter's bottom line.

8. There clearly are limits to growth. Some new growth must go on, of course. And some old growth must make way. The *Global 2000 Report to the President* (July 1980) makes this limit seem frighteningly imminent. In its hundreds of pages it documents what a recent Acid Rain Conference was told: "If all the world's a stage, this must be the Gong Show."

Energy and War; Conservation and Peace

Amory Lovins has made an unequaled and much celebrated contribution toward identifying and fostering the kind of growth that will preserve humanity rather than endanger it. In the book *Energy/War: Breaking the Nuclear Link,* he points out the hazards of the once-bright nuclear hope and, more clearly than anyone, how inevitably the peaceful atom (which we cannot afford) serves as cover for the warring atom (which life cannot afford). It is a book that cannot be ignored by anyone who cares for the Northern Hemisphere. After you read it, put your own genius to work on the most important of all issues — ending the race to blow ourselves up. There is no more critical time to think clearly

157

than when it is hardest to do so, like now. We need clear thought like Richard Barnet's: "No nation can increase its security by lessening the security of its opponent." The great powers are doing that to each other, to all others, and to us.

Because the U.S. has chosen to emphasize nuclear, not conventional, weapons, the temptation is to rely on nuclear threats, and such threats are increasing, in spite of the well-buttressed thesis that a "limited" nuclear war would swiftly escalate to a full nuclear exchange. That full exchange would initially and quickly cost the lives of about a half billion men, women, and children. Almost no living thing would survive the protracted consequence — to the ozone barrier, for example. Damage to it would peak a year after the exchange and let ultraviolet radiation blister people exposed forty minutes to the sun. It would preclude the growth of crops. (This projection of partial-nuclear-exchange consequences was given us in a Department of State briefing urging environmentalist support of SALT II.)

FOE has sought in several ways to obviate nuclear proliferation and the final war, lest all other environmental concerns become academic. We began with our 1970 Vietnam advertisement, "Ecology and War." We have repeatedly warned about the consequences of the U.S. compulsion to have the grossest national product of all. We have put together our *ECO* (our nomad newspaper that travels to many international conferences of importance, including the UN Conference on Disarmament in New York). In the course of all this we exploited Amory Lovins as his ideas developed — in *World Energy Strategies,* in *Non-Nuclear Futures,* in *Soft Energy Paths,* in *Energy/War,* and in *Brittle Power.*

All these books firm up the tread on his soft energy path. They recognize that the nuclear genie is out of the bottle and out of control, but that he can be starved if the U.S. is willing to use its strength wisely, at home and abroad. Using the soft path, the U.S. can back away from nuclear power and nuclear weapons; we can also budget nonrenewable resources, and recycle them again and again; we can mitigate global inequity. In the process, we can use science and technology better, decentralize more and soon enough, spare the environment, make jobs, defuse inflation by making money available for social needs now given short shrift (conservation, education, health, housing, transportation) in our strange infatuation with kilowatts and killer weapons.

Aware of this new route, we can move toward acceptable, sustainable strategies that can spare the Earth the thousands of new Dachaus and Hiroshimas that are otherwise too imminent. The U.S. can pioneer in ending the export of nuclear technology to nations shakier than our own by foregoing it here. We have let the atom become our Maginot Line, and we will not correct that unforeseen error with more reactors and the MX Missile.

Each of us represents total success in the miraculous passing forward of the essential information of life, from its inception on earth some three and a half billion years ago. A tiny bit of each of us now alive is that old, old enough to handle our most important heritage, life, better than we do. That experience, in each of us, is what we now need as never before. Until the superpowers show restraint and back off, they hold the world hostage. The promise inherent in each newborn child is also held hostage.

Getting from Here to 2001

When you next encounter a child, remember that you are meeting a citizen of tomorrow, who, when grown, will be every bit as important as you are now. Wonder for a moment what the child's future will be. Then imagine a world — before the child is ready to vote — with these handicaps, even if nuclear war is prevented:

• Six billion people on an earth already overburdened by four billion.

• Two million fewer species of plants and animals, freshly extinct, thanks to rapacity in our time.

• One billion children, not just today's half billion, too poorly fed owing to overpopulation to use the genius they were born with.

• Twice the chance to contract cancer, because we have poisoned the earth with a technology that raced ahead of reason.

• Too many other handicaps as well, a depressing list of them, man-caused.

These imaginings are not just fantasy. They are based on the best projections our government, after three years' hard work, could come up with, in the *Global 2000 Report.* These dire events will come to pass unless you join the effort to head these tragedies off at the pass; unless you are willing to accept fewer of today's conveniences and persuade others to do the same, so that this child can have tomorrow's necessities; unless you resolve that this child deserves a chance to know a world no less beautiful, no less livable, no less joyful than ours is; unless you say that the world must be better, with more friends of the only earth we'll ever know, and of all the children we'll never know.

If their survival matters, we need a new kind of progress. *Progress As If Survival Mattered* appeared in 1977, a few months into the Carter years. Since then the U.S. has had three further years of Jimmy Carter as president, the election of Ronald Reagan, and almost a year of his presidency; the rise of the New Right, the Moral Majority, and Roth-Kemp economics; Mr. Reagan's appointment of James Watt to the most important environmental office in the world, and a huge outpouring of

159

public protest over that choice. The exploiters' lawyer has been named, as Secretary of the Interior, to guard our nation's parks, wilderness, wildlife, public lands, and dwindling and precious minerals, oil, coal, and soil from these same exploiters. The Strength-through-Exhaustion Department is now administered by people who would seem to require that resources be exhausted before the Second Coming.

The Carter years brought much good. Best of all was the unprecedented achievement in Alaska. They also brought us the *Global 2000 Report,* the projections in which make a new edition of *Progress* vital to environmentalism in the Reagan years. The last few years have brought new diversity to the environmental movement. Professional environmental skills were vigorously sought out by the Carter administration, and influenced early decisions in the State Department, Justice, Interior, Agriculture, the Environmental Protection Agency, and congressional-committee decisions as well. This influence unfortunately was badly eroded as the Carter administration succumbed to the old pressures and went sadly wrong on Tellico Dam, energy policy, Presidential Directive 59 (which added to the insecurity of the superpowers), and the MX Missile (which promises to do the same).

In this new edition, we have written new chapters, thoroughly revised others, added new readings not only from classic literature, but also from recent writing (in which the Worldwatch Institute's contributions have been outstanding).

Here, then, is *Progress* for the Reagan years, to help you get to 1984. While his predecessor was in office, people and organizations interested in conservation had access — a favorite word — to the White House, if not necessarily having power there. People left our staff and that of organizations like ours to work in government. Many of them have now been fired by the Reagan administration, and it is the people who are intent on undoing environmental progress who have the access now. As Jeffrey Knight wrote in *The New Environmental Handbook* (FOE, 1980), now is the time for good environmentalists to come to the aid of the earth by going back to the grassroots, renewing their spirit and reëstablishing their leadership through their love for particular places. People who do not find the Grand Canyon "tedious," as Mr. Watt did, can campaign again, refreshed, to give earth a chance. Opportunity still knocks.

The ill wind of the Reagan administration's attack on public welfare, arms limitation, landscape, and resources has blown some good. People all over the country — all over the world — are acutely aware of what these plans mean for themselves and their communities. Their favorite beach may be despoiled with spilled crude, the park they have worked twenty years to get established may be sold off, the open field where their children play may be covered with new sprawl, or a new

160

factory, or a military dump. Their clean air may be traded off for Detroit's convenience, their protection from hazardous wastes for chemical-industry profits, their prospects of peace for nuclear threats.

People are outraged. At this writing conservationists have gathered a million signatures asking for Mr. Watt's resignation and a reconsideration of the Reagan energy and environmental policies. New groups are forming to protest the arms buildup by the superpowers, the ultimate environmental threat. People are joining environmental groups at the rate they did in the late 1960s and early 1970s; the Sierra Club has gone above 223,000 and National Audubon above 450,000. FOE is growing too, and has been augmented by a FOEPAC, a political action committee to serve its members better in elections to come. With a government so unsympathetic to solving or even considering their needs, people are mobilizing themselves, organizing, building coalitions, joining organizations like ours to fight for their rights, their needs, and their visions for the future. It is up to our allies and FOE to help lead these people, to give point to their alienation and voice to their needs. And we intend to do it.

An old land ethic needs to be rediscovered. Its base is our knowing that we are but brief tenants. We are privileged to enjoy the good things that were left here by predecessors who treated the land as if they trusted us to love it. Those we leave it to are owed the same opportunity: an America as beautiful as ours. A whole world as beautiful.

We can be grateful for the variety of ways that ingenious people have created to save places for themselves and their descendants — special places where what counts is the miraculous interplay of the wild living things that were there, have been spared, and are still there. In humanity's earliest days, such places were safe because people did not yet have the tools to spoil them. Later, when the tools had arrived, places were saved by taboo, or set aside for worship, for kings to hunt in, or for people to be buried in. Some places, of course, were spared by their remoteness or by their hazards, real or imagined. Finally, places were saved by a means that must now be applied with new dedication: the will to share the Earth with living things other than ourselves. And shared, too, by the largest human population of all — the people who have yet to arrive on the planet, but whose genes are here now, in our custody.

David R. Brower, Founder
Friends of the Earth
August 14, 1981

Ten years have gone by. The past is prologue.

161

Dave with Anne Kathryn Olsen in 1989.

The need is not really for more brains.
The need is for a gentler, more tolerant people
than won for us against
the ice, the tiger, and the bear.

The hand that hefted the axe,
out of some blind old allegiance to the past,
now fondles the machine gun as lovingly.
It is a habit men must break to survive,
but the roots go very deep.

Loren Eiseley

CHAPTER 10

NEW PARTY TIME

T HE POLITICAL DECISION-MAKING PROCESS is now in bad repair. We find ourselves confronted with unprecedented human dilemmas and equipped with models for solving them that guarantee old answers to new problems. In the past, situations like this have brought forth new political parties. Elsewhere, Green parties are emerging. For many years I felt that a U.S. Green party would be a spoiler, taking votes primarily from the Democrats, whose environmental record is overwhelmingly, if regretfully, better, thus assuring the worst. I often counterproposed two Green parties, light (liberal) and dark (less so). People were amused, but no one did anything about it, including me.

But I can count. Add up the independents, the disenchanted, and the disillusioned regulars, and you have enough people who want change to save us.

1. Establish the Equity Party

So reversing my own long-held belief, I think it is time for a new party to happen again, a new one that can, without malice or recrimination, pick up the best of what has been achieved and use it with long overdue new ideas. It can accommodate the habits learned on a half-empty Earth to the opportunities now faced, to adjusting American thinking to fit it to a very clearly limited and overused earth. The new party would have Adlai Stevenson's and Loren Eiseley's paragraphs to pledge allegiance to as the basis of all policy, the guiding inspiration for building the quest for equity back into human affairs.

It could be called the Equity party to accommodate greenness and justice. I'm not stuck on the name. All nations who have not already moved in that direction could try it too. The party would have a sound environmental foundation, realizing full well that no party can live on a dead planet, and knowing full well what unsustainable demands a century of the New Satiety has placed upon a finite earth.

The Equity party would also realize that the way to reduce tensions between neighborhoods and nations is to try to eliminate the

163

indignity of the stomach empty of food and the life empty of hope. The party would concentrate on the transition to jobs that heal the earth instead of further tearing it apart, on new goals dependent upon expanding individuals, not the glut of the energy-intensive things they collect but can never take with him.

The Equity party would realize that the old spendthrift goal is finished. The time has passed for anyone to say, "I'll take the easy trip and charge it to the kids."

Such an approach, whether directed by a new party or by the incumbent party, would lead in an opposite direction from the kind of decadent, corrupt corporate and government habits that are leading us into a terminal illness for humanity — indeed, to the Dark Ages by 1984, according to one of the nation's most brilliant scientists in his least optimistic, but not unlikely scenario (Paul R. Ehrlich, in his book *The End of Affluence: A Blueprint for Your Future)*. [People who try to make predictions often fail to recognize how fast the years go by. We are now indeed in a dark age, but too many leaders insulate themselves from the symptoms and too may followers vacuously give consent.]

The Equity party may never need hold office if its new renaissance should reform the tired old parties in time. Each party has had a birth date, and most have had death dates. Some may indeed already be dead without knowing it. There is surely evidence of this in some polls, and in the number of leaders unable to end their unfortunate addictions to concepts of limitlessness.

Whatever it takes to break bad habits — competition from a new party or stimulation by the reawakened within old parties — there are bad habits crying to be broken, and the energy business has more than its share. In the further recommendations that follow, we invite the cooperation of all minorities, including the corporate leaders whose organizational and administrative qualities are essential to the change but who cannot bring it off alone. Some humility is in order. We all have to keep traveling together on this ship, and if there aren't too many of us, we can all have reserved seats.

2. An Investigation of Full or Partial Public Control of Energy

If sacrifices are to be asked — and we think they should be — industry should share in the sacrifice, and especially the energy industry. Its manipulation of prices and resources has contributed substantially to our current inflation and threatened depression. A 73-percent increase in profits cannot be termed a sacrifice.

Oil-price manipulation over the past six years has brought the word "nationalization" to the fore more and more frequently. The very word causes instant polarization, so "public control" is a better term to describe the public's wish to have its government back, to try to run it better than the corporations do. Opponents of public control cite what's wrong with nationalized mail service and nationalized TVAs. Proponents could cite Penn Central, Lockheed, several airlines, and Rolls Royce, not to mention the world's biggest public utility being forced to run to its state government for money. Can we foresee anything better for an oil industry that is trying so hard to accelerate the using up of the world's oil allowance? A Kuwait oilman once asked me, "Why not hurry to use up the oil, and thus end the problem of oil pollution?" That now seems to be oil company (and U.S.) policy. It threatens the future's oil and the present generation's capital in the process.

The polls say repeatedly that the public has lost faith, for all the industry's expensive public-relations blitz, in the industry's ability to conserve, develop, and manage the oil resource for any purpose but the industry's short-term benefit. The public has also lost faith in an administration that enlisted major contributions from oil for the reëlection of a president. The public is not reassured when a political contribution of $100,000 is illegally asked and is illegally received, and when Gulf Oil is thereupon fined only $5,000 for violating the Corrupt Practices Act, thus bringing Gulf's total contribution to the government up to $105,000.

In *The Last Play* (Dutton), James Ridgeway made a strong case for the nationalization of oil. Our own new book, *Cry Crisis! Rehearsal in Alaska* is a case study of what government by oil should not be allowed to do to Alaska and to the Earth. Noel Mostert's revelations about the environmental outrage of oil company supertankers (the *New Yorker,* and also a Book of the Month Club selection in November 1974) should be as frightening a warning to the public as was Rachel Carson's *Silent Spring.*

Moreover, the oil industry is deeply involved in promoting and investing in a further and still more serious environmental threat, atomic energy from fission. We have just published two books exposing the charade of AEC safety hearings and the hazards of the entire nuclear fuel cycle. We will follow with a fourth, *World Energy Strategies,* already serialized in the *Bulletin of the Atomic Scientists.* The book will provide an excellent overview of the need for, and the absence of, energy policy, not only in the U.S., but also in the world as a whole. We think that its factual presentation will make clear that oil-cartel power must be redirected or controlled.

These and other publications, including Wilson Clark's *Energy for Survival,* combined with the daily news, reveal the widespread failure to understand the ecological consequences of that news. We urge a bold step. Bold steps can carry the unwary over brinks, and that is not what we have in mind. What the U.S. does need is an immediate analysis of the consequences, in short range and long, of greatly increased public control of energy. An investigation is needed to determine how public control, in whole or in part, can proceed. It should be a congressional investigation, but there is a question whether Congress is yet free enough of oil domination to conduct it adequately alone.

The Costs and Benefits of Control

We suggest the following questions for the investigation, and further suggest that it be multidisciplinary and that a parallel investigation be multifoundation-funded and free to call the shots as it sees them:

1) Is humanity served best by a public or a private role in:

(a) conducting and applying energy research,

(b) providing capital for exploration and production,

(c) the operation of shipping and marketing, including controls of the rate of use?

2) To what extent could private industry, in spite of its recent record but under revitalized regulation, assume responsibility for various proportions of elements a, b, and c above, so that private and public sectors could keep watch over each other's performance?

3) How should the administering energy agency be structured to avoid being dangerously monolithic and to include private-industry participation in policy and management, but with participation limited, as it now is not, so as to ensure that public interest be paramount?

4) Over how long a period should the increased public management be sustained to break the continuity of the power relations and leadership that has brought the world to its present crisis?

5) In what proportion should the revenue to the government be allocated to:

(a) compensate private management and shareholders,

(b) develop and apply alternatives for energy and equity with primary emphasis on conservation and on transition back to solar energy sources to power the safe progress of civilization,

(c) provide financial aid for Alaska pending review of the present move to drain and export Alaska oil resources, and

(d) substitute a carefully thought out master plan for Alaska that would benefit not just residents and entrepreneurs in Alaska, but also the rest of the country and its friends?

6) What would the likely consequences of such action be, projected to the years 2001, and 2076, compared with the likely consequences of proceeding with the present absence of policy? Specific elements to be compared would include:

(a) energy resource inventories,

(b) other resource inventories, organic and inorganic,

(c) international tension,

(d) prices of key resources, arrived at with energy accounting, and

(e) standards of living, but not standards of using, in the U.S. and other nations.

7) How can the investigation incorporate world model computer studies to encompass the U.S. as well as other nations, e.g., those using less energy per capita than now expended by the U.S.

The foregoing proposals are sweeping, if general. We think an approach of this magnitude is essential if there is to be an adequate reduction in demographic drain globally and if there is to be a more equitable distribution of resources and a consequent reduction of tension and inflation. We think the transition to a lower level of attack on resources would be orderly. We believe the lack of it will not be. The transition should require the kind of leadership and cooperation the U.S. demonstrated well in going into World War II — and in coming out of it.

The peril to humanity is quite severe enough to require this order of effort and to promise that such an effort with fresh approaches fully cognizant of humanity's need for a future will succeed in keeping systems, institutions, and peoples intact.

This country has quadrupled its energy use in half a century and doubled it in a quarter of a century. In the next quarter it should be able to cut that use in half by modifying personal and national goals. By doing so we can give a decent break to subsequent generations, in which there will also be people who need resources, including energy. This kind of long-range thinking has been unhappily absent from almost all public and editorial utterances, and cannot remain so. The public can, and ought to, perfect and finance the few institutions there are for protecting society's future. The public can require that corporations give commensurate consideration to future shareholders of the earth as well as to present stockholders of the company. Laws can be changed to provide for this. The alternative is severe economic and ecological disruption, and little chance for lasting peace anywhere.

Preeminent among energy alternatives is the sun, which has successfully driven the earth's energy systems for four billion years and is not, as some oil company ads suggest, an as yet unproved device. The AEC's study of solar potential shows a promise which, if combined with the totally feasible energy conservation steps suggested by environmentalists, engineers, and poets, can enable the U.S. to get back to living on energy income (the sun's daily ration) by the year 2000, whereupon our standard of living would fall somewhere between that now present in the U.K. and in France.

New evaluations of data suggest that there is little likelihood of population growth anything like the doubling that many demographers have been predicting, and great likelihood of severe reduction of population, solely through the limits of the earth's potential for producing food

167

on a sustained basis. A reasonable look at the pros and cons of Growth as recently practiced should discourage the commitment of major investment of capital to the guess that such growth will go on. A reevaluation of present fossil energy development schemes is thus in order.

The recommendations herein are, we believe, consonant with data about environmental limits that cannot continue to be ignored. These data can lead to decisions that will let people stay aboard our fragile craft. We recommend this effort.

Not Man Apart, mid-November 1974

Asked nearly seventeen years later whether I still support public control of the oil industry this strongly, and with Exxon's arrogance still in the news, I can only say that I prefer public control of the oil industry to oil-industry control of the public, and I am about ready — as I suspect the public is — to move on to the insurance industry.

An Equity party may not wish to be so severe, or need to if the erring industries would support legal reforms permitting them to serve the long-range public interest better, such as allowing a corporation to bypass an opportunity for profit for sound social and ecological reasons, without being sued by stockholders, or requiring environmental impact statements covering new offerings or takeover attempts.

LETTER TO A POLITICAL LEADER

SIX FEET EIGHT is a good height for a stand-out leader of a new political party, and that is how high Tom Stokes rises above sea level, or above whatever he is standing on. We had long talks at lunches and in Village bars while he was the chief New York staff of the tax-deductible Friends of the Earth Foundation. He had radio experience, had helped block the disaster the proposed new freeway on the West Side would be, and his face looked the way Abraham Lincoln's must have when he just came in from splitting wood. Tom wanted to run for office.

I have nothing but admiration for the courage of the people willing to run for office, even those I disagree with. I didn't disagree with Tom. I was, however, beginning to have misgivings about what a third party would achieve in the United States in the present way we vote to give the winner everything and send very competent runners-up out to pasture. The misgivings would take shape later, when I saw, in the New York race for the United States Senate, the two best candidates split the vote, thus letting the poorest become a senator. I would think harder about how to overcome that problem later (that is, I fully intend to).

Meanwhile I was pleased on August 20, 1976, to support what Tom Stokes wanted to try — start a new political party and run for office in it. Even now I would not object if members of our two major political parties would heed it:

Dear Friends:

America's two leading political parties, while they are the best we have developed so far, are disappointing more and more Americans. Tom Stokes is trying to do something about it, and I wish you would try to help him.

The aging parties seem to have rewritten the last two lines of a most familiar four:

Mother may I go out for a swim?
Yes, my darling daughter.
But never, my dear, go out on a limb,
Whatever you do in the water.

Especially an environmental limb. It is as if threats to the one thing you and I cannot live without — the global environment — would go away if each political office seeker would simply ignore those threats.

If Republican and Democratic candidates would face up to them instead of offering the environment to the highest special-interest bidder offering the coziest trade-off, something new would happen. For one thing, there would be a rapid drop-off in the number of voters who, if they register at all, register "independent."

Any citizen of any country, given time for serious thought, will realize that there will be no political party at all on a dead planet. None will be needed to administer an absent humanity. And certainly no citizen needs forty assistants and a Herman Kahn Institute-on-the-Hudson to rationalize that the planet is in no trouble. Any two of one's five senses will make perfectly clear, with a modicum of consecutive thinking, the various alarm signals that are ringing and flashing, whatever the herman kahns of the world may try to do to short-circuit the alarms.

Concerned citizens in many lands are searching for an alternative in politics, an intermediate between the calculated indifference shown by candidates to the Earth's requirements and the hopelessness felt by citizens as the predicament of humanity worsens. Worsen it does — in the home, in the working place, in the streets, and in the outdoors that once made America a beautiful place to live and bring children into.

At least one political party now seems to be dying without knowing it, and the other is developing strange symptoms.

It will not be easy to revise the operative guidelines of politics that force candidates into being amorphous on issues: The less said that any voter could disagree with, the less likely the loss of a vote. You don't get elected with lost votes. Therefore lead from the middle, the safe middle. Fight for the center. Do you remember Shakespeare's lines?

> *Out of this nettle, danger,*
> *We pluck this flower, safety.*

Well, forget them. Expose your position as little as possible and conserve votes. Leave all other aspects of conservation to someone else.

Quite a few people have been thinking about these guidelines to global disaster for some time, intending to do something about them some day.

Tom Stokes has decided to start now, and to see what comes of it. He has learned about great oaks and little acorns, and he has decided that now is the time to plant. I think now is the time for all good men, and the good other 55 percent of humanity, to come to the aid of his planting party. The Renaissance came from people who made the move toward change. The earth is crying for a new renaissance — transition to a human society that is sustainable as a substitute for one that prospers by rushing into its children's resources and wasting them.

Can you add your voice to ours, in your way if not quite in our way?

We want to take a chance for the earth.

We would rather try to be right even if we thereupon harm our chance of being elected.

If there are to be more elections, they had better offer better options, better because we start defining them now.

Perhaps we are a little like bees. To protect their society, as everyone who has learned about bees must know, the worker bee is willing to sting, even though this act is fatal to the specific worker. Merely to hurt, and thus to help protect, the worker bee must die. But few do die. Widely publicized knowledge of how a sting feels makes the sacrifice unnecessary.

The analogy is, like all analogies, a bit too simple, but it helps. If there is to be a sting in what we have to say, it can be viewed as a sharp, friendly warning. It isn't fatal to the new-renaissance party. Its founders will still be around, even if not elected. They will have used the political system for what it was intended to serve — creating, airing, and perfecting ideas so that society can progress in a real sense.

Would you like to be a founder? What is being started, I submit, is politically feasible (in due course) because survival of all we hold dear requires that it be feasible. Humanity, so far, has always managed to come up with the right answer when it has to. We wouldn't want the finish to be too close, and as someone said, if the tree will take a long time to grow, we are already late in planting it.

Tom did not succeed, but I think the arguments in favor of his effort are still sound, and are reflected in the agenda of the U.S. Greens, and indeed improved on there. Perhaps Tom should try again.

I am quite willing to suggest some amendments to the green agenda. It should require that they have more compassion for each other, that they not require the lowest common denominator of consensus, that they accept a bit of hierarchy now and then (old mountaineers know that a leader is essential, cannot lead from the middle or below, and needs to change often enough), and they should not violate Rule 6 so often. (Rule 6. Never take yourself too seriously. The other rules? There are no other rules.)

On Pete Seeger's boat, the Clearwater. Dave Brower is in the center rear. Tom Stokes is in the beard beneath the rigging.

Television interview at Tilden Park in the Berkeley hills, 1990.

Chapter 11

ENERGY, ATOM, AND THE SOFT PATH

———

S O MANY OF MY SPEECHES have included this statement that it must be true: in my fifty years in the conservation business, most of the damage I have seen has come from the mad dash for more energy or the stupid things we did with the power it gave us. As a handy example, we built an oil pipeline across Alaska so that we could have the Exxon oil spill.

Back in 1975 Amory Lovins, who, since 1971, has taught me almost everything I know about energy, calculated that there were twelve energy slaves per person worldwide. That was the per capita equivalent of our use of energy then. The global population, free and slave, then totaled fifty billion, one-third of it in the United States.

The intervening years have not lessened the numbers, the inequity, or the damage. The search for energy has produced mines, drilling, dams, roads, generators, power lines, deforestation, reservoirs, incinerators, radon daughters (from mining for nuclear fuel), and associated environmental and human plagues. We have shared the damage, if not the energy. What our energy slaves have done with it has given us acid rain, global warming, holes in the ozone barrier, too much pavement, gridlock, and toxic materials neither people nor the earth can handle. Energy slaves in the industrialized countries have busily borrowed against the future's standard of living for everyone to fuel the present standard of using for the favored few — us.

Worse, the effort to expand energy slavery, to dominate the world's store of it, is a major motivation for war — preëmptive war if necessary, because war itself has become so dependent on energy. The kind of energy that is free of this threat is the very energy that has safely fueled the earth for its four and a half billion years, the flow of energy from that great fusion reactor in the sky, the sun.

I never really liked dams, and was once willing to seize any alternative to the hydroelectric energy they could produce as they processed the flowing water that solar energy had lifted to the hills. I had high hopes for nuclear energy, but these were finally dashed in 1969 as I began to realize the perils that lay in every stage of the nuclear fuel cycle, from unearthing to re-earthing it. Civilization would surely need an ever-expanding supply of energy, I thought for a while, and was therefore urging greater dependence on coal. By 1978 my thinking was clearer, so much clearer that I still stand by everything I said in the foreword and introduction to a Friends of the Earth book edited by Stephen Lyons, *Sun! A Handbook for the Solar Decade:*

THE PRESENT ERA OF NUCLEAR ROULETTE poses a far greater threat to all living things than the Vietnam war did, because proliferation could stumble us into the final war. The Vietnam war and the subsequent proliferation were triggered by the deepening global addiction to exponential growth in material wants, in energy consumption, and in the buildup of military-industrial strength of the nations competing to secure those wants — to preempt the resources essential for dominance. It is not too late to change course, but it will be too late too soon if too few urge the change.

Vietnam was a stimulus for Earth Day, which worked. Eight years later, the proliferation of reactors and weapons is a stimulus for Sun Day, which will work if enough people recognize its importance. We believe that Sun Day's objectives are important enough to warrant more than one day's attention. We hereby urge the United Nations to declare an International Solar Decade, a ten-year effort to end the nuclear threat and rediscover the sun.

It is rapidly becoming clear that exponential growth of populations and the use of irreplaceable resources can never make sense for long. For example, the current U.S. energy plan calls for a 13.5-percent annual increase in the use of coal. At that rate the U.S. would use up all the world's coal in four decades, having finished off all the world's oil two decades before that. The final half-decade would see the U.S. alone trying to burn up as much as had been used in all previous history. This won't happen, of course. Before the U.S. could achieve this goal, the extra heat would melt the icecaps, the ocean would rise some three hundred feet [one of the numbers being tossed around at that time], and all the most troublesome fossil-fuel-fired flames would be extinguished — in New York, Washington, Brussels, London, Tokyo, Paris, much of Rome, lower San Francisco, and almost all of Los Angeles. To contemplate and lengthen this list is no more ludicrous than is the kind of exponential growth so widely espoused these days, and so infrequently ridiculed. That growth must stop sometime, and it makes sense to stop it while the earth is still livable.

The threat, the alternative, and the urgency are summarized in the following sequences.

1) Exponential growth has led to a destructive race for more and more energy. That race led to nuclear power, the once bright hope, which has turned into the greatest threat to the future — nuclear proliferation, which no one wants.

2) While deploring nuclear proliferation in words, the great powers are racing to exacerbate it.

3) If they succeed, the inevitable war will so damage the world's major civilizations that they can never recover.

4) The U.S., and probably only the U.S., can lead the world back from the nuclear brink to which it led the world with good intentions.

5) Instead of assuming such leadership, the U.S. is pushing reactor sales and, like Russia, getting ever deeper into the nuclear arms race. Both assume that superior sales, armament, and intimidation mean surer security.

6) Each reactor sold to a non-nuclear nation, however, expedites that nation's developing an atomic-weapons capability.

7) Adding to our nuclear capability while denying it to have-not nations won't work. They have reason not to trust the haves. Mistrust and inequity breed sabotage and terrorism.

8) If it is to lead others back from the brink, the U.S. must turn around itself, renouncing nuclear power as the first step; we can do so quickly.

9) Other nations will note, upon analysis, that by moving back also, they can stop wasting themselves on the costly nuclear experiment and invest instead in progress as if survival mattered.

10) Itself freed from the exorbitant cost of going nuclear, the U.S. can allocate resources to the sustainable alternative, derived from the sun's constant gift to the earth. The U.S. and other nations can pursue this alternative at home and abroad to the benefit of all.

11) As its constant gift, the sun sends to earth every few days (estimates range from three to twenty-one) as much energy as there is in all the world's recoverable fossil fuels. The daily gift is stored in rock, water, wind, and living things.

12) The sun has proved its reliability for eons. The nuclear tinkerers cannot prove the same of their gear, and if their tinkering goes on another decade, nothing worth tinkering with is likely to be left.

13) Each day's delay in ending the nuclear experiment makes less likely the chance to put logical solar substitutes in place in time.

14) People are sorely needed now to work the solar side of the street during the next ten years. The opportunity is real, immediate, and not likely to be offered again.

15) The world can then breathe easier. History will admire the brilliance that went into trying to get the atom to work peacefully, but

will admire more the wisdom of choosing not the radioactive, but the sunlit path.

The foregoing points evolved in my own thinking over the past nine years. I have been a conservationist for forty years, twenty-three as a staunch advocate of nuclear power. But I have become a born-again believer in the pleasanter and sustainable solar alternatives. They deserve all the genius we can give them.

Some of the genius is contained in the pages that follow. The rest, we hope, will be elicited and directed by *SUN!;* by Sun Day, the event which occasions the book; and by the International Solar Decade we urge the UN to declare. Declarations made, we may begin the difficult but necessary task of bringing our needs within sustainable limits. Only such an effort, undertaken now, will preserve the planet, and with it humanity.

Limits Under the Sun

One thing the sun will not do is send an exponentially increasing amount of energy our way each year. Although it is actually sending a trifle less each year, it is likely to go on transmitting all we need for several billion years. What happens after that is not our problem.

We can be grateful that the sun's logistics were arranged to provide that one-third of what the earth received be reflected back into interstellar space, lest ours become as uninhabitable a planet as Venus; that a third of that solar energy would vaporize and lift water, which sustains the rivers and soils that supply so much of our energy in food and fiber; that stone and sea and inner space be warmed, and that the solar winds would somehow, though feebly, be echoed in terrestrial winds, bringing and clearing the rain, keeping the pines supple, feeling good on faces, tilting at windmills, and whenever necessary, making waves.

Reverence for the magic that the sun evokes on earth is easy to understand. Yet we have become so enamoured of our technological cleverness that we have almost forgotten what the sun had to do with it, and conjure up such remarks as "Solar energy will not be economically feasible until. . . ." We must rediscover the sun, the energy from which, for those four or so thousand million years, however infeasible it may be, has brought the earth along fairly well. But beware! The River Hubris runs deep.

We can outwit the earth's biosphere by throwing a geometric curve at it — assaulting it in the belief that interminable doubling is good. Russia seems to have gotten the idea first, starting the GNP growth race at the end of World War II. The U.S., not wishing anyone else to have a Grosser National Product, joined the race. Japan won, and now faces the unacceptable cost of victory. Like other not-too-forward-looking nations, such as the U.S., Japan is seeking to cure its growing pains with still more growth, aiming at an annual rate of 8 percent.

How fast does any given growth rate double the demands upon an earth that is not doubling, or upon a sun similarly limited? The easy-to-use number is seventy. Divide it by a growth rate of 8 percent and you get a doubling in nine years. [The way the industrial nations have been operating in their fixation on growth of GNP, that translates into a periodic doubling of the exhaustion of natural resources. Nature abhors a vacuum, such as in the minds of GNP addicts.]

Financial-page writers tend to think this good, customarily liking growth in GNP and not liking to consider or even acronymize National Ultimate Benefit. NUB is just what they are sadly missing. They worry about capital, interest, earnings, losses, inflation, bulls, bears, confidence, and fear, but never or hardly ever about the finiteness of resources. GNP growth of 8 percent isn't happening in the U.S., but wouldn't it be great and strengthen the nation to get it up to that! All too many in this and other lands think so too.

For a moment, then, settle for that growth rate — in GNP, energy generation, telephone calls, traffic waiting to gas up, miles from your garage to your office, distance between you and your sanity. At 8 percent you will need twice as much in 1987 as you have now. Four times as much in 1996. Eight in 2004. When the twenty-first century is sixty-five, one thousand times. Two years before the U.S. celebrates its next centennial and the tall ships sail again, two thousand times as much.

Imagine your grandchildren (or theirs) waking up to two thousand Los Angeleses south of the Tehachapi, extending just beyond where La Paz now is. Nineteen hundred ninety-eight Sundesert reactors clustered in the oasis at Mojave where, it is now alleged, two reactors must be on line in 1985 to avoid stifling the economy and putting people out of work. By the year 2074 California's Governor Edmund G. Brown V will be looking for places to build about twelve more copies of the Peripheral Canal to bring enough water south to all those Los Angeleses — and will probably have to build them offshore.

Soon or not quite so soon, depending upon which exponential growth rate you choose, you end up with the same perplexities: massive overdrafts at the resource bank, overextension of the ability to manage what the debt bought, lessening of the chance to breathe well or at all, diminishing of the sometime joy of living out one's span as the brief tenant each of us is, and extirpation of the hope that our children might fare better than we.

Two questions:

One. Can you find anyone who by 2074 wants even ten Los Angeleses for anyone's grandchildren, or a hundred New York City deficits, or a thousandth as much parking space per car in Paris, or a half-thousandth of the earth's present wild places to serve all those new people who want to get away from it all?

Two. Are any present leaders currently deploring the insistence on the very steps that will produce the foregoing untenable results?

We would like your list of such leaders. We suspect that it will be a short one. We hope *SUN!* and an International Solar Decade, duly decreed by the United Nations, will lengthen that list acceptably.

In our late middle age, when entrepreneurs were trying their best to fill San Francisco Bay, we observed that there ought not be another Los Angeles in a state that deserves only one. Audiences laughed, even in Los Angeles, but didn't quite take the steps to preclude the peripheral Los Angeles that now almost engulfs the first. Both are still, while the oil lasts, operable. New York City, with two centuries's head start, barely is. Detroit hardly fares better, and look what it has done: Count the cities dismembered by its automobiles. Mark how its machines replaced people on farms, foreclosing their chance to live out where night skies still exist. Count the small towns where people's hopes grew so slim that their children left for cities where hopes are slimmer still.

Spring can come to those hopes again, from the sun. The essential limited nonexponential sun.

The Limits to Nuclear Proliferation

Now is the time to move away from the habits humanity got into during the Era of Oil, to avoid the lethal nuclear future the major powers are catapulting the world into. The international race to sell reactors (the U.S. has 60 percent of the business so far) is a race to oblivion unless international nuclear safeguards become real. So far they are a myth, and are likely to remain so. They rely upon treaties that may be abrogated with or without notice, and upon the voluntary and unlikely revelation of state secrets in a still-Balkanized world. "Nuclear safeguards" has such a reassuring ring to it. But what could the minuscule International Atomic Energy Agency's minuscule budget do to protect the global public when the two overwhelmingly largest military budgets were not able to keep a reactor from falling out of the sky on Canada or to know whether it would hit Hawaii or Africa? It is an exaggeration, but not a pointless one, to suggest that the IAEA is too weakly supported to be able to lock the barn door after the horse is stolen, much less before. It is not prudent to expect the impossible. It is prudent to expect that the IAEA cannot begin to prevent a non-nuclear state, once it has been sold a reactor, from making atomic bombs whenever it wishes.

Writing in *International Security,* Clarence D. Long, representative for the Second District of Maryland, member of the U.S. House of

Representatives since 1963, former professor of economics at Johns Hopkins University, and also chairman of the Foreign Operations Subcommittee of the House Appropriations Committee, addressed the nuclear proliferation question and asked if Congress can act in time. He believes that the threat "can scarcely be overstated" and says that "as many as forty countries, typically underdeveloped and unstable, may have nuclear weapons capabilities by 1990."

[A smart student of high-school chemistry has been able to design an atomic bomb that would work. Ted Taylor, atomic scientist, describes that capability well in *The Curve of Binding Energy* by John McPhee. Such a bomb, detonated fifty feet below the reservoir at Hoover Dam, would empty Lake Mead.]

The Stockholm International Peace Research Institute (SIPRI) has predicted that, if such proliferation occurs, nuclear war will be inevitable. The U.S., while proclaiming its wish to enhance human rights and to end proliferation, with President Carter having promised that nuclear power was to be used only as a last resort, is seen to be subsidizing reactors and selling them hard, as if driven to fulfill the SIPRI prediction.

Mr. Long has other worries we should share with all who would like the world to remain intact. Concerned that paranoia caused by nuclear weapons proliferation could compel the U.S. to cover so many bases that the resulting arsenal would have no clear strategic purpose, he continues:

"How could the United States signal in advance its determination to retaliate with unacceptable damage against a nuclear attack if there were no way of identifying the attacker against whom we would then retaliate? Such an attack could be delivered by terrorists or in bombs exploded in ships of false national registry and anchored in our harbors. Indeed, the objective could be to provoke us into nuclear war with the wrong nation."

Another chilling paragraph of Mr. Long's is pertinent here:

"Damage to our own civil liberties could hardly be avoided. National fright typically leads to a huge and pervasive police apparatus. Who can say that our democratic traditions would survive, considering how they have caved in under less pressure in the past?"

Those traditions are in nuclear-caused trouble right now in many countries, we know from Friends of the Earth's sister organizations there. U.S. citizens are probably not aware of the dangers to their own civil liberties — encroachments, we are forced to infer, that could be used for nuclear reactor security — in the powers given to the U.S. Secretary of Energy "to provide for participation of Armed Forces personnel in carrying out functions authorized to be performed" under the act establishing the Department of Energy. Members of the army, navy, and air force may be detailed for service in Secretary Schlesinger's new department pursuant to cooperative agreements. Personnel so detailed may exceed the strength limitations applying to the separate forces; and control of the personnel shifts from the army, navy, or air force to the Secretary of Energy.

U.S. citizens are now still permitted to ask why. Current legislation has provisions that could erode that right. They have, at this writing, been voted by the U.S. Senate, almost unnoticed. With no more public attention, Mr. Schlesinger acquired the right to expand and control elements of the army, navy, and air force. Expressing the foregoing apprehension could become illegal — in one of the few remaining bastions of democracy. Whatever the intent, these moves were made. These moves, and more, can be expected in a world that builds more and more centralized, complicated, hazardous, and vulnerable nuclear power stations. The moves can be avoided, because they are not needed, in a solar economy.

Is the third war after the war to save democracy an inevitable war, as SIPRI fears? "Inevitable? Not if we say no," Garrett Hardin has counseled on another score. Réné Dubos says "Trend is not destiny," and Lord Snow reminds us that "Despair is a sin." Let them be right, and heeded! The consequences of the war SIPRI predicts have been addressed by various writers of scenarios for Armageddon. Harrison Brown, in his chapter "Patterns of the Future" in *The Challenge of Man's Future* (Viking, 1954), was one of the first scenarists: "We are quickly approaching the point where, if machine civilization should, because of some catastrophe, stop functioning, it will probably never again come into existence." He explains that the large resources of high-grade ore and fuels that primitive people could use are exhausted; only an intricately mechanized culture could work with what is left. If this structure is destroyed, civilization has had it. Owing to a vast interdependence — for food, vaccines, antibiotics, hospitals — a forced reversion to agrarian society would result in enormous havoc. He visualizes the atomic war that could force this reversion, but also sees that failure to have alternative energy sources in place in time could result from lack of adequate capital and organization and could also force the reversion to agrarian existence. [Or worse, to hunter-gatherer existence.]

The war to return the world to agrarianism is not inevitable, but nuclear proliferation can make it so. It is well to remember that deeper involvement in Vietnam seemed inevitable, but was stopped. People make wars possible; people got the U.S. out of the tunnel the way it went in. Southeast Asia was not atom-bombed or paved out of existence, as had been suggested. If a war was lost, perhaps a new opportunity can be created that could lead people to flaunt their differences less and accommodate them more.

Opportunities abound for great powers to help small powers find more equity without sacrificing their diversity. Those opportunities will be enhanced, it is our thesis here, not from the 'haves' being more prodigal than ever, disassembling atoms to fuel an accelerating prodigality, but by accomplishing all they can to cease 'wasting their substance in riotous living.' Webster tells us that this is only one of the meanings of prodigality, the one made familiar by the biblical story of the prodigal son. The other meaning more aptly describes the father in the story: 'profusely liberal, giving or yielding abundantly, luxuriant.' Like father, like sun. The sun's prodigality is one we can return to and live with.

Some lands do not have to return. They already know how sustaining the sun can be, and will not forget if they resist the siren song tempting them from solar sea to nuclear rocks. People in those lands are the more fortunate of the two types of people in the world Raymond Dasmann describes in a brilliant concept — *ecosystem people* and *biosphere people.*

A most illustrative measure of the prodigality of Biosphere People is what they have done to the earth's oil. They developed a Freeway Society with an appetite that could exhaust in little more than a century a resource that took some five million centuries to accumulate. The Freeway Society has been a lot of fun. No dust, a love affair with cars, high speed, mobility that encouraged people who had been faithful to abandon cities for one-night stands with glittering shopping centers and soothing second homes half a continent away. These Biosphere People put polyester where the linen was, developed a taste for fast food colored with red number two, coated the land, roiled the waters, sullied the air, throttled the earth, and now dream of colonies in space in which to idyll away their time, forgetting what they had done to Eden.

The sunlit path could be fun too. More could share it longer, not too many at a time. It might even lead humanity to a new Eden.

Now Is the Time to Choose

Freeway or sunlit path? Where would you like to go, or your children to be? Are there things that you have enjoyed that are too good for them? Experiences you had you wish they could share, but cannot because the ingredients are gone?

We suspect that most people would prefer the solar path but feel powerless to influence the choice. They are probably the Unsuspecting Majority and have but to meet each other, marshal their facts and their courage (perhaps with this book's help), and vote the good path in.

People in decision-making circles currently shun having to choose between freeway and path. The routes diverge. The goals are different.

But these people think they can keep a foot on each. Ambidexterity, afoot, leads to problems. Granted, making a choice, making a decision, removes options. But when the boat is pulling away from the dock, one decides or gets wet.

But why can't we go both ways? Ask those who have heavily invested in one, may want to prefer the other, but would rather risk your life than their investment. The reason, simplified, is that the sunlit path is not easily or cheaply switched to, even though it is not so hard or costly as the nuclear alternative. None of us can afford to finance both efforts. There isn't enough capital. There isn't enough time. There isn't enough human genius. And even if there were enough of all these, there are not enough recoverable resources to build both paths with.

Amory Lovins, in his *Soft Energy Paths: Toward a Durable Peace,* was first to stress the point that we cannot have it both ways. He argues for retroactive planning — for ascertaining where we would like the society to be fifty years from now and, by looking back from that vantage point, making sure that we do not wander off the route in ways that would prevent our reaching that goal. A good many people have enough trouble looking forward from where we are. They have more trouble looking backward from where they have never been. Mr. Lovins's critics balk at his last-chance-to-choose thesis. This is unfortunate, because those who are not persuaded to understand it will not choose in time.

A mountaineering analogy may help. When a mountaineer wants to climb a difficult peak, he pauses while he still has perspective and plans his route. He has only so many resources to get him to the top — food, equipment, energy, health, good weather, time, companions, and youth. If he does not anticipate the dead-end ledges and the blind cul-de-sacs by committing them to memory while he is still far enough away to see how misleading they are, then when he is on the mountain itself, with its foreshortened and deceptive perspective, he can fail. If he runs out of just one of those key resources and it cannot be resupplied, he will have thrown away his only chance.

For the nonclimbing capitalist, Mr. Lovins has a compelling argument. He cites a Bechtel Corporation study showing that the Ford-Nixon energy policy (again the policy of Strength Through Exhaustion) would preëmpt three-fourths of the newly formed capital in the U.S., rather than the one-fourth previously devoted to new energy generation. This would reduce by two-thirds the capital that could keep people working in other sectors of the economy — housing, transportation, public health, education, new small businesses and big ones. Most of that three-fourths would be absorbed by nuclear growth, associated with heavily automated technology and providing too few jobs, adding substantially to social stress. There would be a further serious problem, something like that of a hungry serpent with its tail in its mouth: building reactors to satisfy a growth rate postulated to require them would place a heavy demand upon resources. It would also require so much gross energy that there would be a net energy loss as long as the sought-after growth rate persisted.

To expand upon this idea, consider the global nuclear future postulated by Theodore Taylor (of John McPhee's *The Curve of Binding Energy*). Exponential growth would continue until an ultimate population of eight billion people was provided with one-third the energy the average U.S. citizen expends. This future would require, by our calculation, the commissioning of a one-thousand-megawatt reactor (the billion-dollar size) every day, forever, starting now. (Replacement reactors would be needed before the number of reactors got up to full strength.) The billion dollars per day for reactors would be but a fraction of the total cost. But there is little point in adding all the distribution-system and indirect costs here, because they are not numbers a civilization can live with.

What is essential to a sustainable economy is energy conservation. For every dollar spent on it, conservation frees approximately as much energy for useful purposes as would ten dollars spent on nuclear generating facilities.

Applying energy conservation, starting with simple things anyone can do immediately (easier on throttles, thermostats, and lights) and adding new ideas as they become feasible (such as improved windmills and safer walking) — thus cutting energy use 3 percent per year for a while — a given nation could arrive at the year 2001 with a per capita consumption only half what it is now. If the U.S. did so, it would end up with an energy budget close to that of the U.K., Sweden, West Germany, Switzerland, and New York City today. If we cut our consumption of coal 3 percent per year, according to Professor Albert A. Bartlett, coal would last forever. Such a cut might be painless for a while, but it would reduce U.S. per capita consumption to that of Nepal in a century and a half, which would be carrying conservation a little farther than it need go. The soft, sunlit path does not require it. It does, however, require public and private decisions now not to continue the major misallocation of resources still being contemplated. It seems quite obvious that the misallocation to nuclear power and weapons is the most damaging to the chance to switch to the sunlit path in time, and this misallocation creates the longest-lasting liability of all. Continuing to construct hermetically sealed buildings that must thereupon buy their air from energy utilities manifestly misallocates resources and will continue to do so as long as the structures stand unmodified.

Misallocation of resources for wasteful transportation is worth inquiring into in some detail, because it provides so clear an example of how to preclude success by procrastinating.

At this writing President Carter has proposed a ten-year, fifty-billion-dollar transportation program, thirty-five billion of it for highways, fifteen billion for mass transportation. If this program were to be adopted, it would be a clear, if temporary, victory for what former San Francisco Mayor Joseph Alioto called "The Highway Gang" — automakers, oil companies, and highway builders. The proposal would subvert, for this entire critical decade, the chance to make the transition to energy-efficient transportation. The thirty-five billion dollars would be but a minor part of the wrong commitment of capital, time, genius, and resources. The highway building itself would consume a vast amount of energy — cement is energy-intensive. Detroit would be encouraged to delay still longer the essential retooling the late Walter Reuther wished three hundred thousand of his United Auto Workers to undertake to manufacture the essentials of mass transportation, preparing to move people instead of moving cars. Detroit would no longer concentrate on building the overstuffed American car, itself energy-intensive, each requiring some eighteen thousand kilowatt-hours's equivalent to put together.

The oil companies, providing much of the energy it takes to make and lay cement, would also thus pledge their diminishing resource to what already consumes about one-third of the U.S. annual energy budget — gathering resources for fabricating, rolling, and disposing of the Detroit product. There are subtler costs in buildings required to accommodate cars, as well as the fine agricultural land paved to accommodate their overpopulation. Further, the time and funds and management needed to train and equip people to build substitutes will have been frittered away, and oil will be blown faster and faster out of tailpipes that need not have been built. The extra thirty-five billion dollars in capital will have evaporated; it could instead have been made available for such a talented organization as the Army Corps of Engineers, enabling the Corps to shelve its dambuilding and switch to reworking roadbeds and relaying rails. So there would be an expensive, perhaps preclusive delay in getting trains back on the track, to serve the U.S. as they now serve Europe and Japan. Detroit could be making what revived railroads need. After all, parked cars and white-elephant freeways will look silly when the society finally is forced to decide that oil is too precious to be wasted on yesterday's dream, and says farewell, my lovely, to all cars.

It cost something like four billion dollars to build all the U.S. railroads in the first place. With the latest proposed investment in perpetuating Detroit's old habits, some one-hundred-fifty billion dollars will have been devoted to the grand strategy of putting the U.S. railroads out of business. The world's oil will have been repeatedly decimated by the same process. And high though oil costs are getting to be, they are still low compared with alternative energy sources that are all we shall have left for railroad restoration and other essential energy-conservation steps.

Adequately engineered, intelligently planned mass transportation will not have to cost what San Francisco's BART has, but nationwide mass transit, including the electrification of railroads, will come at high cost — in dollars, in energy, in land, and in wit. The longer we wait, the higher the cost in all departments, added to the cost of continuing to build what soon must stand idle.

To recapitulate those costs in all departments: Take the proposed thirty-five billion dollars. Add the customary cost overrun. Add the inflation the proposal encourages. Add the cost of building the cars that were expected to justify the cost. Add the cost of the fuel they will use up until turned off. Add the continuing cost of Manhattanizing cities, of putting the best agricultural land out of action, of opening up the new towns that will soon have to be closed down if the cities are to stay alive. Add the costs of breathing air that cars are making carcinogenic, of crops destroyed by freeway exhaust. Add the cost of an individual's time lost behind the wheel, sweating out traffic, that might otherwise have been devoted to catching up on reading, or talk, or sleep in trains that were fun again. Add the final insult — the cost of all the oil lost because we temporized, kidding ourselves that we could keep a foot on the dock and a foot on the boat.

Does the thirty-five-billion-dollar token down payment look a little bit like a big, continuing, and wholly unnecessary and irresponsible larcenous act, a grand leap for mankind down the wrong path?

A new kind of audit is needed, looking harder than we have been looking at the costs of old habits and the benefits of changing them.

Solar Energy Can Be Human

No energy studies have so far given the public enough credit for being able to conserve. The Big Energy studies seem most timid in this respect, as if no one could be coaxed to substitute a little human energy (renewable for many years) for fossil, fissile, or geothermal energy sources (nonrenewable).

Ivan Illich has impressed many people with his amusing calculation: the average American spends fifteen hundred hours a year working for his car — keeping it fueled, cleaned, repaired, insured, amortized, housed, driven, and whatever else a car requires one to do for it, including contributing humor, health, and part of one's life. The car, in return, carries him an average of seven thousand miles. Thus, Mr. Illich points out, he gets less than five miles per hour, and can walk that fast.

Another friend of ours, of advanced age, tells of being so anxious to get to the Himalaya before it was too late that he put human energy to use, pushing away much food and drink, and walking a fair piece to a bus every day instead of driving to work. This let him put five hundred more miles on his shoes and five thousand fewer on his tires, at a saving of more than $3,000 (and about twelve barrels of oil). Multiply these figures by the number of one-to-a-car commuters, add the value of what their improved health will enable them to accomplish for themselves, their families, and society, factor in what the oil they have saved will be worth when it is really needed, send or bequeath one-tenth of the total to your favorite environmental organization, and a sunlit path is assured. There will be wilderness, parks, and wild forests and rivers for part of that path to wind through and along.

Getting back to our friend, he found that this new discipline not only cut his car's gasoline use by two-thirds, but also that it cut his fat reserve by forty-five pounds, and his lethargy level by enough to get him to an altitude record (for him) of eighteen thousand feet by foot. Mount Everest, which he had feared he should never see, was a mere eleven thousand feet further above, and he felt great.

[Those who have read the first half of my story, *For Earth's Sake,* will know that it was I who felt great.]

To borrow a good line, all who think human energy can save gasoline raise your right foot. Or flick your right wrist; if the automatic transmission had never been invented, wrist-power would by now have saved almost as much oil as exists in the unprecedented Prudhoe Bay discovery. We suspect that if humanity did not have fossil or fissile fuels, we would not waste away. We would simply trim down. The Nepalese have neither, and are rather beautiful.

Concerning the human-energy and other solar alternatives, it does not appear safe to allow more than ten years to get the prototypes in place, not just left in dreams. "What we save in the next few years," Allen Morgan said in 1960, "is all that will ever be saved." Amory Lovins gives us fifty years, give or take a few, to make the complete transition from nuclear and fossil to solar. But we dare not wait that long to start making the transition to the post-oil, post-nuclear era.

Harrison Brown's vision of an attractive goal is as good a stimulus now as it was in 1954:

"The machine has divorced man from the world of nature to which he belongs and in the process he has lost in large measure the powers of contemplation with which he was endowed. A prerequisite for the preservation of the canons of humanism is a reëstablishment of organic roots with our natural environment and, related to it, the evolution of ways of life which encourage contemplation and the search for truth and knowledge. The flower and vegetable garden, green grass, the fireplace, the primeval forest with its wondrous assemblage of living things, the uninhabited hilltop where one can silently look at the stars and wonder — all of these things and many others are necessary for the fulfillment of man's psychological and spiritual needs. To be sure,

186

they are of no 'practical value' and are seemingly unrelated to man's pressing need for food and living space. But they are as necessary to the preservation of humanism as food is necessary to the preservation of human life.

"I can imagine a world within which machines function solely for man's benefit, turning out those goods which are necessary for his well-being, relieving him of the necessity for heavy physical labor and dull, routine, meaningless activity. The world I imagine is one in which people are well fed, well clothed, and well housed. Man, in this world, lives in balance with his environment, nourished by nature in harmony with the myriad other life forms that are beneficial to him. He treats his land wisely, halts erosion and over-cropping, and returns all organic waste matter to the soil from which it sprung. He lives efficiently, yet minimizes artificiality. It is not an overcrowded world; people can, if they wish, isolate themselves in the silence of a mountaintop, or they can walk through primeval forests or across wooded plains. In the world of my imagination there is organization, but it is as decentralized as possible, compatible with the requirements for survival. There is a world government, but it exists solely for the purpose of preventing war and stabilizing population, and its powers are irrevocably restricted. The government exists for man rather than man for the government.

"In the world of my imagination the various regions are self-sufficient, and the people are free to govern themselves as they choose and to establish their own cultural patterns. All people have a voice in the government, and individuals can move about when and where they please. It is a world where man's creativity is blended with the creativity of nature, and where a moderate degree of organization is blended with a moderate degree of anarchy.

"Is such a world impossible of realization? Perhaps it is, but who among us can really say? At least if we try to create such a world there is a chance that we will succeed. But if we let the present trend continue it is all too clear that we will lose forever those qualities of mind and spirit which distinguish the human being from the automaton."

When the age of Harrison Brown's *The Challenge to Man's Future* has doubled, most of you should see what the year after Arthur C. Clarke's 2001 is like. It won't take long. If between now and then, here and abroad, the goal for the machine civilization continues to be the ultimate Mr. Taylor contemplated, most of you will not see 2002. That ultimate has too much population in it, too much appetite, acquisitiveness, consumerism, and other demographic drains. We know we can at long last say *Enough!* soon enough. E. F. Schumacher, in *Small Is Beautiful,* tried to teach us to say it sooner. But economic growth as presently practiced is good to those it self-serves, and is not easily questioned by them.

187

Mr. Schumacher upset them. But there are many people who agreed with him, and many more who will when they read him. Leaders could try to serve that growing audience.

Ultimate is not ahead of us. We passed it a while back. We may not have noticed it then, but we passed it on the day the earth lost the shine we had known, when we forgot to relax and learned to contrive, reached for less and grasped more, when we looked around us and saw fear where love had been.

Ultimate is returnable to. Not a lot more things each year, but fewer, until there is balance again; a little more live and let live, even for scaly slimy things or those that go bump in the night, each like us on its own errand. Ultimate is steady, not dull; dynamically durable; probably more beautiful than what we have been looking at. You could feel needed there. So would friends. No keys. You could walk streets at night, with good talk and laughter, the lights there low enough to let the stars show.

Utopian? Only if you couldn't stand it. If you want it, you have the votes. The sun has enough energy to get you there, joyfully. While it shines on the side of the earth where you aren't, those other suns, so far away and so too long unseen, can keep reminding you of miracles: that they are there, that the only planet you know can be a place to live is here, and that you are here, too, "compounded of dust," as Loren Eiseley said, "and the light of a star."

Sun!: A Handbook for the Solar Decade, 1978

THE END OF THE NUCLEAR EXPERIMENT

W E HAD HOPED THAT THE SOLAR DECADE would be that of the eighties, but will gladly advocate it for the nineties, and we now have more reason to do so. Three Mile Island, Chernobyl, Bhopal, a dying off of forests, a rising ocean, and the opportunity to get sunburned in Australia in 20 percent less time, thanks to ozone thinning, should teach us something. It was Henry Kendall upon whom I heavily relied, although I did not refer to him by name, in an article I prepared for *Newsday* when I made my second visit to Malta (the first was in 1970) for the *Pacem in Maribus* conference arranged by Elizabeth Mann Borghese. The article was reprinted in *Not Man Apart* in August 1972, under a cartoon the legend for which reads: "There's no good reason for Americans to use as much energy for air conditioning as 800 million Chinese use for everything."

MALTA, JUNE 30, SPECIAL — "A star," Alan Watts has postulated for friends, "is a planet on which there was intelligent life that began experimenting with atomic energy." Although he intended this as the briefest of all

188

works in science fiction, some delegates to *Pacem in Maribus,* now being held here, must wonder if there is more truth than fiction in the work.

While the conferees consider how man may more equitably exploit the ocean without killing it, the French forge on with atom tests over the Pacific, the U.S. and U.S.S.R. are adamant about tests near its shores, and the promoters of atomic energy at all costs press on with their own tests wherever they can create a customer for a reactor — at a time when reactors have been revealed to be slow-fused potential disasters.

The chairman of the U.S. Atomic Energy Commission has suggested shooting the lethal, unmanageable atomic wastes off to the sun in rockets. (But how about those short rounds at Cape Kennedy?) Several atomic scientists, deeply troubled by the perils of atomic fission, seek rescue in power from atomic fusion, not yet scientifically feasible. The director of the U.S. Oak Ridge Nuclear Research Laboratory, untroubled, contemplates a world ration of twelve thousand five-thousand-megawatt fission reactors to supply supplemental power for the earth's ultimate population. What their waste heat would do to planetary climate and ocean level is not stated. The resultant atomic radiation's deadly course, Friends of the Earth suspects, would leave no oceans clean enough to worry about, or people to worry.

The time has come, I should like to suggest, for the doom-makers to cool it, to concede that the earth is not only round, but also has limits, and that it is the only earth. As a first step, they can join the move to send reactors back to the drawing board. They will find abundant reasons for this in "An Evaluation of Nuclear Reactor Safety," splendidly documented and startling new testimony that is very much worth struggling through, for all its complex terms and charts. Independent experts here set about letting ordinary people know what the government has not gotten around to telling them about the so-called peaceful atom. The federal agency that should guard against the unprecedented dangers of this atom also sells the atom. It is conflict of interest, squared, and the public is the loser.

Or it would be, except for this contribution by the Union of Concerned Scientists, of Cambridge, Mass., for which they deserve a Pulitzer Prize for honest reporting, long overdue in these matters. They should also win a Nobel Prize for their contribution toward peace between people and the environment, and between them and their own genetic future.

If this sounds extravagant, it will not sound that way to readers who take to heart the duty to themselves, their generation, and future generations and read what amounts to a combined horror and detective story. It is the superbly documented testimony given about the Emergency Core Cooling System problems in reactors before the Atomic Energy Commission on March 23, 1972 — the Great ECCS Snafu.

189

The men who put the testimony together are extremely well qualified. One of them, an atomic physicist, had a key role in the development of reactors. Until this spring he had been a staunch advocate of atomic energy. He now advises that we forget it.

The testimony is beautifully organized. Its sentences, although logical, are not always easy to get through. But you soon sense the drama of this tour de force, and realize you had damned well better get through it because your own life can easily be at stake. Any intelligent layman can get the message. Some parts may be too technical for him, but in that very fact they carry a special message. Someone has to understand these parts, not just approximately, but beyond doubt, or there can be cataclysmic trouble. And the layman, having seen the intricacy of this need, will do well to ask: To whom will I give my proxy in voting on reactor safety? The question affects human heredity.

No one reading this testimony is likely to give his proxy to the AEC, to any of the vendors of atomic hardware, or to the scientists who have been much too timid to warn the public. The Union of Concerned Scientists's testimony has been confirmed by independent scientists who owe nothing to the atomic industry and who are more concerned with the safety of the public than the safety of atomic investments.

This testimony should be read around the world. It will help the world take stock of the alleged energy crises and to conclude that it doesn't really need all the convenience and profligacy of energy the energy producers are trying so hard to sell. The cost of this convenience is simply too frightfully high.

Altogether, the critique consists of 342 pages, including graphs and tables. The skill of the inquiry is something to be admired, as is the conservativeness of the authors, who had every right to be enraged by what they were encountering. My own conversations have been with one author. His overriding concern, as I interpret it, is not that reactor safety is beyond technological achievement, but rather that human fallibility cannot be eliminated from the safety system and the cost to the public of that fallibility will be too high to justify.

Should NASA Turn the Apollo Program Over to the LIRR?

The best minds of science, industry, and government have tackled the task of assuring reactor safety, and even they have failed — both in the task and in reporting their failure. There can be no confidence in what must surely take place as reactors proliferate, as fuel which can be an atomic-bomb ingredient is shipped and reshipped in reprocessing, as obsolescent reactors are mothballed, as waste is shipped to nonexistent safe storage — and as crews of necessarily lower-echelon competence take over an operation where top-echelon competence has failed in forty-three reactor accidents the UCS testimony describes. It brings to

190

mind what the Space Program would be like if NASA should fail and thereupon pass its operations on to the Long Island Railroad. Not that we don't love the institution; we merely concede its limits.

This same physicist told me, "When the lights go dim, we've won!" I know he did not wish to see any human suffering result from a dim-out, real or staged. But neither did he wish to see the massive death and genetic destruction take place that now threaten the world. His is one voice that is trying to let the public find out what it had better know about reactors before trusting the salesman. [The voice? Henry Kendall's, Nobel Laureate.]

At the Barrel's Bottom: Care Less, or Use Less?

I write this in Valletta, on Malta. A bland Mediterranean bathes the edge of this crossroads island much as it must have for the past fifty centuries humanity has known it. The city seems as unaware of what has just been disclosed at the first United Nations Conference on the Human Environment, concluded two weeks ago in Stockholm, as Dr. Edward E. David, Jr., Science Advisor to President Nixon, seems to be.

Dr. David's unawareness of the meaning of Stockholm — that the critical question about the environment is not *how* to exploit but *whether* to exploit — is implied in a recent story in the *Herald Tribune* here. He is to lead a U.S. delegation to Moscow on July 2 to arrange a U.S.-Soviet program to attempt to produce clean energy, tame earthquakes, and exploit the Arctic. What the Administration Energy Policy calls for, a strangely mixed bag, includes an oil pipeline across Alaska's active earthquake country to use up Alaska oil while we look for cleaner energy, a combination attractive to oil and construction companies and puzzling to the public.

We would urge Dr. David and friends to narrow the agenda to the most vital of the world's scientific and technological problems: (a) let people know that atomic energy they have been led to believe is clean is dirty energy, (b) urge them to return to ways of using less energy and share it better. The public demonstrated the ability to use less a mere decade ago, when the energy drain was half what it is now. Using less spares the environment more, and gives survival precedence over convenience.

Except for a few isolated efforts like Consolidated Edison's Save-a-Watt ads, there is no program by government or industry to slow down the exponentially rising, high-powered drive for energy consumption regardless of the environmental costs. Just the opposite is happening, with both government and industry hard-selling the public on demanding more energy, including a come-on for energy to abate pollution (which is like sobering up on martinis). The cost of the increase is soft-pedaled or hidden — unconscionably hidden as we can see in what the Union of Concerned Scientists has disclosed.

The president often asks for TV time to tell the public of important matters. Here is an imminent disaster to warn the nation about. Further, industry might well use its vast promotion budget to tell such essential truth about the waste the fast-breeder reactors, which the president now urges, will breed — a plutonium by-product that must be isolated from living things for five hundred thousand years. But there is silence where there should be warnings. What kind of science advice, the public may well ask, is the president and industry getting?

This is no ordinary risk the public is being exposed to, like the normal mayhem on the highways, or the tragic human losses caused by drug trips, or the continuing ravages of war. It is a threat to the genes that make living things what they are, that make people human. It is a reckless, radical playing around with the building blocks of life. It is atomic roulette.

Atomic Epidemic Worldwide

To add another bullet to the chamber, the International Atomic Energy Agency has known about the ECCS snafu, but its elaborate atom-selling exhibit at the Stockholm Conference breathed not a word of it. Nor was there a word about the unsolved waste problem (revealed by *Saturday Review* and *Technology Review,* not the AEC or the IAEA). Nor a word about the radiation danger the IAEA was downplaying in 1970 at *Pacem in Maribus,* the first Malta Ocean Regime conference. The IAEA was still ignoring this danger in 1971 at an international environmental conference in Finland. The U.S. AEC, after treating scientists Ernest Sternglass, John Gofman, and Arthur Tamplin harshly for their warnings about atomic radiation, then about-faced and set even sterner limits than Drs. Gofman and Tamplin had urged. At Malta, in Finland, and at Stockholm, the UN's atomic energy agency looked very much like the atomic industry's PR Department. The salesman is a specialist. Objective analysis is another speciality. The two cannot reasonably be looked for in a single individual, or a single agency.

We are reminded that no divine order requires that the people of the coming decade must explore, exploit, and extinguish a major part of the Earth's energy capital in order further to disrupt the planet's badly mangled life-support system with poorly disciplined use of that energy.

What the world desperately needs is competent new leadership, capable of moving people from where they are to where they need to go to live out their lives in reasonable freedom with due regard for the only Earth. The world is finding such leadership in the Union of

Concerned Scientists. May other scientists soon share the UCS concern — and prove that they are concerned!

Prepared on request for *Newsday*, August 1972

THE LETHAL NUCLEAR FUEL CYCLE

I F WHAT I HAD LEARNED FROM HENRY KENDALL, professor of physics at MIT and founder of the Union of Concerned Scientists, and Amory Lovins, who would later found the Rocky Mountain Institute, should cause concern, so should some notes I made December 3, 1980, of a conversation with Ted Taylor, subject of John McPhee's *The Curve of Binding Energy*. I had suggested to John that he do a profile on Henry Kendall, but John had found Ted Taylor, inventor of many atomic bombs and well versed on the anatomy of the atoms being split for them and for nuclear power. I started a conversation with Ted in Washington, D.C., in December 1980, referring to his remark to Amory Lovins, Steve Wheeler (FOE's disarmament lobbyist), and me at the November launch of the Committee on National Security.

Ted Taylor had said, as I remembered, that if things proceeded according to present plans, there would be, at a given reprocessing plant fifty years down the road, a big enough spent-fuel inventory to release, if bombed, more radioactivity of thirty- to forty-year half-life than would be released by the detonation of all the nuclear weapons in the world in 1980. If this happened to one plant in Western Europe, Western Europe would be permanently uninhabitable.

He corrected the half-life numbers to twenty to thirty years for Strontium-90 and Cesium-137. According to present plans, the amount of those isotopes in temporary storage at the plant would be of the same order of magnitude as the quantity of those isotopes that would be released by exploding all the nuclear weapons now in the world. The short-term effect would be much bigger in a nuclear war. The effect of these two isotopes would be on the same scale as an all-out nuclear war — but released in one place. The local effects would be massive in the contamination of land with damaging isotopes. He was speaking of the total radioactive hazard after the bombing, not just of the material in the high-level range. Western Europe — or a bigger area — would be made uninhabitable for several decades, maybe thousands of years, considering Plutonium and relatives.

According to present plans for storing high-level wastes at a reprocessing plant, the total inventory of Strontium-90 and Cesium-137 at a reprocessing plant operating ten years or more would be roughly the same as the quantity of those isotopes that would be released by all the nuclear weapons in the world in 1980. Therefore, people should think very carefully if they want to head toward a world in which dozens of reprocessing plants would be distributed widely and be potential targets for nuclear bombardment or sabotage. This is a very serious consideration, since the release of substances from a reprocessing plant to the surroundings could dangerously contaminate very large areas, quite possibly larger than Western Europe.

These reprocessing plants exist now. The number would be much bigger fifty years from now. If someone bombed a certain waste-disposal area at Hanford, we'd have a hell of a mess in the Northwestern U.S. The same would be true of Aldermasten, in the U.K., LaHague in France, soon in Japan and West Germany, and in Russia now. At any time a reprocessing plant is operating at near capacity, it has an inventory of radioactive materials not on the scale of a reactor, but much bigger — in a decade or so, one hundred times or more of the materials. If he were a Swede, he'd wonder about those reprocessing plants now in the U.K. and France.

Without protection, these plants are a tremendous threat. That one would be destroyed is highly unlikely, but . . . If you had asked Taylor, could Three Mile Island happen, he'd have said it was highly unlikely that such a series of mistakes could be made.

I asked Taylor about the ozone story I received in the Salt II briefing given environmentalists by the Carter State Department, predicting the immediate deaths from a full nuclear exchange and a destruction of the ozone barrier that would peak a year later, at which time forty minutes in the sun would produce blisters and no crops could grow.

He had not looked into it. It's hard to believe, he said, but there would be a lot of results none of us have thought of. If ABMs explode in the upper atmosphere, the side effects are essentially unlimited. The list of possibilities is too long to talk about. If one of the current big underground tests were held in the upper atmosphere, it would blow away the magnetic field on that side of the earth, which would dump whatever that field contained there. Three hundred megatons's energy is all the field has.

I asked Ted Taylor if he was going to write any of this down.

"I'm not writing about this anymore," he said. "I'm way overcommitted. I want to accent the positive — energy conservation and solar. There is some indication that this emphasis on conservatisms and decentralization will help alleviate the reprocessing-plant problem."

It is not true, he concluded, that a bad reprocessing accident would equal an all-out nuclear war, but it could be much worse for the people in the vicinity of the accident.

The threat implicit in reprocessing plants exists, and so far as I know, no ameliorating suggestions are being considered — simply

194

because the public here and abroad is unaware of the unacceptably high cost of nuclear electricity. Stating the question another way: How many kilowatt hours of nuclear electricity would be a fair exchange for rendering western Europe uninhabitable? Or the Pacific Northwest in the United States? Or, because the generation of nuclear electricity continues to be a cover for the nuclear activity that continues to produce nuclear weapons, rendering the earth uninhabitable?

The connections exist, the frightening connections. As I said in the early seventies, it is the same atom, whether in a glove or in a fist. The greatest technological hope is the greatest universal threat. It has built an arsenal that within the next thirty minutes, possibly even by mistake, can end the world as we know it.

There is a way out. No one has explained it better than Amory Lovins, in his series of books — *World Energy Strategies, Non-nuclear Futures, Soft Energy Paths, Brittle Power* — and in the continuing efforts of his Rocky Mountain Institute colleagues in Old Snowmass, Colorado. No one has explained more lucidly the way out — energy conservation and energy efficiency. In neither of these ways does nuclear energy have an economically feasible role if the accounting includes the value of a habitable earth.

Something more must be added. If, with conservation and efficiency, we reduce energy use to one-fourth of what it now is, but we permit two doublings of the demographic drain — the combination of population plus consumption — then we are back to square one, and energy conservation will have served as no more than a delaying mechanism. The world must face the hazards in that square now. They are terminal hazards.

As the third millennium approaches, it is obvious that growth is not progress. It is its antithesis. If a course of action is not sustainable, it is not progress. If paradise is to be regained, progress will need to be redefined.

The further news is that the earth can sustain fewer than two billion people if we run out of artificial phosphate fertilizer, which we soon could. We must feed ourselves on the earth's sustained yield rather than on environmental capital, as we are now doing so much. Mineable phosphate is such capital, and so are oil and coal, which will not be replaced in a hundred times longer than man's likely tenancy on earth. We are rapidly using up environmental capital in a most reckless way.

Harvard biologist E. O. Wilson had estimated, I was told in Kyoto in April 1990, that if humanity used resources in the way the United States and Japan are using them, the earth could sustain only two hundred million people. The most radical of the attacks on environmental capital is being launched and accelerated by people who call themselves conservative.

Soon after I returned from Kyoto I met Professor Wilson at the other end of a telephone line and asked if he had indeed been the source of that figure of two hundred million. "No," he said, "but it sounds reasonable."

Our civilization is a confusing one. Nevertheless, we cannot abandon it without causing disaster, nor can we ignore its faults without asking for disaster. We can, however, fix them while it runs.

CHAPTER 12

PLAYING GOD

THE ATOM

W HEN THE GREAT GENETIC ENGINEERING RUSH BEGAN, Friends of the Earth was fortunate in having two women who were deeply concerned about what the recombinant DNA manipulators might be getting the world into. Francine Simring was in the New York Office and Pam Lippe in the Washington office. They put together an advisory council, the most notable member of which was Nobel laureate George Wald. They were provided additional financial support by William Carstens, a retired man from San Diego who wanted to keep the insurance business financially feasible.

Because Bill was in insurance, he was well aware of the difficulty of insuring against nuclear events and envisioned similar difficulty with genetic events. It was our anti-nuclear stance that had interested him in Friends of the Earth in the first place. That stance had been informed by the worry the Union of Concerned Scientists, founded by MIT Professor Henry Kendall, had described concerning the hazards of the nuclear fuel cycle — all of it.

The hazards began with the mining of uranium (the hazard could be carcinogenic, mutagenic, or teratogenic). They continued in the concentration of the ore (also c, m, and t), the accumulation or reconstitution of mining wastes and the release of radon daughters (c, m, and t again), the enrichment of nuclear fuel (requiring the burning of quantities of coal and its disagreeable releases), the loading and burning of the fuel in reactors producing radioactive emissions (the industry likes to suggest they are as innocent as mom's apple pie), the grim threat of fuel meltdowns (that could render an area the size of Pennsylvania uninhabitable), the near misses (Browns Ferry, Three Mile Island), the non-miss (Chernobyl), the storage of spent fuel in reactor-site pools (destruction of which could do in another Pennsylvania), the reprocessing of spent fuel (producing plutonium for more weapons and also

197

producing an inventory of waste like that at LaHague, France, release of which could make Western Europe uninhabitable), transportation of waste on derelict railroad beds (in casks not tested for the severity of stress they could easily receive but not contain), the hazard of ruptured casks (you couldn't drive by an exposed spent nuclear-fuel rod at the highway's edge on a motorcycle fast enough to avoid a lethal dose of radiation), the problem of waste already supposedly disposed of (the still unexplained Chelyabinsk disaster in the Soviet Union, and in Washington State the Hanford leaks and resultant radioactive plume delivered to the Pacific by the Columbia River and extending from Cape Mendocino in California to the northern end of the Washington coast, or the newly discovered, unmanageable, explosive hydrogen build-up in the tanks of high-level liquid waste), the nuclear waste yet to be disposed of (promises of solution deadlines do not solve the problem), the problem of disposing of embrittled, overaged, or otherwise defunct reactors (promises, promises; no solutions), the enormous amount of waste heat (on a planet where the atom's energy was safely stored in the atom instead of being released, further warming an atmosphere that does not need the heat), and the permanent challenge, provided generously and willy-nilly to generations after generations, of minding our waste, sequestering radioactivity from living things, farther into the future than the Neanderthal era extends into our past — these are the principal problems of the nuclear fuel cycle. You will find them under the industry's rug when they let you look in this Age of Disinformation, not to say Deceit.

We therefore had better avoid the nuclear escape from global warming suggested by the nuclear industry. It could be added that when the world follows Sweden's example and phases out and ends the nuclear *power* industry, the nuclear *weapons* industry will have no place to hide.

Fortunately, we escaped still another hazard. We had been promised nuclear energy too cheap to meter. Knowing what damage the industrial nations have done to the Earth with abundant energy they had to pay for, think what could have been done if it had been free! That is now the promise nuclear fusion holds for us, if and when.

All these troublesome problems are with us. If they were foreseen, the people who did the foreseeing chose not to let us know. We can assume that they were driven by a real need to beat Germany's effort to split the atom first, that they welcomed the idea of selling electricity as a by-product of plutonium production, that the utilities especially welcomed the subsidy of two hundred billion dollars from taxpayers, and that in it all there was a mixture of altruism and greed.

This is an assumption. What we do know is that the consequences were not anticipated — were not fended off. They offend still.

One strike against scientists and engineers. Could we learn from it, or refuse to and charge on as blindly with genetic engineering?

Perhaps we could have avoided the danger of strike two, had Wall Street not sensed a great opportunity. A very profitable, presumably beneficial industry was on the horizon; and if we didn't seize it fast and develop it, some other nation would.

The pressure was on. A man of George Wald's stature could resist it. But I remember strolling with him along the boardwalk at Cape May, New Jersey, where we were attending an energy conference a decade ago, and his telling me that young researchers in Cambridge who shared his concern about recombinant DNA were advised by their superiors to keep quiet or else. I reminded him of the great piece he wrote for the *New Yorker* about the Vietnam war, a piece for which there was an unprecedented demand for reprints. We needed as powerful a piece, I said, about a threat that could be even greater — the unleashing, through molestation of a gene, of some entity in due course that would surprise us the way the molestation of the atom had, but surprise us even more if that entity in due course, proved to be something that the immunity to systems of our planet had not learned to fight and subdue — a sort of global AIDS epidemic.

This lets my imagination take off. Suppose we invented an organism that could reduce lignin, the tough structural element of wood, to fluid and the organism got loose and melted down the world's wooden houses and the forests they came from. Or suppose we came up with another organism, one that would devour oil spills and was anaerobic, but it too got loose, not just in crankcases and storage tanks and pipelines, but in the oil-bearing strata themselves, devouring the entire resource. At least that would be a way to end the problem of oil pollution.

A year or so ago my computer picked up the story going around about how the AIDS virus was invented by a collaboration of biological-warfare scientists and genetic engineers, was tested on homosexual prisoners, who were released prematurely (the incubation was still going on) for their contribution to science, whereupon the virus got out of hand. You do not have to believe the story, but you had not better believe something like it isn't possible.

Of course, there are benefits, very tempting and delightful ones. But will we once again begin a cost-benefit analysis and, as we have so often done in the past, assess the benefits but forget to look into the costs, short-range and long?

Almost all of these considerations raced through my mind as I talked with George Wald (the boardwalk is pretty long), convinced that we needed as piercing a look at genetic engineering as he had given our misfortune in Vietnam.

We still do.

Lewis Thomas felt otherwise. He was on the advisory council of Friends of the Earth and its foundation. When he learned that Friends of the Earth was opposing recombinant DNA, he resigned from the council. That was a major blow. As you will see, it led to what I had to say when I was invited to give a paper at the annual meeting, in January 1980, of the American Association for the Advancement of Science in San Francisco.

I quoted Lewis Thomas and a second opinion from Freeman Dyson, a man for whom we also had great respect. He is the father of one of our supplementary sons, George. One of our own sons, Kenneth, has written about both of them in what we think is a classical book, *The Starship and the Canoe*. In that book an alienated son and father are reconciled. I was ready to enjoy his statement about people who would play God.

THE GENE

Whoever can read the DNA language can also learn to write it. Whoever learns to write the language will in time learn to design living creatures according to his whim. God's technology for creating species will then be in our hands. . . . Can man play God and still stay sane? In our real world, as on the island (of Wells's Moreau), the answer must inevitably be no.
— Freeman Dyson in *Disturbing the Universe*

The code word for criticism of science and scientists these days is "hubris." Once you've said that word, you've said it all; it sums up, in a word, all of today's apprehensions and misgivings in the public mind — not just about what is perceived as the insufferable attitude of scientists themselves but, enclosed in the same word, what science and technology are perceived to be doing to make this century, this near to its ending, turn out so wrong.
— Lewis Thomas in *The Medusa and the Snail*

'SCIOLIST' IS A WORD as obscure as 'hubris' was only a few years ago, and I should introduce myself as a sciolist with hubris, and walk quickly away without defining either. A sophomore dropout at Berkeley in the depression that came by surprise, I did eleven years' penance as an editor at the University of California Press, where I gained an editor's tentative knowledge of several fields — eleven years minus three, those three spent learning other fields in World War II. Then, for the seventeen years I was executive director of the Sierra Club, I attended the University of the Colorado River, unaccredited but rather more informative than I had expected. Founding Friends of the Earth ten years ago, I received further education from encounters with supersonic transport and other excesses of speed limits, among them those in nuclear and genetic inquiries.

I also encountered John McPhee, who told me what Russell Train had told him: "Thank God for Dave Brower. He makes it so easy for the rest of us to be reasonable."

Whereupon I have met responsibility number three in the draft for members of the scientific community (which I am not): "When practical, or when called upon to do so, to identify the limits of uncertainty, personal biases, significant sources of support and possible conflicts of interest which are relevant to (members's) opinions or conclusions."

Except that I was perhaps correct in not waiting, before identifying my limits, biases, and other problems, until it was practical to confess them, or until I was called upon to do so.

And therein, I now discover, lies my principal concern about Science, one that is more and more widely shared, I fear: the apparent dictum, "Be ethical when it's practical."

Throwing chronology to the winds, let me explain that concern better. On December 14, 1977, Lewis Thomas resigned from the Friends of the Earth Advisory Council because FOE had filed civil action against the National Institutes of Health on the recombinant DNA question and he did not agree at all with our arguments. With typical speed in answering correspondence, I began drafting a reply between July 5 and July 9, a year and a half later, when I was in Verona, Italy, baby-sitting our latest book, *Wake of the Whale*. Years ago I had read and admired Dr. Thomas's *Lives of a Cell* and on the way to Verona had read *The Medusa and the Snail* and admired it too. I think Dr. Thomas is great, and I was in no hurry to disagree with him, and I am still in no hurry. I have not completed the draft yet. But let me allude to some of my notes, some jotted down in the hotel bar, others noted in a pad by my hotel bedside when jet lag found me stark awake at three in the morning. My draft begins:

Dear Dr. Thomas: You've ruled out "hubris." "Arrogant" is name-calling, and to ask anyone to feign fallibility is assuming, oneself, a touch of divine assignment. How about "smug"?

You argue persuasively (in *Science,* in the *New Yorker,* in the *New England Journal of Medicine,* and in *The Medusa and the Snail*) that Science must be free to inquire. Professor Richard Delgado thinks (in the *Bulletin of the Atomic Scientists,* January 1979, pp. 60 – 62) that "courts will hold that scientific inquiry is entitled to recognition as a first amendment activity, to be accorded the deference that the courts apply when fundamental freedoms, traceable to our colonial heritage, are involved."

But free to inquire without limits? What is good for Science is good for the country? So let none but Scientists define the limits?

To give away my argument to begin with, the moth is free to explore the flame, and pays all the costs of its curiosity. When a child explores flame by striking matches, the child can run away scared and others in the building may pay dearly.

Science is even now in its infancy — the latest blink of time in the long story of life. For example, squeeze the earth's history into the six days of creation, start the first day at midnight on Sunday, and you have, roughly, a day and a half of construction and no life until Tuesday noon. All the rest of the week DNA runs its course, building a remarkable diversity of living things that come and go, with complexity increasing, adversity striking often, but honing and perfecting too. The great reptiles arrived at 1600 Saturday and left the stage (with a few exceptions) five hours later. We came on at about 2355. Eleven seconds before midnight we were still Neanderthal. Agriculture began 1.5 seconds before midnight. Ignoring Isaiah, we laid field to field and built house to house. One-fourth second before midnight we were in enough trouble that Christ hoped there could be peace and good will among us. The industrial revolution, beginning a fortieth second before midnight, pleased us so much that at the close of the latest great world war, two-hundredths of a second before midnight, we decided in our wisdom that GNP is greater than DNA, and let GNP color our thinking: let no one have a grosser national product than ours.

Late in that last blink of time we played, in our scientific infancy, with the ultimate fire. I was told by one of his colleagues that when James Bryant Conant was witnessing the first atomic blast in New Mexico, having been party to the calculations that predicted the duration of the alternate sun's flash, he was alarmed to observe that the flash did not end when it was supposed to lest it ignite the earth's atmosphere. "My God, we've done it!" he exclaimed. We are all witness, alive as we are, to his misapprehension. The atmosphere did not ignite and return the earth to its airless beginnings. The flash winked out, more slowly than planned, but out.

The story would be better if I had asked Dr. Conant and heard it in his own words. But I waited too long to act, a chronic frailty of mine. If any of you know of this firsthand, please let me know, or put it in your oral history. What I report as hearsay evidence could have happened then, and the likes of it could happen now. We are all given lots of curiosity, a fair amount of restraint, and none of the infallibility required for total prescience and the concomitant ability to foresee all possible consequences. Unfortunately, we are not well endowed with curiosity about our fallibility. Other creatures may sense this.

It is not being Luddite, but logical instead — for whatever political value logic may have these days — to maintain that for all the scientific brilliance around us, we have a lot to learn about DNA. The natural engineering that, with no scientist's help, has for three and a half billion years kept life going at no hour-cost at all, and that in each of us can organize and operate trillions of cells for each person's lifetime, has something going for it that research and publication and understanding will someday perhaps catch up with. That something that is going for it could be related to what nostalgia, or emotion, or taboo sometimes command us not to do. Nostalgia, emotion, and taboo can also get us as screwed up as any other informants, but they have been working far longer, with recorded success, than our latter-day scientific intuitions have. They all have limits, and our challenge is to discern those limits.

So we have arrived at the sensitive point. Limits, like nuclear reactors, are fine in someone else's backyard. But everybody, I should like to submit, is in someone else's backyard, there is no away anymore, and now is the time for all good men to take limits seriously. All good women have, already.

My draft petered out on July 8, 1979. I had not figured out how to include a contentious note, scrawled at three-thirty the morning before, about his discrediting of the few environmental organizations that had taken the time to disagree with his DNA perceptions.

There followed some hieroglyphics about how medicine and good intentions could help too much. I remembered, on the one hand, the disaster in my lepidopterous days when I tried to help western swallowtails from their chrysalides out of kindness, and thereby crippled everyone I tried to help. And how on the other hand, without medicine's help, I would not have survived because my mother had to undergo a successful mastoidectomy or I would not have been able to show up a month later, nor my wife to survive infancy without someone's midnight dash for oxygen, nor my oldest son his infancy without penicillin, nor my other sons without medical rescue from serious accidents. Only our daughter didn't need extra help, but how could she have existed if her parents had not survived childhood?

That particular survival having been something I approved of, for all the incipient genetic erosion in the long run, I dropped the subject, and at three in the morning, July 9, jotted down a list of things science should feel a little humility about. It was list of Science-knows-best mistakes. I titled it:

Clay Foot Department

wild oats	treatment of frozen flesh
lantana	Heathrow, the vector
eucalyptus	Apollo wastewater
radiata	Who unblew the DNA whistle?
ARCO grass	Why?
rabbits, Australia	Medical government by AMA
and New Zealand	and pharmaceutical people
English sparrows	CETUS and Cohen
starlings	UC and AEC
mongoose in Hawaii	The U.S. Customs form:
opossum in New Zealand	"anything live?" and mitochondria

Ten minutes later, I added a note to Dr. Teller: "You wear laurels from having helped the U.S. win one of the preliminaries of man's race to oblivion — The Talk Loudly & Carry a Bigger Stick School: If you don't agree, I'll blow you and your environment away."

I ended on a cooler, reasonable note with comments on monoculture, miracle wheat, miracle trees, Dow, my proposed bumper sticker, "A quicker life through chemistry," and a note about Sky Lab, which then was floundering in the sky. I hoped that none of its pieces would hit Three Mile Island.

Most of these items are self-explanatory. (All are clarified at the end of the paper.) The last one is not. The U.S. Customs form requires returning citizens, upon pain of fine or jail, to confess if they are carrying anything alive into the country except themselves, which means that our own government requires us to lie if we want to get home. Everybody is bringing resident *E. coli* along, and the knowing ones hope that the recombinant DNA people have not tinkered with theirs. Only your leukocytes will tell what strangers they are battling at the moment. My temptation, however, has been to say: "Yes. I am bringing a trillion or so mitochondria in with me, and can't do anything about it." My knowledge of this foreign creature comes entirely from Lewis Thomas, and I thank John Updike, and his review of *Lives of a Cell* in the *New Yorker,* for bringing mitochondria and Dr. Thomas my way.

I would like the eighties and the nineties to be a decade of pause and reorganization in the world of science and technology, of concentrating on ameliorating the disturbances of the universe before hastening to disturb more. Of not waiting until it is practical, or one is called upon to do so, to be ethical about confessing uncertainties, biases, and conflict of interest. Of having the stature to admit that peers who differ may be right, and reporting the difference. Of realizing that the public pays the cost of the mistakes that may benefit scientists who err. Of permitting the intelligent lay public to be intelligently informed and intelligently listened to. Of compensating for the enormous power of the ubiquitous political action committees (PACs) and the pitifully inadequate perspective of so many of their goals. Of comprehension, at long last, of the larcenous quality of economic growth (and population growth) as presently practiced. Of the frightful penalties that will ensue if we continue to violate the natural laws governing a sustainable ecosystem, so few of them yet grasped.

James Reston's article, entitled "Plunging into the Eighties," in the December 30, 1979, *San Francisco Chronicle,* said many things that bear repeating here, of which I pick one: "The world is being changed, not primarily by the ayatollahs or even by the contemporary leaders of the principal industrial states. The world is being changed by the fertility of the human body and the mind; by ordinary people who produce more children than they can feed and educate; by science that preserves life at the beginning and prolongs it at the end, leaving to the politicians the problem of finding remedies for this deluge."

This deluge, so well illustrated by the MIT computer graphs of U.S. population — 1776, 1876, and 1976 — needs to be further illustrated by a similar graph of the roots of the population peaks: how far must these excesses reach for sustenance, at whose cost? Without waiting for MIT to produce the illustration, we can well imagine what the roots would look like, and how they grew, from the tentative tendrils of U.S. beginnings to the massive conduits it takes to bring one-third of the world's resources to the homes, supermarkets, and highways of one-twentieth of the world's people. Imaging this contorted maze of roots to sustain the peaks of New York, Chicago, and Los Angeles, we can understand, perhaps, the comment of a black lawyer in Michigan a few months ago: "A lot of countries around the world are thinking, 'Maybe we can't afford the United States any more.'"

This concept has apparently entirely escaped the notice of the subject and author of the recently completed *New Yorker* series, "Master of the Trade." It is a profile of Hans Bethe. By my count, part of the profile violates eleven of the responsibilities of members of the scientific community in the draft presented to AAAS members assembled in San Francisco. Whether the violations are the scientist's, the journalist's, or both bears investigation. I consider it despicable, and fully worthy of the kind of analysis the eminent Berkeley scientist, Professor John Holdren, in 232 pages, has given the infamous Inhaber Report. Some of the highlights are reported in "The Inhaber Affair" in the January 1980 *Omni,* in a piece by an author I am often critical of but more often partial (and gave penicillin) to — Kenneth Brower. Professor Holdren had described the Inhaber Report, in vexation, as "by far the most incompetent technical document I have ever known to have been distributed by grown-ups." It was "the shabbiest hodge-podge of misreadings, misrepresentations, and preposterous calculational errors I have ever seen between glossy covers." The *Wall Street Journal* criticized the invective. Holdren and his colleagues wrote: "We believe that the integrity of the whole process of intellectual inquiry and rational debate is too fragile and too precious — and the costs of misinformation too high — to dismiss so blatant an abuse with a shrug."

I'll borrow from Kenneth Brower's final paragraphs:

"Science *is* fragile. It depends, like the rule of law, on the cooperation and integrity of the people involved. It is not impossible that science, though it leads the way, will be our weak link, the first institution to fail under the pressures of the complex new age it has helped us usher in. Perhaps the end will announce itself as scattered breakdowns in scientific integrity — little cancer cells of myth in the body of science.

"In our scenarios, the deranged scientist who ends the world is always a genius, a Dr. Strangelove. In reality, it may be the opposite. Perhaps the scientist who rings in the End will be a spectacular non genius."

No, on second thought, I'll close by myself. With these lines from Tom Lehrer, as I remember them:

The rockets go up
and where they come down,
"That's not my department,"
Said Werner von Braun.

And add the story, from the Acid Rain conference in Toronto, late in the seventies, about the scientific solution to the loss of Adirondack fish from that rain: "Produce an acid-resistant fish." A critic, remembering coal-mine gas and canaries, remarked, "That's like producing a gas-resistant canary." Or, I might suggest, solving the problem of nuclear proliferation by genetic manipulation, and thus creating radiation-resistant people. That would probably be a better solution than the MX Missile, which amounts to putting the Maginot Line on Amtrak.

Let the principles of scientific freedom and responsibility have this goal: That Science is the search for truth; that truth is beauty, which Science ought not destroy; and that Science will not be the convenience of Enterprise, but will instead be a public trust.

From *Progress As If Survival Mattered,* 1981

CLARIFICATION OF THE
CLAY FOOT DEPARTMENT

A STRANGE THING HAPPENED on my way from the lectern. I had asked if anyone knew of the Conant story firsthand, and indeed a man in the audience had been there and did know it. No one asked, however, about the items in my Clay Foot Department; I list them here anyway.

The first ten items listed were wild oats, lantana, eucalyptus, radiata, ARCO grass, rabbits in Australia and New Zealand, English sparrows, starlings, mongoose in Hawaii, opossum in New Zealand. Except for ARCO grass, all these bits of biota were introduced in alien lands with the best intentions to solve nasty problems, but each of them created a much nastier one — unhappy consequences that had not been anticipated.

The radiata is the Monterey pine, which has been planted in ubiquitous monocultures in Australia, New Zealand, and probably elsewhere because it grows fast in latitudes (north or south) like those of the mid-California coast it comes from. It does well provided it gets support from the right mycorrhiza, the root fungus required by *Pinus radiata* as a symbiont. Unfortunately, monocultures are particularly vulnerable to any pathogen that develops a taste for them and decides to wipe them out.

ARCO grass was my shorthand for an alien grass that Atlantic Richfield agronomists had planned to introduce in Alaska to revegetate the tundra their North Slope operations were tearing up.

My clay-foot list didn't get around to kudzu and so-called Russian thistle, pests that have stayed for dinner in ever-increasing numbers.

The other categories in which learned people exposed their feet of clay have less in common.

Anyone my age remembers when the way to treat freezing was to rub the frozen member with snow. Perhaps the assumption was that the exercise would improve circulation more than the rubbing damaged the tissue. Fortunately, that treatment was replaced.

No one thought, when building the London airport, what a splendid vector for disease transmission Heathrow would be. Hardly anyone worries about it now. But let the biological warfare people, in combination with the genetic engineers, come up with a virus like AIDS, and we will certainly wish science had been more prescient, anticipating consequences instead of attending their unwelcome arrival.

The *Apollo* wastewater incident was amusing in a way. The astronauts were sequestered, quarantined until it could be reasonably ascertained that they had brought back nothing our ecosystem couldn't handle. The men bathed. What did they do with the bathwater? They dumped it in the mother ecosystem, the ocean.

Scientists themselves blew the whistle on recombinant DNA research, perhaps because they agreed with Freeman Dyson that they were indeed trying to play God without adequate training for the role. They then unblew it, ignoring the provision of the draft on the responsibilities of scientists that led to my speech: "When practical or when called upon to do so, to identify the limits of uncertainty, personal biases, significant sources of support and possible conflicts of interest which are relevant to [members's] opinions or conclusions." Take some scientists to a two-martini lunch and ask for their reaction to this standard and why it specifies "when practical" instead of "when ethical."

There is a similar question: How disinterested are the AMA and the pharmaceutical people when it comes to self-government? I love them both and am alive thanks to them, but I do not think they are disinterested. There is conflict, and they resist routes to the resolution of that conflict, such as the provisions of the National Environmental Policy Act that give the public a voice.

CETUS and Cohen is just shorthand for the bitterness I felt when Dr. Cohen, without revealing his financial interest in CETUS, the genetic engineering firm, scolded environmentalists for their public interest.

UC, the University of California, and AEC, the old Atomic Energy Commission, drenched themselves in subjectivity without wishing to confess to it in their respective urges to build nuclear weapons and promote, instead of regulate, the nuclear industry. This is symptomatic of the violation of responsibilities the AAAS was trying to get scientists to cope with. They cannot cope with it as long as they are so dependent on the big grant from the industry that wants its right answer confirmed and wants students trained its way. This is an unrelenting vicious circle that produces what Dr. Sam Epstein calls "indentured academics."

The list could go on. The asbestos epidemic, Challenger, Bhopal, chlorofluorocarbons, and Chernobyl hadn't yet made headlines.

Neither had AIDS, Global Warming, Acid Rain, the Ozone Barrier, Third World Debt, and the extinction of a species of plant or animal, at humanity's own hand, every five minutes, more or less. (Where does that number come from? If you accept the frequently heard estimate that there are fifty million species of plants and animals now on earth, that half of them are in the tropical rain forests, and that we will have eliminated those forests in fifty years, we will be losing a species of plant or animal every single minute without knowing it — every ten minutes, if you accept the low, too low, estimate of five million species. Whether it is every minute or every ten minutes, the rate is unacceptable. And that rate doesn't include the millions of species we are insensibly losing in other ecosystems. When the dusky sparrow was obliterated by the U.S. government's careless disposal of toxics, its loss made the news. Another unknown is that once-in-an-earthtime biological miracles transcend what we have been thinking of as endangered species. We are endangering them with our science, technology, and ignorance, and we should cut it out.)

When I spoke about monoculture, miracle wheat, miracle trees, Dow, and a quicker life through chemistry, I over-optimistically assumed that people would know what I was alluding to. People frequently don't.

Monoculture is something nature abandoned, weeded out in the course of evolution. That is what lies behind the old warning not to put all your eggs in one basket (or, as Ansel Adams once found inspiration to say about a restaurant we were about to go to, "Don't put all your Basques in one exit.") Farmers and foresters continue to violate that law at their descendants's peril. Nature invented biological diversity as the inefficient sustainable alternative, not as a last resort.

Miracle wheat, as presently exploited, violates natural law. It is energy-intensive and, as a monoculture, vulnerable to the first pest that evolves to devastate the waving fields of miracle grain. The temporary increase in yield has been chumming farmers, just as the concept of miracle trees has been chumming timber people. The experiment brings immediate enticing gains and ignores their ominous consequences. It is a little like observing the fact that men are bigger and stronger than women and then concluding that it should be men, not women, that we must cultivate henceforth. Such extrapolations fly in the face of Emerson's Law of Compensation, which encyclopedias ignore but which high school English imprinted in me. It was the precursor of the ecological law, There Is No Free Lunch. For every advantage, there is a disadvantage. Or if it sounds good, watch for the catch.

Specifically, if the tree grows faster, the wood may be weaker, or the tree more susceptible to windfall or pests, or its fertility impaired — to name a few unhappy spinoffs. If there is a better way to grow trees sustainably, nature has had plenty of time to discover it. Not even Harvard should try to add to its curriculum a graduate course in playing God.

Dow and other chemical corporations, please copy. Then look into the cost of restoring the ozone barrier and detoxifying soil, aquifers, and mother's milk. Yes, we all use chemicals, and consist of little else, but excuse me if I prefer those we evolved with.

To close this comment, the AAAS experience led me to two conclusions: First, I should suffer jet lag more often and keep a notebook closer at hand to record what I otherwise seem to forget. Second, in future argumentative encounters between sciolist and scientist I should always ask something like this: "Which scientific conclusion are you most confident about now that you think is most likely to be laughed at twenty-five years from now?"

It would be unproductive for the scientist to ask the same question of the sciolist.

Dave receives his first honorary degree at Hobart College. John Kenneth Galbraith already had his.

CHAPTER 13

RETHINKING

—

CURRICULA

—

Trend is not destiny
– Rèné Dubos

HE SCHOOL OF NATURAL RESOURCES, University of Michigan, was certainly one of the best anywhere in 1970. There were nine hundred students in it then. When I spoke there in January 1989 the enrollment had dropped to three hundred, and I don't think my imminent appearance was the cause, either in Ann Arbor or in the many similar schools I have visited since the first Earth Day. The drop in attendance seems contagious. At breakfast in Ann Arbor, Michael Soulé, Barry Lonik, and I talked about the erosion. I spoke of an idea of mine, one of the many I have done too little about, that could rebuild interest. A major foundation, so well endowed it could not be ignored, should ask all American universities three questions: What natural resource curricula have you had, what do you have now, and what are your plans? Associated questions would bring out the details, such as what the courses are; who the teachers are, or have been, or are expected to be; how strong the academic and financial support is; and, of some importance, what has happened to the students? Other people would be asked for their independent evaluations of the curricula and the product.

Michael Soulé liked the idea and added important suggestions: What complementary studies were the universities offering in other departments — art, history, literature, economics, administration? Should we ask Stewart Brand to make a periodical of it, similar to his *Whole Earth Catalog*? More important, should we seek out the causes of the decline we expected the survey would reveal?

It is my suspicion that universities still feel an obligation to train people for jobs that exist in the outside world and that there simply have not been enough job openings for graduates of schools of natural

211

resources. For years I have been advocating that there be more careers in preservation, in advanced study of ecosystems, in interpretation, all in their relation to a sustainable society. Advocacy accomplishes little, however, without an audience, and my audiences were small and my follow-up nonexistent.

I spoke of a recent conversation with someone at San Diego State University. Receiving notice of a conference on Rethinking Curricula, I telephoned to suggest that the subject of environmental restoration, and curricula relating to it, would be a nice addition to the conference. I had previously suggested such an addition to a conference on engineering at the University of California, Los Angeles. Neither university was persuaded. Someone should be — that, at least, was agreed upon at breakfast in Ann Arbor. A similar agreement was also reached at a faculty seminar at the University of California, Santa Barbara; at a faculty club lunch, University of California, San Diego; at a lunch, Museum of Natural History, San Diego; at a Forestry School party, Yale; at the Land, Air, and Water Conference, University of Oregon; at a faculty lunch at Bethel College, Kansas; at an international meeting of university presidents at Talloires, in the French Alps; and at a seminar at Case Western Reserve University, Ohio. My list of seeds planted goes on, but not of how they germinated. Not much has happened.

Is there anyone out there? Rethinking of curricula is essential. People absolutely must be trained for the fascinating, perplexing, rewarding challenges of environmental and social restoration, and there isn't any time to lose. Which foundation wishes to volunteer, and which publishing house — one willing to budget heavily on promotion?

There is no curriculum dealing adequately with restoration at any university. Nor are there people to teach it. One needs to be sure of one's facts, but to me the fact has been oversold. Facts are the result of selectively isolating a few data from their context. I just selectively isolated the "fact" that opens this paragraph. I feel that it is true.

NEW DIRECTIONS

ANN ARBOR AGAIN, six months later, July 1989. The Sierra Club was holding its third national assembly, this time promoted to an international assembly. Canadians were added, and also two men from Brazil, to receive an award for their impressive role with respect to the Chico Mendes tragedy — the murder of a man with a strong ecological conscience. Early assembly plans had called for speeches from three people who could stir the club up — Edward Abbey, the writer; Dave Foreman of Earth First!, and Dave Brower. Unfortunately, Edward Abbey had died unexpectedly, certainly many years too soon. Dave

Foreman had been jailed, but was released on bond in time. Dave Brower had been asked, two months before, to give the speech at the club's annual dinner in San Francisco. I promised to be gentle in San Francisco, but not in Ann Arbor. Many members urged me to speak out. Which I did. Probably more lucid than my speech was my subsequent letter of July 13 to Doug Scott, the club's conservation director, about the Sierra Club, compromise, and what I thought the club should do about it. The letter is, I am afraid, self-explanatory.

It all appears in *For Earth's Sake*, has been reprinted often, has been (indirectly) criticized but once, has been praised by many Sierra Club leaders, the most generous praise coming from a very kind speaker, as the biggest-yet Eugene conference on Land, Air, and Water was nearing its end: "Dave Brower's letter should be read by every environmental leader every Monday morning."

Did my letter to Doug come out of any philosophy of leadership, or was it just Founder's Syndrome? The term does not appear in Webster, and it can probably be defined best by someone who is not suspected of it. There is a hint of it in a remark William E. Colby made when Anne and I went to his home in Carmel for what turned out to be our last meeting.

Will's recollections were fascinating. He remembered meetings, conversations, even the details of the wall covering. He wove a delightful fabric of the world he had known in his decades of conservation leadership. If we, Anne and I, had any sense, we would surely have taped the talk. We had no sense. But we both remember his saying, "There were giants in those days." A slight suggestion of Founder's Syndrome.

Mitigation arrives when one can look at a baby, a grammar school student, any human being still overendowed with youth, and say, "There will be giants in their days," and add, "there may go one of them." Forgiveness comes when, if you see not just one of them, but several, you move some barriers out of the way. Some. Not too many. As my experience with swallowtail butterflies taught me, barriers can be one of the most useful of teaching devices. Perhaps that is one of the functions people with Founder's Syndrome can perform. If I seem to be talking in circles, just remember that I have been a parent for quite a while, and that's what happens to parents. That may be why parents are provided with successors automatically.

No one can diagnose Founder's Syndrome in me with respect to the Sierra Club. It was founded twenty years before I was, forty-one before I joined it. That is long enough ago to produce a different syndrome: call it Seniority Syndrome. Remember what Colorado Congressman Wayne Aspinall said of it: "The longer I've been around,

213

the better I like seniority." Certainly it was that syndrome that led to my writing to Doug Scott as I did. What my own seniority had taught me drove me into trying to drive compromise out of the Sierra Club, or organizations like it. Compromise is all right in its place, essential in a pluralistic society. But if these organizations pursue it, I insist, they are going in the wrong direction.

Similar biases drive my reaction to practices I have watched in meetings of boards of directors. I have served on many and watched even more, but none so much as the Sierra Club's. I wrote the board what I thought on the way home from a retreat in Wildacres, North Carolina, in 1987.

BOARDS IN RETREAT OR
INTERIM THOUGHTS ON BOARDSMANSHIP

I N MY FIFTY-SIX YEARS in the Sierra Club, seventeen of them as executive director, sixteen as a director, and thirteen as a board kibitzer, I have attended six board of director retreats — two at Clair Tappaan Lodge, and one each in Washington state, Alaska, North Carolina, and Colorado.

The retreats build a fine collegial or family relation among the directors, give them a chance to see some nice country, please the few nondirectors who are permitted to attend — a spouse or two, chairs of the council, of the regional vice-president forum, and of the issues committee, the executive director, two or three department heads, and an occasional extra invitee, such as the executive director of the Sierra Club Legal Defense Fund or an expert witness or two.

At sessions and in between, the participants get to know each other better, and there are some valuable one-on-one sessions for the handling of private concerns, or two-on-two or so for the purpose of solidifying factions within the board. There are many friendly sessions at party time. For the most part there is good humor, even some good jokes, and all this can happen with minimum interference from the telephone — or the members, representatives (lower in echelon) of the club's grassroots.

A retreat is, in effect, a two-to-four-day executive session, in which at times a few others are allowed to listen and, at fewer times, to participate.

This exclusivity spreads to the regular board meetings in San Francisco and Washington, D.C., in the hours spent in "working sessions." They, like the retreat, are actually executive sessions. Some of the decisions made there are subsequently voted upon in the open. But some are implicit decisions, governing subsequent action but not voted

214

upon in the open. Votes in the open are *pro forma*. The audience does not know what the pro and con arguments were.

This is a latter-day development within my experience. Prior to my first retreat in 1983 I had, with just two exceptions, experienced no equivalent either of the retreat or of the closed session in the Sierra Club, and only in the dark days of FOE in 1984, when the main office was closed and the most experienced staff terminated, was so much board privacy indulged in. The Sierra Club board did, of course, caucus briefly on the matter of staff salaries and the election of officers, but these sessions were limited to about an hour immediately precedent to open sessions.

Only two exceptions come to mind. To consider who should be the next club president, an executive session was held at the studio of Ansel Adams on Twenty-fourth Avenue in San Francisco. All I remember from that one was the remark by one director, in Ansel's momentary absence, that "if Ansel were elected president it would destroy the Sierra Club." It would have done wonders for the club.

The other exception was an executive session held at Dick Leonard's house in Berkeley in 1968. I learned about it by accident. The agenda, I learned the morning after, was how to get rid of Executive Director Dave Brower, an objective not to be attained until a year later. My chief question about board retreats is, "What is the price of camaraderie?" It is a question we need to ask of directors and of those who look upon the board, wishing they could do so with more respect than they do.

Anyone who has been in the conservation business for a while has attended many public hearings. The hearing is an important ingredient of democracy. It evolved, in an orderly manner, I assume, from the town meeting. Something distasteful happens to public hearings, however, when the ordinary citizen-witness learns that there was a closed-door session before the meeting at which final decisions were reached; the hearing itself becomes but a charade. Various anti-charade laws are passed from time to time, but it turns out to be very difficult to learn what goes on behind closed doors, even given the usual number of leaks, and it's even harder to know what goes on in telephone conference calls that don't have doors to close on them. Or in assorted tête-a-têtes that cannot even be recorded secretly. Without adding to all this the currently popular device, elsewhere, of shredding documents. Some organizations could use their own Freedom of Information bylaw.

But try to understand why all these less-than-happy things come about. A negligent director whose negligence is not witnessed is not vulnerable to suit. If you want to fire someone without fault or liability, don't let anyone know how you go about it. If you favor Government by

215

the Bottom Line, don't let your constituents know what you cut out that would serve the future well but not this year's bottom line.

Too often boards are seen to avoid unnecessary audiences simply because their presence would be an inconvenience. On the other hand, a board must avoid audiences at times, such as when discussing sensitive personnel matters, or to avoid painful public embarrassment of others, or when attorney-client privileges cannot be broadcast. Democracy started a long time ago, and we can thank the Greeks for what they started. They learned what can be accomplished in the agora, the open marketplace. We must also give the Greeks credit for the word 'agoraphobia,' wondering whether boards suffer from it too much.

TAXES

THE INFLUENCE OF THE PRESENT INTERNAL REVENUE CODE is crucial to the direction that the environmental movement — indeed, the volunteer movement — seems determined to travel. I have argued before other organizations that they, like the Sierra Club, should organize educational, lobbying, political, and litigational arms. The Sierra Club, with its huge membership, has excelled in large part because it has all these bases covered.

Long ago I lost my fear of losing tax-deductible status, and transferred it. I now fear that a big deductible endowment can be a potential albatross. I voiced this fear at the Sierra Club board's retreat in 1987. One director responded, "If the directors show fear of having a substantial club endowment, they will soon be replaced." That seemed almost to end any further effort to address the danger. It exists, however, and it is a serious danger.

In short, the danger is that big contributions to endowment have strings attached to them, implicit or inferred if not obvious. And keepers of stringed endowments put strings on their grants. Moreover, those who receive grants with real or suspected strings are the target, justifiably or not, of suspicion. Club members are quite capable of smelling rats. Even though they may be good reliable white pet rats, there is still that telltale aroma, like that accompanying the running of Chevron ads in *Sierra*. Perception can outrun fact.

Let's probe some examples, whether based in fact or fancy:

1. When the Sierra Club's third executive director resigned, there were some resignations of Sierra Club Foundation trustees. Question. If the Sierra Club Foundation had a fifty-million-dollar endowment, income from which the club depended upon for some eight to ten million dollars in annual support, would the club board have felt forced to act differently? Answer. Right.

216

2. "Bill Hewlett doesn't like the club" was a direct quote I heard at the retreat. Question. What might we change in club direction or tactics that would help Bill change his mind? Answer. Several things, if the importance of endowment is allowed to outgrow its need.

3. The Sierra Club Executive Committee authorized a suit to protect the California condor, and Sierra Club Legal Defense Fund attorneys were ready and raring to go. Nothing happened, and rumor has it that the promise of or arrival of a sizable grant produced the death of the suit. Question. Is something like this possible? Answer. Yes.

4. One of the generous donors to the club when he was a director, president, and honorary president was Walter Starr, a noble conservationist, head of Soundview Pulp, later of Scott Paper, and later president of the Yosemite Park & Curry Company. Question. Did his generosity temper the club's actions? Answer. Yes, it did, and I witnessed the tempering and was tempered.

5. The National Audubon Society has a board of directors that a moment's glance will tell you is not impoverished and is not likely to be liberal. They had a president who, although Republican, was liberal in his views of nuclear power and nuclear war and was critical of Reagan, quite openly. Question. Would such a board tolerate the continuation of Russell Peterson's presidency if that seemed likely to imperil Audubon's tax-deductible funding? Answer. Apparently not.

6. In my mid-years I often heard that Audubon would not do anything to make Laurance Rockefeller unhappy. Question. Did they in those years? Answer. They did not.

7. Did I in those years? Answer. I did, and we got no Rockefeller money.

8. Suppose that in seeking centennial endowment the Sierra Club Foundation gets an endowment of say fifteen to twenty million dollars in tax-deductible gifts and the club itself gets that much, or preferably more, in nondeductible but far more numerous contributions (which Sierra Club Foundation President Allen Brown thinks is possible). Question. Would Brower worry? Answer. Not nearly so much.

9. Remember that Doug Wheeler was advocating that the club seek restoration of its (c)3 tax status, a move that would have put the club back in the league of the organizations I was trying to keep it out of. Question. Did many directors sympathize with my concern? Answer. No.

As I further argued at the Wildacres retreat, the club's big endowment is its members. Treat them right and they will continue to be more important than an enormous chunk of endowment — if that endowment is produced at a cost that is not carefully analyzed, including an analysis of how many strings a given dollar has on it, or are perceived to be on it.

217

You can come up with your own estimate of what the member endowment amounts to. I'll settle for mine:

Contented members will remain so for an average of twenty years, paying almost twice their dues each year, counting the additional contributions, and will remember us in their wills for quite a chunk. The figures I plug in are fifty dollars per year for twenty years, or one thousand dollars with a likely bequest equal to that amount. Multiply two thousand dollars by four hundred thousand [at *this* writing $600,000 plus] and you have a big number — a billion dollars or so.

Fabulous! Or insane? Probably a little of both. But we'll never know if we keep our eye on the bottom line and love the number of dollars in our endowment — at the expense of not keeping members contented by assuring them that what they do to make a difference is more important than the dollars they give.

I'll keep on contending that our spending what it takes, now, to put a world-class (I hate the term) handbook in each two of their hands will repay the investment so handsomely that our heads will swim. But that is just part of it. It is fiscally irresponsible to give lip service to the importance of members and grassroots instead of investing in it.

Moreover, each member can be assumed, or ought to be, to put in fifty hours per year (a mere hour a week) worth ten dollars per hour (both figures insultingly conservative) for twenty years, totaling ten thousand dollars. Add dues and monetary contributions over that time and the total is twenty thousand dollars per member. Multiply that by the number of members and you have trillions in human endowment.

A good handbook could help this happen. A few members might do for us what Dave Welisch did (possibly remembering our prewar ski mountaineering trips): he left the club $750,000.

Or, looking at it another way, a member who chooses not to leave money may well donate an enormous number of hours of volunteer time. For example, take Phil Berry's hours, and multiply them not by ten dollars, but by the hourly rate top lawyers charge. We are all worth that, of course.

I realize that this is not likely enough to happen to justify our spending this endowment right away, but remember what Daniel Burnham is supposed to have said (or was it Henry M. Saylor, if you check Bartlett's quotations): "Make no little plans. They have no magic to stir men's blood."

Can the club afford to make only little plans? Remember also what happens these days to corporations that are undervalued. Wait till Sir James Goldsmith hears about the board's estimate of the Permanent Fund, and Brower's of the value of half a million fully enjoyed members.

218

RECRUITING

IF MEMBERS ARE POTENTIALLY OF SUCH GREAT VALUE, how does an organization go about getting them in the first place? In the Sierra Club, from 1892 to 1969, we did not use direct mail. I don't remember its existing prior to my father's being solicited by mail to join the Save-the-Redwoods League, sometime in the twenties. People joined the club to go on summer outings, local walks, and sometimes just to support conservation. Word-of-mouth was the best recruiter, and an applicant had to be sponsored by a member, later by two members. Joining was difficult enough that people who joined stayed joined. The drop rate in 1950 was about 5 percent.

Full-page cause ads in major papers in the sixties brought in many members, but the drop rate increased to 14 percent by 1968. Sierra Club books brought in many members. So did the IRS, for a while. No one brought in members as fast as Ronald Reagan's Secretary of the Interior, James Watt. When he left office, the Sierra Club had to rely on direct mail for about two-thirds of its new members.

When Friends of the Earth began, Jack Shelton designed our first direct-mail piece. It was a six-page letter that he wrote and I signed, accompanied by a photograph of me looking harried in Glen Canyon [on the jacket of *For Earth's Sake*] and an opportunity, if one elected to join in a high enough category, to receive exhibit-format volumes, *Maui* or *Return to the Alps*. The return on some lists we mailed to reached 5 percent. We were so encouraged by this that we went into debt to cover a much larger mailing. It didn't work. It took eight years to recover from that debt.

Rule of thumb for direct mail for members or subscribers is that it costs a full year's dues or subscription to get a member or subscriber. The net income, therefore, comes from renewals. There is no point going into all this except that without recruiting members, an organization fades away, which is worse than going into debt. There were many painful budget sessions on this issue in Friends of the Earth, which suffered severely from not recruiting new members.

All this leads up to a note I put in *Not Man Apart* in June 1971, enlisting sympathy from the victims of direct mail, "About the Power of Your Name."

OUR ADDRESS IN BERKELEY is the Forwarding Center for five relatives, which means that the mailbox groans a little every time the Friends of the Earth list is traded with a cooperating organization. Having had a role in the trade, we understand what is happening. We suspect other members of Friends of the Earth may not.

Therefore, to help you understand:

1) To build a membership that can sustain an effective organization, FOE has several courses open to it:

a) To conduct a newsworthy conservation program, with emphasis on nondeductible lobbying in Washington and other capitals, here and abroad. This is under way, and we have four registered lobbyists working for conservation on Capitol Hill, all of them good. More coming.

b) To publish books bearing our message and name. There are now sixteen, four in large format, twelve in paperback (three of those published in the U.K.). Some have coupons. More are under way — dozens, in fact. They bring members and royalties.

c) To place conservation ads, with coupons inviting membership and contributions. So far we have done three. One ran only in the *Voter's Guide*. A program is under way. They get the message of our choosing to millions; they pay for themselves and bring in members.

d) Direct mail is our other route. We have traded lists with many organizations and have bought lists from still others. We have not traded with anyone whose message would be dull hard sell. We have tried to select those whose purpose would be of interest to our own members. Since we hope to put a million pieces or more in the mail, and since we would like to hope for something approaching a 2-percent response, we have our work cut out for us.

2) If we don't build a membership, we won't be here. Numbers count, in political effect as well as in the program that can be sustained. We have been reasonably successful, but would understandably like to be more so. FOE incorporated July 11, 1969, but did not announce until the following September. Nineteen months later we hover at the 20,000 mark, and seem to be growing some 2,000 a month. Direct mail has been our most successful tool in this growth. Whatever doubts we have about growth *per se* we set aside when thinking about growth of FOE. We hope you share our philosophy.

3) Sharing that philosophy means a certain amount of sharing your mailbox, and this is not always easy. Competing advertising media (i.e., those relying on other subsidies than those direct mail relies on) have coined and rather muddied the term 'junk mail.' Adverse editorials and other attacks abound. Occasional tricks are resorted to by people persuaded by this criticism — worst of them being the wrapping of various heavy objects in a business-reply envelope and sending them in to harry the hapless or villainous direct-mailer. We have persuaded the P.O. to keep such tricks away from our door, but we probably need to add a point or two more than that to help you members be patient.

If It's Junk in Your Box,
It's Junk on Your Porch
Check your daily newspaper. How many of the pages of ads did you ask for, and how many do you get anyway — and accept as a matter of course, learning to turn rapidly past what doesn't interest you? About 75 percent of your newspaper, we would estimate. Meanwhile we are glad to have the opportunity to judge for ourselves what we want to turn by.

If It's Junk in an Envelope,
It's Junk in a Magazine
Check your magazine, ask the same questions, and see if you don't come to the same conclusion — remembering that the magazines get a bigger public subsidy in second-class mail rates than the direct-mail envelopes get.

If It's Junk on Your Table,
It's Junk on the Tube
Check your daily viewing (or listening) and apply the same tests again, remembering that it's public air that is subsidizing the carrying of the message.

The test, we suggest, is up to you. Is the message good enough to warrant your attention, or isn't it? If not, recycle it. (We don't know quite how to recycle a TV commercial, but would welcome suggestions.)

In short, we have selfish reasons for supporting your right to elect what to read, whether you are exposed to it in an envelope, magazine, newspaper, or commercial. We share the wide concern about ads that lead to over-consuming, but naturally do not think our promotional material will lead to anything of the kind.

The power of your name, multiplied by twenty thousand, can get us an audience far beyond what we could otherwise reach — an audience with something in hand and an envelope to reply in. Direct-mail members are by definition overlapping members, but there is virtue in it. Most citizens support, with varying degrees of reluctance, several organizations that could not exist were they not in the business of taking the environment apart. It is well worth belonging to several that try to hold it together. This is latter-day tithing, and blest be the tithe that binds!

DAVID R. BROWER

P.S. If you can't stand it, please let us know, and we'll try to pull a chip or two out of the computer so that it will skip your name at trade time, but not otherwise. Bear with us if you can. We've got a lot of growing to do.

Not Man Apart, June 1971

LEADING

THE EASIEST WAY TO LEAD is to find people who don't need to be led. This is my opinion. I suspect you would get a different one from the Stanford School of Business. There, however, they deal with people in a price bracket quite different from anything I have had to contend with. Conclusion: If you can't pay enough money, substitute independence and watch what happens.

For much of my life, I did not find it necessary to give orders, primarily because I was not in a position to try. I took orders, but never with any great pleasure. I had to give a few when leading large parties up easy Sierra peaks at Berkeley Echo Lake Camp or on Sierra Club High Trips, or when hollering to people on those trips not to swim above commissary. I had to take a good many as an enlisted man, and gave a few as an officer, but very few. In our military climbing schools the enlisted instructors were expert climbers and knew what to do. The one lieutenant who didn't realize this had to be shipped out.

When I became the Sierra Club chief of staff there were so few staff that it would have been silly to give orders. When there were enough staff to order around, I had forgotten how. In the absence of a hierarchical command, leaders developed faster. I finally put my philosophy in words I spoke gently to myself: find good people, delegate authority and responsibility, talk things over if serious mistakes are made, and try to make fewer yourself. This is not a commercial, nor is it an objective view. Check it out with the victims. Try Amory Lovins first, and see if he can remember my directing him to do anything when he was FOE'S United Kingdom representative. I spent most of my time listening and marveling.

Jeff Knight may have different recollections, but my favorite story about Jeff is the letter he wrote President Carter for me November 4, 1977. Jeff was FOE'S energy specialist in the Washington office and knew far more about the Clinch River nuclear project then I did. A group of us met with the president that day and heard him explain in detail how he had tried all possible ways to oppose the relevant legislation and could not now veto it. Jeff's letter, which I signed and handed to the president as the meeting ended gave five succinct reasons for vetoing the legislation. The president did just that, and the veto was sustained.

It may not work out, but Earth Island Institute consists of many projects essentially run by the people who dreamed them up, have a proprietary interest in them, seek what complementarity they can from the people in neighboring projects, and give as much as they seek. It isn't all as idyllic as it sounds, but it builds leaders and gets things done.

The David Phillips story is a model for me. His dean, physicist Richard Bradley, wrote that David was very good. I did nothing about it but David did — intercepting me in Missoula from his college in Colorado Springs. Come to San Francisco and look FOE over, I said. What isn't it doing that you think it should be, and that you can make happen? If you can suggest sources of funding, that will help. He became FOE's wildlife expert and is now one of Earth Island's executive directors.

What will also work are Earth Island Centers.

The first Earth Island Centers I know of, although they never bore the name, were Ansel and Virginia Adams's studios in San Francisco, Yosemite Valley, and Carmel, and Howard Gossage's public relations office in a rehabilitated firehouse in San Francisco. They had this in common: they were a gallery of sorts, there was good music and a good bar when need be, there was innovative material to look at or read, and exciting people were attracted to them to excite and be excited by others.

More recent examples are the visitor center at Mono Lake, California, and the 3220 Gallery in San Francisco. The Mono Lake center has a constant stream of tourists seeking information, who get it from the gallery, bookstore, slide shows, and guided trips. There are no refreshments, but you can get them next door.

The 3220 Gallery has refreshments, schedules programs ranging from fund-raisers to birthday parties to exhibits, and talks about far-away places. There is an abundance of high-tech computerization and video presentations. It monitors Soviet television so well that people from the Consulate come to watch and find out what is going on back home.

Still another Earth Island Center, this one bearing the name, is housed at the main headquarters of The Nature Company, in Berkeley, California — a commercial network of stores presenting merchandise of high quality and great beauty, based on natural designs. The book department offers an extraordinarily broad selection of current environmental titles and video and audio cassettes. There are superb posters and prints, barometers, telescopes, rain gauges, a wide range of crafts emphasizing natural design, inflatable dinosaurs if you have room for them, and the Wrubel Gallery — wherein Tom Wrubel, founder of the company, was kind enough to exhibit a Brower retrospective — assorted bits of information about my boyhood, battles, and books. I am thus not entirely objective about the place.

As of this writing there are twenty Earth Island Centers. We need twenty thousand to jump-start the Green Century.

They can carry out their mission in widely varied places — in a living or rumpus room, in a loft, store, school, church, gallery, museum, visitor center, senior center, day-care or youth or middle-age center, town or city hall, in organization headquarters, in homes of Audubon and Sierra Club chapter leaders, civil liberties centers, women's and men's clubs, and in intensive care units for legislators.

They can provide any or all of several services — library, gallery, supplies of books or tapes or trinkets, computer terminal, billboard, a clublike feeling, refreshments, music, radio, television, VCR, film, mailing lists, and material to carry home to remind you of what's next.

The center can serve many sectors of society — all who care about Peace On and With the Earth. The people in those sectors can include representatives from existing or forming organizations, not necessarily representing those organizations (it may take the organizations so long to get moving that peace could be declared before they accept a role in seeking it), but potential leaders or innovators committed to helping the unrepresented.

That is just the beginning. Add representatives from schools, academic departments, churches, including workers, investors, managers, learners, interns, professors and nonprofessors, with or without blue or white collars, actual or coming artists. Add all the colors — yellow, brown, red, white, and black and blue (there is some skin so dark that it reflects the sky's blue — the other blues are San Francisco tourists wearing shorts in August) who are willing to turn toward green.

In general, it would be good if all hands were capable of loving and being loved, of checking egos and turfmanship at the door, of committing themselves to creating the melting pot for their block or town, or a broader piece of the planet.

Earth Island Centers should aim at a star. Navigators have been doing just that throughout history. They haven't hit one yet, but their aim got them where they wanted to get. Aim for a better reality.

To get there, it would be well to try to discover others's goals, hopes, needs, demands; where they are coming from, what's driving them, what kind of world they want for children — and for youth, maturity, and the old ones. What will help them discover their aggregate abilities (not power, which corrupts) and how to use them now, to listen eloquently, to see with their hearts, to have fun, to create beauty, and especially to restore beauty to what has been marred.

It might help to remember two posterable quotes:

We want a road map, not a stop sign.
A ship in harbor is safe, but that is not what ships were built for.

And to have on hand a supply of *Operating Instructions for The Third Planet* as illustrated by Ali Pearson.

THE
THIRD
PLANET

Operating Instructions

This planet has been delivered wholly assembled and in perfect working condition, and is intended for fully automatic and trouble-free operation in orbit around its star, the sun. 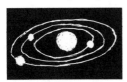 However, to insure proper functioning, all passengers are requested to familiarize themselves fully with the following instructions. Loss or even temporary misplacement of these instructions may result in calamity. Passengers who must proceed without the benefit of these rules are likely to cause considerable damage before they can learn the proper operating procedures for themselves.

A. Components

It is recommended that passengers become completely familiar with the following planetary components:

1) Air

The air accompanying this planet is not replaceable. Enough has been supplied to cover the land and the water, but not very deeply. In fact, if the atmosphere were reduced to the density of water, then it would be a mere 33 feet deep. In normal use, the air is self-cleaning. It may be cleaned in part if excessively soiled. The passengers' lungs will be of help — up to a  point. However, they will discover that anything they throw, spew or dump into the air will return to them in due course. Since passengers will need to use the air, on the average, every five seconds, they should treat it accordingly.

2) Water

The water supplied with this planet isn't replaceable either. The operating water supply is very limited: if the Earth were the size of an egg, all the water on it would fit into a single drop. The water contains many creatures, almost all of which eat and may be eaten; these creatures may be eaten by human passengers. If disagreeable things are dispersed in the planet's water, however, caution should be observed, since the water creatures concentrate the disagreeable things in their tissues. If human passengers eat the water creatures, they will add disagreeable things to their diet. In general, passengers are advised not to disdain water, which is what they mostly are.

3) Land

Although the surface of the planet is varied and seems abundant, only a small amount of land is suited to growing things, and that essential part should not be misused. It is also recommended that no attempt be made to disassemble the surface too deeply inasmuch as the land is supported by a molten and very hot underlayer that will grow little but volcanoes.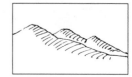

4) Life

The foregoing components help make life possible. There is only one life per passenger and it should be treated with dignity. Instructions covering the birth, operation and maintenance, and disposal for each living entity have been thoughtfully provided. These instructions are contained in a complex language, called the DNA code, that is not easily understood. However,  this does not matter, as the instructions are fully automatic. Passengers are cautioned, however, that radiation and many dangerous chemicals can damage the instructions severely. If in any way living species are destroyed, or rendered unable to reproduce, the filling of reorders is subject to long delays.

5) Fire

This planet has been designed and fully tested at the factory for totally safe operation with fuel constantly transmitted from a remote source, the sun, provided at absolutely no charge. The  following must be observed with greatest care: The planet comes with a limited reserve fuel supply, contained in fossil deposits, which should be used only in emergencies. Use of this reserve fuel supply entails hazards, including the release of certain toxic metals, which must be kept out of the air and the food supply of living things. The risk will not be appreciable if the use of the emergency fuel is extended over the operating life of the planet. Rapid use, if sustained only for a brief period may produce unfortunate results.

B. Maintenance

The kinds of maintenance will depend upon the number and constituency of the passengers. If only a few million human passengers wish to travel at a given time, no maintenance will be required, and no reservations will be necessary. The planet is self-maintaining, and the external fuel source will provide exactly as much energy as is needed or can be safely used.
However, if a very large number of people insist on boarding at one time, serious problems will result, requiring costly solutions.

C. Operation

Barring extraordinary circumstances, it is necessary only to observe the mechanism periodically and to report any irregularities to the Smithsonian Institution. However, if owing to misuse of the planet's mechanism, observations show a substantial change in the predictable patterns of sunrise and sunset, passengers should prepare to leave the vehicle.

D. Emergency Repairs

If, through no responsibility of the current passengers, damage to the planet's operating mechanism has been caused by ignorant or careless action of the previous travelers, it is best to request the Manufacturer's assistance (best obtained through prayer).

Upon close examination, this planet will be found to consist of complex and fascinating detail in design and structure. Some

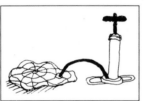

passengers, upon discovering these details in the past, have attempted to replicate or improve the design and structure, or have even claimed to have invented them. The Manufacturer, having among other things invented the opposable thumb, may be amused by this. It is reliably reported that at this point, however, it appears to the Manufacturer that a full panoply of consequences of this thumb idea will not be without an element of unwelcome surprise.
— David R. Brower

These instructions first appeared in The New York Times *in 1975, and were reprinted in* The Reader's Digest *and* Progress As If Survival Mattered. *Illustrations by Ali Pearson.*

Earth Island Institute • *300 Broadway* • *San Francisco, CA 94133*

Dave with Charles Kuralt on Kuralt's receiving the Sierra Club's David Brower Award in conservation journalism, 1989.

OUT TO LUNCH

WHEN THE FRIENDS OF THE EARTH BOARD and I were going through our separation proceedings, the mail was heavy with protestations about who was right and who wasn't. Director Wes Jackson, who heads The Land Institute in Salina, Kansas, was one of those who thought he was right: FOE needed no "ecostars," including me. He was especially right, he thought, about lunch.

Wes is extremely well informed about growing food. He argues that over the centuries the plowshare has done more harm than the sword (although I am sure he would make an exception about what the atomic sword would do to the earth's fertility). He is quite unhappy, properly I think, about what the plow has done. For one thing, it does what nature doesn't. It opens up vast areas of soil to the elements, and nature knows better than to do that. The result is an enormous loss of soil and soil fertility when the rains come, as nature knew they would and therefore kept the soil covered.

So Wes wants the civilized world to treat soil in a civilized manner, to move from an agriculture based on the monoculture of annuals to one based on the polyculture of perennials. Fortunately, the genes of perennial corn were spared [by accident] in Mexico. The last vestige of this species was discovered in Jalisco just before grazing cattle got rid of it. An ear of it is about two inches long. Wes would like agronomists to devote as much time to perfecting perennial corn as they have spent on the soil-wasting annual corn. I agree.

While Wes Jackson is an agro-ecostar with respect to growing food, he lacks one bit of expertise about what to do with food once you have grown it.

One of the best things you can do with food is eat it at lunch. Not just any lunch, but a lunch that is part of a carefully developed passion for finding just the right number of people to discuss over lunch subjects you can never discuss more than five minutes at a time in the office.

The only acceptable substitute for such lunches is a strawberry waffle breakfast at our house. But we are now concentrating on lunch.

Wes was worried about how much I spent for lunch, about the people I took to lunch, and about the alcoholic beverages that were present at the time. He is properly troubled about the agricultural problems we Americans have got ourselves into, and is famous for his ability to address the problem in the earnest voice of a Baptist evangelist. I can forgive him for not having had time to find out what I think lunch is all about and why.

Here, therefore, especially for Wes Jackson, are my criteria for lunch:

1. How many? Never more than five, or there will be too many separate conversations. If you err and have as many as seven, you have to be disagreeable and insist that there be but one conversation at a time.

2. Who? Two criteria. Visiting VIPs should be given lunch companions who are capable both of learning what the VIP has to say and of saying what the VIP needs to learn. These companions should be the staff people most conversant with the VIP's subject, including at least one person to take notes, since I usually misplace mine.

3. Who if there are no VIPs? Department heads whom you have no better opportunity to learn from and talk to, or volunteers or interns who are so poorly paid they can otherwise barely afford a burrito, and have OD'd on the burrito.

4. At whose expense? At company expense, since it is a business lunch, with the only fun resulting from the plenitude of different and interesting things that environmentalists talk about at lunch.

5. But what if there is nothing to cover this expense in the budget? Then charge it to the chairman's (or the president's, or someone's) discretionary fund, set up to cover just such off-budget opportunities. Be sure to have one.

6. Must it be an expensive lunch? No, but not cheap, either, or in scruffy surroundings. And here I must admit how well I rationalize. I like to go to lunch where I have been going to lunch, where the proprietor and staff respond to my loyalty. (In San Francisco it was In the Alley for most of my Sierra Club staff days, and Enrico's, Sinbad's, and Enrico's again [depending on what was close enough to wherever we moved] in my Friends of the Earth and Earth Island days. In New York City it was La Fonda del Sol, as long as it lasted, and the Guard Room or Madison Room at the Biltmore Hotel, while it lasted. New York has not been the same since it lost those national-heritage sites.)

7. But alcoholic beverages? I'm sorry, but I go along with what Abraham Lincoln had to say about General Grant. Nevertheless, you can order Perrier if you prefer.

In summary, the mixture of ages and ideas at lunch is responsible for my looking seventy-nine, not ninety-nine, at my age.

Leaving Paris with Anne in the mid-seventies. (Photo by Edwin Matthews.)

CHAPTER 14

CONSERVATION
AND SECURITY

———

OR REASONS ABUNDANTLY APPARENT in the chapter on the national forests, a good many foresters have been able to restrain their fondness of me, and for this reason I was not selected, although nominated several times, to give the Horace M. Albright Conservation Lecture sponsored by the University of California College of Natural Resources, Department of Forestry and Resource Management. In 1981 the climate changed. By then I had already listened to half the lectures, had known Horace Albright for forty years, admired the series, and jumped at the chance.

Horace Albright heard about it and cheered me on with one of the many letters I received from him, each of them a kind letter, appreciating something I had done, and reminding me again and again that this practice of his was one that I should hurry to emulate. I am still hoping to hurry very soon. His letter of October 30, 1981, arrived a few days before I was to speak.

My Dear Dave:

The University College of Natural Sciences, Forestry Department (John Zivnuska) has written me that you are to give the next lecture in the Albright series, having been appointed Regent's Lecturer for that purpose, and has sent me some copies of the poster issued about your address.

This is just to tell you that I am greatly pleased that you have been selected to give the autumn lecture and I look forward to reading it. My health is still such that I cannot travel anywhere and so cannot make the trip to Berkeley to hear you.

I know it is possible, even probable that you will have something to say against Secretary Watt. I still think he is doing a good job so far as the Park Service is concerned, and I have not noted any serious move on his part detrimental of administering wilderness programs, etc. However, I'm not trying to influence your plan for your lecture. You have always been able to take care of yourself.

You know of course, that I have nothing to do with this series, the selection of speakers or otherwise. It was established back in 1959 or 1960 at the suggestion of Bob Sproul at a tribute dinner given to me in Washington, D.C., on

December 4, 1959, and funds for it were soon subscribed by friends of the Park Service, the University, and I do not know the many others.

I was still a pretty sick man when you were down here in February, so have little recollection of what we talked about. I got the idea you were coming again, and hope you will, both Lady Brower and you. I am quite 'housebound,' am here nearly all the time, must use a walker to get around, etc., and my eyesight is very poor. I cannot read what I have just written above. Years ago I learned the 'touch' system of typing and tried to retain that skill, hence this letter with all its errors. Please forgive them. [There were eleven, all corrected here.] My warm regards and continuing admiration to you good folks.

Faithfully yours,
Horace

P.S. My health is still far from good, but I'm well cared for in the home of my daughter and her husband. I'll be 92 in January. I still miss my beloved wife of 65 years who died of cancer in June, 1980. I miss her terribly. You know she was a classmate in the UC class of 1912, and of Newt Drury's in high school.

H.M.A.

On Armistice Day 1981, appearing in the Life Sciences Building auditorium just fifty years after attending botany lectures there briefly and dropping out of the university, I found the hall jammed with what would be as receptive an audience as I ever encountered. I opened with my sermon about the view of the Earth if reduced to the size of an egg, and its age squeezed to six days, then began the lecture:

LET THE TWENTY-SECOND ALBRIGHT LECTURE BEGIN with words from a book published two years before Horace Albright graduated from this campus (and two years before I was born a few blocks from it).

In 1910, Charles Richard Van Hise wrote in *The Conservation of Natural Resources in the United States,* ". . . the period in which individualism was patriotism in this country has passed by; and the time has come when individualism must become subordinate to responsibility to the many." He realized that "we cannot hope that we shall be able to reverse the great law that energy is run down in transformation, or that we can reuse indefinitely the resources of nature without loss." He wondered what changes in social structure would result "when people begin to feel pinched by meager soil and the lack of coal." (He had already concluded that the greatest use for petroleum would be as a lubricant and had not contemplated that automobiles would use any.) He concluded that "the paramount duty remains to us to transmit to our descendants the resources which nature has bequeathed to us as nearly undiminished in amount as possible, consistent with living a rational and frugal life." He concluded: "In a few thousand years man has risen from the level of the savage to the height of the great creations of science, literature, and art. . . . It is in order that humanity itself may be given an opportunity to develop through millions of years to come under the most advantageous conditions that we should conserve our natural resources, and thus make possible to billions of future human beings a godlike destiny."

And his text ended with a familiar line: "Conservation means 'the greatest good to the greatest number — and that for the longest time.' "

Even as he was writing, people were forgetting a critical part of that definition — "for the longest time." They were already eroding and ignoring the Declaration of Governors adopted May 15, 1908, at the White House conference for conservation of natural resources called by President Theodore Roosevelt. Van Hise himself had not begun to appreciate the devastating forces about to be unleashed by the addiction to exponential growth. He foresaw, for example, that the burning of coal could cause trouble, and cited a physicist who had identified the greenhouse effect by 1896 and had predicted that if the carbon dioxide in the atmosphere increased by two and a half to three times its 1896 value the temperature in the arctic regions must rise eight to nine degrees centigrade and produce a climate as mild as that of Eocene period (abundant vegetation existed in Greenland then). Van Hise suggested that "the coal consumption may become so rapid as to accomplish this in a thousand years or less."

How quickly have we reduced that thousand to two hundred or less! And how firmly have we refused to take individualism out of our patriotism, or extend patriotism to include an ardent love for an entire Earth! But it is not too late. And we can still care about the millennia yet to spin out, and be concerned about the largest population of all. That consists of the billions of people to come, and all the billions of children they will wish to have and see grow up with hope in all those millennia. Their genes are now in our custody. Quite a responsibility, that one!

We have work to do. Today, "the longest time" is being given the shortest shrift in history. There is no greater threat to national security, or to the global security to which our own is inextricably tied, than the present rampant discounting of the future — the economists's greatest sin. It fuels the insane contest now being exacerbated by the superpowers. That contest can, in a moment's confusion, bring the nuclear exchange that would end forever the dream of a "godlike destiny" for humanity. It would also extinguish the biological diversity any benign successors would need. As President Carter said in his farewell address, World War III would be brief.

Ray Dasmann, who gave the Albright Lecture in 1976, says: "We are already fighting World War III and I am sorry to say we are winning it. It is the war against the earth." We were warned of this a decade ago in *Blueprint for Survival,* by Robert [Prescott-] Allen, Teddy Goldsmith, and the team from Britain's *The Ecologist*. More warning came in the Club of Rome's *The Limits to Growth* and *Mankind at the Turning Point*. The alarm was sounded in Stockholm in 1972 at the first major international conservation conference. In spring 1980 the International Union for Conservation of Nature urged, after a long study joined by many nations and scientists, that a world conservation strategy was essential, and they published *How to Save the Earth*, by Robert Allen, but not widely enough. The Brandt Commission increased global anxieties in its study of the North versus South conflict. *The Global 2000 Report to the President* was issued in July 1980 after three years' preparation, to bring the warnings splendidly up to date. The Global Tomorrow Coalition of more than fifty U.S. organizations is trying to keep the warning system operable. Meanwhile, Herman Kahn, Julian Simon, and David Stockman, who must be loved by the Fortune 500, try to dismantle the system; signs saying "Bridge Out" annoy them.

Not to let earlier prophets be forgotten, be it known that all these warnings were anticipated in an extraordinary book published in 1960, drawn from an exhibit assembled by the Sierra Club in 1955, both under the title, "This Is the American Earth." Both were instigated by the 1975 Albright lecturer, Ansel Adams. The text and design were by Nancy Newhall. All in all, I have known fourteen of the Albright lecturers, but worked with Ansel Adams more than with all the rest combined. Most of that work was on the exhibit, the book, and the many good things they led to.

For one thing, *This Is the American Earth* led to nineteen other Sierra Club books in the same format and to ten more published by Friends of the Earth. For another, it led to Justice William O. Douglas, who called the book "one of the great statements in the history of conservation," and soon thereafter served on the club's board of directors. This in turn led to a letter from him to me that is one of the high points of my life. He had attended a Ford Foundation dinner, had there been told that they wanted his recommendations about how to reorganize their conservation program, and he ended his letter with "What shall I say?"

Robert Golden and I (he was on the club staff) put our heads together. With coaching from Dr. Dan Luten, well known in natural-resources circles on this campus and many others, we devised a five-point program. Justice Douglas put it in his own words and presented it to the Foundation, where most of it seems to have been ignored. He asked me to follow up and I tried, first presenting it to the public at the Sierra Club's 1963 Wilderness Conference in San Francisco. (It was also published in the 1964 annual *Sierra Club Bulletin* and in Friends of the Earth's *Not Man Apart* shortly after Justice Douglas died.)

Let me present those five points to you now, briefly and in reverse order. Four of them are as essential as they ever were, and the last is the most important task there is, I submit, for all of us.

We called first for a program to build careers in preservation. We noted the need to balance the "wise use" graduates with guardians of reserves, and to give status to both kinds of careers, not just wise users. We wanted to inculcate ecological literacy in all fields, and still want to. We need guardians of reserves in a broader sense — genetic reserves, places where the biological diversity of the Earth can keep diversifying. Zoos and seed banks are fine for those who like them, but aren't even a down payment on survival.

Next we asked for a crash program for reserving the irreplaceables. Private philanthropy must be relied upon, we thought, for revolving funds with which to buy and hold certain key areas, particularly those in which wilderness and biological diversity are paramount and threatened. The funds would revolve whenever it was politically possible for the government — the commonwealth — to exercise its responsibility for the commons. The Ford Foundation liked the idea and provided a six-million-dollar line of credit to the Nature Conservancy to help carry it out. In our present situation the need is greater than it was then. We need a thousand times that much now, across the whole foundation front.

Third was a plan for the reinterpretation of nature — a conservation education program. The objective would be to inform the public as promptly and thoroughly as possible about ecosystems and peaceful stability — more about which in a moment. The reinterpreters would need to avoid economic and natural-resource clichés and would be prohibited from saying *interface, elitist, input, output, parameter, paradigm, prioritize,* or *holistic.* As Les Pengelly observes, holistic is being used as a noun, an adjective, and a substitute for thought.

Fourth, we wanted a center for the advanced study of ecosystems. This was the brainchild of the late Edward H. Graham, of the Soil Conservation Service, who proposed it in 1961, the year of the first Albright lecture. The center would seek out some Einsteins of biology and give them a chance to speak out freely after some reasonable periods of unharassed thought. Such a center could explain the Law of the Minimum to us (e.g., it doesn't help to have more water than you need if you run out of air, or coal, or grain, or people, or governments). It could help produce such people as Robert MacNamara wanted around to help him invest World Bank funds in ways that would be ecologically sound.

He wanted a thousand trained ecologists then and couldn't find them. In keeping with Dr. Graham's dream, the center might lead us toward ecologically sound agriculture instead of present agricultural mining methods now being followed that could drive society into the ground.

Most important, we wanted the Ford Foundation to make a major effort toward developing a blueprint for the economics of peaceful stability. If the Ford Foundation had listened, I would not have felt the need to give this lecture. And you would not be burdened with my using, as preface to the meat of the lecture, what we said in 1962 about the blueprint for peaceful stability, extracts from which follow, slightly edited:

The "vigorous growing economy" all our leaders keep exhorting us to produce is not possible on an earth of fixed size, and continuing attempts to produce it are *the* basic threat to peace.

The momentum of this phrase is so great that it will take a major effort to offset it and prove we can live without it. The UN is already showing concern about the question, Can the economy withstand peace? The concomitant question is, Can limited resources withstand a constantly expanding expenditure? The answer to the first question is and must be yes, and to the second question, no. Both answers are painfully obvious but universally avoided. There is no better cause than to face them squarely and learn to live with them.

It doesn't take much imagination to demonstrate that unending growth will do our children and theirs out of the heritage they deserve — and that we can survive without that unending growth and *only* without it. Do you know any conservation group that is giving this serious consideration? I don't think you do. It is one of the taboos. I do not think you can find an agency in government yet willing to question growth. But some growth is bad — for instance, malignant growth. One way to combat malignancy is to examine for it periodically. I believe there is malignancy in our economy, and that all conservation will fail unless it is checked. We need to get the checking started. We ought not be lulled by the euphoric statement, "Man's power to mold the world to his liking is almost unlimited."

We would do better to remember Loren Eiseley's warning about "the wounded outcry of the human ego as . . . it learns that the world supposedly made for its enjoyment has existed for untold eons entirely indifferent to its coming."

"The need is not really for more brains," Eiseley said, "the need is now for a gentler, a more tolerant people than those who won for us against the ice, the tiger, and the bear. The hand that hefted the axe, out of some old blind allegiance to the past, fondles the machine gun as lovingly. It is a habit man will have to break to survive, but the roots go very deep."

Elsewhere Eiseley spoke of the machine gun's monstrous successor. "He holds the heat of suns within his hands and threatens with it both the lives and happiness of his unborn descendants . . . caught in a physiological trap and faced with the problem of escaping from his own ingenuity."

Paul Sears has told us this: "As we lengthen and elaborate the chain of technology that intervenes between us and the natural world, we forget that we become steadily more vulnerable to even the slightest failure in that chain."

Joseph Wood Krutch agreed: "It is not a sentimental but a grimly literal fact that unless we share this terrestrial globe with creatures other than ourselves, we shall not be able to live on it for long."

Lewis Mumford adds: "To put all our hope in the improvement of machines is the characteristic inversion and perversion of the present age; and that is the reason that our machines threaten us with extinction, since they are now in the hands of deplorably unimproved men."

So we need a blueprint for an economy that will endure in peaceful stability, that will not require the war with the environment that leads to war with fellow man. The blueprint will not be easily prepared, nor can we keep all our bad habits and live with it. Neither can we keep our bad habits too long and live at all. If we learn the importance of living at peace with our environment, wilderness will be safe. So will we.

Which brings us to Henry David Thoreau: "What's the use of a house [or now we might add a city or a farm, or a small business or a multinational, or a superpower or a symphony] if you haven't got a tolerable planet to put it on?"

I have mellowed enough since 1962 to put the question a different way: What kinds of growth must we have and which kinds can we no longer afford? As the first of two assignments, would you please make your own list of what growth to add and what to subtract? By combining your list and others in some impressive way, we may be able to persuade people with capital on hand to invest it or deny it more usefully, with their goal being the building of a sustainable society, as proposed by Lester Brown of Worldwatch. Investors can make changes faster than governments can. They are rapidly putting nuclear power out of business. Their investment in oil conservation instead of in oil squandering could speedily cool our temptation to risk the society in order to preëmpt Middle East oil. Alternate investment could encourage our and Soviet disarming, and help defuse the population bomb.

In the brief period since the ink dried on the proposal to the Ford Foundation, the earth's population has grown by a billion. When the echo has died on these words and nineteen more years have passed, our present habits will put another two billion people on earth (if we can find enough firewood to cook their food), double the present acreage of the earth's deserts, extinguish a million or two species of plants and animals, and otherwise multiply ecological insults and deplenish the

239

Earth. By then it bristles with missiles — if they have not already been sent on their mission to extinguish us all. If Armageddon had not yet arrived the superpowers would by then have spent some twenty-five trillion dollars on armament — and the opportunity to build a sustainable society on the earth would have been deprived of that much capital, resources, human effort, and human freedom.

Is there a better direction for our society to choose? A way to find friends, not lose them? A sensitivity to what is leading the separate superpowers to join in panic? Can we find an antidote to all this? A rededication to the idea that led us to become a nation, updated with our knowing now that the world flows together or blows apart? A willingness to share resources with the people who are here now, and share also with so many more yet to arrive here, with needs as real as ours, including their need to know that we were capable of thinking of them? More immediately, can we protect our children's right to have a chance to grow up, and our own right to love watching them grow up?

There is a better direction, and the president of the most powerful nation on earth — one that once had a dream — doesn't know it. Nor does the team he selected. He and they are leading us into unprecedented disarray, with malice toward all but a favored few. Call it The Disarrayed Society of Ronald Reagan. The threat of the final war is so huge and so imminent that we can forgive ourselves for not wanting to think about it, but we dare not fail to think about it. People who bury heads in sand these days may all too soon find that sand fused.

In short, President Reagan has sidelined outstanding Republican conservationists, irritated Wall Street, alarmed our friends abroad, frightened the Third World nations by deepening the inequity of our relations with them, and could be driving our supposed adversary, with whom we have never fought, to desperation. He has said it is none of our business who has the bomb and denied having said so. He has said "It is not the business of other nations to make American foreign policy" and then said that he "was misinterpreted." He has crippled energy-saving and oil-substituting programs and has massively increased nuclear subsidies. He supports the Clinch River Breeder Reactor boondoggle and has supported reprocessing of spent nuclear fuel. This could lead to one of the most horrendous of domestic threats. Nuclear weapons expert Theodore Taylor has said that the destruction of a reprocessing plant that had been operating for ten years could release more Strontium-90 and Cesium-137 than would the detonation of all the nuclear weapons now on earth. Were this to happen in Western Europe, the region would be rendered uninhabitable for many years. Reprocessing would also make a mockery of the Nonproliferation Treaty which, weak though it is, is the best the world has achieved so far in slowing the spread of nuclear weapons. He [Ronald Reagan] has said that he believes limited nuclear war is possible. He has rescued the neutron bomb and pushed forward the MX Missile and other moves by President Carter giving the U.S. a first-strike capability. When secretaries Haig and Weinberger contradict each other about firing a nuclear warning shot, he lets it be said that both are right. He has ground the improvement of the national park system to a halt when every delay adds enormously to cost. Let it be added that he has issued a splendid statement in favor of saving whales. For that act we are grateful. Not for the others. We would favor the president's consistent support for corporations if corporations were not so often a device for separating enterprise from conscience — and the hiring of a pride of lawyers to keep the gap intact.

I would urge the president to replace what is becoming known as the Reagan wrecking crew with competent Republicans. There are many: they brought about environmental achievements by President Nixon that most people have forgotten. It would not hurt to add a Democrat or two. Bipartisan moves have worked well in the past. Thoughtful analysis of conservation matters would improve national security by leading away from the Strength Through Exhaustion syndrome that recent presidents, including Mr. Reagan, suffer from. Mr. Reagan is extraordinarily in need of environmental homework; otherwise we could justifiably publish a Ronald Reagan Environmental Handbook, consisting of a three-by-five card file, empty.

We are hoping that the Republicans who carried Mr. Reagan to the presidency will see the immediate importance of persuading the president to make conservation moves in the interest of national security.

The alternative, it seems to me, is that his farewell address be expedited.

These words are harsh, harsher I am sure than were ever spoken in an Albright lecture, harsher than Horace Albright himself has used, far harsher than I like to use or have ever used, but use now because I must. The war that no one wants is inevitable, unless we say no. A chorus of voices in both political parties is saying no and needs to be joined. So do the voices with vast military experience, including words President Eisenhower spoke and President Reagan should memorize. So do the voices of the scientists and engineers working other fields than preparation for war, fields that need the skills of the other half of the professions who are coöpted for war. So do the voices of those who think self-interest has driven us too long, that technology has become too rampant, that serenity and faith and love are all but lost and must not be.

I could list things that these and other people think our change of direction should consist of and that I agree with, but it is far better for you to come up with the list. Perhaps in this way:

You are president. You have a trillion dollars to spend in the next five years to enhance national security, which itself cannot be enhanced without a context of global security. You know how much more important conservation is than did the governors President Theodore Roosevelt summoned to the White House. You know, as you look about you in your own neighborhood, your state and nation and planet, what things need to be done and what seem most important to you. So with this trillion dollars at your disposal — and when did anyone ever offer you that much before, with only one string on it — what would you spend it on between now and the end of December 1986 to increase the earth's security and hence our own? The string? You may not spend it on weapons. You realize, of course, that a nuclear Maginot Line would be far worse than useless. You realize, too, that if you do not spend it on weapons, the Soviet leadership will not need to do so either. So that makes two trillion dollars or equivalent available for healing the earth instead of wounding it further.

While you are thinking of items for your list, I'll reveal that the first item that came to my mind was reforesting the earth — not all the original forest land, of course, but that which should no longer remain derelict. Alfred Heller would spend his trillion dollars on exactly what is being started on the Santa Cruz campus, expanded to global scale — agri-ecology. Combined with Mr. Fukuoka's *One Straw Revolution* (growing crops in a sequence that avoids the need for fertilizers and pesticides) and Wes Jackson's *New Roots for Agriculture* (relying not on monoculture of annuals, but on polyculture of perennials, "growing granola" to avoid plowing), agri-ecology could bring about a sustainable food supply for an otherwise sustainable population.

Visualize the MIT computer map of the U.S. population in 1776, 1876, and 1976. In 1876 Los Angeles is barely perceptible — enough to assure even a Herman Kahn that we can't go on in the next century the way we carried on in the first two.

The other map exists only in my mind — a demographic-drain map to show what resources were required to sustain our new population peaks, a map in which the area of countries is the product of their population multiplied by their resource drain. *Newsweek* published a map on October 26, 1981, that comes close, but not close enough. Something better than gross national product is needed to measure the drain of resources. For example, the U.S., with 5 percent of the world's population, uses one-third of the resources; the remaining 95 percent use the other two-thirds — a ratio of about ten to one. Our 225 million, multiplied by ten, equals 2.25 billion, half the earth's population. On the global map, then, the U.S. would look like Mount Everest. Africa would be flat. I think that if we looked long and hard at such a map, we would realize why a lot of nations are thinking they can't afford us. When I first heard that comment, scenes from Italy flashed through my mind, abandoned castles on hills, castles once comfortably occupied by the affluent

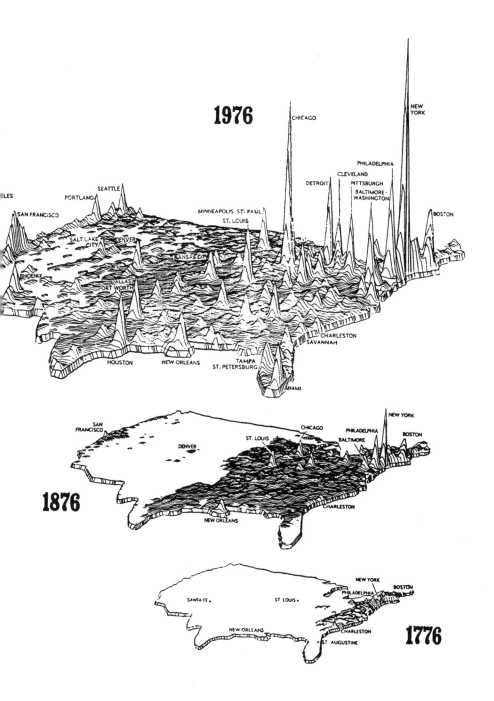

243

who thought that if they kept their supporting peasants ill-clothed and ill-housed and ill-fed enough, the peasants couldn't muster enough strength to cause trouble. You could simply tell them to lift themselves by their own bootstraps, mind the magic of the marketplace, and buy a do-it-yourself covered wagon and go west, as President Reagan has in effect told the Third World.

We have better ideas, and I am sure you do. For the full list of things to spend a trillion on, I refer you to *Progress As If Survival Mattered: A Handbook for a Conserver Society*. But while you are waiting to see it, and before I give you your next assignment, let me try another idea out on you.

One of the nicest angles of all is the 180-degree angle. It enables one to change direction completely and still go straight. It is the face-saving angle, and I suggest that it is time to use it. The superpowers, instead of standing toe-to-toe, ought to stand back-to-back and see not what they can do to each other, but what they can do for the rest of the world. Contemplate a U.S.-Soviet Marshall Plan. Let it invest not in containment or resource depletion, but in resource recovery, in finding ways to avoid fatal battles over what is in the bottom of the barrel, to get our own numbers down, with deliberate speed, to what the bounties of a limited earth can sustain. If this means an orderly retreat from the Land of Self-Interest and Avarice, perhaps we have been there too long anyway. If all this sounds utopian, the alternative is oblivion. Easy choice.

The most important investment toward global security that the North could make, as it looks more at the South's needs instead of so much at its own, is investment in recovery of renewable-resource potential. How can the lesser-developed countries use sun and soil better for their own advantage, even if that means we are deprived of some surfeit? There are various ways of going about this. A first requirement is to change our mindset. Studies help.

Back in the mid-1950s we came up with the idea of a Scenic Resources Review. It was suggested by the periodic Timber Resources Review, and I thought we ought to look at intangibles as systematically. Renamed the Outdoor Recreation Resources Review, which missed the point, it was too limited, and it is time to try again.

Perhaps a global Renewable Resources Review and Intangible Resources Review could carry on where the *Global 2000 Report to the President* left off, and give the present administration something to do besides dismantle the century's conservation gains in order to find money for missiles. Instead of threatening to withdraw support from the United Nations Environment Program, the U.S. could increase support in order to celebrate, in 1982, the tenth anniversary of the Stockholm Conference on the Human Environment [or the twentieth in 1992]. Preparation for that could assist groundwork for still another anniversary — the seventy-fifth (diamond jubilee) anniversary of the Governor's Conference on Natural Resources that Theodore Roosevelt convened at the White House. John F. Kennedy called one, as one would expect; his interest in conservation was obvious in his appointments. In the Roosevelt conference only one voice, that of J. Horace McFarland, spoke in behalf of scenic resources. In the Kennedy conference it was the other way around, and only one voice spoke for utilitarian conservation — Congressman Wayne Aspinall of Colorado. Gifford Pinchot won the first round, John Muir the second.

Ronald Reagan now has a chance to make use of that 180-degree angle. He could call for the seventy-fifth anniversary, in mid-May 1983, a White House Conference on Conservation and Global Security. There is just enough time for sound preparation. He should welcome bipartisan support. Richard Nixon's chief environmental advisor, Russell Train, currently co-chairman of the Year 2000 Committee, knows how to use such support. He has also worked with Soviet conservationists. The conference could have no more important goal than developing means by which a bipartisan world could develop and apply conservation plans for the longest period of peaceful co-existence in the earth's history.

We could remind President Reagan that physicians, who are not notorious for their radical attitudes, have set an example by organizing Physicians for Social Responsibility. They are having an enormous influence, for which we can be most grateful, in awakening the world to the nuclear menace. Perhaps it is time to organize Politicians for Social Responsibility — responsible for seeking a sustainable society on a global scale.

If this is a dream, buy it. Unless you are hooked on nightmares.

We are back to you and your trillion dollars. Assuming that you would not take the easy out — sparing the taxpayers of that burden in the first place — what else would you do? What ten programs would you have the United States design, with your help, to improve the human condition and the life-support system most humans depend upon? What programs now being starved, or not yet thought of, because of our preoccupation with weapons, Trident, MX, cruise missile, throwweight, ground zeroes, missile fratricide, electromagnetic pulse, assorted euphemisms for megadeath, and the needless acceleration of mutations, few of them desirable? Ten is a good enough number to start with. Take your time in making out the list and the allocation of funds to each item. Your papers will not be due until Christmas, a day on which quite a few people on earth remember to celebrate a Prince of Peace who said the meek would inherit the earth and who presumably did not think it would have been subdued and incinerated before they received title to it.

Send your list to me, if you will. Perhaps we can get the Gallop or Harris people to tabulate the data for us. Above all, send a copy to

245

Presidents Reagan and Brezhnev. You may wish also to send President Reagan a copy of President Eisenhower's farewell address, urging that his own be as thoughtful, his intervening performance better. Remind him, if you will, that the 10 percent of the American populace who voted for him (plus the votes he received that were against Jimmy Carter) do not constitute a mandate for him, much less for Mr. Watt, Messrs. Edwards, Haig, and Weinberger, or Senator Laxalt, Joseph Coors, and Mrs. Gorsuch. Or for Mr. Meese — who supported the philosophy of the Governor Reagan who a few years ago was willing to have a blood bath on this campus.

Harsh words again, yes. Derived from fright, and the wish, however poorly put, to motivate you into seeing that this planet does not perish from the Universe because you had part in letting it.

Your list of ten steps toward survival need not be harshly presented. Let your prelude be the words of the man who lost to General Eisenhower: UN Ambassador Adlai Stevenson, in his last speech, given in Geneva in July 1965, left us this wisdom, in the finest conservation message I know about our traveling together, passengers on a little spacecraft.

These words should be in all the places that celebrate the 1945 agreement that war must no longer be the route to resolution. It should be carved in stone at the United Nations centers, translated as necessary, in as grand a manner as can be afforded. It should be ten feet high in the Oval Office, printed somewhere on every calendar. And remembered in every heart, especially the line in which we are spared by "the work, the care and, I will say, the love we give our fragile craft" — love given the earth, ourselves, and our fellow creatures, remember (as we so often do not) that love is the one resource that will be exhausted only if we forget to use it.

The Horace M. Albright Conservation Lecture

The lecture reveals my habit of seeking approval by association. It was reassuring to suggest that people like Thoreau, Eiseley, Sears, Dasmann, Mumford, and Stevenson agreed with me. Having made a few rather provocative statements myself in the lecture, I sought out further contemporary endorsement, and in the printed version added reinforcing words from two ambassadors, a general, an editor, and a senator.

The Window of Opportunity

W. Averill Harriman, former ambassador to Moscow & Undersecretary of State, Washington Post *Op Ed, November 4, 1981.*

We are in danger of ceding our destiny to the whims of nuclear weapons, trusting to good fortune to see us through the nuclear arms race when we should be trusting to ourselves.

The strategic forces of the United States and the Soviet Union carry explosive power more than 100,000 times greater than the Hiroshima bomb. Far from saying "enough," both nations are increasing these forces. . . .

America must take advantage of the window of opportunity it now has to limit nuclear arms. . . .

Negotiations to limit nuclear arms and reduce the risk of war are hardheaded exercises to improve our national security. They signal no approval of other Soviet actions, such as Afghanistan — no more than do sales of American grain to the Soviet Union. They seek, despite the irreconcilable ideologies of our two nations, the common goal that nuclear weapons have made a necessity — the prevention of nuclear war.

In our short time on Earth, we have a choice about the kind of world we leave behind. With nuclear weapons in our custody, our generation carries a heavy obligation. There will be no historian to record one day that we failed on our watch.

Reagan's Military Policy Is in Trouble

*General Maxwell D. Taylor, Army chief of staff under Eisenhower, and chairman of the Joint Chiefs of Staff under Kennedy and Johnson.*Washington Post *Op Ed, November 2, 1981*

With the Reagan economic policy in trouble, his military policy cannot be far behind. Like the voice of the turtle, a swelling chorus of critics and skeptics is rising to question the validity of the goals and programs that constitute a seemingly disjointed military policy. The critics stress the estimated cost of over a trillion dollars in five years and the likely effect on government deficits and social programs. . . .

Implicit in both the criticism and the skepticism is a feeling that the administration does not have a military policy worthy of the name. . . . The administration seems committed to preparing for the least probable threats to the neglect of the most probable.

If the Reagan policy is as deficient as these criticisms (Taylor's) imply, can anything be done to retrieve the situation at this late hour? It would require fundamental changes of policy involving a broadened recognition of the threat, a restatement of policy goals and a new set of guidelines for the structuring of the armed forces. . . .

New stress placed upon the role of the armed forces in securing our national power base in the Western Hemisphere and in protecting the national economy should appeal to the average citizen who wants to wee the relation between increased military expenditures and his own way of life. A modified policy would offer him a reasonable chance to remain safe without going broke in the process.

Perils of Arms Race

George Kennan, former ambassador to Moscow and architect of the containment doctrine, basis of American policy toward the Soviets for decades. In SF Chronicle, November 9, 1981 *(from the* New Yorker*).*

What I see [in the Kremlin] is something quite different.

I see a group of troubled men — elderly men, for the most part — whose choices and possibilities are severely constrained. I see these men as prisoners of many circumstances: prisoners of the antiquated ideology to which their extreme sense of orthodoxy binds them; prisoners of the rigid system of power that has given them their authority; but prisoners, too, of certain ingrained peculiarities of the Russian statesmanship of earlier ages — the congenital sense of insecurity, the lack of inner self-confidence, the distrust of the foreigner and the foreigner's world, the passion for secrecy, the neurotic fear of penetration by other powers into areas close to their borders, and a persistent tendency, resulting from all these other factors, to overdo the creation of military strength. I see her men deeply preoccupied, as were their Czarist Russian predecessors, with questions of prestige — preoccupied more, in many instances, with the appearances than with the realities.

I do not see them as men anxious to expand their power by the direct use of their armed forces, although they could be easily frightened into taking actions that would seem to have this aim.

I believe, too, that internal developments in the Soviet Union present a heavy claim on the attention and priorities of the Soviet leaders. They are deeply committed to the completion of their existing programs for the economic and social development of the Soviet peoples, and I am sure that they are very seriously concerned over the numerous problems that have recently been impeding that completion: the perennial agricultural failures; the many signs of public apathy, demoralization, drunkenness, and labor absenteeism; the imbalance in the population growth between the Russian center and the non-Russian periphery; the increasing shortage of skilled labor, and the widespread economic corruption and indiscipline.

They differ among themselves as to how these problems should be approached, but I doubt whether there are any of them who think that the problems could be solved by the unleashing of another world war.

I believe that until we consent to recognize that the nuclear weapons we hold in our hands are as much a danger to us as those that repose in the hands of our supposed adversaries there will be no escape from the confusions and dilemmas to which such weapons have now brought us, and must bring us increasingly as time goes on.

For this reason, I see no solution to the problem other than the complete elimination of these and all other weapons of mass destruction from national arsenals; and the sooner we move toward that solution, and the greater courage we show in doing so, the safer we will be.

The Reagan Hoax

John B. Oakes, former editorial page editor; former senior editor, New York Times. *NYT Op Ed, November 1, 1981*

While a bemused public and a leaderless Congress look on, foreign and domestic policies that are classic throwbacks to Hoover, Harding, and McKinley arre now being locked into place — with a dash of secretive, imperious Nixonism tossed in.

President Reagan has substituted a mindless militarism for a foreign policy, rattling arms from El Salvador to West Germany,. . . an openended arms race that poses a greater threat to our own internal and external security than all the Communist propaganda that ever emanated from Moscow.

Already, the cost of Reagan policies is devastating to our country in economic strength, in diplomatic influence, in national secruity, in moral statute. . . .

The President's unspoken animus against the environment operates not only via the budget. It takes on immediate life in internal orders, administrative regulations, appointments and firings already executed by such "fronts" as Secretary of the Interior James Watt and Environmental Protection Administrator Anne M. Gorsuch.

Mr. Watt has been busily torpedoing his department's environmental-program function, such as strip-mining control, with Mr. Reagan's "full approval." Mrs. Gorsuch is in effect dismantling the E.P.A., making it impossible to administer the antipollution and tax-substance-control laws it was designed to oversee. Her proposals for a cut-rate Clean Air Act are a guarantee of dirtier air.

Senator Robert T. Stafford, Republican of Vermont, remarked a few days ago: "To make these laws unenforceable because of the de facto repeal achieved through cuts in money and personnel would be to perpetrate a cruel hoax on the American people."

That is precisely what "good guy" Reagan is doing, right across the board. The question is: How long will the American people continue to be hoaxed?

"The world is waiting, and not for us just to arm, arm, arm."
Senator Charles Percy, Republican of Illinois
to the Committee For National Security, October, 1981.

David C. Brower and David R. Brower in Carmel, California, 1991.
(Photo by Sara Harkins.)

CHAPTER 15

THE FATE AND HOPE
OF THE EARTH

I F ANOTHER ROOSEVELT, such as Franklin, were still alive, or a John
Kennedy, or if Jimmy Carter were still president, the idea of another White House Conference of Governors might well have flown.
But as Steve Rauh and I looked over the idea of a seventy-fifth
anniversary of Theodore Roosevelt's conference, we realized that if the
then current administration, Ronald Reagan's, with his chief conservation officer, James Watt, could but understand the need for such a conference, we wouldn't need it. They didn't and we did. Therefore, we
concluded, it must be put together by non-administration organizations.
Here we were, involved with several. Let's go!

One of our first and most important allies was Denny Wilcher. I got
to know him well in two of his roles. He and his team of booksellers put
Sierra Club books on the national map. He had also asked me, when I
was the club's executive director, for a list of Sierra Club donors who had
given fifty dollars or more in extra contributions to the club, fifty dollars
then being about two hundred now. When his bookselling rounds
brought him near those people, he tried to get in touch with them. That
effort brought financial assistance from scores of contributors, including one individual who, in the intervening years, gave half a million dollars to the Sierra Club and Friends of the Earth Foundation in support of
environmental projects I cared about deeply. Denny's help for the conference, motivated by his intense interest in its goals, was invaluable.

He, Steve, and I were all close to the Sierra Club and knew that
the club's support would encourage other environmental organizations
to lend theirs. The club, assured that there would be no financial obligations, gave its support, but too late to be included in the issue of
Earth Island Journal that was to be our principal document informing
people of the conference. We published a compelling poster, and
mailed it, with all the elements of a brochure on its back, to sixty thousand people. We also produced the August 1982 *Earth Island Journal*. I
put the journal together in one hectic day, drawing on some letters, a
list of presenters, and some intense writing on my own part, drawn

251

from nineteen books I pulled out of my home library, and I draw heavily from it in what follows.

When you try to pick conservation out by itself
you find it attached to everything else in the universe.

John Muir, slightly amended.

CONSERVATION IS AN INSEPARABLE INGREDIENT of lasting peace and security, and of the economics of peaceful stability. There is surely an economically feasible route to a sustainable society, one that does not overtax the environment and thus drive civilization to the final quarrel over vanishing resources. A reversal of the superpowers's nuclear arms race is an essential first step, but cannot happen soon enough or last long enough if what causes conflict remains as its vector.

Raymond Dasmann puts the issue succinctly [I hope you have memorized it by now and can uses it often]: "We are already fighting World War III and, I am sorry to say, we are winning it. It is the war against the earth." [I have used this quote many times already and I'll stop when the war ends.] That war is leading directly to the final war, World War IV, the war of people against people and for extinction. If Dasmann's World War III continues, World War IV is inevitable, and likely to be nuclear. If so, as Jonathan Schell has pointed out so compellingly, it will leave no one to remember that we were ever here.

Thirty years of futile attempts at disarmament have proved that fresh ideas are essential, and they are being conceived with refreshing speed. The Union of Concerned Scientists has brought its expertise into a new effort toward nuclear disarmament. Physicians for Social Responsibility have made the need clear to people who will believe their doctor if no one else. The church — at least some of it — is becoming increasingly aware of the armed threat to a sustainable congregation. The environmental movement now needs to extend its traditional scope to encompass a nontraditional but transcendent need.

Some relevant ideas from Friends of the Earth are in my Albright Lecture (reprinted in Chapter 14). The International Project for Soft Energy Paths (a project of Friends of the Earth Foundation) and other derivatives of the work of Amory and Hunter Lovins can lead toward a sustainable society. Richard Barnet, of the Committee for National Security, Washington, D.C. [merged in early 1990 with the Council on Economic Priorities in New York], is broadening the understanding of what security consists of. There is further help from the global interests of the Natural Resources Defense Council, Friends of the Earth International, and from the Global Tomorrow Coalition people who are trying to see that the Global 2000 Report and subsequent recommendations from the Council on Environmental Quality are heeded and expanded.

Countering this are the people who see resources as unlimited and security as a weapons race — people who thought the Vietnam War was winnable and that nuclear war is limitable and winnable. They are dangerously delaying what the superpowers must quickly achieve — a 180-degree turn from the frightening direction they are taking the world. Walter Cronkite put the U.S. need cogently: "We cannot win by force of arms. We must do it by example."

Needed: A New Synthesis of Proved Ideas

Hence our conference on conservation and security in a sustainable society. *Conservation* in the old sense meant stretching the resource budget. It needs now to encompass preservation of the Earth's life-support systems. *Security* sounds nice but is ambiguous: one can be secure in the army, in jail, and in the grave. We have something better in mind. Not a higher standard of living fed by a lowering standard of environment, but a better life, in a society that is sustainable because it has determined that it will not steal from the unborn, and wishes in the words of George Dyson, "to find freedom without taking it from someone else."

Hence the conference itself, and what its participants and advisors can achieve alongside in the months of preparation and follow-up, has a most important goal: to enable the superpowers to understand and to achieve a functional security. This conference should aid enormously and uniquely by showing how conservation and equity can mitigate the causes of war and its drain on the resources that are needed to sustain human progress on the only livable planet we know of.

It is hard to think of anything more important, in these times, to invite you to take part in.

Earth Island Journal to Serve Conference

Earth Island Journal, published by Earth Island Institute, has been asked to be the official newsletter for the First Biennial Conference on the Fate of the Earth. The Institute is a sponsor of the conference. The newsletter is to keep participants informed about the progress of the conference. The participants include not only those scheduled to speak, but also the conference advisors, planners and staff, leaders to be invited, and media. Contributions toward its cost are welcome, as well as contributions toward its content — on the subject of conservation and security in a sustainable society.

Earth Island Institute, incorporated in 1982, seeks to evoke ecological conscience in all spheres of society, and to encourage its growth and development internationally. The name derives from Margaret Mead's allusion to "the island earth." It has been used in publishing by two organizations founded by in 1970 — Earth Island Limited and Earth Island, Incorporated.

The initial program of the Institute included several parts, all related to the principal purpose: a resource library and gallery, an international visiting-fellow sponsorship, conferences and seminars, environmental research, publishing, and awards. Organizations and groups initially cooperating with the Institute are: Friends of the Earth International, Friends of the Earth Foundation; Education Division of the International Union for the Conservation of Nature and Natural Resources; and World College West.

Where Are the Roots of Security?

If the issue of the nuclear arms race was not already urgent, Jonathan Schell's *tour de force* in the *New Yorker*, "The Fate of the Earth," has made it so. Security and armament have seemed synonymous since World War II. They have proved themselves incompatible. Conventional wisdom and extinction need to yield to innovation and survival. Hamlet's old question faces today's — and tomorrow's — humanity: To be, or not to be?

The public's anxiety has been exacerbated by the Pentagon's computer troubles, the Titan Missile and the Wrench, and the chill of the Cold War Revisited. Public concern is accelerating, as we see in the nuclear-freeze campaigns, Ground Zero, UCS teach-ins, the UN Disarmament session, recent and imminent demonstrations here and abroad, their temperatures rising, and in the irrational proposals to reduce armament by investing in more of it. "Like Atlas," Dr. Helen Caldicott says at the end of the film on the Physicians for Social Responsibility, *The Last Epidemic,* "we must take the world on our shoulders." But the film doesn't quite say where to take it.

If the American public is to heed Dwight Eisenhower's suggestion that governments must get out of the way and let people have peace, the public needs help from nongovernmental organizations. If the public is to be willing to insist on reduction of nuclear arsenals, the public needs to see that real security arises not out of having more weapons than anyone else, but out of achieving something more fruitful. To improve national security the public should seek improved global security. The misguided urge to build nuclear Maginot Lines precludes security. And as Richard Barnet says, 'we do not increase ours by decreasing our opponent's.' So how do we increase his security and our own, making a friend of an enemy? It must be possible. We've done it often.

We expect the conference to bring a renewed importance to conservation by showing how it can make friends of enemies. Ever since *conservation* was invented as a word, conservationists have sought security for the environment and have been somewhat successful. The public has responded well and the polls show that it still does. The government has responded, too, in the past, but now in the U.S. the long-term security of a healthy environment is being sacrificed. Immediate economic needs repeatedly are given precedence over long-term necessity. The government still mistakes economic growth for progress. The tremendous ills caused by random growth become ever more pervasive: the greenhouse effect, acid rain, soil depletion, desert-making, loss of essential genetic diversity, proliferation of hazardous wastes and weapons, and corruption of oceans, streams, and aquifers. Security and gross national product are turning out to be antithetical. A more sustainable, not a grosser, national product will best serve us, as well as the generations yet unborn whose genes are in our custody and who cannot vote or speak out except through us. [I'm stuck on this concept.]

Jonathan Schell's *Fate of the Earth* shows the nuclear arms race to be futile and suicidal; the Law of Fear has led to sovereignty, which in turn has brought us to the brink of extinction. There is a better goal and little time to choose it. Schell would have us adhere to the Law of Love, not the Law of Fear. That may sound utopian, but it is preferable to oblivion, now imminent enough to motivate us. We would suggest that the sovereignty that distresses Mr. Schell derives from the aggressiveness that is called territoriality, the roots of which are indeed very deep but nonetheless uprootable. Environmental degradation has been bad enough. Environmental extirpation is unacceptably worse. And we now see that man-caused extinction of creatures and ecosystems is a precursor of our own fate — as Schell puts it, "to absolute and eternal darkness . . . in which never again will a child be born; in which never again will human beings appear on earth, and there will be no one to remember that they ever did." Herb Caen, after quoting this in his column, added, "Have a nice day."

From Growth Race to Arms Race

We can at long last recognize and link between the growth race and the arms race and realize that we need to reject the unbearable race to use up resources that cannot be replaced and to reject the equally unbearable race to build arms. While we are at it, we can reject the race to sequester inequitably the resources that are renewable, including the resource of the human spirit, of love, and of reverence for life. Having rejected races, where do we walk along with others, and not try so hard to be ahead?

In its own way, the conference answers the question with a question: Can there be life after disarmament? If so, disarmament will come more easily. Having disarmed in December, the world won't rush to rearm in January.

So how can we live without arms? To begin with, with the new motivation of imminent oblivion urging us on, we ought to seek out the causes of war other than the one usually identified by the Pentagon or the Kremlin — the lack of enough weapons. There are a dozen or two other causes, all planted by the hand, man's own, that now with woman's help we can and must weed them out.

We hope the conference can begin the shaping of Magna Carta II. Magna Carta I came in 1215 when King John of England was required by his abused barons to grant several liberties, one being that no free man could be arrested, imprisoned, deprived of his property, outlawed, exiled, or in any way destroyed except by legal judgment of his peers or by the law of the land.

The parallel between the need eight centuries ago for law and order and the direr need now for natural law and order to prevent nuclear holocaust provides an extraordinary opportunity. In Magna Carta II the natural world would be enabled to extort certain liberties from *Homo sapiens.* This species, which has so recently and with such hubris assumed the throne, has sought to arrest, imprison, deprive, outlaw, exile, or destroy senior species and habitats on the planet. Their peers did not consent, and there was negligible reference to natural law. This war with the natural world — for that is what the monarch's actions amount to — is not only speeding him to extinction, but also the other lives that make earth unique in the universe.

The reformation of sovereignty may happen faster if we ask ourselves to represent sovereign regions other than our own, to see what it feels like outside. Or to champion the environmental requirements of endangered species. We might well learn to think like a tree, or a condor or a cetacean, or a child born in the U.S.S.R. or in the twenty-fourth century. This kind of creativity will help us all, and only human beings can evoke it. Why not?

Where are the roots of security? Loren Eiseley [again, how does he sound in this context?] had one view of them: "The need is not really for more brains. The need is for a gentler, a more tolerant people than those who won for us against the ice, the tiger, and the bear. The hand that hefted the axes, out of some old blind allegiance to the past, now fondles the machine gun as lovingly. It is a habit man will have to break to survive, but the roots go very deep." [Please memorize this so I don't have to keep repeating it.]

Barbara Ward, in her foreword to Erik Eckholm's *Down to Earth,* looks at shallower roots: "But we must remember that it took many centuries for nationalism itself to become a dominant world force. For a thousand years and more, until the Reformation, ideology and belief were the primary force."

And the deepest roots are the roots of love, which made us all possible. The love of life can restore belief to its role as a primary force, and the conference ought to help this happen.

The Sessions

1. *The Race Against the Arms Race.* Dwight Eisenhower's farewell address is a good point of departure. He was concerned about the arms race and its causes — competition for resources, the military-industrial complex, and the less-talked-about academic-technological complex. The causes of the arms race have hardly changed; the consequences have changed tremendously. Unusable nuclear Maginot Lines are being built, draining human resources and human spirit. The U.S. for one is seeking national strength through exhaustion of national resources. Resources that could sustain us are subverted. They are used up for weapons of destruction; the exhaustion of the resources in itself builds the tensions that can unleash the weapons. Human society has become so expert at making enemies of friends that the extinction of society is imminent. When oblivion seems inevitable, there should be a good market for alternatives — arm in arm not arms vs. arms.

[The subjects, names, and titles that follow are important ingredients (and examples for future conferences) of the Global Coalition for Survival that needs to be built and maintained.]

Session leaders: Ruth Adams, Editor, *The Bulletin of the Atomic Scientists;* Christopher Paine, of the Federation of American Scientists; Arthur Westing, Dean of the School of Natural Resources, Hampshire College.

2. *Conversion to the Economics of Peaceful Stability.* Can the economy withstand peace? Can limited resources withstand a constantly expanding expenditure? Answers to both questions are obvious but ignored. It is time to face them. What kinds of growth must we have, and what kinds can we no longer afford? How can the hidden costs of growth be brought out into the open? What are future generations likely to say about their being so heavily overdiscounted by present-day economists? What critical values are overlooked when we measure progress in units of GNP? What should be factored in if we want, instead of an ever-grosser national product, an improving global standard of life? Are Herman Kahn, Julian Simon, and David Stockman looking in the right direction? John Kenneth Galbraith? Herman Daly? Nicolas Georgescu-Roegen? E. J. Mishan? Or the Unknown Economist? Can we convert to preparation for peace?

Session leaders: David Gold, Council on Economic Priorities; Seymour Melman, SANE; Marcus Raskin, Institute for Policy Studies.

3. *Sovereignty vs. Humanity.* Jonathan Schell, in *The Fate of the Earth,* says that the Law of Fear has led to Sovereignty, and Sovereignty has led humanity to the nuclear brink. Can we find a route back from that brink, or do we take the final giant step for mankind? Is competition the life of trade but the death of traders? In 1910 Charles Richard Van Hise (in *The Conservation of Natural Resources in the United States*) said: "The period in which individualism was patriotism in this country has passed by: and the time has come when individualism must become subordinate to responsibility to the many." "Many" must encompass three times as much as it did then. Having failed in so many attempts to bring about sustainability, ought society now try harder to bring order out of chaos through world government? Or should we just leave it to multinational enterprises — institutions that seem to be ignoring national boundaries rather easily? Do the multinationals have enough goodwill toward the future? Has it yet found suitable soil to grow in? Perhaps investors can change faster than governments can.

Session leaders: Moorhead Kennedy, Cathedral Peace Institute, former hostage in Iran; Nancy Ramsey, Committee for National Security.

4. *The Din of Inequity: North vs. South.* Five percent of the world population (that of the U.S.) demand 30 percent of the globe's resources. President Reagan, in Cancun, would have the Third World rely on the magic of the marketplace. That magic seems to have steadily widened the gap between the Haves and Havenots, be they North or South, East or West, In and Up, or Down and Out. The North could enhance global security by investing in the restoration of renewable-resource potential, helping the South use the sun and soil better for its own advantage, even if that means that the North is deprived of some surfeit. Can we change our mindset and do this? Are the three officers who moved from the Bechtel Corporation into the Reagan Cabinet ready? Will the attempt to reduce inequity through development end up by drowning with cash the very talents and traditions a post-industrial society needs most?

Session leaders: David Chatfield, member, Environmental Liaison Board, Nairobi; Alice Tepper Marlin, Council on Economic Priorities; George Wald, Professor Emeritus of Biochemistry, Harvard, and Nobel laureate.

5. *Food and Soil, Nutrition and Stability.* Taking the long view in his *New Roots for Agriculture,* Wes Jackson has observed the harm that the plow has caused and thinks we had best be careful about what we beat swords into. Nuclear swords, of course, could far outstrip all the plows in history: eroded soil may someday grow something somewhere else, but vaporized soil is not likely to. Globally, the greatest energy

shortage seems to be of firewood, being badly overused by a burgeoning population that is more and more dependent upon starch, which
must be cooked — burning up, in the process, key ingredients of soil
fertility that do not get back to the soil. "It is not given to man to make
wilderness," Wallace Stegner wrote, "but he can make deserts, and
has." His unwise use of livestock has made deserts, and his ten millennia of depending increasingly on starch had made more. Feeding his
growing billions could double the size of the earth's deserts by the year
2000. If we were to use weapons money to heal the earth instead of
destroying it, we could improve nutrition and stability through massive
reforestation and the global practice of agri-ecology as a substitute for
our present mining and burning of soil.

 Session leaders: Joan Gussow, Nutrition Education Department,
Columbia University; Wes Jackson, The Land Institute, Salina, Kansas.

 6. *Smart Energy.* Presidents Reagan and Carter threatened to use
arms to protect access to "our oil" in the Middle East, and President
Reagan now threatens our allies for wanting to buy Soviet natural gas.
The existence of oil offshore in Southeast Asia, Argentina, and the
Falklands has not helped troubled waters. An atmosphere overburdened by the accelerating combustion of fossil fuels threatens lakes,
wildlife, oceans, and people. The proliferation of nuclear power provides
the cover and materials for the proliferation of nuclear weapons. In a
quieter contest, the very growing of food for a growing population
demands more and more oil from a diminishing resource, adding to
tension, decreasing security. Still more subtly, the growing demand for
fossil and nuclear energy has led to overcentralization of energy generation and transmission. This in turn creates an internal vulnerability —
an unprecedented national insecurity — that makes an arms race a
futile exercise. Who needs to waste missiles to cripple the economy of
the eastern states when a handful of malcontents working overnight on
an energy artery in Louisiana could do the same thing?

 All this — and much, much more — spells Dumb Energy, and we
are awash with it. *Smart Energy,* the title of a new book by Denis Hayes,
is probably what we need instead. It needs to be looked into and put to
work soon, before we have used up too much of what remains of low-
cost energy by not being bright ourselves.

 Session leaders: John Holdren, Energy Resources Group, University
of California, Berkeley; Florentin Krause, consultant, International
Project on Soft Energy Paths, and author of a best-selling energy book in
Germany; Arjun Makhijani, energy consultant, India.

 7. *Population and Carrying Capacity.* The earth's carrying capacity,
when people lived by hunting and gathering, could handle twenty-five to
fifty million of them. Agriculture, medicine, science, and technology
have changed all that, at hidden cost. Increase in human fertility has

brought a decrease in soil fertility. The spread of the human monoculture — a most infectious monoculturosis — has shrunk the habitat for other living things upon which humanity is dependent. Coveting of their habitat has led us to poison not only them but also, we find as we discover the Circle of Poison, ourselves. We disdain prophets, doomsayers that they are, and continue to ridicule the wisdom of Malthus. He never dreamed we would sit on the wrong end of the limb we were sawing off. The population bomb that Paul Ehrlich awakened us to so effectively pointed out that unless we solved this problem, we wouldn't even have a ticket to solving the others. Have we gone back to dozing?

Session leaders: Anne Ehrlich, Department of Biology, Stanford University; Avis Ogilvy, Friends of the Earth Foundation; Stewart Ogilvy, formerly with the Population Institute.

8. *Physical Resources: The Environmental Overdraft.* Air, water, and minerals were getting along all right. Then we found fire, and with it changed the earth's ecosystems, but not quite unsustainably, by applying fire to grasses and woods. Next we applied it to grains and multiplied ourselves horrendously, but did not quite subdue the earth. So we applied fire to minerals. Having forced the marriage of coal and iron, we entered the Industrial Age and for two centuries cast ourselves as star in the play *Changing the Face of the Earth.* We are now writing a new play to star in: *Changing the Floor of the Sea.* We argue about how to divide the new riches. Justice William O. Douglas asked whether we should go after them at all. No one has listened. Nor has anyone wanted to pay much attention to the consequences of stirring up all those ocean-bed nodules of copper, magnesium, *et al.,* which might release too much of the *et al.* that is toxic to living things. Side effects, as Garrett Hardin has said, are surprise results, the existence of which we will deny as long as we possibly can. We have become expert in denial and have gotten away with it because of the earth's bounty. Now the environmental overdraft of physical resources may be speeding us to the post-industrial age, or maybe to the post-human age, too fast. There could be mutiny in the bounty.

Session leaders: John Harte, Lawrence Berkeley Laboratory, University of California; Bernard Oxman, University of Florida.

9. *Living Resources: The Meaning of Diversity.* The war against the earth, and the ugliness it produces, is leading rapidly to the ultimate human ugliness, the war of people against themselves. It would be global civil war. If our own generation were the only one to suffer, that would still be unacceptable. But we ought not be the last generation, and could agree with Harvard's Professor E. O. Wilson that the loss of genetic diversity caused by our destruction of natural habitats is the folly for which our descendants are least likely to forgive us. the *Global 2000 Report to the President* gives us some relevant numbers: between

five hundred thousand and two million species of plants and animals, now sharing the earth with us, will be driven off through our efforts by the year 2000 if we do not change our habits. Let us change!

Session leaders: Raymond F. Dasmann, Professor of Ecology, University of California, Santa Cruz, and former consultant to the International Union for the Conservation of Nature, Switzerland; Tom Stoel, President, Global Tomorrow Coalition (of sixty-two U.S. organizations).

10. *Religion and Culture in Global Perspective.* Not long ago Senator Barry Goldwater of Arizona, with a sidelong look at the Moral Majority, began to tally the number of wars that were created by religious zeal and found the number large — not just in history, but in headlines as well. The Cathedral Peace Institute inquired into this subject last April. Lynn White, Jr. (in "The Historical Roots of Our Ecological Crisis") looked into it in March 1967. Some time before that an attempt was made to dissuade people from seeking an eye for an eye, and in a sermon on a mount the audience was told, "Blessed are the meek, for they shall inherit the earth." A disciple, Paul, had a great deal to say about love, and how long it suffered, and how kind it was. The audiences seem to have drifted away, and we suspect that unless they drift back, neither the meek nor the arrogant will be on hand to inherit anything, having been vaporized along with their heritage. The session can advocate our drifting back.

Session leaders: Richard Baker-roshi, The San Francisco Zen Center; Brother David Steindl-rast, Benedictine Monastery.

11. *Education for Stewardship.* The word 'steward' is heard often these days and practiced seldom. The situation has been covered fairly often in a form of teaching that educates through amusement — the comic strip, of course — and Mr. Trudeau, Prime Minister of the Strips, has contributed to the political education of several notables, such as Ted Kennedy, Jerry Brown, James Watt, Anne Gorsuch, Ronald Reagan, and, in a friendlier way, John Anderson. *Doonesbury* has also had a character who has described contemporary education as thought control and wants none of it. Since so much depends upon education, the questions arise, For what? and By whom? Is it to be so practical as to perpetuate the errors of our ancestors? Or is it to become a principal Institution for the Future? Can it deal more magnanimously than it has been lately with the greatest population of all, the people who have not yet been born? If so, there are probably lessons to be learned from natural systems that have lasted far longer than any of ours, and there should be great demand for graduates of the forthcoming Academy of Peace.

Session leaders: Robin Freeman, Berkeley Creators' Association; John Holt, author of many books on education goals; Margot Strom, of *Facing History and Ourselves.*

261

12. *Media: What Happens to the Message?* Having said, "Mankind was given the art of speech so that his thoughts could be hidden," what would Voltaire say now? Man was given the art of print so that his thought could be bought? The art of electronics to make it moronic? Kenneth Brower has postulated that if we had stuck with flippers rather than opting for hands, we might remain here for another thirty million years without burning the place up. To avoid the same hazard, must we avoid media and specialize on body language — or on music and paint (see below)? We want freedom of the press, but can we free the press? Admiral LaRocque has said he thinks it is controlled by the military-industrial complex, and there is all too much evidence that he is right: we get all the war news that fits to print. Another individual, who blew the whistle on Air Force extravagance and took thirteen years, with no appreciable help from the media, to recover from the damage his honesty had cost him, thinks the press is controlled by apathy. And President Reagan thinks there has been too much freedom of information and seems to be trying to back us into the old British Commonwealth spate of Secrecy Acts. "You shall know the truth, and the truth shall make you free." But not too free?

Session leaders: Jerry Mander, Cause-ad specialist and author (*Four Arguments for the Elimination of Television*); Steve Reiner, National Public Radio ("All Things Considered"); Tom Turner, editor, Friends of the Earth (*Not Man Apart*).

13. *The Arts As a Universal Language.* "Lili Marlene" was sung on both sides of No Man's Land in World War II and must still make those who remember it wonder why people who could share its poignancy could not share much else. Four thousand years earlier (*c.* 2300 B.C.) an unknown Chinese poet asked:

What care I who rules the land if I am left in peace?

"From break of day / Till sunset glow / I toil," he said; "I dig my well, / I plow my field, / and earn my food / and drink." We can imagine that his art was the beauty, unbounded, that each new day brought him; that his religion taught him the art and strength of yielding. On a nearby wall is an old Dutch painting, four thousand years younger, that says the same thing.

In 1963 Loren Eiseley told, quite beautifully, of a stone his eyes fell upon, "a stone antedating anything that historians would call art." He hefted it as he groped for words to describe the growing rift between science and art. "I began to perceive the ghostly emanations from a long-vanished mind," he wrote, "that leaves an individual trace behind it which speaks to others across the barriers of time and language." The man who shaped the stone for practical, perhaps brutish purposes, had also embellished it "with skills lost to me . . . until it had become a kind of rough jewel," now speaking across too many millennia to count.

But science has won. It can abolish all memory of art. How had we best mark what we leave?

Session leaders: Jimmy Durham, Foundation for the Community of Arts; André Gregory, of *My Dinner With André;* Alan Gussow, painter.

14. *Magna Carta II.* [Here I repeated for those reading only about working sessions, the thoughts expressed above, and added:] Henry Beston gives *Homo sapiens* their place: "In a world older and more complete than ours they move finished and complete, gifted with extensions of the senses we have lost or never attained, living by voices we shall never hear. They are not brethren, they are not underlings; they are other nations, caught with ourselves in the net of life and time, fellow prisoners of the splendor and travail of the earth."

Learning to think like them — be they cetacean, condor, or sequoia — we can begin to respect their rights, to let trees and wilderness indeed have standing, to let their beauty and peace be shared through the ages.

Session leaders: David R. Brower, Amory and Hunter Lovins, and Garrett Hardin.

15. *Awakening the Body Politic to Its Rights.* [Here I quoted liberally from the foreword to *Progress As If Survival Mattered: A Handbook for a Conserver Society.*] As Dwight Eisenhower once said that the people want peace so much that governments had better get out of the way and let them have it.

The war that nobody wants will be inevitable unless the people, realizing that government is not a spectator sport but a participant sport, insist that governments get out of the way of peace and get intransigently in the way of war. Perhaps the session will agree.

Session leaders: Gerhard Elston, Planetary Initiative for the World We Choose; Lois Gibbs, formerly of Love Canal; Jerome Grossman, The Council for a Livable World.

16. *On Rescuing Cultural Diversity.* Helena Norberg-Hodge, who has been described as a new Margaret Mead, says that grandparents and grandchildren are made for each other. The intervening generation is too fraught to function. In a rough parallel, the preindustrial and post industrial societies are made for each other, and the intervening society, our own, operates in a harried hiatus that is not long for this world. Those of us who want humanity to continue, and who are recognizing the unsustainability of our present habits, would like to see the denizens of the post-industrial era get to it informed. They will arrive there in abysmal ignorance if their grandparents, the people of the preindustrial age who still live in one, are extinguished in a tidal wave of cash and buried in baubles. These people are like Henry Beston's other nations, but worse off. There is no World Wildlife Fund to raise funds and fight their battle for them. They are unarmed. They are the Ecosystem People

Raymond Dasmann has identified, living in vestige cultures that know how to live within their environments's limits, that could inhabit a wilderness in harmony with it. We, the Biosphere People, can't. We can't even light a fire without matches, and certainly cannot navigate by the shape of the waves in daytime or by the shape of the sky at night. These few remnant, earth-sensitive, essential cultures are targets for rampant tourism and the Manhattan Treatment: beads for islands. There has to be a better way for us to go and for them to stay.

Session leaders: Helena Norberg-Hodge and Winona LaDuke.

[The *New Yorker* uses fillers, and I used what follows in the brochure — and in countless speeches since then — to lighten things up.]

Each year Ian McHarg confronts a new generation of college students with a challenge to any imminent professional myopia of theirs and to focus their attention on the place of man in nature. First he tells them of the image conceived by Loren Eiseley in 1961 about what man in space sees as he looks down on the distant earth and asks, "Is man but a planetary disease?" Next, he tells his own story:

"The atomic cataclysm has occurred. The earth is silent, covered by a gray pall. All life has been extinguished save in one deep leaden slit, where, long inured to radiation, persists a small colony of algae. They perceive that all life but theirs has been extinguished and that the entire task of evolution must begin again — some billions of years of life and death, mutation and adaptation, cooperation and competition, all to recover yesterday. They come to an immediate, spontaneous, and unanimous conclusion: 'Next time, no brains.'"

Can Environmental Sanity Reverse the Arms Race?

In summary, what can conservation contribute to the peace and security of a sustainable society? This is the big question being delved into in New York City on October 19 – 21, 1982, at the Cathedral of St. John the Divine, largest Gothic cathedral on earth. The conferees will address three subquestions, each getting its day: (1) What's going wrong? (2) Where do we want to be? and (3) How do we get there?

To Keep the Disarmed from Rearming

Good answers to the three days' questions will expedite disarmament and make it stick. The scientific and technological ability to rearm cannot be obliterated, but it can be diverted to causes that serve humanity instead of destroying it.

As Jonathan Schell says in *The Fate of the Earth*:

"A nuclear holocaust, because of its unique combination of immensity and suddenness, is a threat without parallel; yet at the same time it is only one of countless threats that the human enterprise, grown mighty through knowledge, poses to the natural world. Our species is caught in the same tightening net of technical success that has already strangled so many other species. . . . The peril of human extinction, which exists not because every single person in the world would be killed by the immediate explosive and radioactive effects of a holocaust — something that is exceedingly unlikely, even at present levels of armament — but because a holocaust might render the biosphere unfit for human survival, is, in a word, an *ecological* peril. The nuclear peril is usually seen in isolation from the threats to other forms of life and their ecosystems, but in fact it should be seen as the very center of the ecological crisis — as the cloud-covered Everest of which the more immediate, visible kinds of harm to the environment are the mere foothills. Both the effort to preserve the environment and the effort to save the species from extinction by nuclear arms would be enriched and strengthened by this recognition. The nuclear question, which now stands in eerie seclusion from the rest of life, would gain a context, and the ecological movement, which, in its concern for plants and animals, at times assumes an almost misanthropic posture, as though man were an unwanted intruder in an otherwise unblemished natural world, would gain the humanistic intent that should stand at the heart of its concern."

Earth Island Journal, August 1982

To our surprise and delight, a thousand people arrived at the Synod House, Cathedral of St. John the Divine, for the first conference on the Fate of the Earth. It was an exciting event. It received almost no coverage in the press. It was videotaped by Anita Caselina and crew. A seventeen-minute video resume enhanced many of my subsequent speeches. VCRs are everywhere, and I could introduce the summary and relax while it played, watching the audience reaction and responding when my turn came. A special feature was made of the lively contributions made by Ron Dellums, the member of Congress from my home district and twice the magnanimous nominator of his constituent for the Nobel Peace Prize. Anita produced another feature of the musical component of the conference, contributed by Odetta, Pete Seeger, and Paul Winter and his Consort — which no one, alas, has yet exploited. The proceedings were edited and published through the generosity of Henry Dakin, who had also served on the conference board.

A first biennial conference required a second, which we held in Washington, D.C., two years later. In part because we sent out only ten thousand, not sixty thousand, promotional pieces, and in part also because it was held in conference-jaded Washington, a superb program was attended by only half as many people as the first. The New York conference came out in the black — just. The second fell thirty thousand dollars short, fifteen thousand of which I had advanced — by agreeing, at a last desperate moment, to charge the conference's hotel costs to my American Express card. That advance never returned. It left home without me. Again, the proceedings were published thanks to Henry Dakin's generosity.

The program was, if anything, stronger than that of the first, and a series of good papers ought to be derived for the proceedings of both, in a format similar to that of *Worldwatch Papers*, which are one of the best known and effective achievements of Lester Brown's Worldwatch Institute. That one is on my agenda.

Those who did not get their contributions back should try to feel the way I do about mine: what better could you do with your money? Again and again, as I travel around, people tell me what the conferences did to change their outlook and their lives. Far beyond that, coalitions are growing. There were fourteen sponsors of the first conference, one hundred twenty-five of the second.

There would be 297 sponsors of the third, and once again a thousand participants, in the capital of a nation with but a tenth the population of the United States. In Ottawa several more nations participated, in part because our conference was back-to-back with one held by the International Union for the Conservation of Nature and Natural resources. The 1986 Ottawa conference was videotaped, but the record has inexcusably not been released. A fair gist of the proceedings has appeared, but no more. The conference program, again, was superb. But as happens so often at conferences, follow-through energy is dissipated in the rush to get aboard the flight home. This should be no cause of despair. A conference itself, the creativity its preparation demands, the collegiality of what happens as it happens, the proceedings the participants carry home in their minds if not on paper or on tape, and the motivation the conference adds to what its participants will do with the rest of their lives — all this is enough. But I still want the proceedings from which to draw and repeat the highlights, and the tape for our Earth Island Fortnightly *Video Journal,* forthcoming.

Ottawa was far enough from Nicaragua, and what intervenes, that the Canadians were asked by the Nicaraguan embassy if the next Fate of the Earth Conference could be held in Managua. There were also suggestions that it be held in Sydney, London, and Nairobi.

At a meeting of Fritjof Capra's Elmwood Institute, in Berkeley, Pat Ellsberg suggested that the conference name needed the upbeat of hope rather than the downbeat of fate. Fate is ordained. Hope is possible. We in the United States bought the change, and the Nicaraguans did, but the Canadians did not want to abandon the tradition of the first three conferences. We compromised, with another slight modification. For some reason, foundations seem loath to fund conferences, books, and films. We wanted to be involved in all three at once. If conferences are not fundable, surely congresses ought to be. Therefore, in Managua, June 5 – 9, 1989, we held the Fourth Biennial Congress on the Fate and Hope of the Earth. For reasons not difficult to understand, it took a year longer to prepare. Three years intervened, but the delay was worth it. The governments of Canada, the European Economic Community, Italy, Norway, Sweden, and the U.S.S.R. lent financial assistance. The United States Steering Committee, headquartered at Earth Island Institute, gathered some financial assistance and an enormous component of human energy, and the government of Nicaragua, in the midst of recurrent compacting of staff and agencies owing to the straits of its economy, put in Herculean effort, augmented by ABEN, the Friends of the Earth affiliate in Nicaragua. The names and brief sketches of the people who made the conference possible could overload this chapter.

In New York, a thousand participants. In Washington, the most important city in the world, it says, half that number. In Ottawa, capital of a nation one-tenth the population of the United States, back up to a thousand. In Nicaragua, besieged by earthquake, contras, and hurricane, with a population one-ninetieth that of the U.S., twelve hundred participants, from seventy nations. In the first three conferences, we had heard about the third world. Now we knew. I hope the Managua International Center for Environmental Protection and Restoration will be set up there, with support from all other nations — no exceptions — and that its counterpart will result from the Fifth Biennial Conference on the Fate and Hope of the Earth, scheduled for Zimbabwe in 1991. Equity may still be rediscovered.

Now is the time for the biggest coalition of all — the joining together for a common purpose, without jeopardy to their essential differences — of all spheres of human activity, in all cultures, behind whatever evanescent national boundaries. The Coalition for the Fate and Hope of the Earth.

It's healing time on Earth.

Trish Saar, Dave, and camcorder in Managua, Nicaragua, June 1989.

Bill Travers (with camcorder), Dave Henson, and Dave Brower at a planning meeting in Managua, January 1989.

CHAPTER 16

BARRIERS TO PEACE

B ARTLETT'S *FAMILIAR QUOTATIONS* lists two hundred twenty-two
entries on peace, including "Blessed are the peacemakers,"
which suggests that several people have given some thought
to the concept. They have not been very successful. There
are but two entries for disarmament, which has been even less successful. Love outnumbers hate by ten to one (one thousand two hundred
sixty entries for love!) and that hasn't worked either.

Achieving peace through literature, then, is not the way to go.
How about an economic route, such as Peace through Greed? Can it
be made profitable? Can armed forces and arms-makers learn to live
with it? Can it be made fun, and thus get some prime time on television? Can it be achieved without violence, and thus put Rambo out of
work?

Questions like this come up when you discuss the subject with
Robert Allen. Bob was in the Mountain Troops with me, as I was to find
out long after the war, but was injured by a land mine before we had
quite gotten into combat. I met him when he had become a principal
advisor of Henry Kendall, founder of the Union of Concerned Scientists,
whom I in turn got to know because he was a mountain climber too.
Henry and Bob have been very helpful to some of my ideas, including
the idea that war is old-fashioned and nuclear power and weapons have
made it highly undesirable.

A few years ago, in one of our delightful discussions in Boston,
Bob came up with the idea that a peace conference ought to be held on
such a scale that it would be necessary to rent Switzerland to contain it.
At our meeting in Boston in October 1987 Bob had yet to receive an
acceptable figure for renting even part of Switzerland, so we talked
about alternatives. He gave me an assignment: list the barriers to peace.

Putting my small laptop to work flying home from Boston, I typed
out some pertinent quotations, not knowing that Emerson had said: "I
hate quotations. Tell me what you know." Emerson also said, "By necessity, by proclivity, and by delight, we all quote." He was forty-six when

269

he hated quotes, seventy-three, and thus approaching maturity, as I am, when he delighted in them.

Bob wanted me to think about the hurdles, high or low, that are ahead of us in the race toward peace rather than toward oblivion. So I reached for the wisdom of the people who had agreed with me without their knowing it:

Loren Eiseley, about the need for a gentler, more tolerant race.

Richard Barnet about decreasing the security of our opponent, and "We march toward annihilation under the banner of realism."

Raymond Dasmann, about our war against the earth.

Voltaire: "The world is but one country, and mankind its citizens."

Baba Re Bop (in the cartoon strip, "Farley"): "Improve reality!!"

George Dyson's finding peace, without taking it from someone else.

Dwight Eisenhower about letting the people have peace.

Adlai Stevenson about our little spaceship.

Albert Einstein about the atom's changing all but our way of thinking.

David Brower's sound bites:

We are stealing, not borrowing the Earth from our children.

We need a new renaissance to recognize the Earth's limits.

Daily doses of Rambo will produce no champions of peace.

History never gives peace equal time.

Award Nobel prizes for peaceful physics, and economics.

Develop a Blueprint for the Economics of Peaceful Stability.

Make peace profitable and entertaining.

Onward, Christian soldiers, march away from war!

Beware the Far-Righteous!

Don't just visualize peace. Wage it!

Organize as well for peace, as we do for war!

"One of the troubles," Robert Allen said, "is that people don't know what peace is. You and I do, because we found what a difference it was from our war. So did my wife Carol, and so did your Anne. But most people don't." Few Americans have seen battle, and none of us living have seen it on our native soil. Bob had explained what he wanted to do now — go all out for peace. Get task forces working on all the barriers.

I am still sold on conferences. I saw what the Sierra Club wilderness conferences accomplished, what the Stockholm Conference on the

Human Environment awakened people to, and what groups the Fate and Hope of the Earth Conferences are bringing together. Not for long enough, of course, but they have made enormous contributions if you think about where we would now be without them. So I am fixed on a United Nations Conference on Environmental Restoration (maybe it should be on Restoring the Earth) and offices or agencies within each government helping prepare for the conference and also helping, during the preparatory mode, to forestall further destruction.

Run through the gamut of related words — *restoration, regeneration, renewal, rehabilitation,* and on through a long list, and you get into a positive mood. Problems begin to become opportunities. And in these opportunities, I believe, you will find the most promising road to peace.

I like Bob's idea of task forces. But who is going to do anything about the recommendations they come up with? How do you organize for it? Most of my knowledge of organizing comes from my military experience, wherein the platoon was a key unit. In the platoon, everyone knew everyone else, and they worked together as an effective combat unit. You fought beside and for someone you knew, right there. Of course you were fighting for your country, but that was a far-away abstraction. You were fighting to keep your friends and yourself alive. The infantry company was remote. Battalion very remote. And who cared about regiment or division or army group or theater or Allied Forces? You knew about them, but you cared about your platoon and your squad, and within the squad for its Able, Baker, and Charlie teams, the closest units of all — while they lasted.

But the platoon had something special going for it. That's what I have in mind for the Earth Island Centers — something about platoon size. You set up a facility. You have your meeting place, your gallery, your books and tapes, your computer center, your kitchen/bar, and you draw in people from other interest groups and see what you can do for them and what they can do for you. Above all, you make sure there is some fun in it.

Go beyond the platoon model, or Earth Island Center model. Let people have fun when we get Hetch Hetchy Valley back. As each new species of plant or animal returns to the valley, once the dam has been breached and the reservoir drained, we will have a party. Each new returnee will be celebrated. By the time recovery is well under way, we'll all be enjoying it.

But on with a list of barriers to peace and ways to surmount them:

Religion:
　　Peace must have soldiers, alas — like the onward Christian soldiers, marching on to war. Why not to peace? We shouldn't call them

soldiers. What else? Activists? Advocates? No fun. Peaceniks? No way. Peace First!ers? Perhaps. Earth Islanders? Great, but I'm prejudiced. God's Angels, or Heaven's, or Allah's? Got to watch out for religion, considering how many religious wars the earth has had to put up with — and how many religious people are right now killing people whose religion they don't like. Religions need to provide history a better example to report upon in the future.

There could well be less "multiply and subdue the earth," of God's "terrible, swift sword," of His threatening subsequent generations of innocent children. There could be some rethinking, at least some rechecking of translations, and of the origin of the original writing.

Religion is today, as it has been in for centuries past, a major barrier to peace — a sad example of a fugitive virtue, of the harm that good men can do. I am not irreligious, but I do think that many of the religions I know of are artifacts.

An Economy Based on War:

Conversion is the move toward economic readjustment, toward an economy based on peace, not war. We need more than the idea. We need a constituency. Conversion is an important part of restoration and vice versa. Seymour Melman is great on the subject. So is our Peninsula Conversion Project, in Palo Alto, and we in Earth Island Institute are working, but not hard enough, with Michael Clossen, its executive director. But here we are, several congresses in a row, with Economic Conversion legislation introduced by congressmen Weiss and Mavroules, and the bills getting nowhere. The public doesn't know about them.

Peace must be seen as affordable. In the U.S. at present it isn't, especially in Connecticut and California. California agriculture, which provides one-fourth of the food Americans eat, grosses seventeen billion dollars a year — and the defense industry in California grosses fifty billion dollars, eight billion in San Diego alone. The University of California receives more than one billion dollars of it. How do you get objective instruction with that hurdle in front of you? Connecticut's per capita defense income exceeds California's. Let's convert!

No Profit in Peace:

Conversion and restoration are both profitable. Prove it! Come up with the prospectuses that will invite investment, and encourage diversion of defense funds. Spend them in ways that will produce real security, not diminish it as recent defense expenditures have.

Boredom:

We can add excitement with music, dance, more hugs or outstretched hands, more listening and bringing out what others have inside, finding where they are coming from. Add more parties, more awards. (How about peacemaker awards as varied and ubiquitous as

Colonel North's fruit salad?) Plus more press and TV coverage of heart-warming stories, about champions of the peacefield, doing something new and exciting about the forgotten arts of living — mindbuilding, sharing, loving, discovering, remembering. The Green Century — the Century of Restoration — is going to include a lot of these attributes.

Stabs and Blows:

We need more strokes, fewer blows. TLC, thanks, pats on and not stabs in the back, a World Bank Extending Credit for Good Deeds. When did you last thank half the people you intended to, or any?

Soldiers, Sailors, Marines, Airmen:

Freeman Dyson, in *Weapons and Hope,* thinks we will have to find alternate work for the armed forces — alternate peaceful work — or they will remain intransigent in order to remain employed, and such intransigence won't help. Since the Army Corps of Engineers has already shown the way, keeping engineers busy building levees and dams, why not extend their example? Let them switch [I keep saying] to rebuilding railroads before, not after, we run out of oil. Legislation requiring this needs to be drafted, introduced, and pushed hard.

Find jobs for each branch of the armed forces that will assist conversion and restoration. These can be derived from what we have to know about military government in newly occupied lands. Let them adapt their talents to our own land. Let our defense forces continue such police duties as will probably always remain, find ways to supplement them with peacetime duties that will make their careers more interesting and useful. Like reforestation. Some detached service in Peace Corps functions, minus any disruptive CIA elements. And why not have the CIA concentrate on gathering intelligence on how to restore instead of how to disrupt?

Careers in War:

War creates jobs galore. Let's have some careers in peace.

When Dick Cavett asked me about environmentalists and the loss of jobs, he came up with his own answer, remembering the number of people who were put out of work when the furnaces at Dachau were closed. He quickly changed the subject.

We should have stuck with it. If one man's work threatens another's life, he should change jobs — and probably be trained how to change at public expense. For example, burning high-sulfur coal at current rates causes global threats of acid rain and creates gases that threaten the ozone barrier and add to global warming. People who have been making their living by mining it in West Virginia, Senator Byrd, must be trained for other work — jobs the world can afford — and taxpayers must help.

[In March 1990, Senator Byrd tried to finance just such retraining, but lost forty-nine to fifty, to people who would rather save taxes than save lungs and redirect human energy and talent.]

Likewise, people and corporations making napalm, nuclear fuel and weapons, bombers, missiles, submarines, aircraft and aircraft carriers, as well as conventional weapons, need to move to alternate work the world needs. Economic conversion is the name for it, and I'll gladly pay more taxes to help it happen, if that's what it takes. I'd really rather have General Electric, General Dynamics, Boeing *et al.* pick up the tab if they can afford it more easily than I can.

There is so much preservation and restoration work to be done, and so many young people from all over the world eager to perform it all over the earth that we need the Earth Corps [now called the International Green Circle] that Sam LaBudde, a young man who contributed spectacularly to rescuing dolphins from tuna nets, has suggested.

Conventional Opacity:

A *Los Angeles Times* story on August 26, 1987, was headlined "Soviets Want U.N. Summit Linking Disarmament, Aid." Mr. Gorbachev had proposed a summit conference of the full UN Security Council. The message revived a proposal to finance economic aid with funds saved with defense cuts.

"Washington is opposed to linking disarmament and development," the story continued, "insisting they are unrelated issues."

That is a neat example of Conventional Opacity, all too abundant.

Demographic Transition:

Demographic transitionists believe that the population bomb will be defused when poverty ends, removing the pressure to be prolific in order to be secure; the poverty will end when the standard of living of the South catches up with that of the North and equity reigns supreme.

But how can we move from global pillage to global village when the globe has already been so thoroughly ransacked by those who first discovered the tools of the industrial revolution two centuries ago? As Vandana Shiva, of India, has said, "Ever-expanding and intensifying industrial and agricultural production has generated increasing demands on the world's total stock and flow of resources."

The resources that are left require increasing amounts of diminishing energy if they are to be developed. The Earth's ability to keep renewable resources flowing has been severely damaged. The increasing numbers of people in the South and the increasing overconsumption in the North have combined to ravage both the stock and flow. There are no new globes alongside to draw resources from.

Therefore, it is cruel to hold out the promise to the South, or to coming generations in the North, that there can be more of the same.

Human numbers and appetites have already overtaxed the Earth's resilience. Its abundance of resources has been extirpated. The industrial nations found them, used them up wastefully, and let the end products fall where they may. Nature recycles everything. They recycled practically nothing. The result: global warming, loss of species diversity, acid rain, holes in the ozone, and holes in heads.

The effort to maintain the standard of living based on Gross National Product, a standard that pillage produced for the North, or to achieve it for the South, is a declaration of war against the Earth, and is based on false hopes — a source of terminal frustration.

Global equity must become the global goal. The North must learn to live lightly on the Earth. The South must not forget how to. And the North must, because it alone has the resources, invest in global recycling, restoration, and reparations for the damage it has caused with two centuries of good intentions, self-serving altruism, colonialism, greed, and rapacity — whatever the form of industrial-nation government.

It's Mine!:

The roots of territoriality go deeper than a grapevine's (which can go as deep as 125 feet), so we'll need to starve them from the top. Fewer slaves (see below, *Too Many of Us*). Otherwise you can predict the consequence. Nations, including ours, will develop a Ministry of Foresight, or equivalent.

Looking ahead, they will estimate what resources they will need to continue the present overconsuming habits for the next century or so. They will designate boundaries and surround them with Maginot lines. If those don't work, they will invent ever-more-destructive weapons and somehow find a way to use these in anticipatory retaliation. The solution is to decimate the demographic drain (people multiplied by their appetites for resources) to something the earth can sustain indefinitely. (See immediately below.)

War with the Earth:

What our excessive demographic drain is doing to the Earth amounts to a nuclear exchange in slow motion. The superpower nuclear arsenals can simply do it faster. Overuse is slowly poisoning the soil, the water, the air, space, and the diversity of life. The nearer we get to the bottom of the barrel, the bitterer the fight will be over what's left. *Peace on Earth requires peace with the Earth.* You can't have one without the other.

Too Many of Us:

We are moving from a world that had some blanks on the map and solitude when needed through the crowded-planet mode and on to a mob scene. Mobs can get ugly sooner than anybody. So we look into carrying capacity, avert our eyes when we see the answer, assign the problem to Technology (which seems to create ten problems for each solution), and charge it to American Express, payment deferred, let the kids pick it up. Or we point a finger at the overfertile developing world and avoid looking at what our overconsumption has done to thin the Earth's resource base and fatten us. We speak of an ever-greater global population as if it were an already accomplished fact, which it isn't. If we don't do something about it, nature or our own irascibility will flip to see which of the Four Horsemen — Death, Famine, Pestilence, or War — does it for us first.

Old Growth vs. New Growth:

Conventional wisdom is convinced that a finite planet can sustain perpetually accelerating economic growth, and all our governments and educational facilities teach that Conventional Wisdom. It won't work much longer, and indeed has already cost more than we realize, because hardly anyone is counting. The patterns that will work and have been tested through the eons are out there in nature to guide us. We choose to go indoors, shut the door, and turn on artificial light. What nature says about growth is that old growth gets edited out to make room for new growth, to maintain the essential balance. We have yet to ask about growth — what kind the Earth will no longer tolerate. We avoid thinking about the Law of the Minimum, which tells us, for example, that it matters not a whit how much muscle we have if we run out of heart.

My Country Right or Wrong:

Male chauvinism is not the only bad kind. Back to Voltaire. We had better think of ourselves as citizens of the world. Citing Voltaire, I told a group in Leningrad that I felt free to make suggestions about their city and they should feel equally free to make suggestions about San Francisco. I should have offered them Los Angeles. [In early 1990 a group from Leningrad spent almost a month in San Francisco and made all kinds of suggestions, as well as requests. We are working on them at Earth Island.]

Military/Industrial/Academia/Media Complex:

The only presently successful world government is run by the multinationals, and the most successful (so far) industrial-world government is run by the Fortune 500. This combination of governance provides a lot of money and jobs. "The nations of the world spend $1,700,000 every minute on weapons. . . . One-half the research and development expenditures of the world and 500,000 scientists are concentrated on weapons of destruction" ("Making a Decision About War: Campaign Overview," *Beyond War,* 1987). Grassroots government will arrive when grassroots learn to organize and operate as well as corporations do. Meanwhile, corporate consciences need pricking, and a few changes in the law are needed to let corporations be socially responsible without being sued by their stockholders. All corporations, national and multinational, should be required to come up with plans for what they will do if peace suddenly breaks out. Are they ready for Economic Conversion or for Restoring the Earth?

Liability:

The liability insurance situation being what it is, Good Samaritans had better try a different line of work. The National Park Service finds itself obliged to cut trees, lest they fall on campers, who will thereupon sue the NPS. Some M.D. specialists don't dare continue in their field. They cannot afford the danger.

Isn't it strange how many people, in spite of all this, don't worry about the ethical liability they incur by ignoring what happened in the Nuremburg trials, where knowing nonparticipants became co-conspirators. Now is the time to intervene for peace.

The Void in Government:

If you take a look at the departments of the federal government, and their corresponding committees in Congress, you will note that we take good care of our ways of using the earth, but not of sparing it. The Department of State, as presently functioning, serves primarily as the overseas arm of the Department of Commerce — "to provide a level playing field for American business" (George Bush, February 1990). One that tilts our way? Go down the list, and although you will find everything you want in Alice's Restaurant, including the War Department (renamed not too long ago), you will find no Peace Department. There are too many institutional barriers. It took Japan to put up the original seventy-five million dollars for the United Nations University. Perhaps Japan could fund the feasibility study on our setting up a department in our own government that likes the UN, and is charged with helping the UN do what it started out trying to do when we got tired of war. We might discover ways in which a superpower could aid and persuade rather than bully. The department's duties would include local and global restoration as high priorities. The U.S. could then demonstrate significant interest in the World Heritage, Man in the Biosphere, the UN Environment Program (UNEP), UNESCO, and might even see that we pay our UN dues on time.

Nongovernmental organizations tend to parallel government agencies — or, to put it another way, to try to get the government to come up with "coercion, willingly accepted" (Garrett Hardin) and see that the government abides by its own legislation. A Secretary of Restoration, for example, might give the Secretary of Health, Education, and Welfare a better environment to work in as well as being concerned with UN matters.

277

Pennilessness:

Related to this is the generosity of funding for a giveable earth, and the paucity of it for a liveable one. I am reminded of ecologist Bengt Lundholm's problem in Sweden in 1971. He could get a four-hundred-thousand-dollar grant for finding ways to sink oil spills, but he couldn't get thirty thousand dollars to find out what the oil, once sunk, would do to the sea bottom. Peace has a hard time too. As a poster has indicated, it will be a nice day when the air force'has to hold a bake sale to finance a stealth bomber and when peace and environmental organizations get funded so well that the U.S. won't need to blow money on star wars.

How we fix this I don't know, but it seems as if we should have a better system than the one that requires us to fund bad things willy nilly and tries to penalize us when we ourselves try to fund good things.

The Din of Inequity:

This is a prewar pun of mine. Adlai Stevenson's great line, "We travel together, passengers on a little spaceship," says it all, but I'll go on anyway. It is amazing how thoroughly our foreign policy ignores his sound advice.

We have given our colonies (we don't call them that anymore, but we still treat them that way) the shaft. What we have called "development" has too often consisted of making them dependent on cash at the cost of their own self-sufficiency. We lend them money with which to buy things from us they don't need or that will enable them to produce things we desire. They have thus contributed to our standard of living, and end up owing us money for their trouble — about a trillion dollars so far. Our freedom costs them theirs.

In order not to upset our system of consuming, we upset their system of governing. When they call for a new world economic order, we set up a trilateral commission to make sure any new order pleases us.

Two decades ago The Conservation Foundation, under Russell Train, conducted an Airlie House conference on the ecological harm good aid intentions can cause. Its lessons have been largely forgotten, and we are back on the old road to destruction — of other environments as well as our own.

One of Adlai Stevenson's remarks was "Bought friends don't stay bought." We hardly heard him then and are back to buying again. Investment in restoration for the OUTs (Overused, Underassisted Territories) on earth by the INs (the Industrial Nations) will serve both parties well.

Our Common Future (the Brundtland Report) published by Oxford University Press as "the most important book of the decade" is trying to do something about investment, calling for increased economic growth and sustained development. We need to help define what these can consist of so as to help the OUTs and sober up the INs on something besides more martinis. The Brundtland Commission thinks that poverty is one of the greatest threats to the environment. There was a lot of comment from the Fourth Wilderness Congress audience in Denver and Estes Park which suggested that luxury was the greater threat — luxury and its concomitant overconsumption. The commission has not quite understood Stevenson's advice, Ray Dasmann's about our war against the earth, conducted by the biosphere people (Dasmann's word for the INs) against the ecosystem people (the OUTs), wiping out the native cultural skills that have lasted them for millennia, and selling them our skills, which the environment is already unable to support without irreversible damage. Stevenson and Dasmann on deck. Brundtland, please listen.

The Rising Tide of Apathy:
Lord Snow said, "Despair is a sin," and I like to tell people I am not going to worry about their other sins, but they ought to kick despair. One psychiatrist responded: "Who in this audience has not felt despair?" He didn't want them to feel guilty about it. I had to adjust my thinking, but not very much. Apathy is still the enemy, and despair is its breeding ground. "What can one man do?" or one woman, is the cop-out of the day. A common bumper sticker says, "THE MORAL MAJORITY IS NEITHER." The apathetic majority is both. The earth can't afford it.

Apathy can be cured with large infusions of hope. The opportunity for individual roles in restoration, on spare time if not on career time, are legion, and should encourage hope.

Disagree and Die:
The psychiatrist who told the audience that no one should be ashamed of despair (see ahead, *The Rising Tide of Apathy*) added that one of our big problems is that if people disagree with us we think we have to kill them. He thought we should outgrow this habit. But as Eiseley said, the roots go very deep.

Boundaries of the Mind:
We should let Doonesbury work on this one, Gary Trudeau having spent so much time exploring Ronald Reagan's mind. I am afraid that one of the barriers to peace is in the too many circumscribed minds that consider peace to be non-U (a term invented by Jessica Mitford, author of *The American Way of Death*).

The world hasn't experienced peace for so long that it would seem abnormal. What would the foreign-news sections of the papers have to talk about, if not about quarrels and mayhem. What could a newspaper editorial board decide to feature if there weren't an invasion somewhere, and no little girl has just fallen down a well? I'm back on an earlier subject. What scenarios of a peaceful world can we write to help people visualize peace, as the bumper sticker suggests?

[I was not expecting, when I wrote Bob Allen, that the Berlin Wall would fall — much less that Anne and I would be in Berlin when it fell. Both happened.]

The Dangers in Security:

"In their resolution [of the world's vast contradictions] lies the survival of us all," Adlai said. From time to time, after quoting the full paragraph, I point out that security isn't enough. You can be secure in jail, reasonably secure in the army, with all your needs taken care of (not all, of course, but enough to provide security, until the time comes to cross the line of departure in combat).

Nancy Newhall pointed out that security can be a sedative: "Of all resources, the most crucial is Man's spirit. Not dulled, nor lulled, supine, secure, replete, does Man create, but out of stern challenge, in sharp excitement, with a burning joy."

So we don't want to be secure in jail, in the Marines, or in sleep. Nor, as Richard Barnet said, do we want our security to go so far as to make our opponent insecure.

Other Barriers:

Here in alphabetical order are a few more barriers to peace:

Congenital Nastiness	Distrust
Cruelty	Ego
Deceit	Paranoia
Disinformation	Violation of the Golden Rule
Distortion	Voodoo Politics

The Unturned Other Cheek:

The other cheek that once was turned has been replaced by the chip on the shoulder. Can we learn to take a little abuse better, to consider the source at least, to be like the Navajo parent who is not perturbed by a child's blows? Some anthropologists may remind us of how the mild and meek Indian tribes were overrun by the rough and bold. But hear Lao Tze, in the fifth century, B.C.: "That the yielding conquers the resistant and the soft conquers the hard is a fact known by all men, yet utilized by none."

Nature reminds us that when water apparently yields and rock does not seem to, a Grand Canyon is born.

The Underused Limitless Resource:

The riddle could go: What do you have more of the more you use it? Muscle is a good answer, but love is a better one.

Phobias:

There should be a whole section on this, with names for phobias Webster hasn't learned about yet but nations have.

Enough said about the barriers to peace. My laptop enjoyed the exercise, accepted a few editorial changes, and told my printer what to do two days later. I sent it off to Bob Allen, reminding him of what Daniel Hudson Burnham was supposed to have said: "Make no little plans; they have no magic to stir man's blood." I advised Bob to go ahead with his plans to rent Switzerland. He has not replied yet. I suppose he is still waiting for a fair quotation on renting Switzerland.

If you are tired of people too tired to make big plans (I'm afraid I am) and blamed for trying to make them yourself, you may be excused for repeating the best statement so far — Burnham's or whoever's — on how to plan.

We can go the commandment one better: Thou shalt love thy neighbor better than thyself.

Dave with an Earth Island crew, c. 1987.

CHAPTER 17

RESTORATION, A BLUEPRINT FOR THE GREEN CENTURY

———

ONFERENCES CAN BE ENVIRONMENTAL MILESTONES, and Restoring the Earth Conference; held at the University of California, Berkeley, in January, 1988 was just that. A few hundred attendees were hoped for; a thousand people came, from many disciplines, and left knowing that something new and vital had been launched. Stewart Udall, Secretary of the Interior in the environmentally innovative Kennedy and Johnson administrations, recognized the arrival of a new wave in his opening keynote address. Noel Brown, U.S. head of the United Nations Environment Programme, earned a standing ovation when his closing address confirmed that arrival.

Noel presented ten United Nations Restoration awards to people who had already set brilliant examples of what individuals, without waiting for government, could achieve in environmental restoration. A further award would surely have been bestowed had the United Nations Environmental Programme people and others known what is due David Wingate, who closed the formal conference with a surprise main event. Mr. Wingate had earlier told a small workshop about his twenty-year effort to restore the fifteen acres of Nonesuch Island, just south of Bermuda. At the end of his presentation his tiny audience was hardly able to stop applauding. The Sierra Club's Steve Rauh caught the beauty of it all and persuaded the conference officials to add two hours to the main event in the Wheeler Auditorium.

Watching what one man could do in twenty years of meticulous search for missing parts of the original scene, once again giving nature a chance to integrate them, the audience gave Mr. Wingate the first standing ovation of the three-day conference. If someone will turn his one-hour slide presentation into a book or a video presentation, you will see why. Among other things, you will be waiting for the next ten years to see if the loggerhead turtle hatchlings from eggs he brought to his island's beach sands and released to the sea fifteen years ago will find their way back to the first sand they knew. His audience would be ready, I think, to give a standing ovation to each returning loggerhead.

283

What happened in Berkeley, and what led up to it and will lead from it, is critically important to all of us. And to the biggest population of all — the hundreds of billions of living creatures, some of them human, yet to arrive on the planet, at least as fully deserving as we are of having it not only livable, but also a source of hope and joy. We who are here now cannot guarantee the success of this future, but we can certainly stop trying to preclude it!

Having been in the conservation business half a century, I should have thought harder about restoration sooner.

Unfortunately, many others have overlooked it too. In *Worldwatch Annual State of the World, 1987,* for example, the word does not appear in the index. It is absent also from the index of *World Resources 1987.* Thus it would appear to be missing from the agenda of Worldwatch Institute, World Resources Institute, and the International Institute for Environment and Development. *Our Common Future,* by the World Commission on Environment and Development, alludes to governments which, pressured by their citizens, established environmental agencies and ministries "to clean up the mess" resulting from rapid economic growth following World War II, and adds that "much of their work has of necessity been after-the-fact repair of damage: reforestation, reclaiming desert lands, rebuilding urban environments, restoring natural habitats, and rehabilitating wild lands." Three lines of text do not, however, constitute a restoration movement. So people who have not thought much about restoration have not been alone. Good company. Bad oversight.

In 1986, John J. Berger's book, *Restoring the Earth: How Americans Are Working to Renew Our Damaged Environment* (1986) perked my interest a little, when he addressed the subject at the Third Biennial Conference on the Fate of the Earth in Ottawa in June 1986 I began to wake up.

A booklet-length article really woke me up: "Toward Organic Security: Environmental Restoration Or the Arms Race?" by Carl Casebolt and Steve Rauh in *The Sierra Club Yodeler,* most effective of the club's newsletters, and should indeed be a booklet on its own.

Alert at last, I recalled the program of restoration Huey Johnson initiated in 1977, when he was Secretary of Resources for California Governor Jerry Brown. Huey Johnson's "Investing for Prosperity" proposal would be the precursor of his Green Century Project, the most dramatic of the ideas being developed by the New Renaissance Center he founded, now renamed the Resource Renewal Institute. For the state, he advocated a one-hundred-year plan to improve the state's productivity and environmental quality. Finding his friends laughing at the idea, he went to his ostensible enemies — California corporations.

As Huey Johnson tells it in *Earth Island Journal* (Spring 1987), his first stop was IBM, where he talked to one of the highest-ranking officers. They agreed to help: the work of IBM was to take detail and drudgery out of people's lives, and IBM was certainly interested in enhancing long-term economic and environmental quality. Huey asked, "Can we borrow your lobbyist?" and IBM said, "Help yourself."

Huey then went to Southern Pacific, Bank of America, and other corporations with whom he had been brawling from time to time. They were enthusiastic. Next he went to labor unions, who loved the idea because it would create jobs and enhance the quality of people's lives. The League of Women Voters made Investing for Prosperity their own statewide project.

"Suddenly everybody we talked to wanted to get involved," Huey said. "Then we signed on the environmentalists."

He asked for ideas about what to include in the one-hundred-year plan, and found that people liked to be asked. Some suggestions, he said, were excellent, some off-the-wall, some unpredictable. He put thirty-five projects together and won an appropriation of $125 million a year from state-owned off-shore oil revenues.

His Green Century formula included similar hundred-year plans for every part of the system — conservation and improvement of soil properties; coastline, parks and recreation areas, wildlands, and energy projects — all based on organizing a broad-based constituency for long-term plans for upgrading environmental quality. These were developed by skilled, nonpartisan individuals, and funded with government revenues from publicly owned nonrenewable resources and also from such renewable resources as forests.

In Huey's view, if you link up all the people interested in air, agriculture, water, energy, forestry, wildlife, for example, you have a powerful political base that's determined to deliver a positive future. "When you get them all together," Huey concluded, "it's just like sending an avalanche through a tea party."

The rest of us can do it. We have to. War has become unthinkable, primarily because of the nuclear issue. So what are people going to do now? Although their traditional focus of energy and skill unfortunately has been on war, the environment can absorb it all.

John Berger's book tells of several ingenious individuals who each take on a different restoration assignment: A grandmother, Marion Stoddart, leads the project that makes the Nashua River an economic and aesthetic asset to New Hampshire once again. Twenty-two-year-old Thomas Gordon adopts Maine's ailing Lake Annabessacock and clears it up. Francis Smith, a New England plumber of thirty-seven, cleans up the Quashnet River well enough that it is ready for reintroduction of sea-run eastern brookies, absent for one hundred fifty years. Ed

Garbisch, fifty-one, a former chemist, organizes an armada that creates flourishing artificial marshes, earning good money doing it. Tony Look, at sixty-nine, does wonders for the Big Basin redwoods. Other dynamic individuals take on, in turn, mine reclamation in Pennsylvania and New Mexico, prairie restoration in Wisconsin, toxic wastes in Michigan, falcon breeding and urban renovation in California.

THE DAN JANZEN STORY

JOHN BERGER'S NEWS IS GOOD. So is the news revealed in the lead article in the January 15, 1988, issue of *Science* by Professor Daniel Janzen of the University of Pennsylvania and ecological advisor for the Foundacion Neotropica, San Jose, Costa Rica. Since mid-January 1988 I have been unable to make a speech without alluding in some way to environmental restoration, and in most of them have I talked about the work of Daniel H. Janzen. The opening paragraph of his two-page article, "Tropical Ecological and Biocultural Restoration," frightened me then and frightens me still, but the rest is most encouraging:

"The increasingly vigorous efforts to protect some of the relatively intact portions of tropical nature come too late and too slow for well over half the tropics — especially the half best suited to agriculture and animal husbandry. Its relatively intact habitats are gone. Its remaining wildlands are hardly more than scattered biotic debris. The only feasible next step is conservation of biodiversity by using the living biotic debris and inocula from nearby intact areas to restore habitats. If this step is not taken quickly, natural and anthropogenic perturbations will extinguish most of the habitat remnants, small population fragments, and the living dead — the organisms that are living out their physiological life spans, but are no longer members of persistent populations."

Those two phrases need to be spoken slowly. Scattered biotic debris. The living dead.

Who has done the scattering? Who has given the death sentence? We have. And if knowing that the earth's life forms survive us is important to us, we can find joy in what Daniel Janzen is undertaking in his effort to restore the dry tropical forest in Costa Rica. There should be weekly bulletins on his progress.

If this were an anthology of the writings of others, I would happily include all his article right here. It ought to be in all environmental anthologies, just like Garrett Hardin's "The Tragedy of the Commons" and "The Historical Roots of the Ecological Crisis," by Lynn White, Jr.

Rescue of tropical species and habitats, Dan Janzen says, has abruptly become urgent. With the production of genetically engineered crop plants and animals that flourish in tropical rain forest habitats, millions of farmers and entrepreneurs will push into the habitats. The biotic debris will go first. Thousands of species of organisms will be obliterated. Restorationists seeking intact patches of forest still have some to choose from, but they are not interchangeable.

"The sites, though very interesting, do not represent the full sweep and glory of tropical biodiversity. To reduce this imbalance requires restoration of the wild habitats that once occupied the lands that today support most tropical civilizations — dry forests, volcanic soils, riparian alluvia, coastal plains, islands, intermediate elevations. . . . Restriction of conservation to the few remaining relatively intact habitat patches automatically excludes more than 90% of tropical humanity from its direct benefits; restoration is most needed where people live. . . . Restoration at such a habitat's margins is essential for its long-term survival.

"But even in small areas, populations must be restored before new trouble arrives."

Professor Janzen lists places where restoration has taken place naturally "if there is an adequate inoculum of plants and animals, and if it is permitted to invade and grow." However, he warns, "It is critical that the potential for restoration does not become yet another rationale for the obliteration of relatively intact tropical wildlands."

Where should one look for help?

"Choose an appropriate site, obtain it, and hire some of the former users as live-in managers. Sort through the habitat remnants to see which can recover. Stop the biotic and physical challenges to those remnants. The challenge is to turn the farmer's skills at biomanipulation to work for the conservation of biodiversity.

"Explicit and public agreement on management goals is imperative." Public agreement, of course, is not enough. "How does one know what habitat to restore? The simplest thing to do is let the organisms decide." Time will also do some deciding:

In general, a canopy of woody plants (and substantial faunas) will appear on the restoring site within one or two decades, mature-appearing forests will appear in one to five centuries, and truly pristine forest and faunal structure is a matter of millennia.

The earlier start, therefore, the better. Accepting triage will be painful but necessary "to get scarce resources focused on particular sites and not to ladle funds onto the living dead for nostalgic reasons." Government ownership is critical because private owners are not able to bear the unpredictable costs of fire, pesticide damage, irrigation projects, new legislation, mining, squatters, logging, and new agricultural varieties.

"Human cultures," he continues, "evolved in mutualism and conflict with the natural world . . . by far the most diverse and evocative intellectual stimulation known to humans. Tropical humans are experiencing nearly total loss of this integral part of their mental lives. It is as though they are losing their color vision and most of their hearing. Ten thousand acres of rice is one of the dullest habitats on earth.

"Obliteration of tropical wildlands and human intellectual deprivation go hand in hand.

"It is critical that diverse and imaginative education programs be taught within the restoring wildland, and local peoples be intellectually involved in the restoration and management process. To save what is restored, the doors of the library must be open very wide. Yes, some books will be stolen, lost, worn, incorrectly shelved, and unappreciated. That is the tax that a conserved wildland must pay for survival in tomorrow's tropics. . . .

"Choose a community of 300 subsistence farmers anywhere in the tropics, purchase three adjoining farms, turn them into a public conserved wildland, give it back to the community, and you will get 280 votes favoring its presence and permanence.

"There will be plenty of problems. One area's plan will not likely fit another's. School education programs in one place may not work as well as ecotourism. Cattle grazing may be helpful here, harmful there. The wrong genetic material may be introduced and for a while mask long-range damage. A wildfire may destroy restoration gains and what was left of the inocula. Restoration projects may be mislabeled as 'colonial imperialist.' The new understanding of restoration may disrupt religious and business traditions.

"And all this," Daniel Janzen concludes, "is to say that humans have won the battle against nature. Humanity makes its living by preventing restoration. It is up to us to accept the responsibility of putting the vanquished back on their feet, paws, and roots. We can do it. Even defeated, tropical nature has too much to offer for us to accept a world without it."

How can we expedite restoration programs when inertial tendencies are so prevalent? One such tendency leads some people to suspect that the very name will lead to abuse. And there are undoubtedly hordes of developers who would jump at the chance to say "We'll restore it there later if you'll let us destroy it here first." They have been doing this for some time with the words "mitigation" and "enhancement," which, a friend of ours once said, "are runner-up prizes in a loser's game."

Just change the order: require that they restore it first, and do it well enough that they will build in their restored area instead. Build a separate and equal Grand Canyon somewhere else and put your dams there.

Restoration and preservation are complementary. If, on the one hand, it costs a trillion or so dollars to restore what was destroyed to make a few billions in profit — the bill is likely to be very high for cooling the global greenhouse — industry and its customers will be reluctant to repeat the mistake because they can't afford it. If, on the other hand, you are looking for the pattern that will tell you how to restore an ancient forest, but have clear-cut and lost the pattern, you are out of luck.

This is a long way of saying that preservation and restoration are inseparable — you can't have one without the other. Just as you cannot have peace on earth without making peace with the earth.

Remembering Nancy Newhall's axiom: "The wilderness holds answers to more questions than we have yet learned how to ask," we had better not burn, pave, or shred those answers.

TOMORROW'S MARSHALL PLAN

ONE WAY TO SPARE THOSE ANSWERS, a way to link conservation and security, would be a U.S.-Soviet Marshall Plan devoted not to resource depletion, but to resource rescue, an investment in recovery of the earth's renewable potential. In the First Biennial Conference on the Fate of the Earth, held in New York City in 1982, Steve Rauh, many associates, and I tried to get environmental and peace organizations working together toward this goal. Success was modest.

A year later, at a peace conference in Prague, I was co-chair of a dialogue on economic conversion, and was pleased to find that people both East and West thought conversion a good idea, a chance to see whether socialists or capitalists could convert faster to a peaceful economy. But I soon learned how long, and with what little success, others had been working on the subject, including Professor Seymour Melman of Columbia University and New York Congressman Ted Weiss. Again and again legislation had been introduced, had been fought by the Department of Defense, and had received support from too few to warrant field hearings, themselves a good way to encourage the building of a constituency for conversion. An Economic Adjustment Act isn't a concept that fits easily on a bumper sticker or into a thirty-second commercial.

But conversion is something to organize around, and can be a crucial motivation for an economy that need no longer be so dependent on manufacturing and exercising the sinews of war. Conversion and restoration can be the best of companions in the rescue operation the Earth's life-support system requires.

I like Kenneth Brower's way of putting it (in the 1968 foreword to the two-volume Sierra Club book *Galapagos: The Flow of Wildness*):

"A living planet is a rare thing, perhaps the rarest in the universe, and a very tenuous experiment at best. We need all the company we can get on our unlikely journey. If an island is washed away mankind is the less: One species's death diminishes us, for we are involved in life. The more varied the life the better. There is no requirement that our voyage be a monotonous one."

Or a lonely one. Beyond caring about other species, we need to restore a few other things:

Foresight, for example — the ability to look ahead on behalf of future generations. To seek alternatives to destructive energy-producing and energy-wasting habits, and to destructive sources of economic growth. To strive for excellence in education, in health care, in housing, in the arts and the media, in crafts, in transportation, in manufacturing, in research, and in methods of investing in all these.

There is more. We can restore the ability to live in peaceful stability. The Chinese once did it for three centuries but seem to have forgotten how. We would be hard put to find where modern civilization has done it for three years. We can restore the reverence for the land and the life on it (and not too much of that life our own species) that earlier Americans had. We can reassemble the essential natural systems that worked so well before we got too clever — systems we inherited, tinkered with, lost parts of.

By restoring our own ingenuity, we can expedite the transition to an economy based on peace. We can keep people on their present payrolls but rewrite their job descriptions. For example — an example I am forever repeating but doing little about — let the new job description allow the Army Corps of Engineers to keep up some military duties, but leave rivers alone for a while and get the railroads running like Japan's and Europe's while we still have enough low-cost energy to get the job done.

Add an Earth Corps element to all military training. Military people learn map-reading for military operations that deface what is on the map. Let them extend their skills enough to restore what they and others have defaced.

Soldiers learn how to give first aid to people. Could they not also learn, in their own small ways, how to apply first aid to the economies of erstwhile, present, or imagined enemies? Making friends of them could broaden a soldier's outlook on life. I saw a little of this happen during and immediately after my combat days in World War II, even without our being trained for it. In the middle of combat we shared food with the people dispossessed by war. In the first postwar months we learned, in applying temporary military government, how to rebuild local economies. In postwar Japan, Dr. Daniel Luten, later to be chairman of Friends of the Earth, was a principal conservation advisor to General MacArthur with excellent results. And, of course, there was the Marshall Plan, invented by a five-star general. Think what would happen if `humanitarian aid' for the Contras were invested in restoration of Nicaragua as a whole, with the Contras changing their former role to one of healing a badly torn country.

Perhaps what we need most to restore is the better reality we once had. Call it the American Dream.

The dream is not hard to discern, even by people who have not yet experienced it. On a few occasions when I was expected to make a speech to a group of young people and there were only a dozen or two in the audience, I have turned the tables on them and asked them to make the speech. Forming a circle and each speaking in turn, they would give their answers to the simple question: What kind of a world would you like your children to grow up in — or the children of others if you choose to have none of your own? Try it sometime, and try not to be moved by the answers (but don't try too hard). The answers are beautiful. If there is time, go around the circle again, so that complementary comments can come out, leading toward a hope-building conclusion: We have a consensus. We have the votes. All the rest is just administrative detail. Let's go for it!

LESSONS FROM STOCKHOLM

ADMINISTRATIVE DETAIL, however, is fundamentally important to the project. How do we go about going for it? What strategies will work? What alliances will we need? How can we stimulate the action? What is our timetable? Who should lead and advise? Who should follow? How do we pay for it? And what progress has been made lately in this direction, all over the world, to encourage us? Lots of questions.

Let's start with the last one, and go back to the 1972 Stockholm Conference on the Human Environment. Peter Stone wrote an informative, lively, grossly underappreciated book about it. The briefly almost successful British publishing house I started, Earth Island Ltd., put the book out but did not get it around nearly well enough. I still have a score of copies of *Did We Save the Earth at Stockholm? The People and Politics in the Conference on the Human Environment* in my basement, and they can be most useful in preparing for yet another UN conference. Peter does not claim that we saved it, but exclaims how the work started at that conference, by one hundred thirteen nations and five thousand people, gave the earth another chance. The assembled nations agreed on a seven-paragraph declaration, on twenty-six principles, and on one hundred nine recommendations for action at the international level. The sixth recommendation ends with the only italicized sentence in the whole series: *"To defend and improve the human environment for present and future generations has become an imperative goal for mankind — a goal to be pursued together with, and in harmony with, the established goals of peace and world-wide economic and social development."*

291

Principle Three was the briefest of all: "The capacity of the earth to produce vital renewable resources must be maintained and, wherever practicable, restored or improved." The concept of restoration is addressed nowhere else in the final action, nor does the word or any derivative of it appear in the index. There is frequent mention of 'improving,' and 'development' is ubiquitous. There is no mention of the word 'wilderness.' All this is understandable. It took five years to put the conference together and it was important to keep things on familiar ground and to develop consensus. Now is a good time to explore the perimeter of that familiar ground, to step over the boundaries boldly here and there, and especially to inquire into the opportunities to restore what people, with their affinity for control, management, improvement, tinkering, and development, contrive to disrupt, knowing not what harm they may do.

Broken eggs will have to remain broken. Extinct species will have to stay where they have been sent — banished forever. But broken toys can be fixed with glue; broken hearts can be mended with love; exhausted fields, left fallow, can renew themselves — almost; dashed hopes can be put partly back together as long as life lasts. We need only get over the current feeling that while there's life there's hopelessness, and answer the ever-repeated question, "But what can I do?"

The thing to remember is that the very effort of trying to restore will inform us, persuade us to take it easy the next time we are tempted to treat an heirloom roughly. An engineer knows that the budget for what he is building must include O, M, and R — funding for operation, maintenance, and replacement. If you are counting on a long operation, you had better set aside a reserve fund for that faraway day of replacement — something the mining industry rarely thinks of if you include replacement of what was there before the boomtown became a ghost.

To an engineer, replacement usually requires using an artifact.

Restoration will require many artifacts. But restoration has more going for it — it has the earth's natural forces of renewal, just waiting there for their chance to put things back together. Grass can take care of pavement. Restore rail service to the likes of what they have in Japan and Europe; give a John Jeavons or a Wes Jackson or a Boone Hallberg, respectively from California, Kansas, and Oaxaca, a chance to restore the sustainable agriculture the world knew before it became addicted to oil and its pesticide and fertilizer and ground-compacting derivatives. Freeways breed gridlock. Farm a few instead!

Think what the United Nations organizations could do if their charge included restoration.

UNESCO could call attention to the need and to past successes, such as Huey Johnson's Investing for Prosperity program for California,

Daniel Janzen's restoration of dry tropical forest in Costa Rica, or David Wingate's twenty-year devotion to a little, devastated island.

MAB (Man and the Biosphere Program) could fill a wish list overnight, establishing major biosphere reserves while there is still time (and allowing women a role in the biosphere).

WHO (World Health Organization) would find new opportunities in what a healthy environment could do for world health.

FAO (Food and Agriculture Organization) could easily spend what the world military operations cost in making soil productive again, free of its present addiction to oil.

The Industrial Development Organization could busy itself with the logistics, making sure that developers who call wild land "raw land" are tranquilized or kept miles away from what is being developed.

The World Meteorological Organization would have much less to worry about as we looked more to the continuing flow of sunshine for our energy needs rather than disrupting so much with the flow of chlorofluorocarbons and of squandering fossil fuels through our tall stacks and tailpipes.

The UN Development Program would be encouraged to play with the hand the world has dealt it, concentrating on development that heals the earth rather than maiming it.

The UN Volunteer Program (UNCHE), along with the UN Environment Program and the Environmental Liaison Board and Center, could enlist an unbelievable amount of help from the NGOs of the world, and could well come up with a better name than NGO — nongovernmental organization. Margaret Mead properly objected to naming something for what it is not.

The United Nations Conference on Environmental Protection and Restoration should take place in 1992, the twentieth anniversary of the UN Conference on the Human Environment held in Stockholm. So far, the key words `protection' and `restoration' have been omitted from the announcement, and the word `development' has been added. If protection and restoration are not added to the agenda of the UN conference in Brazil in June 1992, look for me on the nearest soapbox.

Remember that the 1972 Stockholm Conference would have been succeeded even if it had not been held, thanks to the enormous amount of work that went into the planning. All those preparatory documents were by no means going to be lost and forgotten. But for all the foreboding, the conference was held, was successful, and spawned good works globally, including the opportunity to improve upon them. Mr. Peter Stone points out, it wasn't so much the long speeches that accomplished this as it was the meetings and sharing that went on in the corridors and at the bars.

The minimum of three years necessary for planning a new conference can produce a much-needed bold concentration of genius, power, and magic focused on what can become the essential ingredient of peace. We can have a global Marshall Plan for global restoration participated in by all the earth's people in behalf of themselves and their descendants.

If a new UN agency is born of this effort, it can pay for itself soon in the increased environmental protection and productivity that will result. Or the work can be shared by the existing agencies — provided they solemnly swear they will not use cosmetics instead of action.

The new UN agency could follow the U.S. example of NEPA — the National Environmental Policy Act — and the Environmental Protection Agency and Council on Environmental Quality that resulted from NEPA. The UN set up its own EPA in 1972, UNEP — the United Nations Environment Programme. (British spelling seems to be a product of the Me Generation. What good do those last letters in *programme* do?)

Russell Train, key advisor of the Nixon administration in its support of NEPA and first head of EPA, attended the Stockholm conference on behalf of the United States and materially helped things move. You will recall that this is the same Judge Train who fathered the idea of the UN World Heritage when he was president of the Conservation Foundation, and who also thanked John McPhee for my being around and making it so easy for "the rest of us to be reasonable."

I consider Russ Train to be the outstanding Republican conservationist. The newly merged Conservation Foundation and World Wildlife Fund, U.S., is fortunate to have him as its chairman. He was one of the first to appreciate the ecological disasters that well-intentioned development efforts have produced far and wide. The U.S. suffered from his absence from the inner councils of the Reagan administration. It would be a far different and better world had he not been excluded.

It will take a Russ Train, or someone separate but equal, to get a NERA up and moving — a National Environmental Restoration Act, with the necessary family of agencies and regional offspring that can make it work. I was advocating a National Restoration Agency until a friend reminded me that the acronym NRA is bad news for people who don't like getting shot at. An alternative NRS was suggested — a National Recovery Service, augmented by a federal Restoration Finance Corporation. People who remember the Franklin Roosevelt administration will remember the two predecessors — the National Recovery Administration and the Reconstruction Finance Corporation, the latter initiated by Herbert Hoover.

It would be helpful if legislation were enacted to create this service in time for it to help the proposed UN conference to achieve its goal. This would be the kind of example I think other nations would like the U.S. to be setting.

FOR DICTATOR PRO TEM

IF I WERE DICTATOR for a week or so, my benevolence would include the following:

1) I'd have Russ Train and Huey Johnson meet with some people of their choosing but also of my choosing, and I would not be surprised if there were some overlapping.

2) My choices would include Robert McNamara, former president of the World Bank, in addition to other duties; Amory Lovins, benign terrorist with numbers; Hazel Henderson, the economist who calls economics a form of brain damage; someone to represent what Margaret Mead and Barbara Ward would be thinking had they not left us too soon; Barber Conable, current president of the World Bank; Gus Speth, head of World Resources Institute; Norman Myers, biologist who could write a book about what the restoration legislation should encompass; Robert O. Anderson, the environmentalists's oilman; Donald Kennedy, president of Stanford University; Barbara Boxer and Ron Dellums, neighboring members of Congress who should be introducing the legislation; Dale and Betty Bumpers, who know respectively of how the Senate and the peace movement could help; Jesse Jackson, who had the best environmental platform of all presidential candidates; David Rockefeller, because we want this to go somewhere and the Trilateral Commission could move it; Jimmy Carter, because he knows what should happen and this will help history treat him better; Jerry Brown, for the same reason; and Paul and Anne Ehrlich, to keep the program from straying too far.

3) Normally, I would not tell such a stellar group how to go about its business. Since I have dictatorial duties for the moment, however, I would require that several action items be on the agenda. (I won't start a new series of numbers; one is enough.)

4) Have the NRS legislation drafted and sent out to states, not for review, but for copying before my term of office has expired.

5) The legislation is to set up the U.S. National Recovery Service with a charge similar to that given the EPA, and with a concurrent President's Council on Environmental Restoration that will have powers equal to the Office of Management and Budget (since the OMB has been dedicated principally to the expenditure [so-called `development'] of resources, and the CER must see that enough investment takes place to allow future OMBs to have something to expend).

6) Federal departments must not only consult with the NRS, but also cooperate, which requires mutual agreement. There is no federal agency that cannot assist, if it has to, the national restoration program.

7) Each agency will be directed to provide its own portion of a Blueprint for the Green Century. The number-one criterion for the blueprint is that it project the kind of world sought for the centennial of the NRS and that it determine what the U.S. role is to be in getting there equitably and ethically (this need not, for a change, be considered heretical). Also, each agency will outline steps that need to be taken or avoided, as the case may be, if such world is to have a chance to arrive at the year 2100 in better than acceptable shape. No, I am dictator. It must arrive in superior shape.

8) One budget shall be presented. Not a bare-bones budget. I would reject it. Not an optimum budget. Optimum is too timid, and no one would accept a mere optimum performance from any professional team. The budget must be fully adequate for the job ahead. Read my lips.

9) The budget should be footnoted with the kind and number of jobs the program would create and the improvement in environmental capital that would result.

10) The banking types in the meeting are required to handle the troublesome world debt my way: the debt is to be forgiven, not merely rescheduled to rationalize further loans to cover still greater interest payments — provided that the debtor nation invest the amount of the forgiven repayment in environmental protection and restoration. The restoration is the important part, because that keeps people working and gets the country's environment back on its productive feet. Since the debt is unlikely ever to have been paid anyway, the obligation should be shared by those who profited from what the debt bought (and let's identify those things) and the rest of us, who were going to have to pay it anyway and might as well have a better world for our trouble.

11) Perfection in the legislation and the blueprint is not required. The perfect is the enemy of the good, as someone said, and it is important to get this planet back in running order promptly. We can fix the enabling legislation or the activating blueprint while we run.

12) This one is next to last. What we will accomplish with this effort, while we are at it, will improve the security of our enemies-of-the-moment. We are not going to improve our security or theirs if we go through life with guns pointed at each other's heads or make each other nervous for subtler reasons. This leads to what will achieve a mutually assured future through economic conversion.

13) Note on the importance of conversion: if we are ever to get over our overdependency on the military-industrial-academic complex (MIAC), we must fashion a supercarrot. Somehow the war-dependent people who have rationalized that their well-being and global security are synonymous must be persuaded to alter their rationalizing.

One by one, we need to find alternatives to MIAC-dependent jobs that will provide similar challenge and income.

There is nothing new in this observation. What is also not new is that neither this nation or others I have heard about has accommodated this observation.

Thus peace continues to escape us, or we it.

The war budget, periodically hyped-up by the Defense (War) Department fantasies about enemy arms buildup, has deprived other needs of society disastrously.

The principal (and deprived) needs are health; education; equitable opportunity to be fed, well-clothed, and well-housed; transportation; industrial progress; and environmental protection and restoration.

Taking each of these again, one at a time, we need to pair the MIAC capabilities with those needed in making the transition to the alternatives, here and abroad, in the first, second, third, and fourth worlds.

Many of the MIAC industries are already diversified enough that they could make the transition once they were persuaded to seek alternative markets, or were required to depend on alternatives.

Academia will probably adjust to corporate needs without much trouble, because much of their financing will be determined by those needs, as has been true too long.

The public is probably more than ready but has heard little about the opportunity.

The armed forces will have the hardest time making the transition; but, as Freeman Dyson has pointed out in *Weapons and Hope,* it is important to find these people something else to do. Until Paradise arrives, in the arms of Ecotopia, and Sin has left the planet, armed forces will be needed to police the errant. That does not mean that they should not have alternative work in between missions, missions that we hope will be rarer and rarer — those requiring them to shoot up places and people.

The Corps of Engineers provides the readiest example. Their mission requires that they be able to build things in a hurry and organize a civilian component quite successfully. At present, they successfully organize the industrial and political forces needed to build dams and dikes and dredge harbors and channels. The Corps could be kept successfully busy on restoration, thus compensating for their past excesses. Let them dismantle the Hetch Hetchy dam for practice.

Let us find parallel opportunities for other armed forces, with emphasis on environmental *protection* (the army used to protect the national parks) and *restoration* (patterned after the CCC).

Perhaps there can be transfers to Father Hesburgh's proposal of the new Peace Army, or whatever he calls it. I prefer Sam LaBudde's Earth Corps idea, with renewed United Nations muscle and innovation in support, for its new name, the International Green Circle.

Congress after Congress has introduced legislation to get economic conversion under way. It is an inseparable component of restoration. But in Congress after Congress, the legislation has languished. Enact it!

Arms-race suppliers — the warlords of old and their progeny — need to be asked that simple question: "If peace breaks out, what is your fall-back position?" Responsible CEOs ought then to lobby hard for the conversion that could assure them a future.

Superpowers please add this item to a summit agenda soon.

I should like to go on, but the rest would be more administrative detail, which is boring. Furthermore, my term as dictator does not have long to go, and we are going to have to get together to decide how to make this thing work. I think we can persuade people that it is going to cost something, but that it is a good investment in the only planet worth knowing. And it is really going to cost us if we don't make the investment. Before departing my dictatorship, I would decree that funds will come from an assortment of sources:

1) Set up Restoration districts, like Marion Stoddart's Nashua River Watershed Association, members of which made the necessary minor contributions. They were a local land trust of sorts.

2) Vote a Restoration tax, like what you pay to have your garbage disposed of, however poorly it is disposed of now.

3) Restoration bonds. These could be statewide, and big. Unlike most bonds, they would be an investment, not a method of deferring current obligations.

4) Restoration insurance. Entrepreneurs would take out their policies to cover restoration costs when they have ended their exploitation. This would be an alternative way of putting up restoration bonds and different from (3) above.

5) Restoration sinking funds. A variety of the restoration insurance, but pay-as-you-go self-insurance. The nuclear industry should have built a sinking fund of $200 billion or so, but neglected to.

6) Restoration tax write-offs, check-offs, and rebates. Each of these is slightly different, and all are used by exploiters for immediate benefit. Long-range costs should be accommodated too.

7) A Restoration Corps, variant of the Peace Corps, in the UN, U.S., and in neighborhoods (to cover all levels). The Peace Corps gets (and earns) $180 million a year. That's a good start.

8) Restoration homesteads. The opportunity to homestead derelict land and thus acquire title, assuming the obligation of restoring the mess you acquire.

9) Restoration claims. Related to (8) but like mining claims. Stake them out, do initial restorative work, and when you have done enough, patent the land.

10) Restoration awards. Follow the precedent now set by the United Nations Environment Programme (the ten UNEP Restoration Awards handed out in Berkeley by Noel Brown).

11) Restoration job descriptions. Each corporation with, say, twenty-five or more employees would set up an in-house position of restorationist or, in larger firms, a restoration department. We would have then an adequate basis for ecological careers in university curricula. It is assumed here that ecological literacy could serve in all other restoration goals, from housing to transportation to agriculture to medicine to philosophical approaches to whatever humanity is up to.

12) Huey Johnson-like offices in government at all levels, funded out of the general revenue — like Huey's $125 million a year for restoration.

13) Ditto in NGOs, even if they can't raise $125 million.

14) Continuing restoration conferences, in order to build a constituency, with legislative and political clout, to obtain all the goals listed above.

15) Transfer restoration talent funds from the arms race to the survival race.

16) Add a restoration division to the World Bank.

17) Restoration pricing. It is time for us to pay the environmental cost of things we buy — adding enough to the manufacturing, distribution, and profit we already pay for to assure that the environment that produced the basic parts can be restored and remain producing those basic parts just as well next time, and all the subsequent next times. The Earth is tired of subsidizing us, giving and giving, and getting nothing back.

OUR LESS COMMON FUTURE

THE NEED FOR A GREEN CENTURY IS IMPLICIT in the Brundtland Commission's book, *Our Common Future,* for which Norway's Prime Minister Gro Harlem Brundtland chaired the three-year inquiry into problems and opportunities on five continents.

She attended the Fourth World Wilderness Congress in Colorado in September of 1987, along with some two thousand people, including delegates and others from sixty nations. (Eastern bloc nations listened in, but did not formally participate, and we hope for better luck next time.) Her prepared statement, together with her response to questions from the floor, led me to conclude that she is one of the world's most brilliant women. The book about her commission's study is described by Oxford University Press as "the most important document of the decade on the future of the world." If only Oxford agreed well enough to get the book widely distributed! It has not been. Five of its paragraphs powerfully reinforce the relationships between conservation and security that have been stressed in the four biennial conferences on the Fate and Hope of the Earth (New York, 1982; Washington, D.C., 1984; Ottawa, 1986; Managua, 1989).

"The deepening and widening environmental crisis presents a threat to national security — and even survival — that may be greater than well-armed, ill-disposed neighbors and unfriendly alliances. Already in parts of Latin America, Asia, the Middle East, and Africa, environmental decline is becoming a source of political unrest and international tension. The recent destruction of much of Africa's dryland agricultural production was more severe than if an invading army had pursued a scorched-earth policy. Yet most of the affected governments still spend far more to protect their people from invading armies than from the invading desert.

"Globally, military expenditures total about $1 trillion a year and continue to grow. In many countries, military spending consumes such a high proportion of gross national product that it itself does great damage to these societies's development efforts. Governments tend to base their approaches to `security' on traditional definitions. This is most obvious in the attempts to achieve security through the development of potentially planet-destroying nuclear weapons systems. Studies suggest that the cold and dark nuclear winter following even a limited nuclear war could destroy plant and animal ecosystems and leave any human survivors occupying a devastated planet very different from the one they inherited.

"The arms race — in all parts of the world — preempts resources that might be used more productively to diminish the security threats created by environmental conflict and the resentments that are fueled by widespread poverty.

"Many present efforts to guard and maintain human progress, to meet human needs, and to realize human ambitions are simply unsustainable — in both the rich and poor nations. They draw too heavily, too quickly, on already overdrawn environmental resource accounts to be affordable far into the future without bankrupting these accounts. They may show profits on the balance sheets of our generation, but our children will inherit the losses. We borrow environmental capital from future generations with no intention or prospect of repaying. They may damn us for our spendthrift ways, but they can never collect on our debt to them. We act as we do because we can get away with it: future generations do not vote; they have no political or financial power; they cannot challenge our decisions.

"But the results of the present profligacy are rapidly closing the options for future generations. Most of today's decision makers will be

300

dead before the planet feels the heavier effects of acid precipitation, global warming, ozone depletion, or widespread desertification and species loss. Most of the young voters of today will still be alive. In the Commission's hearings it was the young, those who have the most to lose, who were the harshest critics of the planet's present management."

In the present world of INs and OUTs, the INs still treat the OUTs as colonies, although they call them Developing Nations instead, as a cosmetic for further exploitation. The few INs use most of the world's resources, are leaders in environmental destruction, and have so far staved off the hopes of the far more numerous OUTs for a new world economic order. The din of inequity grows steadily louder. The OUTs, unable to win by force of huge military expenditures, could be driven to thinking hostile thoughts about the INs, these thoughts leading to hostile, inexpensive acts — sabotage and terrorism. It takes little imagination to carry the scenario further, but let's try something else. For destruction let us substitute that fresh alternative, Restoration.

TOWARD A NEW RESOLUTION

IN MY JUDGMENT, a preponderance of the audience at the Fourth Wilderness Congress was not happy with the Brundtland Commission's main prescription for ending the gross global inequities it saw as leading to further environmental destruction and probably to global conflict. Poverty, the commission concluded, was the greatest threat, along with inequity. The solution was economic growth so that the gap between the INs and the OUTs could be narrowed, poverty eliminated, and the needs of the OUTs met with sustainable development.

Professor Raymond Dasmann first gave voice to the audience's unspoken concern. Abandoning his prepared text, he explained why he thought *economic growth* and *sustained development* were but buzzwords unless we knew what the concepts contained, and we weren't being told. He feared that the attempts of developers and environmentalists to "cooperate" would be a replay of *Godzilla vs. Bambi*. That evening, at bar time, I showed him my draft of a resolution the Congress could pass, and he liked it.

We disagreed with the commission's idea that the declining world environment, the result of the economic growth and development carried on since the Industrial Revolution, could be corrected with more economic growth and development. For the past twenty years we had been hearing that economic growth would narrow the gap between rich and poor nations. But growth and development had widened the gap. If, however, new economic growth were based on investment and payout from environmental restoration, this in itself could lead to sustainable development in the right places. It could be sustained not just for the few years corporations are usually constrained to think about, but in perpetuity.

I submitted a resolution in behalf of Earth Island Institute, supported by delegates from several organizations. It passed, minus the sales message in the preamble, without dissent.

RESOLUTION ON ENVIRONMENTAL RESTORATION
Estes Park, Colorado, September 14, 1987

Preamble: The United Nations Conference on the Human Environment in Stockholm in 1972 brought global recognition to the need for reform in human attitudes toward the environment. The United Nations Environment Programme and its subprograms resulted. Many people soon felt that environmental protection needed to be linked to economic growth and sustainable development. Belief is now widespread that economic growth and sustainable development are inseparable from environmental protection.

The questions not covered in detail at the Fourth Wilderness Congress are these:

1) What can economic growth be based upon and what can sustainable development consist of on a limited Earth?

2) How much of the economic growth and development since the Industrial Revolution have been dependent on the mining of nonrenewable and renewable resources?

3) If the basis of economic growth in the past has depended on resources that are being exhausted, what must the new growth and development consist of if they are indeed to be sustainable?

It is axiomatic that there can be an environment without an economy (the environment existed for more than four billion years before the first economist appeared), but there can be no economy without an environment. Environmental destruction is widespread and is accelerating.

An important and virtually untested way to determine the extent and the reversibility of environmental impairment and destruction is to undertake to restore those elements which have been impaired and destroyed. Is restoration possible and economically feasible in whole or in part? The effort to determine this, to find out what resources of science, technology, and human genius and spirit are available and what they cost, is an obligation to the future. It can determine what course the human family, now rapidly becoming aware of what its past has cost the Earth and the future, now ought to follow. We are less likely to destroy what we cannot afford to restore — including a future for our children.

Several times Congress has heard words related to restoration — heal, redeem, recover, and rehabilitate. What these words connote was not dwelt on. The word *restoration* places heavy demand on us, if we remember the effort to put Humpty Dumpty together again, but we ought not to back away from the demands.

The Stockholm Conference of 1972 would have been worthwhile even if it had not been held, owing to the study and exchange of ideas required of those around the world who prepared for the conference. It is now urgent to proceed beyond the Stockholm declarations.

NOW THEREFORE BE IT RESOLVED:

1) that the United Nations be urged to begin preparation for a Conference on Environmental Restoration in 1992, to celebrate the twentieth anniversary of the Stockholm Conference of 1972 and to ascertain the environmentally feasible routes to economic growth and sustainable development throughout the world that will respect and protect the irreplaceable resources of information that exist in the remaining living wildernesses of the world;

2) that the individual governments participating in the United Nations be urged to establish agencies or services (a) to further the preparation for the conference and (b) to advise their respective governments of interim courses of action to preserve the opportunity to carry forward the recommendations of the Conference on Restoration;

3) that nongovernmental organizations be urged to support this resolution vigorously;

4) that the Executive Committee of the Congress appoint a committee to follow up on this resolution; and

5) that the media inform the public of this resolution and participate in the preparation for the conference and in covering its deliberation and conclusions.

The Resolutions Committee's chairman, Robert Prescott-Allen explained that the Wilderness Congress did not establish follow-up committees; if I wanted action on the Restoration resolution, the ball was in my court.

BACK FROM THE BRINK

I BEGAN TO LEARN about that court more than twenty years ago when the Conservation Foundation's stars Russell Train, Ray Dasmann, and John Milton got me thinking vaguely about international conservation, and when Jerry Mander wrote the ad asking people to think of the earth as the Conservation District in the Universe — as Earth National Park. I have argued that only one-tenth of the earth remains essentially uninterrupted by man and his technology. We have the capability of grinding our way through that vestige in a decade or so. We shall then have to go back where we have been and do better there, repairing, renewing, and restoring as best we can. But how much better to go back now, encroaching no further on the world's wildness! Leave it for Nancy Newhall's reason.

I thought the argument was a good one. The 10 percent arrived by intuition. At the Wilderness Congress, Mike McCloskey, the Sierra Club's chairman, presented an inventory of the world's remaining wilderness that totaled the figure at 34 percent. That number included rock, ice, and sand that I had never counted in the first place. Wild, yes. Endangered, hardly. I asked Mike, "What would the number be if you edited out those inhospitable places?" It would take some reaching to put those numbers at his fingertips, but the 10 percent did not seem unreasonable. Whatever the number, the attack of exponential growth on wildness can get rid of it; and whether it would take ten or thirty years is not worth arguing about. One way or another, getting rid of it will avail us little. We would lose the very patterns we need to restore things well — patterns tested and proved through the eons. Without wilderness the world's a cage. While it lasts — and it should be permitted to last forever — it can remain, to quote Wallace Stegner, part of our Geography of Hope.

Although we still have an appreciable wilderness to go through — preferably to save — we have reached the edge of an abyss in other respects:

Air that is destroying lakes and forests cannot be good for anything that breathes, and isn't even good for statuary.

An atmosphere being warmed so seriously that sea level is rising will not be helpful in Venice, Holland, and Florida, where saltwater will invade freshwater domain.

We may need the ozone barrier more than we know.

Water from aquifers so polluted that it should not be served to children and pregnant women probably ought not be mixed too freely with Bourbon. Aquifers are being mined as well as polluted.

Land that pollutes these aquifers because it is becoming addicted to unnatural chemicals should say no to such drugs. And soil needed for growing food and fiber needs restoration, not pavement.

In our own misuse of energy we are co-conspirators in crimes against the air, the water, the land, children, and other living things.

It will surprise no one these days that life itself is at still further risk — on the only place in the universe it exists, so far as we know. From time to time it has been profitable to represent God. It has now become quite lucrative to play God. Pandora, we find, had more than one box, and we seem determined to open them all. We do not yet know how to handle the consequences of freeing the atom, and we may find it equally puzzling to cope with our freeing of DNA. We repeatedly prove the adage that the love of money is the root of all evil.

If the consequences of such errors fell only on those who profit from them, the rest of us might find it acceptable. We ourselves could accept the consequences of our own apathy. But what can we say about a species that inflicts tragedy on the innocent bystanders, all the other forms of life, forms that earned their place long before we showed up? What will the Great Auditor record about the brief tenant, *Homo hubris?*

But wait! We haven't stepped over the brink yet. We can indeed turn around and step forward.

After his Healing Time on Earth address, Noel Brown was reminded of the proposal for a United Nations Conference on Environmental Protection and Restoration in 1992. He arranged for further discussion of the conference with me in his New York office. That discussion, a few days later, revealed widespread support for the conference, that Sweden would be ready to host it as the twentieth anniversary of the Stockholm Conference and the concurrent environmental forum held by nongovernmental organizations. Friends of the Earth leaders from six countries had there published a daily paper, the famous *Stockholm Conference ECO,* which delegates read during speeches that were dull and which the media used for reference as they reported to the world.

Noel Brown now urged that there be another parallel environmental protection and restoration conference in Stockholm arranged by nongovernmental organizations to bring attention to subjects the nations themselves might not get around to. Sobeit! If not a parallel conference, at least alternate theater.

But once we have met old and new friends and ideas at conferences, and have recharged others, or been recharged ourselves, what do we do about following up, filling the interstices between conferences with good altruistic deeds?

THE WAY OUT

ALTRUISM IS FINE, especially if it is selfless, and may someday supersede our less admirable attributes. Until then, we had better find out how to exploit humanity's most dependable trait, self-interest. This is not too discouraging. Robinson Jeffers, mindful of the wholeness and beauty of life, speaks of the essential "knowing that it survives us," and that the most selfish self-interest includes the urge to know. It is something potent to work with. We want Beethoven's symphonies to survive us; the art of Leonardo and Michelangelo and the Beatles; the writings of Shakespeare and Plato and Mark Twain and possibly even of Gore Vidal; the vegetation and wildlife that graces what we look upon; certainly our children, even many of someone else's children; and conceivably even AT&T. And not just that these survive us, but also that they enjoy being around and being useful.

None of these wishes will come true if we fail to change course. The warning signs are all around, and hardly anyone can miss them. Put the questions fairly: Do you feel more secure and content these days, and is this the kind of world children can grow up in joyfully? In the all-but-unanimous negative answer, there is plenty of support to work with.

Does the change in course mean economic ruin? To the contrary, failure to change will ruin more than the economy. But can the change in course be profitable? I think it can be and that nations will find out how to make it so. That's why we need a United Nations Conference on Environmental Protection and Restoration Program, and the innovative cooperation of government and private entities, global and local.

That's why we need a United Nations Earth Corps. Why we need a Restoration Finance Corporation, not just for the United States, but for the planet. And the International Green Circle for the heart all this will require.

Corporations can comprehend the need, given a fair presentation. Any well-run corporation knows that in order to succeed it must find a need, and in order to fill it, must plan, build, recruit, operate, maintain, and replace. Good CEOs, looking around, can certainly see plenty of evidence of the impending catastrophe coming the world's way because the budget cutters have for so long been deferring essential mainte-nance and replacement, environmental and human.

In the military, no sensible field commander would conduct an extended operation without pausing to reorganize. The industrial age needs that pause. Planetary reorganization requires a major investment in the restoration of the life-support system. Coming generations, for all the problems of their own, need something better to live on than the dregs of a civilization that knew only how to pillage.

What happens during the pause can be exciting. It will be exhila-rating to restore health, our own and the Earth's, and to rediscover mutual respect, compassion, a bit of serenity now and then. To hear more silence that we have not been hearing lately. And to renew acquaintance with the prescience, intuition, and wit it took humanity so long to develop in the first place.

These remarks are getting pretty heavy, but so are the times. There are ways to lighten them up. The ball is in your court.

Everest: The West Ridge, 22, 31
Everyman's Genius (Austin), 9
Extinction, 208, 239, 265, 291
Exxon, 168;
  oil spill by, 173
Farquhar, Francis, 1, 2, 21, 30;
  Sierra Club Bulletin and, 3-4
Farquhar, Marjory Bridge, 1, 2
Farquhar, Samuel, 30, 63
Fate and Hope of the Earth conference,
  271, 298;
  Fourth Biennial, 65;
  Fifth Biennial, 267-68
Fate of the Earth, The (Schell), 254, 255,
  258;
  quote from, 265
Fate of the Earth conference, 265-66;
  First Biennial, 289;
  Third Biennial, 284;
  Fourth Biennial, 267
Federal Power Commission, 78, 120
Federal Timber Hearings, 95
Federation of Western Outdoor Clubs, 85,
  95, 121
Fern in Rain, Mount Rainer National Park
  (Adams), 14
Fifty Seven Year Index: Sierra Club
  Bulletin, 4
Films, 44-48, 63-65, 67-68, 266
Fishing High (film), 44
FOE. See Friends of the Earth
Food and Agriculture Organization
  (FAO), 292
Ford Foundation, 105, 236, 237, 238, 239
For Earth's Sake (Brower), 114, 186, 213,
  219
Foreman, Dave, 212-13
Forest Practices Act, 130
Forest Service, 5, 6, 46, 69, 71, 73, 105;
  booklet by, 91-92
Forsyth, Alfred, 113
Fox, Stephen, xii
Frankfurt Book Fair, 8, 31
Frazer, Ben, 113
Freeman, Robin, 261
Freeway Society, 181
Friends of the Earth (FOE), 26-29, 32-33,
  35-37, 40-41, 67, 107, 120, 126, 137-
  39, 142, 149-51, 158, 161, 174, 179,
  189, 197, 200, 215, 222, 223, 230-31,
  252, 267, 283;
  founding of, 106, 125, 155, 201;
  incorporation of, 220;
  merger of, 128;
  publishing by, 20, 147-48, 153, 236,
  305-6;
  recruiting by, 219;
  tax status of, 127, 132

Friends of the Earth Advisory Council,
  201
Friends of the Earth Foundation (FEF),
  155, 168, 251, 252, 254;
  merger of, 128
Friends of the Earth International, 110,
  252, 254
Friends of the Earth PAC, 128, 161
Fritz, Emanuel, 38
Fruge, August, 2, 30
Fukuoka, Mr., 242
Fund-raising, 33-34, 251
Gaines, David, 36
Galapagos Islands, 105, 107;
  Darwin and, 98, 103
Galapagos Islands National Park, 106
Galapagos: The Flow of Wildness, 103,
  104, 289
Galbraith, John Kenneth, 210, 257
Gandhi, Indira, 152
Garbisch, Ed, 285
Garfield, James, 50
Garnett, William, 30
Garrison, Lloyd, 113
Garrod and Lofthouse, 30
Garroway, Dave, 20
Gasahol, 157
Genetic engineering, 197, 199, 203, 207
Georgescu-Roegen, Nicolas, 257
Gibbs, Lois, 263
Gilliam, Harold, 62
Gillick Press, 31
Girard, Alexander, 27
Glacier National Park, 82, 111
Glacier Peak Wilderness, 53, 54, 76
Glen Canyon, slide show on, 55-56, 57
Glen Canyon Dam, 55, 56, 112, 113, 114,
  121
Global 2000 Report to the President, The,
  157, 159, 160, 236, 244, 252-53, 260-
  61
Global Coalition for Survival, 257
Global Tomorrow Coalition, 236, 252
Global warming, 208, 275
Gofman, John, 192
Gold, David, 258
Golden, Robert, 236
Goldsmith, Sir James, 218
Goldsmith, Teddy, 235
Goldwater, Barry, 261
Gorbachev, Mikhail, 274
Gordon, Thomas, 285
Gorsuch, Anne M., 246, 249, 261
Gossage, Howard, 36, 125, 223
Goudy, Frederick, 30
Governor's Conference on Natural
  Resources, 235, 245, 251
Grabhorn brothers, 30

POSTSCRIPT

L ET'S SAY THAT I TRIED TO PUT THE BALL IN YOUR COURT, but it hit the net, and my euphoria fell with it. It has not recovered. The tragedy in the Gulf has put it about six feet under. I want to get that euphoria back, and spread it around. Hence this final chapter.

My euphoria began to peak on November 10, 1989. I was to make my last speech after a tour of several German cities for the U.S. Information Agency. There was a hint as we boarded the train in Nuremburg that something big was in the wind. The train traveled all day through the ecological chaos of East Germany. Early in the evening we reached Berlin to hear church bells ringing and find the streets overflowing with people overwhelmed with joy. The Berlin Wall had fallen.

Surely no one would want to bother to hear my talk at a time like this. A small group nevertheless showed up, including two men from East Berlin who had heard that I was to give a talk. Another young man from East Germany joined a few of us in a nearby bar after the talk. He told us that it was the happiest day of his life. I was told that the bars did not close that night in Berlin—and later told that they never do.

Since our whole family had been traveling in Europe in 1961 and were in France, and duly apprehensive, when the wall went up, we had good reason for our own special delight as it fell. That delight grew in January 1990, when on my home fax machine an invitation to attend a global forum in Moscow appeared, signed by Academician Yevgeni Velikov, whom I had met in Aspen when he received the third Windstar Award in 1988. I couldn't make that meeting, but heard all about it when attending a conference, along with two hundred others, held immediately after the global forum. Its aim was to promote joint U.S.-U.S.S.R. projects.

There we planned an International Green Circle project that was to take us to Lake Baikal in August. I was to be in Kyoto in early April at a Renewing the Earth conference, at the Mall in Washington to say my few minutes' worth about the International Green Circle to a crowd of some 125, 000 on Earth Day, in Kathmandu in May to visit our granddaughter and her parents and talk restoration, in Europe again with the same sermon at a meeting at the Tufts University Talloires campus of university

321

His Holiness the Dalai Lama and Dave Brower in San Francisco, 1991. (Photo by Justin Lowe.)

presidents from around the world. All this was in addition to a busy domestic travel schedule, constantly expanding on Noel Brown's theme, "It's Healing Time on Earth." I explained it all easily: I was trying to use up all the jet fuel and thus end the problem of stratosphere pollution.

In Kyoto I remembered my first visit, back in 1976, under the aegis of the U.S. Information Service. They wanted me to speak in seven cities about pluralism in America. As I explained earlier, I didn't know what pluralism was (I do now), but that didn't matter. I gave my own speech instead.

Speaking slowly, and thus with more careful thought than usual because consecutive translation gave me time to do so, I tried my best to worry the Japanese about the hidden dangers in the celebrated growth of their gross national product. They were then happy with an 8 percent annual growth in GNP.

I told them the bad news. If you insist on the 8 percent, I said, then by the time a Japanese baby born now is old enough to vote you will need thirty times the resources you now require, and when that child retires, two hundred times. Right now (remember, it was 1976) your papers are saying that all the world's forests, combined, cannot provide the wood products Japanese industry needs today. What will you do for wood products when you need thirty or two hundred times as much of them, considering that the ancient forests we are all depending upon cannot be renewed? (Monoculturous forest plantations are no substitute.)

I did not mention the inventory of other resources already ransacked by the industrial nations. In 1976 the list was not so alarming as it is now.

Nor could I be concerned about the game of musical chairs that was to be played internationally fourteen years later as the imminent end of the Cold War found power shifting from seat to seat.

The imminence of new reigns of terror seemed all too clear in April 1990. How, in Rumania or South Africa or Armenia or Azerbaijan or Lithuania or Georgia or the Ukraine or Ireland or the Middle East or India or China—and the list goes on—how does it happen that the change in power is accompanied by so much violence and hatred?

How indeed, in our own country, can there be such resistance to the ending of the Cold War, such acceleration of the arms race, with President Bush making others run ever faster to keep up with us?

Is there something, I ask, that we can work together on, side by side, even with people some of whose ideas, such as their religious ideas, we strongly disagree with—work together toward a goal that we can share joy in as we work toward it, and jubilation as we attain it?

Returning from Kyoto, I became obsessed with the idea of running a full-page ad in the national edition of the *New York Times*. I wanted it to run in May. Obstacles kept it from running until August 13, under the heading "On Human Survival and Healing the Earth." I wrote the introduction. The body of the text was Mikhail Gorbachev's address to the Global Forum. My remarks were brief, and appear below, along with excerpts from the address, all of which is available from Earth Island Institute on request. It should be available everywhere.

LAST JANUARY, THREE WEEKS AFTER TIME magazine named Mikhail Gorbachev "Man of the Decade," he addressed the Global Forum on Environment and Development for Survival in Moscow and gave the most compelling environmental speech any world leader has ever made.

In it Mr. Gorbachev suggested that an "International Green Cross" be established. We have talked about this idea to nearly 200, 000 people in Canada, Japan and the United States, and nearly two-thirds have expressed their willingness to commit a year of their lives to it.

We have decided to pursue the creation of such an organization as a project of Earth Island Institute. We are calling it the International Green Circle. Just as the International Red Cross repairs damage the earth wreaks on structures and people, the International Green Circle would help repair the damage people and structures have done to the Earth and each other.

The International Green Circle comes at a moment in time—on the eve of the twenty-first century—when it is needed most. Your interest, participation and support are essential if we are to fully realize its potential.

[Excerpts from] Mr. Gorbachev's remarkable speech follows. The breadth, scope and substance of his environmental vision set a new standard against which all world leaders should be measured. I urge you to read it closely and ask your friends to do the same. Also please send the coupons or write your own letters.

And join us as we begin a decade of healing the Earth.

David R. Brower, Chairman, Earth Island Institute

Address by Mikhail Gorbachev
to Participants in the Global Forum on
Environment and Development for Survival
Palace of Congresses, the Kremlin, 19 January 1990

The five days which you have spent here in Moscow, in an atmosphere of intense creative communication, your meaningful discussions and final conference documents you adopted, all justify the conclusion: an important step in molding mankind's ecological self-awareness has been made.

The threat of a military thermonuclear catastrophe was understood earlier. The scientists also made an irreplaceable contribution to

324

this. International forces at all levels—political, diplomatic and public— have already been mobilized to stave off this threat. We are witnessing the first results. But a second threat, the assessment of which until recently was clearly inadequate to its gravity—the threat to life on Earth as a result of damage to the environment—has emerged.

The great minds of the past foresaw the consequences of the thoughtless "conquering" of nature by man. They warned that humankind could kill itself by destroying the vegetable and animal kingdoms and poisoning the earth, water and air. At the end of the twentieth century, we have a very acute crisis in relations among man, society and nature. Paraphrasing Immanuel Kant, it is safe to say that the ecological imperative has forcefully entered the policy of states and people's everyday life. It is becoming unconditional, and not only because perhaps irreparable damage has been done to nature. The new scientific, technical and technological revolution, all the consequences of which we do not know yet, can make this damage irreversible. As distinct from some absolute pessimists, we are not fatalists. But the hour of decision—the hour of historic choice—has come, and there is no reasonable alternative for man because he is not predisposed to suicide. Humanity is a part of the single and integral biosphere.

We provide ourselves with vital resources due to the products of the biosphere of the past, and we should not forget that clean water, oxygen in the atmosphere, and soil fertility are a result of the interaction of hundreds of thousands of varieties of plants and species of animals and microorganisms which make up ecosystems. The stability of ecosystems and, hence, the quality of the environment depend on the preservation and maintenance of biological diversity and equilibrium of the biosphere. Your Forum has said in no uncertain terms that something should be substantially changed in the factors for further progress in order to ensure man's initial right—the right to life. We agree with this conclusion.

I must admit that in the Soviet Union we only recently came to understand the vital importance of the ecological problem to a proper extent at the level of policy. The war danger stood in our light. Fewer words are needed here. But the gist of the matter lies not only in this. After the revolution, having started industrializing our country, we were not inclined to "divert our attention" to secondary questions, as it seemed to us at that time, especially to spend our limited funds on this. The size of our country and its riches encouraged this ecological carelessness.

Even when the pollution of the environment in some regions began to acquire a dangerous scale, this was not properly assessed at once. It is our scientists—to their credit—who sounded the ecological alarm, and the public followed them. Having changed the philosophical approaches to the problems of the development of society, *perestroika* has also altered our views on ecology. A detailed report on the national ecological situation, the first in the history of the Soviet state, has recently been published in our country. An unbiased analysis of our woes and dangers was made in this "green book." The pollution of the atmosphere in some big cities exceeds the permissible level. The state of the water resources spells grave consequences for the vegetable and animal kingdoms. Soils degrade, harm is being done to people's health, and full possibilities of future generations is being called into question...

There is yet another factor to which I would like to draw your attention. There are ecosystems on the territory of this country that have not yet been affected by human activity. Therefore, we attach great importance to the creation of preserves and other protected territories. By 2000 their area is to increase approximately three times. These are unique nature laboratories situated over a vast territory from the Arctic Islands to Central Asia. They may serve as standards of primeval nature and sites for international ecological cooperation.

The ecological situation in different countries is different. Many countries have accumulated valuable experience in nature conservation and attention and practical use. The ecological crisis we are experiencing today is tragic but convincing proof that the world we all live in is interrelated and interdependent. It appears that all people everywhere realize this now...

This means, however, that we need an appropriate international policy in the field of ecology. Only if we formulate such a policy, shall we be able to avert catastrophe. True, the elaboration of such a policy poses unconventional and difficult problems which sometimes affect the sovereignty of states...Here are our main ideas on this score.

First, the Soviet Union fully supports the Nature conservation plans and actions of our global universal organization, the United Nations and its agencies. We want the UN Conference on the Environment and Development, which is to be held in Brazil in 1992, conducted at summit level. It would be right if that conference discussed the question of drafting an international code of ecological ethics. Binding on all states, it should contain common standards of a civilized attitude to nature. Such an action would symbolize the willingness of the international community, represented by its top leaders, to arrange life in the twenty-first century in accordance with new laws. The 1992 conference could also adopt a global program of action on environmental protection and rational use of natural resources. Such a program should embrace the protection of the world climate and the animal and plant life on our planet, and preservation of biological diversity, without which it is impossible to preserve the regulating properties of the biosphere and, consequently, of life on Earth.

Second, the Soviet Union finds it necessary to develop an international legal mechanism of protecting unique natural zones of global importance. This primarily refers to the Antarctic. The thick Antarctic icecap is an invaluable treasury of the Earth's past, of its geological and ecological history. Significantly, the Antarctic has become the world's first nuclear-free zone and the first territory ever fully open for international research programs. The Soviet Union shares the concern of many scientists and public figures over the exploitation of the Antarctic's natural resources. Our grandchildren will never forgive us if we fail to preserve this phenomenal ecological system. The U.S.S.R. is ready to join the program for creating a life-support system for the Antarctic continent which is our common laboratory...

Then again, do not tropical forests and coral reefs—the ecological heritage of mankind—need our common care and concern? Or what about such natural phenomena as Lake Baikal?

Third, the Soviet Union believes that the world is in urgent need of an international mechanism for technological cooperation in nature conservation. Our civilization is indivisible and demands united efforts in this area as well. We are for developing an international system of exchanging ecologically clean technologies effectively accessible to all nations. Also, we are ready to open our territory for inspection in order to dispel all fears that technologies might not be used according to their purpose...

Fourth, the transition to new forms of cooperation worthy of the 21st century has highlighted the need to create an international mechanism of ecological monitoring control. Today, measures for building ecological confidence could be based on the methods, procedures and instruments similar to those used in arms control, including opening up of on-site inspections. We could begin by national nature preserves.

Fifth, the right to a healthy environment is one of the basic human rights. However, we should also ensure the right of the individual and groups of people to participate in drafting ecological policies... At the moment, the member states of the European Communities are actively debating the organization and functions of a European Environmental Protection Agency. The Soviet Union supports the idea of setting up such an agency and is ready to join its work from the very beginning. Many ideas deserve attention.

Among them is Austria's initiative to set up international nature-protection units called "UN Green Helmets." Perhaps it would be useful to institute a kind of international green cross that offers its assistance to the states in ecological trouble. The Soviet idea of setting up a UN center for urgent ecological aid has the same purpose. The center's chief mission, as we see it, is to organize international groups of experts to be sent to the sites of ecological disasters. Soon, the UN Secretary General will receive the list of Soviet experts and researchers whom the Soviet Government will be ready to send to such places at its own expense on instructions from the center.

Sixth, and last but not least, the Soviet Union believes that the time has come when the limitation of military activity is needed not only for lessening the danger of war but for protecting the environment. The best thing to do here would be to ban all nuclear tests. Before this authoritative international forum I reiterate the Soviet Union's readiness to ban nuclear tests completely, for all times, and at any moment, if the US does the same.

The convention on and the prohibition and complete elimination of chemical weapons which, we hope, will be signed soon, misses the need to ensure an ecologically safe method of accomplishing this task. Here, too, international cooperation would be extremely welcome, for we are going to eliminate tens of thousands of tons of these lethal weapons. Generally speaking, military activity on land, in the air and in the seas and oceans, and even in outer space—should be run with due account taken of its ecological planning to introduce certain limitations on the flights of military aviation, and on the movement of the land forces and of warships. We are also prepared to sign international agreements on the score...

In conclusion, I would like to say the following: the problems you have discussed and the documents you have adopted are a call for the triumph of the trinity of scientific knowledge, human reason and universal moral principles. This task is as magnificent as it is difficult. I wish all of you—and all of us—every success.

New York Times Ad, 1990

The trouble with running the ad on August 13 was that most of that day's paper was devoted to Iraq's invasion of Kuwait.

THE CHEMICALS OF WAR

ONE YEAR AFTER THE GORBACHEV SPEECH, hope has been dissolved by the chemicals of war, the War in the Gulf that I had been predicting for a decade if the U.S. insisted on the Strength Through Exhaustion energy policy the Reagan administration locked us into.

An Op-Ed by Amory and Hunter Lovins in the January 21, 1991, the *Los Angeles Times* focused sharply on the war's cause. The headline, "The Energy Saboteurs Are in the White House," was followed by a subhead, "Policy: The Administration perpetuates our dependence on gulf oil, instead of profitably eliminating the need."

"Three times in the past 17 years," the op-ed opened, "the oil dependence that keeps us over a barrel in the gulf has enabled fanatics

328

halfway around the world to scramble America's economic and political life.

"As long as that dependence continues, we'll be subject to similar disruptions. But it's not fate. We don't need to continue to depend on oil from the gulf—and it's cheaper not to, for us and for our allies.

"Shaking the gulf oil habit isn't fanciful. For nine years through 1985, the United States was making such rapid progress in saving oil that, if we'd just kept up the same pace, we'd have needed no Persian Gulf oil. But instead, the Reagan Administration's 1986 rollback of light-vehicle efficiency standards immediately doubled oil imports from the gulf."

If we had moved toward 32-miles-per-gallon cars, the Lovinses pointed out, we could have displaced our need for any gulf oil. Instead we were opting for 0.56-mpg tanks.

Earth Island Institute was one of the few environmental organizations that thought the Gulf war was a threat to the environment. On January 29 we teamed up with Greenpeace in a well-attended press conference, at which I gave a short prepared statement:

THE GULF WAR WILL END EVENTUALLY. There will be a cease fire negotiations, and a peace treaty. Will this happen before or after irreparable cost to human lives, global economies, and the Earth?

We must demand that it happen before, not after.

It is essential that citizens and their organizations call for an immediate cease fire and for serious, not cosmetic, diplomatic negotiations.

In serious negotiations the U.S. needs to bear several key points in mind:

• Pretend no longer that we ourselves are without sin.

• Remember the tragedy of Tibet at China's hands, a tragedy that far exceeds the horror of Kuwait but is met with our silence.

• Regret our own brutal past in Central and South America.

• Recall that we ourselves helped arm Saddam and voiced no objection when his Kuwait strategy was made known to us.

• Accept as fact that the world is interconnected. This truth cannot be repealed by dislike of the word "linkage."

• Realize that our demand for lots of cheap oil destabilized Iraq and, if continued, will destabilize civilization.

• Move toward the internationalization of oil, administered by the United Nations.

• Insist on an end to disinformation and needless censorship.

• Understand the present alarming consequences of our refusal to accept the end of the Cold War—our pretending to begin disarmament but continuing to build and test ever more brutal weapons. Gorbachev's manifest intentions—glastnost and perestroika—have been rendered vulnerable to recalcitrant generals and Soviet citizens locked in the past.

A valid new world order cannot be dictated by the United States. It can come from the "courage of patience" (Eisenhower), the end of leaders' "persistence in error" (Ellen Goodman), and a determination, from here on, not to plot to blow the Earth up, but to organize globally to restore it. The world's best efforts toward rebuilding the damage and encroachment on freedom wrought by the Industrial Age will require innovative leaders and a major investment. There is no more rewarding investment, none that in the long rage can be so profitable.

Press Statement, 1991

There were a few photo bites on local television, a front-page story with a color photo in the little Richmond paper in the East Bay, and no coverage at all in the main San Francisco or national papers. But we learned that afternoon by telephone that the story had reached Bangkok!

For the following few weeks the media became addicted to bang bang, their investigative reporting being essentially so tranquilized they had to be spoonfed. Being objective, they balanced peace rallies with war rallies, giving equal time to each, although the numbers participating were widely disparate. They usually picked the tattiest of the participants to speak in behalf of peace. Fairness and accuracy in reporting were put on hold.

Then suddenly, after more than one hundred thousand sorties, the U.S. put the war on hold and Greenpeace and Earth Island held another press conference on March 1. It was skimpily covered. I had more to say—but only the readers of *Work in Progress* will know what I said:

CAN PEACE IN THE GULF REMAIN BIG NEWS?

What this county needs now is a new Gettysburg Address, but the likes of Mr. Lincoln are unavailable.

May I begin with a most appropriate quotation from Omar Khayyam, part of which Herb Caen alludes to frequently?

"The moving finger writes, and having writ, moves on: nor all your Piety and Wit shall lure it back to cancel half a Line, nor all your Tears Wash out a Word of it." [Capitalization is Omar's.]

We are tempted to celebrate a victory. In a more sober moment we will realize we should be celebrating a wake.

The moving finger, we ought to comprehend, is not writing well of us. We, with our allies and high tech, have smashed a nation one thirtieth of our combined size, have killed, maimed, or otherwise crippled no one knows how many of its human beings in the process, created no one yet knows how many new enemies, and established a new world disorder with a war that could have been avoided.

Having disempowered one of the many ruthless dictators we have supported, and having done so in six weeks instead of six or so months, we are being persuaded to think we stand tall. If indeed we are standing tall in the saddle, we may need to ask ourselves on which of the Four Horsemen we are standing so tall.

We are gathered here for what will end up as sound bites or photo ops, occupying slightly more space in the print media than in the electronic. I keep reminding myself that we should watch the Soviet Union closely and, if they can make democracy work, try it ourselves.

What fuels democracy is Truth, not sound or photo bites. What we are getting is an overdose of disinformation, carefully spooned out and rarely evaluated or interpreted. We worship, but do not practice, freedom of speech. We have a Freedom of Information Act that is anathema to the Administration. The media, by and large, serve their client, not the people. Their client is the Advertiser, for all too large a part representing the Fortune 500 and the Multinationals, themselves largely overseen by the undisciplined who exhaust the pool of fossil and nuclear energy and other irreplaceable resources.

In a strange and most regrettable way the client and his servant government and media, are co-conspirators in a grand larceny whose most pitiful victims are the unborn.

The finger moves on, and it is our obligation to give it something far better to write about.

We can hasten to restore the damage done, not only by this latest eruption of international violence, but also by the damage to the only life support system we know of in the universe. It is unprecedented damage, made possible by two and a half centuries of the Industrial Revolution and its ingrained habit of taking and taking from the Earth, and not giving back.

We in the United States can aspire to lead in a Decade of Restoration—regenerating as well as we possibly can, reassembling what has been taken apart, sometimes with the best of intentions, too often wantonly. The Old Testament advised us to multiply, replenish the Earth, and subdue it. We have multiplied and subdued all too well, admiring the benefits but not counting the costs. We have forgotten to consider the benefits of replenishing.

Such victory as we may be about to experience demands a touch of humility, a rediscovery of compassion, and genuine, not opportunistic, support of the United Nations.

And we certainly deserve a sustainable global energy policy, which may in the end require internationalization of the world's remaining resource of oil. What we have now is an energy tragedy. It is the illogical assumption, which President Bush seems determined to perpetuate, that there is Strength in Exhaustion—that the faster we squander the energy that drives our society, the stronger we shall be.

It is exactly this kind of logic that led to the Gulf War and will inevitably, if allowed to continue, lead to still worse disasters.

We are now realizing, considering what has happened to the Earth since that speech, that we have been extirpating, not liberating, the world's resources. The new deserts we have created since 1965 would, if they had remained fertile, feed China. The soil we have lost further, to erosion, pavement, and poison, would feed India. The forests we have destroyed would cover the United States east of the Mississippi [these figures from the Worldwatch book, *State of the World 1991*].

In my own 78.7 years the population of the Earth has trebled, of California has been multiplied by twelve, and the world as a whole has used up four times as many resources as in all previous history. We are surrounded by institutions—government, universities, corporations, media, and overconsumerism—that think this exhaustion can go on and that science and high tech will save us. That is science fiction.

What can save us, if you don't mind my using a word the media avoid, is what Adlai Stevenson alluded to—the love we give our fragile craft, the crafts and all its passengers, here and forthwith. Love is one resource that becomes more abundant the more it is used. . . .

Press Statement, 1991

You have seen the Stevenson lines before [see page 278] and may even have remembered them by now. I repeat them for the entertainment value in what happened to them in the summer of 1990, when I used them at Lake Baikal. They were recorded, translated into Russian, then translated back into English:

"Let's suppose that we are completing an enormous trip . . . We are passengers of a small space ship, dependent on its workmanship, its air resources, its fuel, trusting to it our safety, security, survival. We have trusted our preservation, safety and peace to the care of the whole world. I am speaking of the love we give to our fragile ship. We cannot support its normal work with semi-slave, semi-successful, semi-desperate, semi-confident half-measures with respect to the enemies of humanity, just as we cannot be semi-free in the exhausting of the world's resources up to the very last day. No ship, no crew can travel with such inconsistencies."

Later in my talk Thoreau's "In wildness is the preservation of the world" became "The savior of mankind is in wild nature."

Neither wild nature nor investigative reporting could rescue the press conference. Public radio and ABC gave us a few sound bites and one photo bite. All eyes and ears were on how to welcome the troops back home.

My Albright Lecture in 1981 was abrasive enough to require reinforcement from the writings of people distinguished by their acumen, long ago and now. The trauma the Gulf war brought so pervaded what I was saying and writing that I looked for further reinforcement. After all, polls showed that some 90 percent of the American public voted yes on the war, and it was lonely out there in the remaining 10 percent.

One of the strange habits I can't overcome is tearing pages out of newspapers (or whatever, but not books) that contain articles I could expect to refer to sometime, in articles, interviews, speeches, or perhaps even in an autobiography. The price for old newspapers will plunge whenever the time comes to recycle what I have accumulated over the past half century, all of it irretrievable unless someone wants to help me understand what I was collecting, and file it in an orderly manner.

Not quite all is irretrievable. The March 1991 pile is right where it ought to be and fathomable...The challenge, at this moment, is to pretend that I am a television news editor and see how to reduce material already written succinctly and well into a few brief bites, feeling well-deserved guilt for having tried.

Thus I can reduce what Richard Reeves said in the March 1 [all dates will be 1991] *San Francisco Chronicle* in "The Fields of Death":

Modern war does not end when the troops stop shooting and go home. The carnage continues for 20 or 30 years as men and women working the land or walking on old trails step on land mines or children pick up small mines that look like stones or even toys.

That was his lead. On to the final paragraphs:

War, despite the videotapes of smart bombs and the reassuring talk of modern military men, is what it has always been: War is hell. And, like hell, it tortures forever in parts of the world abandoned after the famous victories and defeats, leaving the landscape littered with death and pain.

On the same page, in a letter entitled "Saved From The Truth," Allan Jacobsen writes:

"We hit the jackpot," said an American pilot Tuesday, referring to the bountiful quarry available for air strikes as the Iraqis pulled out of Kuwait. War dehumanizes everybody. George Bush claims this is a war of principle—a "just" war. What principles were strengthened by our victory? That mass murder is an acceptable foreign policy, that large countries can destroy small countries, that the mass media can now take their place as "part of the weaponry of war" (as Samuel Day Jr. said), that wrong can get away with masquerading as right and lies be accepted as truth? That the peace movement is a bunch of fussbudgets and traitors?

On to the last lines:

Now we can go back to sleep, while our world continues to fall apart around us, secure in the knowledge that Big Brother is watching over our starving souls.

The real war is just beginning.

Then Georgia Wells, writing about "Homecoming Attitude," wondering whether President Bush's wanting to give the returning troops a heroes' welcome begs the question:

Will these returnees, I wonder, buy it when they learn of this administration's plans to accelerate the manufacture of arms? Will they favor the proposed gearing up of the war machine under the guise of "turning the economy around"? Will they ask themselves what part these armaments might play in the establishment of Bush's "new world order"?

Going down these mindless paths will lead America into future and more devastating wars. For it is a delusion that a nation can realize economic health by committing itself to dependency on the unhealthiness of its defense industries.

Or has history taught us nothing?

On the same day, "Lessons of Victory," Anthony Lewis's column in the *New York Times,* alluded to the battle of Agincourt in Shakespeare's "Henry the Fifth."

Victory in the war with Iraq leaves us with feelings of awe...How did it happen? What are the consequences?

Mr. Lewis gives credit to outstanding political and military leadership. Going it alone would not have worked. The United Nations played a crucial role.

If Mr. Bush's talk of a new world order is to have any meaning, the United Nations will have to play a much greater part in the future in preventing war. The UN system can work; we know that now. And prevention is far better than war.

That is a practical point, not just an idealistic one. For a fourth lesson of the Persian Gulf war is that neither the United States nor the world can afford to repeat it.

We fought the war on money promised from others. The U.S. will not want that to be a pattern, making itself a provider of mercenaries.

So much for March 1.

On March 20 Tom Wicker's column in the *New York Times* was headed, "An Unknown Casualty."

With the Persian Gulf war over and won, the Air Force has chosen to disclose a fact that few television viewers or newspaper readers could have suspected while the fighting was going on: The famous "smart bombs" made up only 7 percent of all the U.S. explosives dropped on Iraq and Kuwait.

In fact, in spite of all those TV scenes of precision-guided bombs going down the chimneys or in the doors of Iraqi targets, 70 percent of the 88, 500 tons of bombs dropped on Iraq and Kuwait in 43 days of war missed their targets. This is not a condemnation of the Air Force, which did an outstanding combat job, and voluntarily made these facts public—after the war. It is a damning commentary on the controlled information policy exercised by the Pentagon during the war. And it's no compliment to the American press or public, both of which too tamely accepted military censorship...

334

Americans watching at home did not realize that they were seeing only what their Government and military permitted them to see—not including the bodies of dead Americans or "collateral damage" in Iraqi cities.

Nor did the press and television, to their discredit, protest as effectively as they should have, or always make it as clear as they could have, that much of what they conveyed—like the can't-miss version of Air Force bombings—was not only controlled by the military but prettified for home consumption. Thus was the First Amendment badly wounded in Desert Storm—though war-giddy Americans seemed not to know about or mourn this national casualty.

On April 1, the date the *Chronicle* reprinted his "What the U.S. Has Wrought in the Persian Gulf," Anthony Lewis wrote:

A United Nations mission has reported on what it found in Iraq. The allied bombing, it said, had had "near-apocalyptic results."

There is no running water in Baghdad or other cities. There is almost no electricity. Sewage systems do not work. There is little or no fuel. Hardly anyone can get to work. Hospitals are without medical supplies. Industry has virtually stopped operating. Food is extremely scarce.

"The Iraqi people may soon face a further imminent catastrophe, which could include epidemic and famine, if life-supporting needs are not rapidly met," the mission said.

In answer to the report, the President symbolically washed his hands of responsibility. It was Saddam's fault, he said, for seizing Kuwait and thus bringing on the war...

The misery of the Iraqi people is being intensified now by civil war. Saddam's forces have crushed rebellion in the south and they are doing the same against the Kurds in the north.

Here again the United States cannot escape responsibility. For it was Bush's decision to go to war when and as he did that encouraged the rebellion.

Yet, Bush's policy is to sit by passively while Iraqi helicopter gunships spray napalm and acid at the rebels. He described Saddam as a modern Hitler, but he is allowing Iraqis who oppose the tyrant to be slaughtered...

In a January column, I wrote that it was a just war, if not a wise one. I was wrong. The cause was just—the cause of undoing Saddam's aggression. But the war was worse than unwise. When the cheering stops, the reality of destruction and political abdication will remain.

Columnists have deadlines. So do the writers of autobiographies who do not especially wish to be published posthumously. And the *New York Times* for April 3 is the last issue available for this bite on the press and the Gulf war.

If only the thinking on the Op-Ed page for April 3 had prevailed as the year began! In that one page Leslie H. Gelb is concerned that President Bush's zeal to avoid the prime sin of military intervention has let him commit the second sin of passivity.

Mr. Gelb's concern moves to the United Nations: "Silence fills the halls of the UN. The Security Council surprised itself by authorizing war

335

against Iraq. It surprises few today by returning to form and scampering away from all responsibility for postwar Iraq turmoil."

Flora Lewis's column is headed, "America Deserts The Rebels Cynically":

The justification for the war is being put in doubt by the coalition's willingness to let Saddam Hussein snatch victory, over his own people, from defeat at allied hands.

Hypocrisy is too weak a word for a policy of bombing the daylights out of Iraq and then asserting no responsibility at all for its internal affairs, after calling on Iraqis to overthrow their tyrant.

"Smoke Over Kuwait," by Tom Wicker should have brought mainline environmental organizations to their feet but failed to do so:

About six million barrels of oil, weighing roughly a million tons, around 10 percent of the world's daily oil ration, are going up in smoke every day from the 550 Kuwaiti wells set afire by Iraqi occupiers.

None of the fires have yet been put out, and at the projected extinction rate of five days per well, the job could take as long as two years. Meanwhile, the burning wells emit a daily load of 50,000 tons of sulfur dioxide—a prime cause of acid rain—and 100,000 tons of sooty smoke into the atmosphere. The remainder is mostly carbon dioxide.

Scientific experts disagree on how bad the environmental consequences might be. But U.S. authorities seem to have been worried about causing a real disaster. Just as they controlled information about the desert war itself, they also clamped down on discussion by the Department of Energy officials in this country about "environmental impacts of fires/oil spills in the Middle East." This is reported, along with details of the conflagration and its results, by John Horgan in the May issue of Scientific American.

The order limiting information to "the media"—a copy of which was obtained by Mr. Horgan—was issued in writing on Jan. 25, just after the war began, by the D.O.E. office in San Francisco. A department spokesman told me that the purpose was to deny "information useful to the Iraqis." But it was the Iraqis who set the fires, and the same office told Mr. Horgan the order was not rescinded until March 22, well after hostilities ended, by telephone.

Was it feared in Washington that dire environmental forecasts about oil-well fires might dim enthusiasm for the war? That seems possible, since Saddam Hussein threatened to destroy Kuwait's wells if the allies tried to drive him out; by January few could have doubted that he would do it.

There's no doubt that Kuwait itself has suffered what Raymond Henry, an American firefighting expert, called an environmental "catastrophe." Daytime temperatures beneath the thick smoke clouds are far below normal, hospitals are jammed with respiratory patients, "black rain" is damaging crops and water supplies, and the fierce fires rage on.

Farther away, estimates vary. Some authorities predict a globalwarming effect owing to an increase of as much as 5 percent in emissions of carbon dioxide. Others foresee a sort of "nuclear winter" caused by the 30-odd million tons of smoke the burning wells are expected to emit in a year. Richard Crutzen of the Max Planck Institute has calculated [that] by the end of the year the northern hemisphere would be cooled by two degrees Celsius.

Other experts dispute such predictions; but even one of them, Richard Small of the Pacific-Sierra Research Corporation, told Mr. Horgan that "we have never seen a pollution event of this scale." Damage, he said, might be felt over an area extending 1, 000 kilometers from Kuwait.

Saddam Hussein's forces, of course, actually set the fires and caused this immense environmental threat. He had plainly warned that he would do it, however; so the U.S., by its decision to launch the war anyway rather than rely on non-combat pressures, bears some responsibility.

The Administration insists that it had no real alternative to war. But if environmental damage from Kuwaiti fires proves as bad as the pessimists predict, the resulting damage and casualties may again appear out of proportion to Iraq's offense. Already a UN report concludes that Iraq has been bombed back to the "preindustrial age," its infrastructure destroyed, its people beset by famine and disease. Was that degree of destruction unavoidable and warranted?...

As for environmental damage, Joel S. Levine of NASA, an authority on biomass burning, told Mr. Horgan that Kuwaiti well fires were "the most intense burning source, probably, in the history of the world."

Mr. Wicker, we are sadly pleased to note, told his readers what Earth Island and Josh Karliner had presented, with detailed documentation, in our press conference in January. Press and television coverage then was minimal.

Must war continue to be too exciting a show to miss?

William Witt is staff photojournaist, University of Northern Iowa Office of Public Relations, and chairman of the Sierra Club-Iowa Chapter. He has kindly allowed me to quote from a text he developed from a speech presented March 13 at the Forum of the University's College of Humanities and Fine Arts. He does not speak for the Sierra Club; I would gladly have him speak for Earth Island anytime he wants to:

It has been 20 years or more since I saw the phrase "pyrrhic victory" appear in public print, but Donald Kaul's recent comparison of our stunning demolition of Iraqi armies to the battle of Agincourt put me in mind of it. Since "pyrrhic" Pyrrhus operated in a time when the most effective propaganda media were columns of smoke on the horizon and columns of fleeing, terrified civilians begging refuge at one's gates, a thumbnail sketch of his character and accomplishments might be useful to CNN-oriented audiences.

War was simpler then. Pride and plunder moved armies. King Pyrrhus of Epirus was a practical soldier and a sound tactician who avoided ego clashes and kept up morale by the booty principle. "Take the money and march" seems to have been his philosophy, but we remember him today for his assessment of the battle of Asculum in 270 B.C. The Epireans defeated the Romans at Asculum—but at the cost of their best men. "One more such victory and we are lost," Pyrrhus said, as he surveyed the carnage...

This brings us back to Donald Kaul's calling Desert Storm "the most glittering victory accorded the English-speaking peoples since Agincourt 575 years ago." Why? Because although Agincourt, like Desert Storm, represented a stunning triumph of superior technology and tactics, it also resembled Asculum in its long-term consequences. Agincourt, it may be argued, helped induce Henry V and his successors to spend the next 150 years trying to maintain a politically, economically, and strategically untenable foothold in France.

In the final analysis Agincourt was mainly a propaganda victory. For England it foreshadowed a long century-and-a-half marked by ongoing struggles with the Irish and Scots, and a series of bloody royal intrigues that culminated in the civil war between the houses of Lancaster and York. Throughout, the English periodically had to sacrifice energy, lives, and capital to try to hold their shrinking French territories and commercial claims. If the propagandist had not been Shakespeare, the era would have left little glory to history.

Out of the vortex of Desert Storm, the bombing of Baghdad, the cataclysm before Basra, George Bush and his propagandists have broadcast to the world a series of images that King Pyrrhus would have relished. There are the columns of smoke; there, the cowering, obeisant armies; here, the abject citizens begging sanctuary. It's powerful stuff, all of it. And Bush and his generals have done their rhetorical best with it. Yet there is something deeply unsettling about it all—something that whispers "weakness" beneath the swell of strong words, a muffled clanking sound below the ringing pride, something that drags and scrapes like the long chain of consequences that followed Agincourt...

I can't find anything new or hopeful in this new world order our Commander-in-Chief keeps referring to. We're a nation of petroholics, lurching around the globe like a drunk with a hand grenade staggering through a nursery, yet the cure the President offers is more smart bombs and an energy program that's nothing more than drill, burn, and waste—a welfare scheme for oil....

A world order founded on avarice and bellicosity is neither new nor orderly. Our pride and our cleverness are propelling us toward a triumphal entry into oblivion. Let's set a truly good example for the world and temper our might with patience, compassion, self-discipline, and restraint. A real new world order affirms that the path of conservation is the path to lasting peace.

GOING AROUND IN GREEN CIRCLE

UNEP'S NOEL BROWN, SPEAKING at the New England Environmental Conference at Tufts University in March 1991, was not at all happy about Desert Storm. If there was to be healing time on Earth, which he had urged three years earlier at the Restoring the Earth Conference in Berkeley, it was essential to trade Desert Storm for Desert Flower. The audience, not one likely to contain the war-giddy, broke into applause.

To find a place to plant the seed for that flower would require an enormous program of restoration of the land ravaged by Desert Storm. Early estimates of the restoration engineering required were around $100 billion, with the Bechtel people likely to get at least a lion's share of the work.

The estimate is probably far too low, and cannot possibly include the cost of capping 550 burning oil wells. Henry Kendall told me at Tufts that the well casings had been destroyed some thirty feet below the surface. It would seem to require a miracle to extinguish the fire and cap even one well in the five days mentioned above, much less find enough survivors and material to handle the other 449.

Then there is the cost of the damage done. How much will it cost to undo the damage wrought by acid rain, not just to current forests and crops, but also to soil and aquifers? Or, if the greenhouse effect is expedited, as it surely must be, to begin to repair or protect against that damage? If the unexpected surprise arrives, as usual, the ozone barrier will require a restoration job that is beyond our present knowledge or intuition.

Add the damage imminent in that barrier and in the unusable space above it if the military's infatuation with star wars, and the atmospheric damage attendant upon space shots, not to mention sending out crews to clean up the high-speed junk already cluttering the vast desert of space. This junk will be outrageously augmented by the tests star-wars increments will require before they can be counted on to work in a space environment that will no longer, in all likelihood, allow them to survive until they are supposed to be needed.

While we are working on estimates so huge that require us to think beyond the familiar "the sky is the limit" ceiling, we can easily exceed the $200 billion estimate for trying to clean up after the nuclear power/nuclear arms production and storage facilities.

How, for example, would one go about estimating the cost of cleaning up the Ogalalla aquifer to start with, followed by all the other aquifers in the world rendered undrinkable, or nearly so, by our fascination with altering the world's chemistry?

What is the cost of restoring to its fertility a mere twenty years ago the soil which, had it not been lost, could feed the population of India.

Or the cost of restoring the deserts man has created in the last two decades which, had they not been created, could grow enough food (once we could afford the irrigation works and find safe water to fill them), to feed the people of China?

Or to get closer to home, what would it cost to put the soil lying idle in the Gulf of Mexico back in place in the Mississippi bioregion where it could do some good again?

These 'opportunities' (remember that Howard Zahniser thought that was a more stimulating word than 'problems') are overwhelming. Let's try one that is only whelming, and perhaps manageable.

What would it cost to abandon the present determination to use the atmosphere, instead of the land and water, as a dumpsite. Remember that incinerators make deserts in slow motion. The organic material they burn needs to be returned to the soil that created it—the soil that has invented the best converters and storers of solar energy that the Earth has yet come up with.

339

Perhaps we should settle for simply being underwhelmed, starting out with renewal projects in which we get out of the way and let nature do the work—far enough out of the way to allow nature to do so while humanity is still around to enjoy the benefits.

Putting some boundaries around civilization will help wildness preserve the world. This will require making some vast tracts available for restoration, relieving the burden of too many human feet and the grasp of too many greedy hands. It will also require our learning how to use the scattered biotic debris and living dead Daniel Janzen speaks of as inocula in trying the restore traumatized ecosystems. It will require investing for prosperity, as Huey Johnson got California to do, in regenerating forests, soil, wetlands, and streams. Or the persistence of John Berger's Restoring the Earth organization, the model restoration projects he has described, or the one hundred fifty-two of them he helped get started in his own San Francisco Bay region.

Think, too, of the restoration in Vietnam being undertaken by Vietvets. Of what the current models of the old Civil Conservation Corps are accomplishing. Of what private and public agencies and organizations can achieve, voluntarily or for profit.

Of what the International Green Circle can do to catalyze all the forces it will take to grow that Desert Flower—not as a monoculture, but with all the biological diversity we have left intact and that may rescue us yet.

All we need to do, to put it simply, is to make war obsolete and to make peace exciting

Could there be a more useful game?

Let parliamentary, religious, corporate, academic, and environmental leaders and followers take hold. Organize from the grassroots down, as a friend of mine once spoonerized it. Or did he? Was he unintentionally right? Grassroots know damned well that they have to look down for sustenance.

Do it your way.

Or start out by helping us do it our way in Earth Island's International Green Circle Project. We are looking for participants, challenges, ideas, teachers, sources of funds, and affiliates.

FRIENDS OF LAKE BAIKAL

OUR MOST DRAMATIC IGC PROJECT at this writing is Russia's Lake Baikal. The Blue Gem of Siberia, Lake Baikal, is what you'd have if you excavated the Great Valley of California to a depth of more than a mile (but averaging only half that) and filled it with all the water in the Great Lakes, then moved it far enough north to touch Admiralty Island.

To make it more interesting, add the nearby cities of Irkutsk, Ulan Ude, and Severobaikalsk, some small picturesque communities, archaeological sites that need exploring, unclimbed peaks, and ice thick enough in winter to support railroad tracks and, indeed, a train.

To make it still more interesting, add some thirteen hundred species of plants and animals, in the lake and along its shores, that occur nowhere else. Add fresh-water seals, the likes of which exist nowhere else except in streams flowing into Quebec's James Bay.

To counteract all this, add polluting industries and agriculture, enough to kill the lake in sixty years if nothing is done about them. Whereupon it would take six hundred years, some Soviet friends tell us, to restore the lake.

To spare humanity the cost of so long and tedious a task, a group of us thought we should try to prevent the lake's being killed in the first place. I call this effort an International Green Circle project. We have a long way to go, and the slower we move, the longer the way. Either way, you have but to visit the lake, as a fully accredited and committed eco-tourist or eco-student, to know that the effort is worthwhile, either way.

Eliot Porter was aware of Lake Baikal as early as the mid-sixties. That is when he told me that he wanted to do a Sierra Club book about the lake. Russell Train, John Milton, and Raymond Dasmann wanted to see it in the World Heritage. So, to my great surprise, do a good many Soviet citizens.

I was not ready for a different surprise. In 1988 the Earth Island office called me at home to say someone from Moscow was trying to get in touch with me. Moscow, Idaho, I presumed. But it was the original Moscow, and would I be willing to attend a conference at Lake Baikal to investigate ways of saving it, all expenses paid?

Could I make a deal? I wanted Anne to go too. Could we get there on our nickel and they pick up the rest of the expenses? Michael Kinsley, from Amory Lovins's Rocky Mountain Institute, Anne, and I were the only Americans arriving at Listvyanka, on Baikal's shore beside the Angara River, that carries Baikal's waters in due course to the Arctic Ocean.

There were some two hundred Soviets. Andrei Serenko was assigned to us to tell us what the Soviets were saying and tell them what we were saying. We had seven days of meetings and four days and three nights on the lake.

It was October 1988, and Farley Mowat's *The Siberians*, which we read as we traveled, told of sudden October storms that sank Baikal ships.

Ours only rocked. The best part of the whole meeting, which would have been impossible without *glastnost,* was our learning that the

Soviets government had just signed the World Heritage Convention and that many of our new Soviet friends wanted Baikal in the World Heritage. Would I bring some people over next year to help it happen?

I was back in Moscow in January 1990, immediately following the Global Forum that I just missed, finding Andrei looking for me and ready to interpret some more as we attended a Citizens' Summit to inquire into joint Soviet-American projects. I came with one hundred fifty Americans, but that was not the group I had been asked to bring. At that meeting, however, I met the people who could put a group together, and they did. And we were at the lake in August.

Some two dozen of us met with some three dozen of them, including representation from the Supreme Soviet, for a period of nine eventful days. We came up with a long series of recommendations, the beginnings of a book, a documentary, plans for two continuing studies, recollections of fascinating places we scattered to visit in large groups and small, and much more, including my own twelve hours of videotape. What a memento!

We also came up with a tri-city Soviet committee to encourage conversations that were not being held, a feeling of urgency, and an American Baikal Watch.

Baikal Watch, although I consider it a model Green Circle project, is also an Earth Island project on its own. Fran Macy was co-leader of our expedition. I bore the same title, but John Knox, one of Earth Island's two executive directors, bore the load. Gary Cook heads Baikal Watch.

Whiling away his time as our expert on biology and eco-tourism, Professor Jim Butler, of the University of Alberta, composed some words that sang:

We the undersigned have been joined together in the Lake Baikal Environmental Expedition to share insights, concerns, and potential solutions toward the ecological restoration of one of the great natural regions of the world—Lake Baikal, U.S.S.R.

We have gathered in working seminars beside this magnificent landform in the warmth of friendship and the strength of determination that Baikal, one of the treasures of the world, shall endure, recover, and perpetuate its ecological integrity, continuing as it has for centuries, to nourish those people who seek the fruit of its womb and the serenity of its spirit. The knowledge of its intricacies will long strain our intellects. Its seven named winds, and not mankind, should rule its dominion.

Be it the intent and spirit of this delegation that we hereby:

•Reaffirm to organizations and governments, both regionally and globally, the significance of Baikal as a global treasure.

•Commit our intellect and our conscience, individually and collectively, locally and globally, to the environmental restoration and perpetuity of the Lake Baikal ecosystem.

Support the intent of the collective recommendations which emerged from our working groups in the belief that they provide initial steps of a long journey on the path of the resolution that will be supported by commitments of action eventually to contribute toward an elevated quality of life.

Each of us, independent of culture, representation, and nationality, affix our signatures to this declaration as a symbol of our national and collective commitment to the integrity of this unique natural wonder, which was born to this land long before governments laid claim to it, and long before our industrial vision had cancered its life blood.

May this declaration symbolize the birth of a new vision, a new cooperation, and a new relationship between mankind and Baikal.

What a new group of us will have discovered on our next trip to Lake Baikal, in late July and early August 1991, will have to be explained later. I do not believe that my publisher is prepared to present this part of my autobiography in looseleaf format.

On Seeing Others

IN THE FIRST VOLUME OF THIS EXERCISE, *For Earth's Sake,* there is a chapter on Family and one on Friends. Readers have observed and possibly have regretted the apparent limits therein revealed about my friends, so many of whom are no longer with us.This happens to almost anyone entering his eightieth year, and I don't like it. I miss every one of them.

But I need fewer condolences than most people. I have an addiction, pleasant to me, of feeling compelled to make a speech whenever I am confronted with an audience of ten or more. The blessing in all this is that I usually find myself talking to younger people (there are very few who can't be so described). Much younger people. Students. College students, but occasionally one or two schools lower.

Most of them listen patiently. I listen, too. Three years ago I formed a new habit—stopping a speech suddenly when I have about another third to go, and asking for questions or, preferably, statements. People are thereby relieved of pretending a statement is a question. It is great to watch the relief in people's faces as they start listening to each other rather than to a patriarch.

If the statements thin out, it's time to hurry the session to a close and wait for the few enthusiasts to come up with more questions and stick around to hear the questions and answers.

Almost always the question will be asked, "How come you haven't burned out?" Fifty-five years of environmental tasks and talks should provide enough fuel for burnout, but haven't. Because of people like you, I can say, and I don't make that up. It is utterly true. People like you make my euphoria possible.

There is always a bit of advice about commitment, the Goethe quote about boldness, and the insistence they not violate Rule Six and thus forget to have enough fun. Remember that you'll be my age much sooner than you think, I say, so just remember what Theodore Roosevelt said: "I'd rather wear out than rust out."

I remember all the people like them, many of whom, through the years, have struggled with me in the Sierra Club, Friends of the Earth, Earth Island, or the Fate and Hope of the Earth conferences. There will be people like them in the Green Circle. The formula is simple. Get them engaged, give them a few suggestions and the reins, and bask in the glow of what they accomplish. A hug or two won't hurt.

Serendipity keeps showing up. I had just spoken about James Bay II at Yale and had drifted toward the exit at the rear of the Forestry School hall, chatting with people on the way because it's fun. I noticed a tall young man standing very patiently to one side, finally had a chance to hear what he wanted to say, and he handed me a sealed envelope. Should I open it now, I asked, and he said no, just when I had time later. Serendipity was waiting in the envelope:

Dear Mr. Brower,

At the reception in Boston, someone said you are as close to a Wise Man as the environmental movement has. I beg your wisdom, and I will try to be brief."

I have decided that I must spend my life trying to save the earth. I have good parents, go to a good high school, will go to a good university; in short, I am privileged. The effect I will have on the environmental movement should be commensurate with the advantages I have in life. I have such a great life that I have an equally great responsibility to use all my resources to the fullest.

Yet sometimes I feel like all our efforts are in vain. You said before *Encounters With the Archdruid* was written there was only ten percent left, we could no longer afford to compromise. I shudder to imagine what compromises have been made since then, and what has been destroyed.

I have to think that the only possible way to save us and the earth that we know is a radical change in society, something like that advocated in *Deep Ecology*. At least once with equally sweeping effects. However I can't see how such a change could ever come to pass, not in time, anyway.

As if that weren't enough, in *High Technology: Construction of Disaster*, John H. Broomfield writes, "We have created a technology that assumes infallibility but is operated by fallible humans. Accidents resulting from human error are a certainty. Weapons of war are made to be used. There is no historical precedent of a major weapons system being developed and never used."

This seems like good reason for hopelessness.

When adults patronize me and tell me that I believe what I do because I'm young and liberal, and my views will soften as I grow older, I look to your example as proof of the fact that as one grows old one never has to soften.

But my question to you: What kept you going? How did you deal with such doubts, which no doubt occurred to you? You have done such great things in the face of such odds? I ask not for one pearl of wisdom that will revolutionize my thinking as a panacea that will cure all my doubts. But I want to help, and I feel like I can do more if I believe there is hope of success.

I would cherish your reply more than you know.

Thank you for your time,
Justin Ruben (the one with the big hair)

To avoid burning out one needs to have at least one consecutive success. If I got just one letter like that, I couldn't burn out. I did, so I won't. My advice to me is that I write some letters like that to people who really deserve them.

I promised the one with the big hair that I would surely answer his letter. His having asked not for one pearl of wisdom was a mistake. I am going to send him this whole damned book, a guaranteed way to keep him from getting one pearl of wisdom.

THIRTY FOR THE NINETIES

N O ONE HAS ASKED ME, BUT SOMEONE MIGHT, what I would like to concentrate on between now and my entering my ninetieth year, more specifically, July 1, 2001. Should that happen, I would give priority to celebrating it. No other priorities. I'm against them. Prioritization is a device for not getting things done, for escaping the obligations listed last.

Well, one more priority: find people who like one of the items on the following long agenda, and provide downfield blocks while they run with the ball. Not too far downfield, however.

Following, unalphabetized, unnumbered, and unprioritized, are what I want to see happen. When these are well under way, call me to see what I have most recently added to the wish list.

International Green Circle:
Start it rolling and roll with it. Wherever we go to heal, listen eloquently, look with heart, and see ourselves as others see us (and improve what they see).

Growth, birth, and hubris control:
Run cost-benefit analyses of all three, with special attention to cost.

UN Conference on Environment and Development, Brazil:
Beware of development; stress restoration and protection.

General Agreement on Tariffs and Trade (GATT):
Disclose and remove the hidden environmental threats.

Yosemite:
Consider improving management and give credit where due for the protection and restoration already provided.

The Regreening of America:
Make sure the green is in operations, not public relations.

Fate and Hope of the Earth Project:
Gather people together in many places around the world, including this agenda in its agenda.

Magna Carta II and III:
Give power to other species and rediminish the sovereign's, which has been rebuilding since Magna Carta I.

Eco-Tibet:
Support HH the Dalai Lama's proposal for a Tibetan peace park; help restore Tibet's splendor.

Eco-curricula:
Infuse in present curricula what this agenda needs taught to its perpetrators.

Eco-tours:
Make them big and eco enough to thwart unsound development.

National Biosphere Reserve System:
Hang the reserves together, as we have done for parks and forests. Invent new ways to add privately preserved land.

Earth Island Conservancy:
Involve members and foundations in private preservation while government gets its act together. Urge Sierra Club et al. to do the same. There are millions of acres to save, following the Nature Conservancy's example.

Earth Island Voters:
Organize to reach all voters for support of environment, peace, and equity.

Earth Island Law Center:
Help it grow to complement other centers' support for the whole Earth.

Earth Island Action Group:
Get it moving, nondeductibly, for maximum legislative reach.

Council for Primeval Forests:
Work with the forest protection groups willing to be courageous enough to stop further compromises and come up with alternatives (see my letter to a Conservation Director in *For Earth's Sake*).

World Heritage Library:
Get going on the rest of the one hundred volumes originally planned.

Manifesto for the Earth:
Make a beautiful Sierra Club exhibit format book of Ansel Adams's idea, together with a traveling exhibit.

These Are the American Antiquities:
And another one, with a traveling exhibit, celebrating the National Park Idea.

The Wildness Within Us:
Finish and publish the DRB prospective (another long foreword, and a favorite quotation and photograph from books DRB edited for every day of the year).

Support FAIR:
Fairness and Accuracy in Reporting is what we are not getting and need to get.

Earth Island Weekly Journal:
Step up the frequency and merge with selected other journals so that people have vital information on hand soon enough to act on it.

Earth Island Video Journal:
Described in the chapter 3 of this volume.

Energy Strategy Instead of Tragedy:
As the bumpersticker says, WAR IS NOT AN ENERGY POLICY. Get a comprehensive Earth Island Energy Project going in close cooperation with the Rocky Mountain Institute.

Earth Island Affiliates:
Find them, engage them, and work diligently with them.

James Bay II and III:
Stop both attacks—on the Cree and Quebec wilderness—in their cradles. If II is stopped, III will not start.

Truth Squads:
Organize teams to give the media something more to cover—not just the entrepreneurs' side, but ours too.

EIEIO:
Establish the Earth Island Environmental Information Office to help the truth squads—and to lighten up the conversation when we answer the telephone with the acronym.

Operation Desert Flower:
Put Noel Brown's idea to work, an ideal assignment for Green Circlers!

347

Recover Travers:

That I have even thought of the foregoing thirty (was anyone counting?) is in no small part due to the remarkable management Bill Travers has provided me. His wife Debbie recruits for the Peace Corps and overreached, recruiting Bill. Arrange to make the Peace Corps an arm of the International Green Circle.

While I am making this assignment, everyone who has read this book has earned the right to help any or all items on the agenda, with Earth Island or wherever. Until we raise the funds all the items will be self-rewarding.

Is the ball in your court now?